THE BIG ◆QUESTIONS

A Short Introduction to Philosophy
Fifth Edition

ROBERT C. SOLOMON
University of Texas at Austin

HARCOURT BRACE COLLEGE PUBLISHERS

Fort Worth   Philadelphia   San Diego   New York   Orlando   Austin   San Antonio
Toronto   Montreal   London   Sydney   Tokyo

Publisher   **Christopher P. Klein**
Acquisitions Editor   **David Tatom**
Product Manager   **Steven K. Drummond**
Developmental Editor   **Pam Hatley**
Project Editor   **Laura J. Hanna**
Art Director   **Vicki Whistler**
Production Manager   **Melinda Esco, Debra Jenkin**

Cover image: Vita P. Solomon, collage/painting of Auguste Rodin's *The Thinker.*

ISBN:0-15-503686-6
Library of Congress Catalog Card Number: 97-73638

Address for orders:
Harcourt Brace & Company
6277 Sea Harbor Drive
Orlando, FL 32887-6777
1-800-782-4479

Address for editorial correspondence:
Harcourt Brace College Publishers
301 Commerce Street, Suite 3700
Fort Worth, TX 76102

Web site address:
http://www.hbcollege.com

Printed in the United States of America

7 8 9 0 1 2 3 4 5 6   039   9 8 7 6 5 4 3 2 1

PREFACE

It was the fall of 1806, in the college town of Jena, in what we now call Germany. It was about the time when most students and professors would have been getting ready for their classes, with mixed annoyance and anticipation. The professors would have been finishing up their summer research; the students would have been doing what students usually do at the end of the summer.

But this year school would not begin as usual.

Napoleon's troops were already approaching the city, and you could hear the cannon from the steps of the university library. French scouts were already in the town, walking around the university, stopping for a glass of wine in the student bars, chatting casually with the local residents, many of whom were in sympathy with the new French ideals of "liberty, equality, and fraternity."

As the battle was about to begin, a young philosophy instructor named **Georg Wilhelm Friedrich Hegel** was hastily finishing the book he was writing—a very difficult philosophy book with the forbidding title *The Phenomenology of Spirit*. But "spirited" is what the book was, and it perfectly captured the tension, excitement, and anxiety of those perilous days. It was the end of an old way of life and the beginning of a new one. The book was a vision of consciousness caught in the midst of gigantic forces and looking for direction in a new and terrifyingly human world. It was an appeal for hope and thoughtful effort toward universal understanding and a belief in what was then innocently called the "perfectibility of humanity."

Transfer the situation to our own times—it was as if life in America were about to change completely, with all our old habits and landmarks, our ideas about ourselves and the ways we live, replaced by something entirely new and largely unknown. We talk about "future shock" and "megatrends" but, in fact, most of what we consider drastic changes in American life are mere shifts of emphasis, the not always convenient advantages that accompany new and improved technologies and techniques. If so many of us can get so melodramatic about computers, television, and the Internet, how would we react to a *real* change in our lives? Hegel and his students felt confident, even cheerful. Why? Because they had a **philosophy**. They had a vision of themselves and the future that allowed them to face the loss of their jobs, even the destruction of their society and the considerable chaos that would follow. Their ideas inspired them and made even the most threatening circumstances meaningful.

I recently asked my American students, who had been reading Hegel's philosophy, to characterize their own views of themselves and their times. The answers were less than inspiring. For many of them, the word "dull" seemed to summarize the world; others spoke of "crisis" and "despair." One said that life was "absurd" and another that it was "meaningless." I asked why. The answers were that gasoline was expensive, that most of them weren't getting the job interviews they really wanted, and that television programs were bad. Everyone agreed that these events were less than tragic, hardly "absurd," and didn't make life "meaningless." Everyone agreed that the

Georg Wilhelm Friedrich Hegel was born in Stuttgart in 1770. While he was a college student, he was enthusiastic about the French Revolution (1789–95) and an admirer of Napoleon. Hegel was teaching at the University of Jena in 1806 when Napoleon marched in and took over the town, ending the eight-hundred-year-old Holy Roman Empire and initiating widespread reforms throughout the German states. It was in this atmosphere of international war and liberal hopes that Hegel formulated his philosophy, which centered on the notion of "Spirit," by which he meant the unity of the world through human consciousness. His method was **dialectic**—that is, he tried to demonstrate how contradictory views can be reconciled and shown to be, in fact, different aspects of one underlying phenomenon—ultimately, of Spirit. Hegel is still considered one of the great synthesizers of human knowledge and values; his *Encyclopedia* (first published in 1817) is a short synthesis of the whole of human life, including logic, science, and psychology as well as philosophy, art, religion, metaphysics, and ethics. He died in 1831.

old specter of nuclear war and terrorism had put a damper on our optimism, but we also agreed that the likelihood of such catastrophes was debatable and that, in any case, we all had to live as best we could, even if under a shadow. But why, then, in these times of relative affluence and peace (compared to most of the world throughout most of history) were our answers so sour? What were we missing that Hegel and his students, confronting the most terrible battles ever known, seem to have had—something that made them so optimistic and fulfilled? Again, the answer is a philosophy.

Philosophy, religion, and science have always been closely related. The emphasis shifts, but the point is the same: the importance of ideas and understanding, of making sense out of our world and seeing our lives in some larger, even cosmic, perspective. *Ideas* define our place in the universe, our relations with other people; ideas determine what is important and what is not important, what is fair and what is not fair, what is worth believing and what is not worth believing. Ideas give life meaning. Our minds need ideas the way our bodies need food. We are starved for visions, hungry for understanding. We are caught up in the routines of life, distracted occasionally by those activities we call "recreation" and "entertainment." What we as a nation have lost is the joy of thinking, the challenge of understanding, the inspirations as well as the consolations of philosophy.

This is odd, however; for America, more than any other nation on earth, was founded on ideas, was built upon philosophical principles. And yet how many educated Americans can even name a living American philosopher? Or, for that matter, how many of us know anything about the philosophical history that, toward the end of the eighteenth century, gave birth to this nation? We recite ideas that are two hundred, in some cases two thousand, years old without any attempt to understand them, without any awareness that many men and women have lived and died for them, without even trying to be critical about them, to work them into our vision of the world. That is philosophy: philosophy is simply *thinking hard* about life, about what we have learned, about our place in the world. Philosophy is, literally, the **love of wisdom**. It is the search for the larger picture, the demand for **knowledge**—the kind of knowledge that allows us to understand our lives and the world around us. It is, accordingly, the insistence on the importance of **values**, a refusal to get totally caught up in the details of life and simply go along with the crowd. Philosophy and wisdom define our place in the universe and give our lives meaning.

When undergraduates ask questions about the meaning of life and the nature of the universe, it is philosophy that ought to answer the questions. But thousands of students, not trained in hard thinking but starved for ideas and understanding, will retreat to the easier alternatives—pop philosophies of self-help, exotic religions, extreme politics. . . . If the hard thinking of philosophy does not address the big questions, then perhaps these easier alternatives will. The difference between philosophy and the popular alternatives is ultimately one of quality—the quality of ideas, the thoroughness of understanding. Since we all live by our ideas anyway, the choice becomes not whether to do philosophy or not do philosophy, but whether to accept a cheap and unchallenging substitute or to try the real thing. The aim of this book is to give you an introduction—to the real thing.

THE SUBJECT OF PHILOSOPHY

Philosophy is sometimes treated as an extremely esoteric, abstract, and specialized subject that has little to do with any other subjects of study—or with the rest of our lives. This is simply untrue. Philosophy is nothing less than the attempt to understand who we are and what we think of ourselves. And that is just what the great philosophers of history, whom we study in philosophy courses, were doing: trying to understand themselves and their times and their place in the world. They did this so brilliantly, in fact, that their attempts remain models for us. They help us formulate our own ideas and develop our own ways of clarifying what we believe.

Throughout this book, I have tried to introduce at least briefly many of the great philosophers throughout history. (Brief biographies are included in the chapters and at the end of the book.) But philosophy is not primarily the study of *other* people's ideas. Philosophy is first of all the attempt to state clearly, and as convincingly and interestingly as possible, *your own* views. That is *doing* philosophy, not just reading about how someone else has done it.

This book is an attempt to help you do just that—to *do* philosophy, to state what you believe, using the great philosophers and the great ideas of the past as inspiration, as a guide to ways of putting together your own views, to provoke the present alternatives that you may not have thought of on your own. The aim of the book—and at least one aim of the course you are taking—is to force you to think through your ideas, connect them, confront alternative views, and understand what you prefer and why you prefer it. Some students inevitably think that once they are speaking abstractly, it doesn't matter what they say. So they talk utter nonsense, or they express ideas they have never thought about, or they recite mere words—for example, the popular word "value"—without having any sense of what they as individuals believe to be true. I had a very bright student one year who claimed he did not exist. (I didn't convince him otherwise, but I gave him a grade anyway.) Some students even feel that it doesn't matter if they contradict themselves—after all, "It's only ideas." But if it is through ideas that we see the world, if they determine how we feel about ourselves and live our lives, then our ideas make all the difference. So it is urgent—as well as intellectually necessary—that you ask, at every turn, "Do I really believe that?" and, "Is that compatible with other things I believe?" Good philosophy, and *great* philosophy, depends upon the seriousness and rigor with which such questions are asked. And it is the aim of this book to help you ask them, to help you build for yourself a philosophical presentation of your own view of the world.

It may sound as if it is an overwhelming task to summarize your views about the meaning of life and the nature of the universe in a single course. But no matter how crude your first efforts, this kind of integrative critical thinking—putting it all together—is essential to what you will be doing all through your life: keeping your priorities straight, knowing who you are and what you believe. In this course, which may be your first introduction to philosophy, the idea is to get you started. And once you begin to think about the *big questions* you may well find, as many students and almost all professional philosophers have found, that it is one of the most rewarding and most accessible activities you will ever learn—you can do it almost anywhere, at any time, with anyone, and especially alone. And if it seems difficult to begin (as it always does), it is because you are not used to thinking as a philosopher, because our ideas are inevitably more complex than we originally think they are, and because, once you begin thinking, there is no end to the number of things there are to think about. So consider this as a first attempt, an exploratory essay, a first difficult effort to express yourself and your opinions—not just on this issue or that one, but concerning the whole of your view of the world. It is *doing* philosophy, even if it is only for the first time, that makes it so exciting and challenging.

The first chapter of the book consists of a set of preliminary questions, in order to get you to state your opinions on some of the issues that make up virtually every philosophical viewpoint. Some of the questions you will find amusing; some of them are deadly serious. But between the two, the outlines of what you believe and don't believe should begin to become clear. Each succeeding chapter also begins with a set of preliminary questions. And again the point is to encourage you to state your beliefs on these subjects before we begin to develop the views that philosophers have argued. Each chapter includes a discussion of various alternative viewpoints, with brief passages from some of the great philosophers. Special terms, which probably are new to you but have become established in philosophy, are introduced as they are needed, as a way of helping you make distinctions and clarify your beliefs more precisely than our ordinary language allows. (A glossary containing most of these terms—which are boldface in the text—appears at the back of the book.) Each chapter ends with a set of concluding questions that will help you locate your own views among the alternatives of traditional philosophy. There is a bibliography at the end of each chapter containing suggestions for further reading; you can explore those topics that interest or challenge you, since no textbook can substitute for original works.

For the Instructor

This fifth edition is easier to use and more flexible for teaching a variety of individually structured courses in introductory philosophy at both the college and advanced high school levels. The addition of two appendices, *Deductive Logic Valid Argument Forms* and *Common Informal Fallacies,* not only allows the text to be more simple and straightforward but also for these topics to receive focused attention. I expanded the final chapter on feminist and non-Western philosophies. As in the fourth edition, my intention for this and all chapters is to make such material available to those instructors who choose to use it but dispensable for those who do not. The discussion in every chapter is more or less self-contained, and the chapters can be used in just about any order. Some instructors prefer to start with the "God" chapter, for example, others with the more "epistemological" chapters on "Knowledge," "Truth," "Self," and "Freedom." I find that the opening chapters, with their broad collection of both playful and serious philosophical questions and varied discussions of the "Meaning of Life," are helpful in loosening up and relaxing nervous first-time students and getting them to talk in a more free-wheeling way than they do if they are immediately confronted by the great thinkers or the most intractable problems of philosophy. So, too, I find the opening questions are helpful for getting students to think about the issues on their own before diving into the text. To encourage students to write and think about philosophical questions, to get them used to *interacting* with the text and arguments, I added space between each question, in which the students can write their own responses and comments directly in the book. The closing questions to each chapter, by the way, also serve as handy exam questions.

ACKNOWLEDGMENTS

I thank all those readers, both students and colleagues, who responded kindly and critically to my earlier text, *Introducing Philosophy* (Harcourt Brace Jovanovich, 1977; Sixth Edition, 1997). The present text, *The Big Questions,* Fifth Edition, is a fresh attempt to reach an audience no longer addressed by that book, and I am indebted to all who pointed out the need for the new book and helped me develop and refine it.

I especially thank all those people who taught me the joys and skills of philosophy, and how to teach it. First of all, there is my father, Charles M. Solomon, who always encouraged me in "that thinkin' stuff." There is Robert Hanson, who first thrilled me with Parmenides and Heraclitus at Cheltenham High School, and Doris Yocum, who taught my first philosophy course. I learned so much about teaching philosophy from Elizabeth Flower, James Ross, Peter Hempel, and Frithjof Bergmann, and I continue to learn from great colleagues like Bob Kane and Paul Woodruff. I also thank Donette Moss, Winkie Conlon, and Shirley Hull for their much-needed care and attention, and Jon Solomon for his advice on exotic matters in the book.

For their encouraging reviews and helpful suggestions, my thanks to Stephen Waters; Mark Gilbertson, Texas Lutheran University; Victor Guarino, Indian River Community College; Michael Thomas, College of the Redwoods; Thomas E. Moody, California State University-San Bernardino; Stanley M. Browne, Alabama A&M University; Ronald Duska, The American College; Albert B. Randall, Austin Peay State University; Emrys Westacott, Alfred University; Gary Prince, West Los Angeles College; and Janet McCracken, Lake Forest College.

Karen Mottola helped me tremendously with this edition, and I owe her a special debt of appreciation. I am also grateful to David Tatom and Pam Hatley of Harcourt Brace College Publishers for their editorial expertise during publication of the fifth edition. Thanks, too, to Bill McLane.

Special thanks to (most of) the students in Plan II Philosophy at the University of Texas at Austin.

Robert C. Solomon

Contents

INTRODUCTION
DOING PHILOSOPHY

Auguste Rodin, The Thinker, *detail, The Metropolitan Museum of Art, New York, gift of Thomas F. Ryan, 1910.*

INTRODUCTION
DOING PHILOSOPHY

The unexamined life is not worth living.
— *Socrates*

Know thyself!
— *Oracle at Delphi (Socrates' motto)*

Philosophy consists of our views—our beliefs and attitudes about ourselves and the world. Doing philosophy, therefore, is first of all the activity of stating, as clearly and as convincingly as possible, what we believe and what we believe in. This does not mean, however, that announcing one's allegiance to some grand-sounding ideas, or, perhaps, some grand-sounding word, is all that there is to philosophy. Philosophy is the development of these ideas, the attempt to work them out with all their implications and complications. It is the attempt to see their connections with other people's views—including the classic statements of the great philosophers of the past. It is the effort to appreciate the differences between one's own views and others' views, to be able to argue with someone who disagrees and resolve the difficulties that they may throw in your path. One of my students once suggested that she found it easy to list her main ideas on a single sheet of paper; what she found difficult was showing how they related to one another and how she might defend them against someone who disagreed with her. I pointed out that she was saying something like this: She would really enjoy playing quarterback with the football team, as long as she didn't have to cooperate with the other players—and then only until the other team came onto the field. But playing football is cooperating with your team and running against the team that is out to stop you; philosophy is the attempt to coordinate a number of different ideas into a single viewpoint, and holding out for what you believe against those who are out to refute you. Indeed, a belief that can't be tied in with a great many other beliefs and that can't withstand criticism may not be worth believing at all.

Socrates was perhaps the greatest philosopher of all times, though he never wrote a word. (All that we know of him comes down to us from his student Plato and other philosophers.) Socrates was born in 470 B.C. and lived his whole long life in Athens. He had a spectacular gift for rhetoric and debating. He had a much-gossiped-about marriage, several children, and lived in poverty most of his life. He based his philosophy on the need to "know yourself" and on living the "examined life," even though the height of wisdom, according to Socrates, was to know how thoroughly ignorant we are. Much of his work was dedicated to defining and living the ideals of wisdom, justice, and the good life. In 399 B.C. he was placed on trial by the Athenians for "corrupting the youth" with his ideas. He was condemned to death, refused all opportunities to escape or have his sentence repealed, and accepted the cruel and unfair verdict with complete dignity and several brilliant speeches, dying as well as living for the ideas he defended.

BEYOND BUZZWORDS
AND VERBAL SPAGHETTI

To defend your ideas is quite different from insisting, no matter how self-righteously, on the mere sound of a word. To say that you believe in "freedom," for instance, may make you feel proud and righteous, but this has nothing to do with philosophy, or, for that matter, with freedom, unless you are willing to spell out exactly what it is you stand for, what it is that you believe, and why it is that this "freedom," as you call it, is so desirable. But most students, as well as many professional philosophers, get caught up in such attractive, admirable words, which we can call "buzzwords." These sound as if they refer to something quite specific and concrete (like the word "dog"), but in fact they are among the most difficult words to understand and they provide us with the hardest problems in philosophy. "Freedom" sounds as if it means breaking out of prison or being able to speak one's mind against a bad government policy; but when we try to say what it is that ties these two examples together, and many more besides, it soon becomes clear that we don't know exactly what we're talking about. Indeed, virtually everyone believes in "freedom," but the question is *what* it is that they believe in. Similarly, many people use such words as "truth," "reality," "morality," "love," and even "God" as buzzwords, words that make us feel good just because we say them. But to express the beliefs these words supposedly represent is to do something more than merely say the words; it is also to say what they mean, and what it is in the world (or out of it) to which we are referring. Buzzwords are like badges; we use them to identify ourselves. But it is equally important to know what the badges stand for.

Some buzzwords seem to be ways of identifying ourselves—the words "science" and "art," for example. How many dubious suggestions and simple-minded advertisements cash in on the respectability of the word "scientific"? What outrageous behavior is sometimes condoned on the grounds that it is "artistic"? And in politics, what actions have not been justified in the name of "national security" or "self-determination"? But such buzzwords not only block our understanding of the true nature of our behavior; they can also be an obstacle—rather than an aid—in philosophy. Philosophers are always making up new words, often by way of making critical distinctions. For example, the words "subjective" and "objective," once useful philosophical terms, now have so many meanings and are so commonly abused that the words by themselves hardly mean anything at all. Would-be philosophers, including some of the more verbally fluent philosophy students, may think that they are doing philosophy when they merely string together long noodle chains of such impressive terms. We call this "verbal spaghetti," and it is to philosophy what a howling dog is to music. Philosophical terms are useful only in so far as they stay tied down to the problems they are introduced to solve and retain the carefully defined meanings they carry. Buzzwords become not aids for thinking but rather *substitutes* for thinking, and verbal spaghetti, despite its complexity, is intellectually without nutritional value.

The abuse of buzzwords and the ease with which some people can overwhelm serious discussions with verbal spaghetti explain the importance of that overused introductory philosophical demand, "Define your terms." In fact, it is very difficult to define your terms, and most of the time, it is unnecessary and a waste of time. You know quite well what you mean. But when certain philosophical terms enter our discussion, it is clear why this incessant demand has always been so important; many students seem to think that they have learned some philosophy just because they have learned a new and impressive word or two. But that's like believing that you have learned how to ski just because you have tried on the boots and skis. The truth, however, is to be found in what you go on to do with them.

ARTICULATION AND ARGUMENT: TWO CRUCIAL FEATURES OF PHILOSOPHY

Philosophy is, first of all, **reflection**. It is stepping back, listening to yourself and other people (including the great philosophers), and trying to understand and evaluate what it is that you hear, and what it is that you believe. To formulate your own philosophy is to say what it is that you believe as clearly and as thoroughly as possible. Often we believe that we believe something, but as soon as we try to write it down or explain it to a friend we find that what seemed so clear a moment ago has disappeared, as if it evaporated just as we were about to express it. Sometimes too we think we don't have any particular views on a subject, but once we begin to discuss the topic with a friend it turns out that we have very definite views, as soon as they are **articulated**. Articulation—spelling out our ideas in words and sentences—is the primary process of philosophy. Sitting down to write out your ideas is an excellent way to articulate them, but most people find that an even better way, and sometimes far more relaxed and enjoyable, is simply to discuss these ideas with other people—classmates, good friends, or family—even, on occasion, a stranger with whom you happen to strike up a conversation. Indeed, talking with another person not only forces you to be clear and concrete in your articulation of your beliefs; it allows you—or forces you—to engage in a second essential feature of doing philosophy: **arguing** for your views. Articulating your opinions still leaves open the question whether they are worth believing, whether they are well thought out and can stand up to criticism from someone who disagrees with you. Arguments serve the purpose of testing our views; they are to philosophy what practice games are to sports—ways of seeing just how well you are prepared, how skilled you are, and, in philosophy, just how convincing your views really are.

Articulating and arguing your opinions has another familiar benefit: stating and defending a view is a way of making it very much your own. Too many students, in reading and studying philosophy, look at the various statements and arguments of the great philosophers as if they were merely displays in some intellectual museum, curiously contradicting each other, but, in any case, having no real relevance to us. But once you have adopted a viewpoint, which very likely was defended at some time by one of the philosophical geniuses of history, it becomes very much your own as well. Indeed, doing philosophy almost always includes appealing to other philosophers in support of your own views, borrowing their arguments and examples as well as quoting them when they have striking things to say (with proper credit in a

Articulation—putting your ideas in clear, concise, readily understandable language.

Argument—the process of supporting your ideas with reasons from other ideas, principles, and observations to establish your conclusions and overcome objections.

Analysis—understanding an idea by distinguishing and clarifying its various components. For example, the idea of "murder" involves three component ideas: Killing, wrongfulness, and intention.

Synthesis—gathering together different ideas into a single, unified vision. For example, the Pythagorean notion of the "harmony of the spheres" synthesizes mathematics, music, physics, and astronomy.

footnote, of course). It is by *doing* philosophy, articulating and arguing your views, instead of just reading about other people's philosophy books, that you make your own views genuinely your own, by working with them, stating them publicly, defending them and committing yourself to them. That is how the philosophies of the past become important to us, and how our own half-baked, inarticulate, often borrowed, and typically undigested ideas start to become something more. Philosophy, through reflection and by means of articulation and argument, allows us to **analyze** and critically examine our ideas, and to **synthesize** our vision of ourselves and the world, to put the pieces together in a single, unified, defensible vision. Such a synthesis is the ultimate aim of philosophical reflection, and scattered ideas and arguments are no more philosophy than a handful of unconnected words is a poem.

CONCEPTS AND CONCEPTUAL FRAMEWORKS

The basic units of our philosophical projects and viewpoints are called **concepts**. Concepts give form to experience; they make articulation possible. But even before we try to articulate our views, concepts make it possible for us to recognize things in the world, to see and hear particular objects and particular people instead of one big blur of a world, like a movie camera that is seriously out of focus. But in addition to defining the forms of our experience, concepts also tie our experience together. Concepts rarely occur in isolation; they virtually always tie together into a **conceptual framework**.

An example of a concept would be this: as children, we learn to identify certain creatures as dogs. We acquire the concept "dog." At first, we apply our new concept clumsily, calling a "dog" anything that has four legs, including cows, cats, and horses. Our parents correct us, however, and we learn to be more precise, distinguishing dogs first from cats, cows, and horses and then later from wolves, coyotes, and jackals. We then have the concept "dog"; we can recognize dogs; we can talk about dogs. We can think about and imagine dogs even when one is not actually around at the time, and we can say what we think about dogs in general. We can refine our concept, too, by learning to recognize the various breeds of dogs and perhaps to distinguish between dangerous dogs and friendly dogs. On certain occasions, therefore, the concept takes on an undeniably practical importance, for it is the concept that tells us how to act, when to run, and when to be friendly in turn. But the concept "dog" also becomes a part of our vision of the world—a world in which dogs are of some significance, a world divided into dogs and non-dogs, a world in which we can contemplate, for example, the difference between a dog's life and our own. (One of the great movements in ancient philosophy was called **Cynicism** after the Greek word for "dog." The cynics acquired their name by living a life of austerity and poverty which, to their contemporaries, seemed little better than a "dog's life.")

Empirical knowledge—knowledge based on experience (whether your own experience or the observations and experiments of others), for example, "The temperature in Chicago today is 17°F."

A priori **knowledge**—knowledge that is independent of ("before") any particular experience, for example, "2 + 3 = 5" or "A + B = B + A."

Some concepts have very specific objects, like "dog." These specific concepts, derived from experience, are often called **empirical** concepts. We have already seen this word "empirical" referring to experience (for example, knowing the various breeds and behaviors of dogs). We shall see it again and again; the root *empiri-* means having to do with experience. Through empirical concepts we make sense of the world, dividing it into recognizable pieces, learning how to deal with it and developing our ability to talk about it, to understand and explain it, and to learn more and talk more about it. In addition to such specific concepts, we make use of a set of much more abstract concepts, whose objects are not so tangible or empirical and which cannot be so easily defined. These are *a priori* concepts, because they are conceptually *prior to* empirical concepts. One example is the concept of "number." However important numbers might be in our talk about our experience, the concepts of arithmetic are not empirical concepts. Mathematicians talk about the concept of an "irrational number," but there is nothing in our everyday experience which they can point to as an example of one. To understand this concept requires a good deal of knowledge about mathematics, since this concept, like most concepts, can be defined only within a system of other abstract concepts.

The *a priori* concept of "number" raises problems far more difficult than the empirical concept of "dog," and it is with the most difficult concepts that philosophy is generally concerned. Because philosophical concepts are abstract, there may be far more room for disagreement about what they mean. For example, the concepts of a "good person" and the "good life" seem to mean very different things to different people and in different societies. So, too, the concept of "God" creates enormous difficulties, in fact, so many difficulties that some religions refuse to define God at all, or even give Him (and not always "Him") a name. Within the Judeo-Christian and Islamic traditions, there are very different conceptions of God, even within the Bible. When we begin to consider some of the other conceptions of God—for example, the Greek conception of Zeus and Apollo; the Hindu concepts of Vishnu and Shiva; or some modern conceptions of God as identical to the universe as a whole, or as a vital force, or as whatever a person takes to be his or her "ultimate concern in life"—you can see that simply agreeing on the word still

THE FIELDS OF PHILOSOPHY

For convenience and in order to break the subject up into course-size sections, philosophy is usually divided up into a number of fields. Ultimately, these are all interwoven, and it is difficult to pursue a question in any one field without soon finding yourself in the others, too. And yet philosophers, like most other scholars, tend to specialize, and you, too, will probably find your main interests focused in one of the following areas:

Metaphysics—the theory of reality and the ultimate nature of all things. The aim of metaphysics is a comprehensive view of the universe, an overall worldview. One part of metaphysics is a field sometimes called **ontology** the study of "being," an attempt to list in order of priority the various sorts of entities that make up the universe.

Ethics—the study of good and bad, right and wrong, the search for the "good life" and the defense of the principles and rules of **morality**. It is therefore sometimes called "**moral philosophy**," although this is but a single part of the broad field of ethics.

Epistemology—the study of knowledge, including such questions as "What can we know?" and "How do we know anything?" and "What is truth?"

Logic (or **philosophical logic**)—the study of the formal structures of sound thinking and good argumentation.

Philosophy of religion (or **philosophical theology**)—the philosophical study of religion, the nature of religion, the nature of God, and the various reasons for believing (or not believing) in His existence.

Political (or **social-political**) **philosophy**—the study of the foundations and the nature of society and "the state," an attempt to formulate a vision of the ideal society and implement ideas and reforms in our own society to better achieve this.

Aesthetics (or **the philosophy of art**)—the study of the nature of art and the experiences we have when we enjoy the arts, including an understanding of such concepts as "beauty" and "expression."

leaves open the hardest questions: What is God like? What can we expect of Him? What is involved in believing "in" Him? What is our *concept* of God?

The concept of "freedom" is particularly difficult; some people think that freedom is being able to do whatever you want to do. Others think that freedom makes sense only within the rules of your society. But it is not as if the word "freedom" *already* means one or the other; the word and its meaning are open to interpretation, and interpretation is the business of philosophy. This is not to say, however, that what we might disagree about is simply the

> *The Ethiopians make their gods black-skinned and snub-nosed; the Thracians say theirs have blue eyes and red hair. If oxen and horses had hands and could draw and make works of art as men do, then horses would draw their gods to look like horses, and oxen like oxen— each would make their bodies in the image of their own.*
>
> *—Xenophanes*

meaning of a word. What we disagree about is the *concept,* and the concept in turn determines the way we see the world.

The concept of "self" is like this too. In a purely grammatical sense, the word "self" just points to a person—for example, to *myself* when I say, "I presented myself to the dean." But what is this self? Again, it is not defined by the word, which only points. Is my self just the *I,* the *voice* that is now speaking, or does it refer to a whole human being? Does it include every trivial and insignificant fact about me? (For example, the fact that I forgot to brush my teeth this morning?) Or does it refer just to certain **essential** facts—for instance, the fact that I am a conscious being? Is my self a *soul?* Or is my self perhaps a social construction, which must be defined not in terms of one person alone but in terms of my society and my particular role in it?

The concept of "truth" is an important concept in philosophy. Is the truth simply the "way things really are"? Or does it depend upon the nature of what and how we believe as well? Could it be the case that we are all caught up in our limited view of the world, unable to see beyond the concepts of our own language and our own restricted range of experiences?

The most abstract and controversial concepts of all are not those through which we divide up the world into understandable bits and pieces but rather those grand concepts through which we try to make sense of it all together. Religion is the traditional vehicle for this total understanding, but in our culture religion has been challenged by science, by art, by the law, and by politics for this ultimate role, as well as by philosophy.

These all-embracing pictures and perspectives are our ultimate **conceptual frameworks**—that is, the most abstract concepts through which we "frame" and organize all of our more specific concepts. The term "conceptual framework" stresses the importance of concepts and, therefore, is central to the articulation of concepts that makes up most of philosophy. But what we are calling a "conceptual framework" can also be viewed, from a more practical perspective, as a set of values and a way of looking at life, a way of living, or, in our contemporary vocabulary, as a **life-style**. If the emphasis is shifted to politics and society, the same thing can be called an **ideology**—that is, a set of ideas about the nature of society and our political roles within it. But an ideology also depends on concepts and so is a conceptual framework too, as well as a kind of lifestyle. If we shift to a more historical viewpoint, we find that historians sometimes refer to the same thing as a **climate of opinion**. If we shift the emphasis away from the concepts through which we give form to our world and emphasize instead the view of the world that results, we can use a popular philosophical term, **worldview** (which is often left in German, **Weltanschauung**, since a number of German philosophers used it quite often in the last century or so). But whether we use one term or the other, with one emphasis or another, the important point is that we in some sense already have such viewpoints, through which we give shape to our world and define our lives within it. When we articulate them in philosophy, we are not just creating an arbitrary structure of ideas; we are making explicit and clarifying what we already believe, in order to be more aware of our ideas, in order to be able to defend them, and, sometimes, in order to be able to change them.

Our conceptual framework, our lifestyle, our ideology, our climate of opinion, or our worldview is usually taken for granted, as the intellectual ground that we walk on. But, sometimes, it is necessary to examine that ground, to look carefully at what we usually take for granted. If we are planning to construct a house, it is a good idea to investigate the ground we will build on, especially when something seems wrong—the soil is too soft or it is on a fault and susceptible to earthquakes. This is often the case, too, with our conceptual frameworks; as soon as we look at them, they may seem to be soft, ill-formed, perhaps in danger of imminent collapse, or liable to total disruption by a well placed question or confrontation with someone who disagrees with us. This is a common experience among college freshmen, for example; they come to school with certain religious, moral, political, and personal views which they have always taken for granted, which they have never questioned or been forced to defend. Then they meet someone—a roommate, a teacher, a friend in a course—and these lifelong views are thrown into total chaos. Students who are not prepared for intellectual confrontation may find that they are no longer so sure; then they get defensive, even offended and belligerent. But with time and some philosophical thinking, the same students again become clear about what they believe and why. Before the ground was examined, it might have been soft or near collapse, but once they see where they stand, they can fill in the holes, make it solid, protect themselves against unexpected idea-quakes, and renew their beliefs with a confidence much greater than before.

It is possible, of course, that you will find yourself using two or even more conceptual frameworks—for example, a scientific framework in school, a pleasure-seeking (or **hedonistic**) framework for Saturday night, and a religious framework on Sunday morning. The question then becomes, How do these different frameworks tie together? Which is most important? Are they actually inconsistent with one another? If our lives are to be coherent, don't we have to unify our various beliefs so that they all hang together? What makes an understanding of concepts and conceptual frameworks so important and rewarding, ultimately, is the fact that in understanding them, we are also in the process of *creating* them, and in so doing enriching them, developing

RELIGION AND SCIENCE: EINSTEIN

It is easy to see why the churches have always fought science and persecuted its devotees. On the other hand, I maintain that the cosmic religious feeling is the strongest and noblest motive for scientific research. Only those who realize the immense efforts and, above all, the devotion without which pioneer work in theoretical science cannot be achieved are able to grasp the strength of the emotion out of which alone such work, remote as it is from the immediate realities of life, can issue. What a deep conviction of the rationality of the universe and what a yearning to understand, were it but a feeble reflection of the mind revealed in this world, Kepler and Newton must have had to enable them to spend years of solitary labor in disentangling the principles of celestial mechanics! Those whose acquaintance with scientific research is derived chiefly from its practical results easily develop a completely false notion of the mentality of the men who, surrounded by a skeptical world, have shown the way to kindred spirits scattered wide through the world and the centuries. Only one who had devoted his life to similar ends can have a vivid realization of what has inspired these men and given them the strength to remain true to their purpose in spite of countless failures. It is cosmic religious feeling that gives a man such strength. A contemporary has said, not unjustly, that in this materialistic age of ours the serious scientific workers are the only profoundly religious people.

—Einstein, *Religion
and Science*

them, solidifying them, and giving new understanding and clarity to our everyday lives.

Doing Philosophy with Style

The quality of a philosophy depends upon the ingenuity with which its ideas are presented, the thoroughness with which they are worked out, the care with which one idea is tied to another, the vividness with which the entire view comes across to the reader. The greatest philosophers in history—Plato, Aristotle, and the German philosopher Immanuel Kant—did not believe anything very different from most of their contemporaries, including other philosophers whom they knew and talked with every day. But they became the great philosophers of our tradition because they presented their ideas

THREE IMPORTANT NAMES TO KNOW

Plato (427–347 B.C.) was a student of Socrates and the leading spokesman for Socrates' ideas. He was shocked by Socrates' execution and dedicated his life to developing and spreading his philosophy. In 385 B.C. he set up the Academy to educate the future leaders of Athens in morality and philosophy in general.

Aristotle (384–322 B.C.), a student of Plato, strongly disagreed with many of his teacher's theories. Aristotle was an accomplished scientist as well as a philosopher, and his ideas ruled most of the sciences—especially biology—until modern times. He was the tutor of Alexander (who became "the Great") and later founded his own school (the Lyceum) in Athens. When Alexander died, Aristotle was forced to flee, commenting that he would not let Athens "sin against philosophy a second time."

Immanuel Kant (1724–1804) was, in the opinion of many philosophers, the greatest philosopher of modern times. He spent his entire life in a small eastern Prussian town (Königsberg). He was famous for his simple, regular life (He never married, and his neighbors were said to set their clocks by his punctual afternoon walks.). And yet this somewhat uninteresting professor was also an enthusiast of the French Revolution—and a revolutionary in his own way, too. His ideas turned many of the traditional views of knowledge, religion, and morality upside down.

with eloquence, defended them so brilliantly, and put them together in monumental constructions which are wonderful (if also very difficult) to behold. Philosophy is first of all articulation and argument, but it is also articulation and argument *with style*. Every philosophy, and every essay or book in philosophy, is essentially *making a case*. That is why philosophical training is so valuable for students going into law, or politics, or business, or—ultimately—almost every career where articulation and argument are important. But disjointed articulation and argument not aimed at making a case to some particular audience (even if that audience is only your roommate or philosophy instructor) is without a point or purpose. Philosophy should be persuasive. That means that, in addition to evidence of hard-thinking and a display of wisdom, philosophical writing should be somewhat entertaining, witty, dramatic, and even seductive. It is working out common views in ways that are not at all common. But whether philosophy is the somewhat modest thinking of a first-year philosophy student or the hundreds of pages that make up the classic texts of the great philosophers, the activity is the same—to try to articulate and clarify and present one's own view of the world as attractively as possible. It is possible to appreciate philosophy only by participating in it, by being a philosopher, too. And by the time you have completed this course, you too will be a part (if a small part) of that long tradition that has come to define the world of "Western" philosophy, and a little bit of "non-Western," too.

1. *Your ideas:* Without ideas, articulated clearly, there is nothing to think or write about.

2. *Critical thinking:* Ideas unqualified and uncriticized, undeveloped and unargued, are not yet philosophy. One of the most valuable tools you can carry away from a philosophy class is the ability to read and think critically, to scrutinize ideas as well as gather information.

3. *Argumentation:* Philosophy is not just stating your opinions; it is providing arguments to support your opinions, and arguments against objections to your views. The best philosophy always includes a kind of point-counterpoint format. Don't just state your views. Argue for them, and anticipate the kinds of objections that will probably be raised against you, countering them in advance. ("Now you might object that. . . , but against that I want to point out that . . .")

4. *A problem:* Philosophy does not consist of random speculations and arguments about some topic or other. It is motivated by a problem, a real concern. Death and the meaning of life are philosophical problems because—to put it mildly—we are all concerned with questions about life and death, *our* lives and deaths. Problems about knowledge arise because someone somewhere challenged our ability to know as much as we think we know, and philosophers ever since have been trying to answer that challenge. (For example, How do you know that you are not dreaming right now? Or, How do you know that the world wasn't created five minutes ago, with all of its fossils and supposedly ancient relics, and with us and all of our memories of the alleged past?) Philosophy may begin by wondering about life and the world in general but it comes into focus on a problem.

5. *Imagination:* A list of your ideas with qualifications and arguments might count as philosophy, but it would be uninspiring and dull. Don't be afraid to use metaphors and analogies. As you will see, some of the greatest philosophers developed their views of the world into visions that are as much poetry as philosophical essays.

6. *Style:* Anything in writing is readable only if it is written in a lively style. The rules of good essay writing apply to philosophy, of course, but so do the rules of entertaining—be exciting, attractive, appealing, persuasive. No matter how exciting an idea or incisive a criticism, it always gets across better when presented with eloquence, with a personal touch and an elegant turn of phrase.

Socrates might have said, "Everyone should think about his or her life, because at least sometimes that helps us out of hard situations and makes life more valuable," but probably no one would remember it. Instead, he said, "The unexamined life is not worth living," and a hundred generations have been struck by the boldness and bluntness of his statement, whether or not, on examination, they have agreed with it.

But that one aphorism only encapsulates a philosophy; it is not itself a philosophy. What does that one striking statement mean? Its meaning is the whole body of Socrates' philosophy, with all of its ideas, images, and arguments. Your philosophy, too, is nothing less than the whole of what you believe, articulated and argued as convincingly and as elegantly as you can.

For more on philosophical style—and writing a philosophy essay or exam—see Appendix I.

A
LITTLE LOGIC

The Beatles, UPI/Corbis-Bettmann.

A LITTLE LOGIC

The central problem of logic is the
classification of arguments, so that all those
that are bad are thrown into one division,
and those which are good into another. . . .
— *Charles Sanders Peirce*

Philosophy consists of ideas, grand theories, and visions, articulated in speech or in writing and presented in the clearest way possible. In the presentation, therefore, it is crucial to give **reasons** for your ideas, to *support* your theories with a variety of examples and considerations which will show that your philosophy is more persuasive than its alternatives (or at least as persuasive). Accordingly, the key to good philosophical presentation development is what we call an **argument**. In ordinary language, we sometimes think of an argument as a violent quarrel, filled with hostility and mutual resentment. This need not be the case, however; an argument is nothing more than the process of supporting what you believe with reasons. "I know that I am not dreaming right now because I never dream this vividly, I just pinched myself and, besides, if I were dreaming I'd probably be snoring right now." An argument ties your belief to other beliefs and helps persuade someone else to accept what you believe. A good argument can be presented in a perfectly coolheaded and amiable manner. Indeed, the best arguments are always defined by a process of careful thinking which we call **logic**, often described as the "science (and the process) of proper reasoning."

Philosophers use a variety of arguments and argument-types. So, of course, do politicians, salespeople, television talk show hosts, and each one of us, every time we are trying to convince someone of something we believe or trying to think something through for ourselves. There are arguments by **example** ("Let's look at a particular case") and arguments by **analogy** ("Life is like a novel. There is a beginning and an end; it can be dull or exciting; there will surely be conflicts and bad scenes; there is suspense; the plot thickens. Therefore, the most important thing in life is to live an interesting life, develop your character, and don't just play it safe."). There are arguments based on extensive scientific research and there are arguments that are very abstract and largely verbal (concerned more with the words used to describe a phenomenon than with the phenomenon itself). There are arguments based on nothing more than a vicious attack on one's opponents, and there are arguments that—despite their appearance—are not really arguments at all. In general, we might divide arguments into two classes—good arguments and bad arguments—depending on the *relations* between various statements. ("Truth" and "falsity," on the other hand, apply to the statements themselves, never to the arguments.) But what counts as a good or a bad argument depends upon what kind of an argument it is. As a useful way to understand arguments and what it is that makes them good or bad, it is convenient to divide them into two very general categories, to which philosophers and logicians (that is, those who study logic as their essential interest) apply the names **deduction** and **induction**.

DEDUCTION

In a deductive argument, one argues for the truth of a conclusion by *deducing* a statement from a number of others. An example that might be familiar to you is any proof of a theorem you learned to formulate in high school geometry. Some statements are assumed to be true from the outset (for example, statements which are true by definition and statements so obviously true that they need not be proved at all, called **axioms**). Then, new statements are deduced, or **inferred**, by means of a number of established **rules of inference**—that is, the laws of thought, such as "A statement cannot be both true and false at the same time" or "If either A or B, but not A, then B." A deductive argument is thus a progression from one true statement to another; the second statement is established as true, too; in fact, a deductive argument is sometimes defined as an argument whose final statement—or **conclusion**—is guaranteed to be true by the truth of the first statements—or **premises**.

The best-known deductive arguments are called **syllogisms**. An example of a syllogism is:

> All philosophers are wise.
> Socrates is a philosopher.
> _____
> Therefore, Socrates is wise.

What is important in such arguments is the form of the component statements:

> All P's are Q's.
> S is a P.
> _____
> Therefore, S is a Q.

When a deductive argument proceeds correctly according to this form, we say that it is **deductively valid** or simply **valid**. Arguments that are not valid are **invalid**. Deduction guarantees that our conclusions will be at least as certain as the premises. If the premises are certainly true, then the conclusions will certainly be true as well. But it is important to emphasize that an argument can be valid even if its premises and conclusion are false. For example, the following syllogism correctly follows the above form and is therefore valid:

> All cows are purple.
> Socrates is a cow.
> _____
> Therefore, Socrates is purple.

This is a valid argument, even though both the premises and the conclusion are false. But without true premises, even a valid argument cannot guarantee true conclusions. A good deductive argument must also have premises which are agreed to be true. Notice that, contrary to common usage, philosophers restrict their use of the words "valid" and "invalid" to talking about correct and incorrect arguments; the words "true" and "false" apply to the various statements that one makes in an argument—its premises and its conclusion. Thus, the claim that "three plus two equals eight" is false, not invalid; and the argument "If Socrates is a man and all goats eat cabbage, then Socrates is a goat" is invalid, not false (whether or not its premises or conclusion are false). When an argument is both valid and has true premises (a good argument, in other words), it is called a **sound** argument. An argument is **unsound** (a bad deductive argument) if its premises are false, or if it is invalid. A good deductive argument, then, has two essential features:

a) It is a valid argument.

b) Its premises are true.

A detailed discussion of valid argument forms can be found in Appendix II.

INDUCTION

Inductive arguments, on the other hand, do not guarantee the truth of their conclusions, even if all the premises are agreed to be true. The most familiar form of inductive argument is **generalization** from a number of particular cases—for example, noting that every animal we have seen with sharp front teeth eats meat, and concluding that *all* animals with sharp front teeth eat meat. But notice that although we might be absolutely sure that we are correct about the particular cases—that every animal we have seen does in fact eat meat—we might still be wrong in our generalization, our conclusion that *all* such animals are meat eaters. Thus it is essential in any inductive argument to begin with a well chosen number of particular cases and to make sure that they are as varied as possible (that is, to have what social scientists usually call a "random sample"). Inductive arguments can be **strong** or **weak**; depending on the weight of the evidence for the conclusion, the quality of the sample, and the plausibility of the generalization. Inductive arguments are not evaluated as valid or invalid; in fact, given the definition of validity as the guarantee that the conclusion is true if the premises are true, *no* inductive ar-

DEDUCTIVE AND INDUCTIVE LOGIC

Deductive logic guarantees the truth of the conclusion, *if* the premises are true.

Example: If Moriarty didn't do it, then the Spiderwoman did. We know that Moriarty was in prison at the time, so the Spiderwoman must have done it. (Premises: "If M didn't do it, S did" and "M was in prison at the time.")

Inductive logic does not guarantee the truth of the conclusion, but only makes it more reasonable for us to believe the conclusion (compared with other possible conclusions).

Example: The pipe tobacco is the same kind he uses and the footprints match his shoes. He was seen in the neighborhood only an hour before the crime and he was heard to say, "I'm going to get even with her if it's the last thing I do." The best explanation of the evidence in this case seems to be the conclusion that he is guilty.

gument is ever deductively valid. (That is not a mark against it, of course. Inductive arguments have other functions; they are not supposed to be deductively valid.)

Although generalization is the most familiar example of induction, inductive arguments can be used to support virtually every statement of fact. For example, if you believe that Julius Caesar was murdered in Rome on March 15, 44 B.C., that is a statement of fact which you cannot directly observe today. The argument for its truth must therefore be inductive, based on information you have read in history books, colored by imagery from a play by Shakespeare, to be further verified—if you are curious—by an investigation into the **evidence** available in chronicles of the period, records of Roman politics, and perhaps a few relics from the times. In such inductive arguments, it is the **coherence** of the evidence that provides the argument—that is, the various elements of the argument fit together well. In a criminal trial, for instance, evidence is presented in favor of two contradictory statements of fact ("The defendant is guilty" versus "The defendant is not guilty"). The inductive question in the mind of the judge and the jury—and probably earlier in the mind of the detectives who worked on the case, too—is whether the evidence for conviction is more coherent than the evidence against. It is worth noting that what Sherlock Holmes and Dr. Watson continuously point to as Holmes' "amazing powers of deduction" are for the most part powers of *inductive* reasoning, drawing factual conclusions from scattered and sometimes barely noticeable evidence.

One of the most important ingredients in inductive reasoning is the **hypothesis**, the statement that an experiment is supposed to prove or disprove. You are probably familiar with hypotheses in science, but we use hypotheses throughout our lives. Induction would be a waste of time if we did not have some hypothesis in mind. Just as a scientist tries to organize his or her research around a particular topic and a specific claim, we organize our attention around particular concerns and specific hypotheses. "Who killed the judge? It must have been either Freddy or the thug. Which hypothesis is the more plausible?" Not only science but almost everything we know and want to know depends on hypotheses and inductive reasoning, from looking for the car keys in the morning ("Now, I'm sure I left them somewhere near my books") to speculating on the existence and the nature of black holes in space.

From the preceding discussion, it should be clear that much of what passes for argument is not that at all. For example, many people seem to think that simply stating and restating their opinion—forcefully and with conviction—is the same thing as supporting it with arguments. It is not. Stating your opinion clearly is the essential preliminary to formulating an argument, but it is not the same thing. An argument goes beyond the opinion itself, supporting it by deduction from other statements or with evidence based on experience. Some people seem to think that a single example will serve as a complete argument, but, at most, a single example serves as *part* of an argument. Most inductive arguments require many examples, and they must deal with examples that *don't* fit the hypothesis, too. Every argument is bound to meet up with several counterarguments and objections, so even a single argument is rarely enough to make one's case.

Similarly, many people seem to think that an appeal to **authority** will settle the case, but in most philosophical disputes, it is the nature of authority itself that is in question. If someone insists that God exists because it says so in the Bible, the question immediately shifts to the authority of the Bible. (A person who does not believe in God will probably not accept the authority of the Bible either.) If someone defends a political position because his mother said so or, for that matter, because Thomas Jefferson said so, the question then moves to the authority of the arguer's mother or Mr. Jefferson. One of the main functions of philosophy is to let us question authority and see for ourselves what we should believe or not believe. Simply to appeal to authority is not necessarily to show respect for that authority, but it is to show disrespect for ourselves. The truth can always stand up for itself, and what we believe isn't worth much if we are unwilling to test it with criticism.

CRITICIZING ARGUMENTS

One of the most crucial philosophical activities—but by no means the only one—is **criticism**. Criticism does not necessarily mean—as in everyday life—negative remarks about someone or something; it means carefully examining a statement, testing it out, seeing if in fact the arguments for it are good ones. But this does mean that, whether it is our own statements or other people's statements that are being examined, it is important to find out what is *wrong* with them, so that they can be corrected or strengthened. One way to criticize a deductive argument, for example, is simply to show that its premises are not true; if it is an inductive argument, to show that the evidence on which it is based is falsified or distorted. Another way to criticize an argument is to show that it consists of invalid deductive arguments or weak inductive generalizations. A particularly powerful way to do this is by the use of **counterexamples**. For instance, if someone claims, "All American men love football," he or she can be refuted if we can find a single American male who does not like football. Any claim that takes the form "All X's are Y's" or "No A's are B's" can be refuted if we can point out a single counterexample—that is, a single X that is not Y, or a single A that is a B. If a philosophy student says, "No one knows anything for certain," a familiar response might be to hold up your hand, stick out your thumb, and say, "Here is a thumb: I know *that* for certain." This may not be the end of the argument, but it is through such general claims and counterexamples to them that philosophical arguments are made more precise.

Even if all arguments seem to be sound, a philosophy can be shown to be in trouble if it is **inconsistent**, if the conclusions of its different arguments **contradict** one another. In the same way, one can rise doubts about a philosophy's acceptability if it can be shown that it results in **paradox** and, consequently, must be thoroughly reexamined. For example, suppose a philosopher argues that God can do absolutely anything. For instance, He can create a mountain. He can move a mountain. But now a critical listener asks, "Can He create a mountain so large that even *He* can't move it?"—and we have a paradox. Either He can create such a mountain but then can't move it (and so cannot do everything), or He cannot create such a mountain (and so cannot do everything). The paradox forces us to reexamine the original claim that God can do absolutely anything. (Perhaps it can be revised to say something like, "God can do anything that is logically possible.") Notice that this is a form of **reductio ad absurdum** argument, a "reduction to absurdity," in which a position is rejected because it results in a paradox. But even when a philosophy does not contain outright inconsistencies or lead to paradoxes, it may be **incoherent**, such that the various claims have virtually nothing to do with each other, or mean very little, or can be interpreted only in an absurd way. A philosophy can be accused of **begging the question** repeating as a supposed solution the very problem that it is attempting to resolve. An example of begging the question is the argument, "Other people exist. I know because I've talked to them." And a philosophy can be accused of being silly or trivial, which is just about the most offensive thing you can say, indicating that it is not even worth your time to investigate it further. It is much better to say something false but interesting rather than silly or trivial. (A common way in which philosophical claims can turn out to be trivial is when they express what logicians call *tautologies:* for example. "A is A.") An argument can be ***ad hominem*** (or ***ad feminam***), aimed at the person but ignoring the issue completely. Accusing someone who disagrees of being an atheist, a communist, or a Nazi is an all-too-familiar example of an *ad hominem* argument. Such bad arguments, in general, are called **fallacies**, whether or not they are formally

A **paradox** is a **self-contradictory** or seemingly absurd conclusion based on apparently good arguments. Sometimes the paradox is merely apparent and requires restating; on occasion a well formulated paradox has brought about the total rethinking of the whole of a branch of science, philosophy, religion or mathematics. Some examples are:

"This sentence is false." (If that is true, then it's false, but if it's not true, then it must be true.)

"There is a barber who shaves everyone in town who does not shave himself." (Does he shave himself?)

"God is all-powerful, so he could create a mountain so huge that even He could not move it."

If Achilles shoots an arrow from point A toward point B, it first must cover distance A–C, which is half of A–B; then it must cover distance C–D, which is half of C–B, and then D–E, which is half of D–B, and so on, each moment covering half the distance it has covered in the moment before. The paradox is that if the arrow keeps moving forever, it will never reach point B.

invalid. (A *formal* fallacy is one that violates the proper rules of inference. An *informal* fallacy may not break the rules of inference but "cheats" by sneaking in ambiguous terminology, biased language, evasion of the facts, and distraction.) A list and discussion of such fallacies can be found in Appendix III.

In emphasizing criticism, it is important to point out, as a matter of balance, that philosophy is nevertheless an especially *cooperative* enterprise. Ar-

Here is a famous paradox invented by Zeno of Elea in the fifth century B.C.

THE BASIC CONCEPTS OF LOGIC

An **argument** is a sequence of assertions, or statements to back up a viewpoint or idea. The **conclusion** is an assertion that is supported by all the other assertions. The assertions are thus the **reasons** for accepting the conclusion. Those assertions that are assumed to be true (for the sake of that argument) are called **premises**. Arguments can be either **deductive** or **inductive**: deductive arguments *guarantee* the truth of their conclusion if they are both valid and have all true premises; inductive arguments do not guarantee the truth of their conclusions, no matter how impressive the evidence. Deductive arguments are said to be **valid** or **invalid**. (Arguments are never true or false.) Invalid arguments are also called **fallacies**. Individual assertions or statements are **true** or **false**. (They are never said to be valid or invalid.) A deductive argument that is both valid and has true premises is said to be **sound**. (Otherwise, it is **unsound**.) An inductive argument that is well supported by its evidence is called **strong**, a poorly supported argument is called **weak**. **Logic** is the use of, and the study of, good arguments.

gumentation and criticism are not hostile or defensive. They are ways of making your ideas and their implications clear—clear to yourself as well as to other people. Socrates used to say that his truest friends were also his best critics. Indeed, we would distrust a friend who was never critical and never argued. ("If you were really my friend, you would have told me!") Arguments and objections take place within an arena of shared interest, and with a common concern for reaching the truth. But, just as important, arguments and objections and mutual respect between people who disagree are absolutely essential in a pluralistic democracy such as our own, where everyone's opinion is respected and it is most unlikely that we will all agree. But to say that everyone's opinion is respected is not to say that everyone's opinion is of equal value; the depth of thinking and the quality of argument make some opinions better and more plausible than others. At the same time, cooperative respect, mutual concern for the importance of argument, and honest disagreement are the preconditions for life as we want to live it.

In developing your own thoughts about the various questions of philosophy, you will inevitably find yourself using both deductive and inductive arguments, and it is perfectly normal to catch yourself—or your friends—using some incorrect arguments as well. What is important, however, is that you can recognize these forms when they appear, and that you are aware—even in only a preliminary way—of what you are doing when you argue a position or an idea. Arguments aren't the whole of philosophy; an argument can't be interesting if the statements it is intended to support are trivial or uninteresting. But the best ideas in the world can be rendered ineffective and unheeded if there are no good arguments used to present them.

CLOSING QUESTIONS

Examine the following arguments. Are they inductive or deductive arguments? Are they valid and sound? If they are invalid or unsound, why? Is there anything else wrong with them? (You may want to consult the Appendices II and III.)

1. The philosopher from northern Greece is a well-known homosexual. Therefore, his claim that the universe is ultimately made up of atoms should be ignored.

2. Every event in the world is caused by other events. Human actions and decisions are events in the world. Therefore, every human action and decision are caused by other events.

3. If God exists, then life has meaning. God does not exist. Therefore, life has no meaning.

4. All cows are purple.
   Socrates is purple.
   Therefore, Socrates is a cow.

5. William James and John Dewey both called themselves pragmatists. They are the leading American philosophers. Therefore, all American philosophers are pragmatists.

6. Believing in God makes people moral—that is, believers tend to do good and avoid evil.

7. If I try to doubt that I exist, I realize that I must exist if I am doing the doubting. Therefore, I must exist.

8. We haven't seen a fox all day. Therefore, there must be no foxes in the area.

A **tautology** is a trivially true statement. Some examples:

A man is free if he is free.

You can't know anything unless you know something.

I wouldn't be here if I hadn't arrived.

What about the following? Are they tautologies?

Business is business.

Boys will be boys.

A rose is a rose is a rose.—Gertrude Stein

Become who you are.—Friedrich Nietzsche

9. If you don't agree with me, I'm going to hit you.

10. God must exist; the Bible says so.

11. He must be guilty; he has a criminal face.

12. If she were innocent, she would loudly proclaim her innocence. She is loudly proclaiming her innocence. Therefore, she must be innocent.

13. "The state is like a man writ large." (Plato)

14. "Freedom's just another word for nothing left to lose." (Kristofferson)

15. "I have terrible news for you. Mary is going out with Frank. I called Mary on Saturday night, and she wasn't home. Then I tried to call Frank, and *he* wasn't home, either!"

BIBLIOGRAPHY AND SUGGESTED READINGS

A good introduction to logic is Robert J. Fogelin and Walter Sinnott-Armstrong, *Understanding Arguments,* 5th ed. (Harcourt Brace, 1997). The standard introductions to symbolic logic are Irving Copi, *Introduction to Logic* (Macmillan, 1961) and W. V. O. Quine, *Methods of Logic* (Holt, Rinehart and Winston, 1959). A short and useful introduction is Wesley Salmon, *Logic* (Prentice-Hall, 1963). A good and very practical book, with many good examples, is Merrillee Salmon, *Introduction to Logic and Critical Thinking,* 3rd ed. (Harcourt Brace, 1995). A good discussion of fallacies is Morris Engel, *With Good Reason* (St. Martin's, 1986). A wonderful student handbook on logic is Anthony Weston, *Rulebook for Arguments* (Hackett, 1987). An excellent introduction to critical thinking is Larry Wright, *Practical Reasoning* (Harcourt Brace Jovanovich, 1989).

CHAPTER ONE
PHILOSOPHICAL QUESTIONS

Raphael Sanzio, The School of Athens, *fresco, detail, 1509–11. Stanza della Segnatoura, Vatican Palace, Rome. Art Resource, New York.*

PHILOSOPHICAL QUESTIONS

*It is now some years since I detected how
many were the false beliefs that I had believed
to be true since my earliest youth. And since
that time, I have been convinced that I must
once and for all seriously try to rid myself of
all the opinions which I had formerly
accepted, and begin to build anew, if I
wanted to establish any firm and permanent
structure for my beliefs.*

—*René Descartes,* Meditations

Philosophy begins with nagging personal questions. Quite often, our philosophical awareness begins in disappointment or tragedy, when we first start wondering whether life is fair, or whether there is ultimately any reason for our childish confidence that, in the long run, "things will work out right." Sometimes, philosophy begins when we find ourselves forced to make difficult decisions that will affect the rest of our lives, and other people's lives, too—for example, whether to attend college or enter a trade or the military, whether to get married, whether to have children. We all find ourselves needing to justify ourselves from time to time—living in relative luxury in a world in which millions are starving; attending college when it sometimes seems as if we are not really getting much out of it; saying that we believe in one thing when our actions (or *in*action) would seem to indicate that we believe something quite different.

Our philosophizing can begin with a trivial incident; we catch ourselves lying to a friend and we start thinking about the importance of morality; we suffer from (or enjoy) a momentary illusion or hallucination and we begin to wonder how it is that we know anything is real, or even that we are not dreaming all the time. We have a quick brush with death (a near car wreck, a sudden dive in an airplane) and we start thinking about the value and meaning of life. In such moments, philosophy takes hold of us, and we see and think beyond the details of everyday life. *Doing* philosophy, in turn, is thinking further about these dramatic questions, which can suddenly become so important to us.

PHILOSOPHICAL QUESTIONS

Philosophy, simply stated, is the experience of asking such grand questions about life, about what we know, about what we ought to do or believe in. It is the process of "getting to the bottom of things," asking those basic questions about ideas that, most of the time, we simply take for granted, never think of questioning, and probably never put into words. We assume, for example, that some acts are right and some are wrong. Why? We know that it is wrong to take a human life. Why is this? Is it always so? What about in wartime? What about before birth? What about the life of a person who is hopelessly sick and in great pain? What if the world were so overcrowded that millions would die in one way if others did not die in another? However you respond to these difficult questions, your answers reveal a network of beliefs and doctrines that you may never have articulated before you first found yourself arguing about them. And not surprisingly, the first time an individual tries to argue about questions he or she has never before discussed, the result may be awkward, clumsy, and frustrating. That is the point behind philosophical questions in general: to teach us how to think about, articulate, and argue the things we believe in; to clarify these beliefs for ourselves and present them in a clear and convincing manner to other people, who may or may not agree with us. Very often, therefore, philosophy proceeds through disagreement, as when two philosophers or philosophy students argue with one another. Sometimes the dispute seems trivial or "just a matter of semantics." But since what we are searching for are basic meanings and definitions, even arguments about the *meaning of words*—especially such words as "freedom," "truth," and "self," for example—are essential to everything else we believe. With that in mind, let us begin our study with a series of somewhat strange but provocative questions, each of which is designed to get you to think about and express your opinions on a variety of distinctly philosophical issues. (It helps enormously if you write down your answers to each question *before* you read on in the text.)

René Descartes was born into the French aristocracy in 1596. As a young man, he discovered the connections between algebra and geometry (a field that we now call "analytic geometry"), established the mathematical basis for a number of sciences, and used mathematics-like thinking in philosophy and theology. An early Enlightenment thinker, he developed a method of thinking based on individual reason that did not allow for appeal to any authorities, except for the "clear light of reason" itself. His approach was to doubt everything until he could prove it to his own satisfaction. The first premise of his philosophy was the indubitability of his own existence (see Chapter 7). He died in 1650.

OPENING QUESTIONS

1. Is there anything you would willingly die for? What?

2. If you had only a few minutes to live, what would you do with them? What if you had only a few days? Twenty years?

3. A famous philosopher once said that human life is no more significant than the life of a cow or an insect. We eat, sleep, stay alive for a while, and reproduce, so that others like us can eat, sleep, stay alive for a while, and reproduce, but without any ultimate purpose at all. How would you answer him? What purpose does human life have that is not to be found in the life of a cow or an insect? What is the purpose of *your* life?

4. Do you believe in God? For what reason(s)? What is God like? (That is, what is it that you believe in?) How would you prove to someone who does not believe in God that God does indeed exist and that your belief is true? (What would change your mind about this?)

   If you do not believe in God, why not? Describe the Being in whom you do not believe. (Are there other conceptions of God that you would be willing to accept? What would change your mind about this?)

5. Which is most "real"—the chair you are sitting on, the molecules that make up the chair, or the sensations and images you have of the chair as you are sitting on it?

6. Suppose you were an animal in a psychologist's laboratory but that you had all the mental capacities for thought and feeling, the same "mind," that you have now. You overhear the scientist talking to an assistant, saying. "Don't worry about that; it's just a dumb animal, without feelings or thoughts, just behaving according to its instincts." What could you do to prove that you do indeed have thoughts and feelings, a "mind"?

   Now suppose a psychological theorist (for example, B. F. Skinner of Harvard University) were to write that, in general, there are no such things as "minds," that people do nothing more than "behave" (that is, move their bodies and make sounds according to certain stimulations from the environment). How would you argue that you do indeed have a mind, that you are not just an automaton or a robot, but a thinking, feeling being?

7. Suppose that you live in a society where everyone believes that the earth stands still, with the sun, the moon, and the stars revolving around it in predictable, if sometimes complex, orbits. You object, "You're all wrong: the earth revolves around the sun." No one agrees with you. Indeed they think that you're insane, since anyone can *feel* that the earth doesn't move at all, and you can *see* the sun, moon, and stars move. Who's right? Is it really possible that only you know the truth, and everyone else is wrong?

8. "Life is but a dream," says an old popular song. Suppose the thought were to occur to you (as it will in a philosophy class) that it is possible, or at least conceivable, that you are just dreaming at this moment, that you are still asleep in bed, dreaming about reading a philosophy book. How would you prove to yourself that this is not true, that you are indeed awake? (Pinching yourself won't do it. Why not?)

9. Describe yourself as if you were a character in a story. Describe your gestures, habits, personality traits, and characteristic word phrases. What kind of a person do you turn out to be? Do you *like* the person you have just described? What do you like—and dislike—about yourself?

10. Explain who (what) you are to a visitor from another planet.

11. We have developed a machine, a box with some electrodes and a life-support system, which we call the "happiness box." If you get in the box, you will experience a powerfully pleasant sensation, which will continue indefinitely with just enough variation to keep you from getting too used to it. We invite you to try it. If you decide to do so, you can get out of the box any time you want to; but perhaps we should tell you that no one, once they have gotten into the happiness box, has ever wanted to get out of it. After ten hours or so, we hook up the life-support system, and people spend their lifetimes there. Of course, they never do anything else, so their bodies tend to resemble half-filled water beds after a few years, because of the lack of exercise. But that never bothers them either. Now, it's

your decision: Would you like to step into the happiness box? Why or why not?

12. Will a good person (one who does no evil and does everything he or she is supposed to do) necessarily be happy, too? In other words, do you believe that life is ultimately fair? Will a wicked person surely suffer, at least in the long run? (If not, why should anyone bother trying to be good?)

13. Do you believe that it is wrong to take a life under *any* circumstances?

14. Have you ever made a decision that was *entirely* your own, that was no one's responsibility but yours? (That is, it was not because of the way your parents raised you, not because of the influence of your friends or television or books or movies, not because you were in any way forced into it or unduly influenced by someone or by certain circumstances.)

15. Is freedom always a good thing?

16. Do you want to have children? Why?

Some of these questions seem frivolous; others are clearly "profound." But they all are aimed at getting you to articulate what you believe about yourself and the world. More important than your beliefs, however, are your reasons, for it is in your **reasons** for believing what you believe that your philosophy will begin to unfold.

Let's look at the questions one by one, and you can compare your answers with those of some of the famous philosophers in history as well as with the responses of other students. (It may be a good idea to compare and contrast your answers with those of your friends and classmates. They may well have thought of angles that did not occur to you, and you may have some answers that did not occur to them.)

1. Is there anything you would willingly die for?

The philosopher **Socrates** went willingly to his death because he believed he had an obligation to respect the laws of his city even when

Socrates is in prison, condemned to die. His friend Crito has arranged an escape.

> CRITO: *I know some people who are willing to rescue you and get you out of the country. Why throw away your life?*
>
> SOCRATES: *My dear Crito, I appreciate your warm feelings, if, that is, they have some justification. Tell me this: Isn't the really important thing not to live but to live well?*
>
> CRITO: *Why, yes.*
>
> SOCRATES: *And to live well means the same thing as to live honorably or rightly?*
>
> CRITO: *Yes.*
>
> SOCRATES: *Then in the light of this we must decide whether it is right for me to get away without an official discharge. Is it not so that one ought to fulfill all of one's agreements, provided they are right?*
>
> CRITO: *One ought to fulfill them.*
>
> SOCRATES: *Then consider the logical consequence. Suppose while we were preparing to run away from here the Laws and Constitution of Athens were to come and confront us and ask, "Do you imagine that a city can continue to exist and not be destroyed if the legal judgments pronounced in it have no force, but can be nullified and destroyed by individual persons?" Suppose they said, "Was there a provision in the agreement between you and us [the Laws and Constitution] for you to disobey, or did you agree to abide by whatever judgments were pronounced?" What are we to say, Crito? Are we not bound to admit that we must obey?*
>
> CRITO: *Indeed we are bound, Socrates.*
>
> SOCRATES: *That, my dear friend Crito, is what I seem to hear them saying, just as a mystic seems to hear the strains of music, the sound of their arguments rings so loudly in my head that I cannot hear the other side. Do you wish to urge a different view?*
>
> CRITO: *No, Socrates, I have nothing more to say.*
>
> SOCRATES: *Then give it up, Crito, and let us follow the proper course, since God points out the way.*

—Plato, *Crito,* abridged

those same laws condemned him to death (see above). (He died by poisoning. He was forced to drink a cup of hemlock, and was dead within half an hour.) His friends tried to convince him to escape. He himself thought he was condemned unjustly. But his respect for the laws and for his own sense of honor were so strong that he decided that the most important thing for him to do would be to show his belief in his own principles by dying for them. In modern times, in our own country, the young patriot Nathan Hale went down in history during the Revolutionary

War. As he was about to be hanged by the British, he said, "I only regret that I have but one life to lose for my country."

Some students say that they would willingly die to save the lives of members of their immediate family. (Some cautiously qualify their answers, adding that they would do so only if risking their own lives would mean a fairly good chance of saving the lives of others.) Some students say they would give their lives "for Jesus," but they are not very clear under what circumstances such a sacrifice would be called for. A few veterans have said they would give their lives for freedom but, having fought in Vietnam, they were highly skeptical about what would count as a fight for freedom. It is worth noting that very few students in my classes have written that they would die for "honor" as such. Socrates did, though, and most of his fellow Greeks also would have considered death preferable to shame in the eyes of their countrymen. And quite a few students have said that there is really *nothing* they would willingly die for. What does that indicate about their values and what they think is most important in life?

2. If you had only a few minutes (a few days, twenty years) to live, what would you do with them?

There is an old quip that there are no atheists in foxholes. The idea is that when faced with death, we all search for some ultimate source of support. Of course, the foxhole example can represent desperation and terror as well as some latent religious impulse in all of us, but the point has been made again and again that the thought of death brings out the philosopher in all of us. Would your last thoughts turn to God? Why? Would they turn to your best friends? Your family? Your work? Your frustrated ambitions for the future? Unfinished business? Sex? A final meal? A last hearing of your favorite record? A farewell note to the world? In the 1970s movie *The King of Hearts,* the hero says in panic, "We've only got three more minutes to live!" The heroine replies with excitement, "Three whole minutes. That's wonderful!"

3. What purpose does human life have that is not to be found in the life of a cow or an insect? What is the purpose of *your* life?

The question of the "meaning of life" is, perhaps, the big question of philosophy. There is an enormous difference, we suppose, between the significance of the life of a mosquito, for example, and a person. But what is this difference? One suggestion is that we alone have a special place in God's creation and a special role to play. But what is that role, and why are we so sure that mosquitoes don't have it, too? Can life lack meaning even if we are God's creations? How does one know what one's assigned role is?

Can life have meaning if there is no God?

It is sometimes suggested that human life is meaningful because we, unlike cows and insects, are *conscious*. What does this mean—and what difference does it make? Does being conscious—even being thoughtful and philosophical—guarantee that life is meaningful? What are we asking for when we ask about the "purpose" or "meaning" of life?

4. Do you believe in God?

Most college students have no trouble answering this at all; even those who aren't sure what to believe are quick to say that they aren't sure what to believe. Of all philosophical questions, this one is probably the most thought about, because it is obviously so important—even if it is, compared with most of our concerns in life, distinctly philosophical. But what is much more difficult is to say *why* we believe and *what* it is that we believe in. Many people will recognize that they believe in God because they were brought up to do so. Is that a legitimate reason for believing? Many Americans seem to feel that a reason for believing in God is that it makes them happier and more secure—a reason that would have horrified the original Christians. *Is* this a reason, and if so, does it really matter what you believe in so long as you're happy? And if you believe in God, what does that signify about the rest of your life? For example, there has been a dispute in Christianity ever since the third century A.D., about whether belief in God is a matter of faith (as argued by the philosopher **Saint Augustine**, for instance) or a question of "good works" (as argued by the monk Pelagius, Augustine's contemporary). If you believe in God, does that mean that other people should, too? Do you have an obligation to convince them to do so? Or is belief in God your own personal concern, and nobody else's business? If you believe in God, how do you account for the amount of evil and suffering in the world? If you don't believe in God, can you still think that life has any ultimate meaning? In fact, if you don't believe in God, is there any reason for the universe to exist at all?

5. Which is most "real"—the chair you are sitting on, the molecules that make up the chair, or the sensations and images you have of the chair as you are sitting on it?

We tend to think of "reality" as what is most true, most obvious, most evident to our senses. But sometimes what is evident to our senses turns out to be an illusion, and what is obvious turns out to be untrue. Scientists tell us that our belief that the chair is obviously and evidently a solid object is in fact not correct. Rather, they tell us that the chair is an enormous complex of invisible particles, atoms, and molecules in various arrangements, electrons whizzing around at tremendous speeds, and mostly empty space. On the other hand, a philosopher or psychologist might tell you that what is so obvious and evident to your senses is not the chair itself, but rather your sensations, particularly those of sight and touch, from which you *infer* the existence of something causing these sensations.

6. What could you do to prove that you do indeed have thoughts and feelings, a "mind"?

   One of the basic but continuously debated distinctions in philosophy is the one between those aspects of us that are *physical,* tangible, explainable through the techniques of physics, chemistry, and biology—our *bodies*—and those that are *mental,* that have to do with our *minds.* The problem is that mental events and processes—such as our feelings and our thoughts—can be known directly only to the person who has them, whereas our physical traits can be observed by almost anyone. But how, then, can anyone ever *know* that anyone else has a mind as well as a body, if all that one can ever observe is another's body? Usually, of course, we *assume* that the visible movements of a person's body (his or her behavior, gestures, speech) are expressions of mental processes, which are not visible. But how could you prove this? And how could you prove that you have a mind (thoughts and feelings) to someone who did not assume that your bodily movements were expressions of mental processes? How would you argue with someone who claimed that you (and he) did not have a mind at all?

7. Suppose that you alone believe that the earth moves around the sun, rather than vice versa. Is what you believe true?

   There was a time, about 500 years ago, when only a few people believed that the earth moved around the sun. The most famous was **Copernicus**, whose theory is accepted by virtually all scientists, but it is worth noting that our ordinary way of talking is still riddled with words and phrases such as "sunrise," "sunset," and "summer constellations" as if the earth were indeed stationary. The fact is, even in this scientific climate, that most students are incapable of giving any convincing reasons for believing the Copernican theory rather than what would seem to be the obvious testimony of the senses. If you were not surrounded by an entire society that kept insisting that the earth does in fact move around the sun, what reasons would you have for believing it at all?

Nicolaus Copernicus (1473–1543) was a Polish astronomer who advanced the then-heretical theory that the sun was the center of the solar system, with the planets revolving around the sun in simple circular orbits. His theory not only established the foundations of modern astronomy but delivered a traumatic blow to the human pretension that the universe revolved around the earth and ourselves.

But you are stubborn, and you insist. Is what you believe—against everyone else and against most facts of common sense—*true?* Well, that depends on what we mean by "truth." If the truth is "the way things really are," then it doesn't matter how many people know it or deny it. But suppose that part of what we mean by "truth" has to do with what people believe and agree to? For example, it is impossible that only one person should know the meaning of a word in English; a word has meaning in English because English speakers agree on its meaning (more or less). Truths of arithmetic—such as "2 + 5 = 7"—depend in part on **conventions**, general agreement about the meaning of certain symbols (such as "2" and "+"). Could this be true of scientific theories about the world, too?

8. Suppose the thought were to occur to you that it is possible, or at least conceivable, that you are just dreaming at this moment, that you are still asleep in bed, dreaming about reading a philosophy book. How would you prove to yourself that this is not true, that you are indeed awake?

This has long been one of those standard questions that philosophers use to test the rigor of their theories of knowledge. Or, as the French philosopher **Descartes** states the question in his *Meditations,*

How often has it happened to me that in the night I dreamt I found myself in this particular place, that I was dressed and seated near the fire, whilst in reality I was lying undressed in bed!

Of course, there are very few philosophers who would actually say that they are dreaming right now, but having to **prove** it forces them to be very clear about what they think knowledge is, what they think reality is, and how we can in fact know anything at all. If you say, for example, that reality is "what you experience" or "what you believe" at any given time, then it may be impossible to prove that what you now think is real might not be just a dream.

What implications does this problem have for all of the other things that you believe?

9. Describe yourself as if you were a character in a story.

Part of the problem of finding an adequate conception of ourselves is that we spend almost all our time seeing ourselves "from the inside" rather than "as others see us." "From the inside," however, it is all too easy not to see ourselves at all; we do not see the gestures or hear the words that would give us a strong impression of someone we are meeting for the first time. For just this reason, people are often shocked to see themselves on film or hear themselves on tape. Many people, in fact, think of themselves as if in a kind of daydream, with very little contact with what—to anyone else—would be the most obvious facts about them. This exercise is designed to correct some of that, to get you to look at yourself "as others look at you," and to try to say what is *essential* about you. But it is also a way of asking what it is that you really value, in others as well as in yourself. What do you admire? What sort of person do you want to be?

A German philosopher once said that the test of who you are is whom you admire. Do you admire athletes more than artists? Do you admire people with wealth or power? Do you admire a person who stands up for what he or she thinks is right but becomes a martyr as a result? And do you admire a person because you wish you were like him or her? Or for some other reason? Some people admire athletes because they are enjoyable to watch, for instance, but they do not emulate them. Some people admire Jesus, not so much because of the kind of person He was (about which we know very little) but because He was the Son of God. But if you admire people who are very different from yourself, that raises the possibility that you admire people who make you feel inferior; why would a person do that? Do you admire people in order to provide inspiration and perhaps a measuring stick for yourself? Or just to be amused? Or in order to *discourage* yourself? What would you have to do to become a person you would admire? (Or, perhaps, are you already?)

Writing up a list of virtues (see Aristotle's list on p. 265) is a way of seeing what we value in ourselves, what kind of a person we think is ideal (assuming, of course, that you aren't just thinking like a babysitter, for whom the virtues in one's wards are that they sit quietly and do nothing bothersome). Try to arrange your list in order—that is, with the most important virtues first. Is being honest, for example, as important as being considerate? Is being neither a borrower nor a lender as important as helping friends in need? Is being cautious as important as being courageous? Or is being polite as important as being entertaining or provocative?

10. Explain who you are to a visitor from another planet.

"A student at the university" will obviously not be very informative. (The creature will look up "university" and "student" in its American dictionary, but what will this tell it?) You say, "I am a human being." What does that mean? The creature pulls out a weapon that you guess to be a ray gun and you hurriedly try to talk it out of disintegrating you. What would you say? What reasons can you give that are not just of personal importance (that is, reasons that would be understood only by you and people like yourself—for example, "I have to take my midterm exam in two days" or "I've still got books out from the library")? What is particularly impressive about being human, being a student, being *you?*

11. Would you like to step into the happiness box?

The point of the question is obvious enough. What do you value? If it is pleasure and contentment, you obviously ought to get in the box. (Are pleasure and contentment the same thing as "happiness"?) If, on the other hand, you think life is about relationships with other people, fulfilling ambitions, and *doing* something, you certainly won't get in the box. But then again, if the reason you like to have friends and lovers is because you *enjoy* them, if the reason you like success and accomplishment is because they give you pleasure, then why not just get in the box? There you'll find genuine enjoyment and pleasure, without the hassle of other people, and without having to work, sweat, or worry about the possibility of failure. After all, isn't that what you really want?

12. Will a good person necessarily be happy, too? Is life ultimately fair?

One of the central ideas in our way of looking at the world is our belief that virtue should be rewarded and evil should be punished. In fact, of course, this is not always the case. Governments try to catch and punish criminals, but they do not always succeed. The events of life sometimes punish the wicked and reward the good, but—unfortunately—not all that often. It is in part to serve this belief that so many religions invoke God (or *karma*) to provide some assurance that things will come out right. But even in Christian theology, the question arises whether we can believe that God does fulfill this function (see "The Problem of Evil" in Chapter 3). But it doesn't follow from this that there is no reason to be good—or not to be wicked—if there are no guarantees of ultimate reward and punishment. The Greeks, for example, did not believe in ultimate rewards and punishments, but they did believe in the importance of *honor,* and this, we might say, was its own reward.

13. Do you believe it is wrong to take a life under *any* circumstances?

Two contexts in which this question comes up immediately are the controversial question of abortion and the age-old dilemma of war. But what the question also provokes is a sense of the very nature of morality. Do moral principles hold *no matter what?* Suppose you had a chance to save an entire city by sacrificing one innocent child (as in the ancient Greek tragedy *Iphigenia,* in which the warrior Agamemnon sacrifices his daughter Iphigenia to assure victory in the Trojan War). Or suppose God said to you—as He said to Abraham—that He wanted you to take the life of your child to prove your faith? On the other hand, would it be right to extend the life of a person suffering horribly from incurable cancer artificially? Is life by itself worth more than anything else? And as we encounter other societies, there is the question whether we have the right to impose our moral laws (even if we consider them absolute for ourselves) on differing cultures. If a band of cannibals has long practiced the custom of killing and eating the weakest among them, do we have the right to say that they are wrong? And you can't just reply, "Yes, because killing is immoral" if you already admit that the rule has exceptions. Why pick on the poor hungry cannibals?

14. Have you ever made a decision which was *entirely* your own?

Most of my students have come down hard on the word "entirely." Some of them have said, "Well, of course, not *entirely* my own." And they have all agreed that there were always at least some influences on every decision—from family and friends, something recently read or some half-hidden influence, some nagging feeling, some half-forgotten childhood fear that is nevertheless still effective. But then opinions begin to split into two opposite sides. Some students have argued that this set of influences, taken all together, wholly determined their decision. That is, there was no way they could have chosen to do otherwise, and anyone who knew them well would have recognized that. On the other side, some students have argued that no matter how powerful or numerous the influences on a person, he or she is *always* free to choose. If nothing else, we can always choose exactly the opposite of what everyone else expects, even the opposite of what we know we ought to choose, just in order to prove that we are free to choose for ourselves.

This question has become one of the most controversial in philosophy. It is commonly called the **free will and determinism problem**, and many philosophers have chosen it as the central issue of their entire philosophical worldview. On the one side, there are philosophers who call themselves **determinists**; they believe that everything that happens, even our most carefully deliberated and (apparently) freely chosen actions, is totally caused, or "determined," by a set of prior conditions and influences. And this means that there is no such thing as a "free choice," since no one ever "chooses" to do anything that he or she is not determined to do anyway. On the other side are the philosophers who believe that a person is always responsible for his or her actions, even if he or she seems forced into them. Thus some of these thinkers, who call themselves **existentialists**, would say that a soldier who panics has in some sense *chosen* to panic and should be held responsible for his actions. Other freedom-minded philosophers have argued that there is a "gap" in the causal laws of nature, so that, no matter how many causes operate on our decisions, there is always at least a little bit of room within which we are free to choose and be responsible for our choices. And others, noting the fact that branches of modern science such as quantum mechanics do not presuppose determinism since they base themselves on probabilistic models of reality, argue that there is no longer any reason to suppose that the scientific view of things is incompatible with a belief in free will.

According to the determinist's view, we are mainly victims of forces beyond our control; according to the other views, we are always responsible for our actions. From the rivalry between these two views, some of the most important differences in philosophy have emerged.

15. Is freedom always a good thing?

Suppose there were a society in which the people have to act according to the orders of a dictator, but they obey happily and the society runs smoothly and is free from many of the problems—such as crime, unemployment, and economic scarcity—that plague most modern societies. The only problem is that no one (except perhaps the dictator) is free. There is no freedom of speech or of the press. Everyone is raised in the same religion, and the punishments for any form of eccentricity or unusual behavior or belief are severe (usually death). How could you convince the members of such a society that they were missing out on something essential? The problem, as in question 14, is that we routinely speak so highly of "freedom," without qualification and without any attempt to understand its meaning, that, when called upon to do so, we find ourselves simply insisting that "freedom is good." Good for what? It is not necessary for happiness or a well-run society; indeed, it is easy to find or imagine societies in which people are both happy and prosperous but not, in our sense, free. But what is "our sense," and does it always make sense? Is freedom a *means* to happiness and prosperity? Or could it be that freedom is an end in itself, one feature of human life that should be defended no matter what? Why would this be? What if freedom is sometimes harmful (for example, the freedom *not* to wear seat belts)? What if one person's freedom threatens the freedom of others (for example, freedom of speech for Nazi advocates of violence and intolerance or the freedom of an unstable and potentially dangerous schizophrenic)?

16. Do you want to have children? Why?

Most people have children for terrible reasons—or for no reason at all. They have them to keep a floundering relationship together. They have them because they are temporarily lonely. They have them because they forgot to use a contraceptive or miscalculated the time of the month. But having children is one of the most important decisions anyone can ever make. And it is a decision with the longest-lasting personal consequences. It is a decision that reveals a great deal about the way we deal with the world—or fail to deal with it. Do we want to provide some future for the family name? Why? Do we need more hands around the house to help with the chores? (Don't bet on it.) Do we look forward to having absolute authority over someone? (It doesn't last very long.) Do we need someone to inherit the throne after we're dead? (Not applicable to most of us.) Do we think that having children will give us a sense of immortality? Could it just be a matter of curiosity? Vanity? Are we willing to sacrifice that much of our time and energy? Or do we not consider it a sacrifice at all?

We can look at another Socratic dialogue, this time between Socrates and "Diotima," an imaginary wisewoman to whom Socrates pretends to be talking. This dialogue is from Plato's *Symposium:*

DIOTIMA: *All men, Socrates, have a procreative impulse, both spiritual and physical, and when they come to maturity they feel a natural desire to beget children. . . . There is something divine about the whole matter; in procreation and bringing to birth the mortal creature is endowed with a touch of immortality. Procreation is the nearest thing to perpetuity and immortality that a mortal can attain.*

SOCRATES: *Diotima, am I really to believe this?*

DIOTIMA: *Certainly, and if you will reflect you will see that the ambition of men provides an example of the same truth. You will be astonished by its irrationality unless you bear in mind that the love of fame and the desire to win a glory that shall never die have the strongest effects upon people. For this even more than their children they are ready to run risks, spend their substance, endure every hardship and even sacrifice their lives. Consider the great poet Homer, for example. Who would not envy him the children that is, the great poems,* **The Iliad** *and* **The Odyssey** *that he has left behind, children who have won for their parent immortal fame and glory?*

BIBLIOGRAPHY AND SUGGESTED READINGS

Plato's *Symposium* is available in a delightful new translation by A. Nehamas and Paul Woodruff (Hackett, 1989). René Descartes' *Meditations,* the standard starting point for a great many introductory philosophy courses, is translated by D. Cress, 3rd ed. (Hackett, 1993). The last days of Socrates—his arrest, trial, imprisonment, and execution—are described by Plato in the dialogues *Apology, Crito,* and *Phaedo,* all of which are translated by G. M. A. Grube in *The Trial and Death of Socrates* (Hackett, 1974). For a delightful, but very biased, general introduction to philosophical problems, see Bertrand Russell, *A History of Western Philosophy* (Simon and Schuster, 1945) or the same author's shorter but more difficult *Problems of Philosophy* (Oxford University Press, 1912). Or, see Robert C. Solomon and Kathleen M. Higgins, *A Short History of Philosophy* (Oxford, 1996).

CHAPTER TWO
THE MEANING OF LIFE

Caspar David Friedrich, Wanderer Uber Dem Nebelmeer. © *Elke Walford, Hamburg.*

THE MEANING OF LIFE

"Maybe I did not live as I ought to have done,"
it suddenly occurred to him. "But how could
that be, when I did everything so properly?" he
replied, and immediately dismissed from his
mind this, the sole solution of all the riddles of
life and death, as something quite impossible.

— *Leo Tolstoy*, The Death of Ivan Ilych

OPENING QUESTIONS

1. Fill in the blank: "Life is _____."
Some examples:

Life is a puzzle, except that you don't know what the picture is supposed to look like, and you don't even know if you've got all the pieces.

Life is a maze, except that you try to avoid the exit.

Life is a poker game. (It requires luck, but you can win with a high pair and you can lose with a flush.)

Life is win or lose. A few people win. Most are losers.

Life is an adventure.

Life is a learning experience.

Life is a blessing.

Life is suffering.

What does your answer say about you and how you see yourself? What are your ultimate goals? Expectations? Hopes? Fears?

2. Suppose an angel is sitting on a cloud, watching the parade of human activities below—the way we would watch a colony of ants hurrying along in their daily business. What would the angel say about the flurry of activity? What would it amount to, in the angel's eyes?

44

3. Name three or four things that you would not like to leave undone at your death. How many of these things have you already accomplished or begun? Which of these things could you now be doing, but are not? (Why not?)

4. The philosopher Albert Camus suggested that life is like the task of the Greek mythological hero Sisyphus, who was condemned to roll a rock up a mountain, only to have it fall back again; and he had to do this forever. Is life indeed like this? Why?

What is the meaning of life? This is *the* big question—the hardest to answer, the most urgent and at the same time the most obscure. Careful thinkers often avoid it, aware that the question is vague, that the meaning of the word "meaning" is itself ambiguous, that the answers are not always literal truths that can be defended by argument and reason. And yet, it is reason that makes an answer possible; and it is reason that makes the question necessary.

THE MEANING OF MEANING

For most of us, the question about the meaning of life is most likely to arise in a time of confusion, when we are depressed, or when some incident has upset our values and expectations. In everyday life, when we aren't studying philosophy or thinking in general about things, life seems crammed full of meanings—there's a term paper to write, an oil filter in the car to change, a good party to look forward to or remember, the prospect of an important job interview sometime in the next few weeks. But when we begin to think abstractly, as we inevitably do at times, it becomes obvious to us that none of these small goals and expectations could possibly count as the meaning of life. And so we look at bigger things—happiness in general, doing well in life, success, influence, love. But then the ominous message of Ecclesiastes hits home: "All is vanity," and soon to pass away. And so we begin to look beyond life itself for the meaning of life—the ultimate question of philosophy.

What is the meaning of life? First we should ask, what is the meaning of "meaning" in this question? Sometimes, the meaning of something (a sign, a word) is what it refers to, something beyond itself. Thus the sign "Beware of the dog" presumably refers to some dog, probably unseen, presumably large and possibly ferocious. The name "Socrates" is the name of Socrates. Thinking of meaning this way, we would say that the meaning of each of our lives is whatever our individual lives refer to. But what would this be? One might say that each of our lives in some sense refers to other people around us—family, friends, associates—so that the meaning of life is other people. Or one might say that each of our lives refers to the larger community, to the nation, or to

THE MEANING OF LIFE: FROM ECCLESIASTES

Vanity of vanities, saith the Preacher, vanity of vanities; all is vanity. What profit hath a man of all his labour which he taketh under the sun? One generation passeth away, and another generation cometh: but the earth abideth for ever. . . . All things are full of labour; man cannot utter it: the eye is not satisfied with seeing, nor the ear filled with hearing. The thing that hath been, it is that which shall be; and that which is done is that which shall be done: and there is no new thing under the sun. . . .

I said in mine heart, Go to now, I will prove thee with mirth, therefore enjoy pleasure: and, behold, this also is vanity. I said of laughter, it is mad: and of mirth, What doeth it? I sought in mine heart to give myself unto wine, yet acquainting mine heart with wisdom; and to lay hold on folly, till I might see what was that good for the sons of men, which they should do under the heaven all the days of their life. I made me great works; I builded me houses; I planted me vineyards: I made me gardens and orchards, and I planted trees in them of all kind of fruits: I made me pools of water, to water therewith the wood that bringeth forth trees: I got me servants and maidens, and had servants born in my house; also I had great possessions. . . . Then I looked on all the works that my hands had wrought, and on the labour that I had laboured to do: and, behold, all was vanity and vexation of spirit, and there was no profit under the sun. And I turned myself to behold wisdom, and madness, and folly: . . . I saw that wisdom excelleth folly, as far as light excelleth darkness. The wise man's eyes are in his head; but the fool walketh in darkness: and I myself perceived also that one event happeneth to them all. Then said I in my heart, as it happeneth to the fool, so it happeneth even to me; and why was I then more wise? Then I said in my heart that this also is vanity. . . . Therefore I hated life; because the work that is wrought under the sun is grievous unto me: for all is vanity and vexation of spirit.

But let us hear the conclusion of the whole matter: Fear God, and keep His commandments: for this is the whole duty of man. For God shall bring every work into judgment, with every secret thing, whether it be good, or whether it be evil.

— Ecclesiastes *1:2–9,*
2:1–17

humanity as a whole. Or one might say that our lives refer to our Creator, so that the meaning of life is God. But the concept of "reference" becomes stretched very thin here, and one might well object that a life doesn't refer to anything at all. It just *is*. However, this seems to leave us without an answer to the question of the meaning of life, but perhaps the problem is with the notion of meaning as reference.

We can say that particular words and signs refer, but they do so only within the context of a language, a community of shared meanings. The written word *pepino* doesn't mean anything to a person who doesn't speak Spanish. The word *fore!* may be meaningless to someone who doesn't play golf. Reference is a contextual affair, and so it is in life, too. The meaning of our particular acts can be explained by reference to goals and conventions ("He did that in order to impress the recruiter" or "He did that in order to signal a lefthand turn"). But can we similarly explain the meaning of our whole lives? A rare person does dedicate his or her entire existence to a single goal—winning the revolution or finding a cure for cancer—but most people are not so singleminded and their lives don't have a meaning in this easy-to-define sense. But this doesn't mean that their lives lack meaning. In linguistics, we can ask the meaning of the word *pepino,* but we cannot intelligibly ask for the meaning of the whole language. The question "What is the meaning of Spanish?" is nonsense. So, too, we might say, asking for the meaning of life *as a whole* is nonsense. But this seems to deprive us of any possible answer to our all-important question.

When people ask about the meaning of life, however, they often have in mind just such reference to something beyond them, something outside of their lives. These references may be extremely important. They may even be the most important things *in* life. But it is worth pointing out that, in a sense, they do not fully answer the question; they only postpone it. There are four such answers worth mentioning: thinking of one's children as the meaning of one's life, thinking of God as the meaning of one's life, thinking of an afterlife as the meaning of one's life and, in despair, concluding too quickly that life has no meaning.

Children as Meaning

Many people would say that the meaning of life lies in their children and their children's children. But this answer has an odd consequence, as soon as you start to think about it. If the meaning of life lies not in their own lives, but in someone else's life, what is it that makes *their* lives meaningful? *Their* children. But what makes their *children's* lives meaningful in turn? Their children, and so on. In this way people have always tended to project abstractly into the future, to a place of total peace and happiness—what philosophers call a utopia. And this is how they would like their children, or their children's children, or their children's children's children, to live. But how does this make their *own* lives meaningful? And what is the meaning of life for those distant relatives happily living in Utopia? The question remains for them. Successful couples often look back to their years of struggle together and agree that *those* were the best years of life. And is simple happiness itself so obviously the meaning of life?

God as Meaning

A traditional answer to the question of the meaning of life is: God. In fact, it has often been suggested that for people who believe in God the question does not even arise, and that in the days before people doubted His existence, the meaning of life was never in question. But this simply is not true. The great philosopher Saint Augustine, the most devout of Christians, asked that question more persistently than any atheist. So did Martin Luther and an enormous number of Christian thinkers before him and since. To think that believing in God by itself *answers* the question of the meaning of life only pushes the question back one step further. *Why* has God created us? What does He expect from us? Why did He create *us?* Some people think that God created us as something special, not only "in His own image" but with a mission to accomplish for Him here on earth. But why would He do that, since he can do anything? To prove a point? (To whom?) To satisfy His vanity? (The Jehovah of the Old Testament was, after all, a jealous God: perhaps a vain God, too.) Why should we think that we have been created for a special mission or purpose? And if so, what is that mission? What is that purpose? The question thus repeats itself, as the great thinkers of Christianity have long recognized; what is the meaning of our lives? Belief in God seems only to make the question more urgent; belief does not solve it.

Afterlife as Meaning

People also believe that the meaning of life is to be found in another life that is our reward or punishment for this one. But whether or not you believe in such an "afterlife," this answer to the question is odd, too; to say that this life has meaning only by reference to the next one is to say, as Ecclesiastes openly argues, that this life itself is insignificant, meaningless. But what is it that we are to do in this insignificant life so that we will be rewarded in the next one? Simply have faith? Do good works? Live life to the fullest? Realize our artistic or social potential? Convert the heathens? Learn to cook? Again the question repeats itself, and one might also ask: If this life is so insignificant, what would make the next one any more meaningful? Is it the fact that this one is so short and the next one is so long? But if life—even a few minutes of life—has no significance in itself, then what significance can eternal life have? If you're bored by sitting in a class for an hour, it won't make you any less bored if you are told that the class will be extended for ten more hours. On the other hand. Christian thinkers, especially in the past several centuries, have often argued that the rewards of the next life will be available only to those who live *this* life to the fullest. And there is our question again: What is it to live life to the fullest? What is it to find this life meaningful?

THE MYTH OF SISYPHUS (AS TOLD BY CAMUS)

The gods had condemned Sisyphus to ceaselessly rolling a rock to the top of a mountain, whence the stone would fall back of its own weight. They had thought with some reason that there is no more dreadful punishment than futile and hopeless labor.

• • •

If this myth is tragic, that is because its hero is conscious. Where would his torture be, indeed, if at every step the hope of succeeding upheld him? The workman of today works every day of his life at the same tasks, and this fate is no less absurd. But it is tragic only at the rare moments when it becomes conscious. Sisyphus, proletarian of the gods, powerless and rebellious, knows the whole extent of his wretched condition: it is what he thinks of during his descent. The lucidity that was to constitute his torture at the same time crowns his victory. There is no fate that cannot be surmounted by scorn.

• • •

The struggle toward the heights is enough to fill a man's heart. One must imagine Sisyphus happy.

— Albert Camus, *The Myth of Sisyphus*

No Meaning at All

On the other side of the question, there are those philosophers—and a large portion of today's students—who would say that life has no meaning at all. The word that is often used to express this view is **absurd**. "Life is absurd," they say, which means that it has no meaning. Again, this is a view that has been held both by people who believe in God and by people who don't, although it is clear that the most troubling and final statements have come from those who do not. For example, the French philosopher **Albert Camus** said in his book *The Myth of Sisyphus* that the absurd had become a widespread sensibility in our times.

At any streetcorner the feeling of absurdity can strike any man in the face. . . .

It happens that the stage sets collapse. Rising, streetcar, four hours in the office or the factory, meal, streetcar, four hours of work, meal, sleep, and Monday Tuesday Wednesday Thursday Friday and Saturday according to the same rhythm—this path is easily followed most of the time. But one day the "why" arises and everything begins in that weariness tinged with amazement.

Albert Camus was born in Algeria in 1913. He was an outspoken journalist and throughout his life adopted a difficult middle stance in politics, between the radicals and revolutionaries on his left and the harsh authorities of Nazi occupation and colonial injustices on his right. His first published novel, *The Stranger,* made him an instant celebrity in Europe; it is still one of the most popular novels on American college campuses. His philosophy was based on his view that life is essentially "absurd," that the universe will never satisfy our expectations for meaning and justice. His reaction, however, was not that life is therefore not worth living but rather that we have to *make* it worth living by rebelling against this absurdity, by refusing to participate in the injustices of the world and by living life to the fullest. He died in a car crash in 1960.

It is important to emphasize that each of these answers may have extreme importance in a person's life. One can certainly dedicate oneself to one's children, and many people have always done so. It is possible (though more rare than people usually say) to devote one's life to God, and many people do. But it is just as important to realize that these noble answers leave open our question, for they just transfer the question one step down the line. What is the meaning of our children's lives? What is the kind of life to live in service of God? We need an answer *in* our lives, not just beyond them.

The same might be said of the reply that life has no meaning, that it is all absurd. Camus sometimes argues that position on the basis of his atheism; if there is no external meaning, then there can be no meaning at all. But external meanings may not be the meaning of life, and it does not follow from the absence of God (if in fact He does not exist) that life is without meaning.

It is worth noting that linguists now insist that meaning must be found *within* the context of language. A word has meaning not just because of its reference but, more important, because of its sense in the language. Thus we might say, by way of analogy, that the meaning of life is to be found in the context of our lives—the sense they make and the sense we give to them—rather than in reference to anything outside of life. Devotion to God answers the question of the meaning of life insofar as one actually *lives for* God. Children answer the question insofar as one actually lives for one's children. Ironically, **nihilism**—the view that life has no meaning—can also provide life with a meaning, if one actually dedicates one's life to the proposition that life has no meaning, and deflating the false and sometimes self-righteous and vicious meanings that people think it has. Camus seemed to have lived his life that way.

THE UNBEARABLE HEAVINESS OF BEING

The greatest weight.—What, if some day or night a demon were to steal after you into your loneliest loneliness and say to you: "This life as you now live it and have lived it, you will have to live once more and innumerable times more; and there will be nothing new in it, but every pain and every joy and every thought and sigh and everything unutterably small or great in your life will have to return to you, all in the same succession and sequence. . . ."

Would you not throw yourself down and gnash your teeth and curse the demon who spoke thus? Or have you once experienced a tremendous moment when you would have answered him: "You are a god and never have I heard anything more divine." If this thought gained possession of you, it would change you as you are or perhaps crush you. The question in each and every thing, "Do you desire this once more and innumerable times more?" would lie upon your actions as the greatest weight. Or how well disposed would you have to become to yourself and to life *to crave nothing more fervently* than this ultimate eternal confirmation and seal?

— Nietzsche, *The Gay Science*

THE MEANINGS OF LIFE

Life is like the Olympic games; a few strain their muscles to carry off a prize, others sell trinkets to the crowd for a profit; some just come to look and see how everything is done.

— *Pythagoras*

Life is like playing a violin in public and learning the instrument as one plays.
— *Samuel Butler*

Life is just a bowl of cherries.

— *Anonymous*

Life is a bowl of pits.

— *Rodney Dangerfield*

The question of the meaning of life is not one of those questions that require or allow for a specific answer. Indeed, it is more of a metaphor that is required, an image, a vision of life in which you can see yourself as having a definite role, a set of reasonable expectations, and—what makes this so important—your vision in many ways determines the life you will lead. For example, suppose you go into business, or perhaps to school, with the attitude that life is "dog eat dog" and everyone for himself. You will greet everyone as a threat and a rival; you will not be wholly honest, and in any case you will not generally enjoy others' company. People will begin to sense your competitive hostility and distrust you, perhaps even testing your intentions with small acts of provocation. And soon you will find yourself indeed in a "dog eat dog" atmosphere—one that you have largely created yourself. So the question of the meaning of life is not just a matter of discovery; it is also an important act of creation. Your own philosophy is only in part the expression and clarification of the view you already have of the world, for the philosophy you formulate will also be an instrument for forming that view. Thus some philosophers who have had a gloomy or pessimistic temperament have willfully formulated rather cheerful and optimistic philosophies, not in order to deceive themselves but in order to *change* themselves, and some of them have succeeded remarkably well.

The images we use to talk about life define the meaning we find, or don't find, in it. Thus your answers to opening questions 1 and 4 in particular should give you a fairly clear indication about the general view of life you seem to accept, even if your answer is playful or poetic. (It is in play and poetry, as well as in doing serious philosophy, that our views become clear to us.) If you stated that "Life is a game," for example, then you said that you think life shouldn't be taken very seriously (whether or not you yourself do take it seriously), that it doesn't add up to anything in the end and that the best way to live is to enjoy it. On the other hand, if you stated that "Life is a gift from God, to be used wisely," you said that you think life is indeed serious, with a more or less definite mission (which you have to learn) and a fairly clear-cut sense of success and failure (in God's judgment). In what follows, I have listed and briefly described a number of grand images of life and its meaning (or lack of it) that have appeared in history and in students' papers. Of course, the list is not at all complete; you may well want to add some images of your own, which may be even better than the ones I have listed here.

Life as a Game

If life is a game, it is not to be taken so seriously, as we said above. A game is a self-contained activity, and even if it does add up to something (as playing basketball increases your coordination, or as running track increases your endurance), the significance of the game lies in the playing itself. ("It's not whether you win or lose, but how you play the game.") But then again, some people see games as fiercely competitive. (Thus Vince Lombardi's famous line, "Winning isn't everything; it's *the only thing!*") And to see life that way is to see it as a perpetual contest in which you win or lose. If you think life is a game, therefore, it is also important to ask what kind of game. Some games are played for fun alone. Some games are played to prove your superiority (arm wrestling); others are played to kill time (solitaire). Some games are distinctively social (bridge); some are intentionally anxiety-producing (poker for high stakes); some are aimed at hurting the opponent (boxing); and some are aimed at helping others (turning charity into a game, for example, to see who can collect the most money for the cause). The notion of life as a game has been used by many writers: two decades ago, for example, the most popular book on the best-seller list was Eric Berne's *Games People Play* and some philosophers have suggested that language, economics, and philosophy itself are games. To think of life as a game is to put it in a certain perspective, in order not to take it *too* seriously, in order to emphasize the importance of obeying the rules and, perhaps, the centrality of being a "good sport," enjoying oneself and, if possible, winning. But we tend to use the words "winner" and "loser" in a dangerous way. For example, what kind of standards are we setting for ourselves when we declare that the second-best football team *in the world*—the team that just lost the Super Bowl—"is a bunch of *losers*"?

Life as a Story

"Life imitates art," wrote the British dramatist and essayist Oscar Wilde, twisting around Plato who wrote that art is an imitation of life. It is obvious that we live, not just moment to moment or (most of us) for some single great goal, but rather we follow a rather detailed script, a story, a narrative, which (to at least some extent) we make up as we go along. The outlines of the story and our roles in it are probably provided by our culture, first our families, then by the circumstances in which we find ourselves. To think of life as a story is to think of life in a particular temporal way, as a plot unfolding, as the development of character and personality. (The German philosophers of the nineteenth century talked about life as a *Bildungsroman,* a story of personal development as a young person goes through the various quests, disappointments, and discoveries of life.) We often find ourselves making decisions about our lives using the standards we also use in evaluating literature or a movie: Is it interesting? Is it boring? Does it have enough suspense? Is it in good taste? Is it well-timed? Is it carried out dramatically, or overdramatically, "overacted"? Is this action in line with the character of the hero (namely, *you*) The American novelist John Barth (in *The End of the Road*) suggested that each of us is the hero of his or her own story: "The character Polonius," he writes, "did not consider himself a minor character in *Hamlet*." One could rewrite *Hamlet* from Polonius' point of view (as, indeed, playwright Tom Stoppard has wonderfully rewritten Hamlet from the point of view of two even more minor characters, Rosenkrantz and Guildenstern, in his play, *Rosenkrantz and Guildenstern Are Dead*). *Hamlet,* of course, is a tragedy. But some people live their lives as comedies, as farce, others as adventure stories—choosing glamorous jobs or dangerous hobbies—and do whatever is dramatically required to add to their list of swashbuckling episodes. According to this view, it is not the end goal or outcome of life that gives life meaning but rather the quality of the story, the quality with which one lives out and develops his or her role or roles. To choose the wrong role (one for which one is unsuited and untalented) or not to recognize one's role—or to have too many roles or incoherent roles—is to damage the meaning that one finds in life.

Life as Tragedy

One incontrovertible fact is that we all die. But this fact can be ignored; or death can be viewed as an inconvenience, as a passage to another life, or as ultimate disaster. If we look at our lives as less dramatic and less well written versions of *Hamlet, Macbeth, Othello,* or *Faust,* we can indeed find the crucial ingredients of tragedy in every one of us—some tragic flaw, some error in judgment, some fatal contradiction—that get played out through life until everything ends in death. The philosopher Camus ends his novel *The Stranger* with a character declaring, "All men are brothers, and the same end awaits them all—death." Opposed to the game metaphor, the tragedy metaphor makes life into a serious and unhappy process, punctuated by pleasures, perhaps, but ultimately an inevitable progression of a tragic plot that can have only one end. To live well, in this view, means to play one's tragic role well—to bear it heroically, perhaps making some grand soliloquies along the way.

Life as Comedy

"Life is a joke." Well, perhaps not, but it may be refreshing to think of life that way in contrast to the idea that life is tragic. Laughter is too often ignored as an essential ingredient in life, perhaps, even, as *the* essential ingredient in the good life. Plato does not write much about laughter, but he certainly displays a profound sense of humor throughout his Socratic dialogues. The sixteenth-century Dutch philosopher Erasmus wrote one of the most profound books about human life, which he called *In Praise of Folly,* a celebration of human foolishness. Nietzsche's fictional prophet Zarathustra is taught (by his animal friends) not to be so serious, to enjoy laughter and levity. Of course, there are many kinds of humor. There are jokes, including both good and bad jokes, offensive jokes, and "shaggy dog" (tediously protracted) jokes. Some thinkers would emphasize the importance of sophistication in humor, but others would say that laughter itself is what is important, not what the laughter is about. (Offensive jokes, as opposed to merely bad or silly jokes, on the other hand, perhaps should not count as "humor" at all.) Jokes, however, tend to be rather contrived and limited in time, and a person who spends all of his or her time playing or telling jokes (a "jokester") too easily becomes a tedious and pathetic person to have around. But then there are more serious comedies, not one-line stand-up humor but a protracted story of ambition and frustration, desire and disappointment, all treated not in terms of what Camus called The Absurd but rather as absurdity in a humorous sense. Tragedy and

FROM *THE STRANGER*

[In prison, awaiting execution, Meursault:]
Then all day there was my appeal to think about. I made the most of this idea, studying my effects so as to squeeze out the maximum of consolation. Thus, I always began by assuming the worst; my appeal was dismissed. That meant, of course, I was to die. Sooner than others, obviously. "But," I reminded myself, "it's common knowledge that life isn't worth living, anyhow." And, on a wide view, I could see that it makes little difference whether one dies at the age of thirty or three-score and ten—since, in either case, other men and women will continue living, the world will go on as before. Also, whether I died now or forty years hence, this business of dying had to be got through, inevitably. Still, somehow this line of thought wasn't as consoling as it should have been; the idea of all those years of life in hand was a galling reminder! However, I could argue myself out of it, by picturing what would have been my feelings when my term was up, and death had cornered me. Once you're up against it, the precise manner of your death has obviously small importance. Therefore—but it was hard not to lose the thread of the argument leading up to that "therefore"—I should be prepared to face the dismissal of my appeal.

From The Stranger, *by Albert Camus, translated by Stuart Gilbert. Copyright 1946 by Alfred A. Knopf, Inc. Reprinted by permission of Alfred A. Knopf, Inc. and Hamish Hamilton, Ltd.*

comedy can be combined, in "black humor" or in irony. At the end of a great Humprey Bogart–John Huston movie, *The Treasure of Sierra Madre,* the old man (played by Walter Huston, John's father) has lost everything, but he breaks out in uproarious laughter and encourages the others to do the same. It provides the only possible "happy ending" to a story of greed, disappointment, and death. It is hard to deny that all of us could use a little more humor, not only in our lives (television provides more than enough of that) but *about* our lives, in the way we see our own faults and foibles.

Life as a Mission

Christianity has often taught that life is a mission, the mission being to get others to become Christians, too. But not only Christians accept this view of life as a "calling." The German poet **Wolfgang von Goethe**, for example, described his mission in life as the creation of poetry to give the German people

Johann Wolfgang von Goethe (1749–1832) is still considered to be the greatest German man of letters. He was also a scientist, a lawyer, a civil servant, an artist, an adventurer, a physicist, and a politician. He made important discoveries in botany and wrote essays on Newtonian physics. Goethe wrote in virtually every literary genre, from simple love poetry to long and involved epic plays, the most famous of which is *Faust,* which he worked on for over sixty years. He once claimed to "teach poetry to speak in German," and Hegel followed him in philosophy. Both the poet and the philosopher used the biological imagery of growth as the basis of their work, combating the largely mechanical imagery that dominated the age after Newton.

a sense of cultural identity, and the philosopher Hegel took it as his mission (about the same time as Goethe) to use philosophy to clarify for everyone the meaning of the world following the French Revolution. Political radicals often talk of their life as a mission—to liberate oppressed people or to get rid of tyranny in their homeland. Scientists sometimes feel they have a mission to fulfill in the expansion of knowledge or the development of a cure for some dread disease, and people with children often feel that their mission is to raise their children well and do what they can to make the world a better place for them to live in. If one's mission is primarily moral, it will vary according to one's moral philosophy. A utilitarian like Bentham would aim to change things in order to promote the greatest happiness of the greatest number. An ethical rationalist like Kant would urge that our goal should be to cultivate our moral personality and make the world a better place by practicing our duty as prescribed by reason.

Life as Art

"Live your life as a work of art," wrote the German philosopher **Friedrich Nietzsche**. But he did not have a story in mind, more an art like sculpture, in which one lives by creating a shape for oneself, "building character," developing what we call "style." The German philosopher **Friedrich von Schelling** saw the whole of life as God's work of art. (We are, in effect, His apprentices.) Artists often describe their sense of mission in life as simply "to create," but it is the activity itself that counts for them as much as the results of their efforts. The ideal of this view is, appropriately, to live *beautifully,* or if that is not possible, to live at least with style, "with class" we might say. From this view, life is to be evaluated as an artwork—as moving, inspiring, well designed, dramatic, or colorful, or as clumsy, uninspired and uninspiring, or easily forgettable.

Friedrich Nietzsche (1844–1900) spent most of his life attacking Christianity and Christian morality and making some unforgivable comments about women. He declared himself an "immoralist" and insisted instead on the *aesthetic* value of life. And yet, he is generally recognized as one of the great moral philosophers of all times (see Chapter 7).

Friedrich von Schelling (1775–1854) was a German philosopher who was a friend and great admirer of the romantic poets of the early nineteenth century. His philosophy places unusual emphasis, therefore, on the importance of creativity and the centrality of art. Indeed, he interprets God not only as a Creator but ultimately as the Great Artist, who is still creating the universe, through us. Schelling was one of Hegel's best friends in college, and the two developed their philosophies together, until they quarreled and went their separate ways.

Life as an Adventure

Life as a story, life as art—these are inspiring images, but the virtues of life then become the virtues of literature or sculpture: their shape and timing, their appeal to onlookers. But life can be aesthetic and exciting without being like art, without the necessity of always thinking about the shape of the whole or what it looks like to an observer. There is also the thrill of living "to the fullest," taking chances, enjoying challenge and the rush of adrenalin. Seeing life as an adventure is like that. It is living life by taking risks, even risking life, and thrilling in that sense of skill and uncertainty. It is certainly not an image for everyone. (There is an old Chinese curse: "May you live in interesting times!") But for those who see life this way, there may be no other way to live. Everything else is boring and tedious. And unlike life as art or as literature, life as adventure never plans a proper ending. When it's over, it's just—over.

Life as Disease

Life viewed as tragedy has a sense of grandeur about it; life viewed as a disease is rather pathetic. Sigmund Freud, for example, said several times that "the goal of all life is death," a view that has been around since ancient times. Not many years ago, the neo-Freudian American philosopher Norman O. Brown wrote that "man is a disease" and in the early 1980s, a large number of books were published describing the "disease" of modern life, of Western civilization, of capitalism, and so on. But to be "sick" presupposes some sense of what it is to be well, and the all-important question for anyone who uses

THE MEANING OF LIFE: NIETZSCHE

Concerning life, the wisest men of all ages have judged alike: it is no good. *Always and everywhere one has heard the same sound from their mouths—a sound full of doubt, full of melancholy, full of weariness of life, full of resistance to life. . . . Even Socrates was tired of it. What does that evidence? What does it evince? Formerly one would have said (—oh, it has been said, and loud enough, and especially by our pessimists):* "At least something of all this must be true! The consensus of the sages evidences the truth." *Shall we still talk like that today? May we?* "At least something must be sick here," *we retort. These wisest men of all ages—they should first be scrutinized closely. Were they all perhaps shaky on their legs? late? tottery? decadents? Could it be that wisdom appears on earth as a raven, inspired by a little whiff of carrion?*

• • •

When one finds it necessary to turn **reason** *into a tyrant, as Socrates did, the danger cannot be slight that something else will play the tyrant. Rationality was then hit upon as the savior; neither Socrates nor his "patients" had any choice about being rational: it was* de rigueur, *it was their last resort. The fanaticism with which all Greek reflection throws itself upon rationality betrays a desperate situation; there was danger, there was but one choice: either to perish or—to be* **absurdly rational**. *. . . One must be clever, clear, bright at any price: any concession to the instincts, to the unconscious, leads downward.*

— *From* Twilight of
the Idols

this metaphor is: What would count as a *healthy* life? Immortality? A life of antlike social productivity? A life of unblemished happiness? A life of continuous love without a hint of hostility? These may all be desirable, or course, but to desire them does not mean that not to have them makes life a disease. And yet, much of our language these days is caught up in such "health" metaphors. (Another word for much the same view is the word "natural"; natural is healthy, unnatural means disease or deformed.) We talk about a "healthy economy" and we think of what we used to call games now as "exercise" to promote health. And life itself, viewed through the health metaphors, is bound to seem like a fatal disease, at least ultimately, since there seems to be no cure for it.

Sigmund Freud (1856–1939) is not usually thought of as a philosopher. As one of the greatest thinkers of modern times, though, he has changed our conception of ourselves and our minds as much as any orthodox philosopher, even while rejecting some of the favorite premises of most philosophers. For example, he argued that the clarity of self-knowledge discussed by such thinkers as Descartes may often be an illusion, that most of our ideas and desires are in fact the product of the *unconscious,* in which forbidden urges and wishes are repressed and often distort what we think we know so clearly. And yet Freud himself continued to be the great defender of rational thinking, and his whole technique of psychoanalysis, he once wrote, was aimed at nothing less than making the unconscious conscious, and so putting its contents within the realm of rational understanding and control.

Life as Desire

This view is often linked to the Sisyphus myth of life as constant frustration. The Greek allegory in this case is **Tantalus** (from whose name we get the word "tantalizing"), who was condemned by the gods to be tied just out of reach of a bunch of grapes; he spent all eternity reaching for the fruit, but never managed to get any. The modern version of this story is *Faust,* which has been written into some of the most brilliant plays of modern times, one (*Dr. Faustus*) by the English writer Christopher Marlowe in 1589, another (*Faust*) by Goethe, already mentioned. Faust lived for his desires; when one was satisfied, it was immediately replaced by another. The image of life is that of continuous wanting, one thing after another, with no end in sight. A person wants to earn "just enough money to support myself," and does so, only to find that now he or she wants something more, which becomes the focus of life until it is acquired, but then it, too, is not enough. What one wants is something else. And so on and so on. This is not to say that life is frustration, for such desires can usually be satisfied. It is rather the life of desire after desire, in which nothing is ever ultimately satisfying. It is desire, as well as the satisfaction of desire, that gives life meaning. Not to desire, on the other hand, is to be already dead.

Life as Nirvana

The opposite view of life as desire is life as *not* desiring, the overcoming of desire. Freud called this the "constancy principle" in his early psychoanalytic works, the "nirvana principle" later on. In his view the goal of life is to attain as restful a state as possible, without tension or desire. The word nirvana

> *We are put on this earth to help others, but what the others are here for I cannot say.*
>
> — *W. H. Auden*

comes from Buddhism and means "at peace" in Sanskrit; the goal of Buddhism is to loosen the hold of our desires and reach a state of tranquility where nothing bothers us. The Buddhists even say that nirvana and death are very similar (and thus nirvana includes an equanimity toward death), and Freud, too, sometimes referred to his principle as the "death wish." In Western philosophy, the sense of peace is sometimes promoted as the goal of philosophical activity or **contemplation** (see p. 62).

Life as Altruism

Altruism is acting for the benefit of others, even if there is no benefit whatsoever to oneself. Some people see themselves as being here on earth to help others less fortunate than they are. It is a view of life that has a very definite sense of mission, as well as quite clear-cut views of success and failure and of what ought to be done. For some people, life as altruism is a one-way enterprise; they help others in order to give their own lives meaning, but they expect nothing in return. For other people, life as altruism is a *general* ideal, and their hope is that, some day, everyone will selflessly help everyone else.

Life as Honor

It is a concept that has changed over time, but for the Greeks in Homer's *Iliad,* for instance, life was essentially a matter of living up to the expectations of your community, of proving yourself in battle and not disgracing yourself in any way. This was not to say that you couldn't behave badly: Achilles went sulking in his tent like a child when the king took one of his favorite slave girls away from him. But he established his honor again when he returned to the field of battle to avenge the death of his best friend. For the Greek heroes, honor was more important than life itself, and given the choice between death

> *Do not value either your children or your life or anything else more than goodness.*
>
> — *Socrates,* Crito

Stoicism is a philosophy that flourished for centuries, from 300 B.C. (not long after the death of Aristotle) to the fourth and fifth centuries A.D. (near the end of the Roman Empire). The Stoics viewed most human desires and emotions as irrational, and held that in order to live in harmony with the universe we need to control our passions and live the simple life of integrity and duty. Seneca, who lived at the court of the emperor Nero, was the most famous of the later Stoics; like Socrates, he was condemned to death for his popularity and ideas. The school also included a Roman emperor, Marcus Aurelius, and hundreds of lesser figures who were powerful spokesmen in their times. Most of the Stoics did not share Seneca's fate, but virtually all of them stressed the importance of maintaining one's sense of honor and integrity above the transient events of life.

with honor and life without it, they would not have hesitated for a moment. But the concept of honor has not been limited to military heroes. Socrates died for his honor, too, not in battle but in a prison cell, in order to show that he valued his principles more than life itself. Our own concept of honor is not so clear, however; American soldiers have died with honor, of course, but the more general sense of honor—as the guiding principle of life—is surely not so evident in daily American life as it supposedly was in ancient Athens. But we do have a sense of *duty,* and many people would say that, whatever else, the meaning of life is doing your duty—to God, country, family, friends, and employer.

Life as Learning

A common image is the view of life as a learning experience. Of course, *why* we are learning all of this is an open question; but some learning, at least, is satisfying for its own sake. This satisfaction, presumably, is what the learning of life is all about. We have a bad experience (being walked out on by a boyfriend or girlfriend, being thrown out of school for smoking) and we "chalk it up to experience." Some people feel compelled to experience as much as possible, to "try everything at least once," just in order to know what it is like. For them, "living life to the fullest" means doing everything. But notice that the same expression means something very different from other viewpoints: The person who sees life as a mission lives life to the fullest by taking every opportunity to carry out his or her mission, and the person who sees life as tragedy takes that phrase to mean to suffer dramatically. A popular metaphor today is that life is a "growth experience" and that living is a matter of "developing your human potential." This view of life was also popular in Germany almost two hundred years ago, and it can be found, too, in Greek philosophy—for example, in Aristotle. Does it make sense to ask what we are

"Four Noble Truths" of Buddhism:

1. Life is suffering.

2. Suffering arises from desire.

3. Desire can be eliminated.

4. One can eliminate desire by following the "right way."

learning *for?* The age-old answer is that learning leads to **wisdom**, and accordingly, the life of **contemplation** (continual learning and thinking) has been the suggestion of philosophers ever since ancient times.

Life as Suffering

Here we can raise again the vision of Sisyphus pushing his rock up the mountain only to have it fall back again. We sometimes look at life as just one repetition after another, ultimately adding up to nothing. A character in one modern novel commits suicide when she looks at her toothbrush and realizes that she will have to brush her teeth again and again for the rest of her life, a prospect that, when thought of all at once, indeed seems pointless. Sometimes you fix something, knowing that it will only break again soon; you learn how to do something for the seventeenth time, knowing that you will have forgotten it in a week. You get a high school diploma just in order to go to college, just in order to get a B.A., just in order to get into medical school, just in order to get an M.D., just in order to intern, just in order to study surgery, just in order to practice surgery, just in order to live the good life you wanted to live while you were in high school, but then you are too old and too busy to enjoy it. Some people would say that this is absurd, in just the same way. But it is worth mentioning that Camus thought that Sisyphus' life was meaningful, despite the absurdity of his task, because he reacted to his frustration with a kind of defiance. Is there anything analogous to this in our lives? The great pessimist Arthur Schopenhauer also thought that life is frustration. Our desires are ultimately irrational and pointless, he says. The answer, he proposes, is **detachment** through either aesthetic contemplation or ascetic self-denial. Schopenhauer's answer is similar to that of the ancient philosophy called **Stoicism**, which also teaches that most of our passions are irrational and are best ignored through the detached wisdom of reason.

Life as an Investment

Since we live in a society in which business plays such a major role, it is natural that we should sometimes think of life as business. ("The business of America is business," said Calvin Coolidge, a businessman who happened

Thus Camus, a latter-day Stoic, began his *Myth of Sisyphus* with the striking statement, "There is only one serious philosophical question, and that is suicide. Whether life is worth living or not amounts to answering the fundamental question of philosophy. All the rest . . . comes afterwards. . . . One first must answer."

also to be president.) To think of life this way is to think of the years of our lives as so much capital, which we invest in various enterprises—a career, a particular school, marriage and children—in order to get a certain return. What it is that is returned is never all that clear, and so the standards for a good investment versus a poor one are a matter of considerable dispute. A father might consider his son to have "wasted his talents" (that is, to have made a poor investment) because he decided to be a poet, while the son may accuse the father of having "sold out" for going into business as he did. It is fairly easy to confuse the metaphor with its most prominent manifestation, and think of the actual money a person earns in life and the estate he or she accumulates as a test of success. A moment's reflection, however, will prove that this is not always a dependable measure, and if a good investment is measured by what one has at the end, there is a very real question about how this, rather than the activity of living itself, is the meaning of life.

Life as Relationships

We have said too little directly about love and marriage and friendship, but it has been obvious to many people that the most important thing in their lives, and what gives their lives meaning, is human relationship—not the grand and abstract sense of being part of humanity or a citizen of a great nation but the very particular relationship one has with another person or a few other persons. Thus people say that what really counts in life is friendship, or the most important thing in life is love. But it is worth pointing out a curiosity about the metaphorical term "relationship"; why do we describe something so important with a word that is so bland? Why do we think of the union of two

ARISTOTLE, ON FRIENDSHIP AND THE GOOD

The excellent person is of one mind with himself, and desires the same things in his whole soul. The excellent person is related to his friend as he is to himself. The friend is another himself. Hence friendship seems to be one of the features of the good life.

people as a "relating" of one separate being to another, rather than thinking in terms of a union to begin with? Indeed, much of our language about "relationships" presents us with this unflattering picture of two lonely souls trying to "get through" to one another, trying to "communicate" or "break down the barriers." But then, on the other hand, there is a much more inspiring picture of all of us already connected, perhaps—as Hegel argued—in one all-embracing Spirit. In this view, it is the distance between us, not intimacy, that is the aberration. The meaning of our lives is our network of relations with other people; ideally, the meaning of life is **love**.

CLOSING QUESTIONS

1. Give your preference for the following images of life. Rate them on a scale of 1–5, with "5" indicating that you wholeheartedly agree, and "1" indicating near-total disagreement. Are there some (for example, life as disease or frustration) that you think may be right even though you do not like them? Mark these with an "x." Feel free to add other images of your own.

   Life is
a game	——
a story	——
a tragedy	——
a mission	——
comedy	——
art	——
an adventure	——
a disease	——
desire	——
nirvana	——
altruism	——
honor	——
learning	——
suffering	——
an investment	——
relationships	——

2. Suppose one of your friends tells you that the meaning of life is nothing other than "get yours while you can." What would you think of this? Would you try to talk him out of this view of life as selfishness? How would you do so?

3. A traditional American Indian saying goes "Leave the earth as you found it." Many Americans, by way of contrast, are told that they should "make their mark on the world." What are the comparative virtues and vices of these two very different ways of thinking, and how would you try to reconcile the two? What are the two very different "meanings of life" that they offer?

BIBLIOGRAPHY AND SUGGESTED READINGS

Ecclesiastes is in the Old Testament; I have used the King James Version. Johann Wolfgang von Goethe's *Faust* has been translated many times, recently by Walter Kaufman (Doubleday, 1961). Nietzsche's view of life as art begins with his study of the Greeks in *The Birth of Tragedy,* trans. Walter Kaufman (Random House, 1967); his attack on Socrates and the life of reason is best summarized in *The Twilight of the Idols* in *The Viking Portable Nietzsche,* trans. Walter Kaufman (Viking, 1954). Albert Camus' *Myth of Sisyphus,* trans. Justin O'Brien (Vintage, 1955), is one of the classic books of the absurdist tradition in modern literature, and should profitably be read along with Camus' powerful short novel *The Stranger,* trans. Stuart Gilbert (Vintage, 1946). Arthur Schopenhauer's pessimism is exemplified and expounded in his *Studies in Pessimism* translated by Thomas Bailey Saunders (Macmillan, 1908). Sigmund Freud's vision of life is perhaps best argued in his classic *Civilization and Its Discontents,* trans. James Strachey (Norton, 1962). For a variety of views on the meaning of life, see David R. Cheney and Steven Sanders, *The Meaning of Life* (Prentice-Hall, 1980). See also, for a good popular approach, Thomas Moore, *Care of the Soul* (HarperCollins, 1992).

CHAPTER THREE
GOD

William Blake, The Ancient of Days, *Whitworth Art Gallery, University of Manchester, England.*

GOD

*I am the Lord thy God . . . Thou shalt have no
other gods before me. . . .*

— Exodus 20:2–5

*No man hath seen God at any time; the only
begotten Son, which is in the bosom of the
Father, he hath declared him.*

— John 1:18

*I am the sacrifice! I am the Prayer! . . .
I am the Father, Mother, Ancestor and Guard!
The end of learning! That which purifies
I am . . . the Way, the Lord, the Judge,
The Witness, the Abode, the Refuge. . . .
Death I am, and immortal life I am
Visible Life and Life Invisible.*

— Bhagavad Gita, 2:11–20

There is no god but Allah.

— Qu'ran III

OPENING QUESTIONS

1. Do you believe in God?

If your answer is "yes," you are a **theist** (no matter what particular conception of God you believe in).

If your answer is "no," you are an **atheist**.

If you say, "I don't know," you are an **agnostic**.

2. What are the most prominent features of God? (This question is just as important if you are an agnostic or an atheist; it is important to know what it is you *don't* believe in or don't know; perhaps you don't believe in a fatherly God who looks after us but do believe in some vital force or "prime mover" that got the universe going in the first place, for example.)

Is God all-powerful (**omnipotent**)?

Is God all-knowing (**omniscient**)?

Did God create the universe?

Does God care about human beings?

Does God have emotions?

If so, which ones?

    love

    jealousy

    anger (wrath)

    hatred

    vengeance

    mercy

    others

Is God distinct and separate from the world He created?

Is God knowable to us?

Can He take or has He ever taken human form?

3. *Why* do you believe in God? Or why *don't* you?

BELIEVING IN GOD

In most people's philosophies, the belief or nonbelief in God is one of the most important single concepts. It is God who ultimately makes sense of the universe, who gives life meaning. If we believe that life ought to be fair, for example, it is important to believe that there is some powerful being who will make things come out in some fair way—if not in this life, then in another. To believe in God allows a person to have that confidence; not to believe takes it away. Thus the French philosopher Camus believed passionately in justice but felt that, because he was also an atheist, there could be no guarantee, in fact little likelihood, that justice would ever be realized. And so he defended the "absurd," by way of protest. If there were no God, there could be no justice, and if there were no justice, then life was without a meaning.

On the other hand, many people believe in God just because they cannot see, from their perspective, any ultimate justice in the universe. Again, it is God who makes sense of things, despite the apparent "absurdity" of life. The

Søren Kierkegaard (1813–1855), one of the most important philosophers of modern times, is often recognized as the father of **existentialism**. He lived his entire life in Copenhagen, and after a short period of wild living and a brief engagement to be married he devoted
his life to spelling out "what it means to be a Christian." His basic
point: To be religious is to make a passionate, individual choice, a
"leap of faith" against all evidence, even against reason itself. Faith is
something personal, not a matter of doctrine, churches, social groups,
or ceremonies.

*The thing is to understand myself, to see what God really wishes me to
do; the thing is to find a truth which is true for me, to find the idea for
which I can live and die.*

— *Kierkegaard,*
Journals *(at the
age of 22)*

Book of Job makes this point powerfully, and the Danish philosopher Søren
Kierkegaard used it to prove that "the absurd"—far from leading to atheism—
is the premise of true faith in God.

To believe that God *exists* is not the same as to believe *in* Him. The
eighteenth-century philosopher Voltaire, for example, said he believed in God
as a hypothesis for physics, since there had to be some initial force to start up
the universe, which Voltaire believed to be like a giant watch, ruled over by
Isaac Newton's laws of motion. But Voltaire also said that "God is no more
just or moral than he is blue or square." In other words, God played no role
in his view of life and its values at all; God had nothing to do with justice or

Voltaire (1694–1778) was the leading philosopher of the French
Enlightenment. He was a skilled critic and a dedicated political reformer who used his connections with the courts of Europe and the
aristocracies of France and England to promote religious tolerance
and other enlightened reforms. He was continuously at war with the
Catholic church in France. Although he was not an atheist but rather
a **deist** (see p. 81), he rejected Christianity as an institution and
once bragged, "I am tired of hearing how only twelve men established the Christian church; I should like to show that only one can
destroy it."

How Do I Think About Religion?

I believe what I do (about religion) because:
- ☐ **1.** I have thought about and justified it to myself.
- ☐ **2.** It gives my life meaning.
- ☐ **3.** It sounds good to other people.
- ☐ **4.** I've never really thought about it.
- ☐ **5.** My parents told me so.

When I go to a religious service, I feel:
- ☐ **1.** Awed and overwhelmed by emotion.
- ☐ **2.** Peaceful and joyful.
- ☐ **3.** Comfortable and secure.
- ☐ **4.** Nothing in particular.
- ☐ **5.** Uncomfortable, bored or angry.

Hearing talk or reading about "spirituality":
- ☐ **1.** Makes me think long and hard about what it means.
- ☐ **2.** Reminds me of what is really important.
- ☐ **3.** Makes me think that the speaker/author is feebleminded.
- ☐ **4.** Turns me off.
- ☐ **5.** Makes me crazy.

Organized religion and religious institutions:
- ☐ **1.** Are the only true vehicles for spiritual values.
- ☐ **2.** Embody the spiritual identity of a community.
- ☐ **3.** Are important social, not spiritual, institutions.
- ☐ **4.** Are contrary to the true idea of religion.
- ☐ **5.** Are socially irresponsible, parasitic institutions.

Adapted from George Fowler's "Religious Consumer Index"

reward and punishment, nothing to do with the rules of morality, and nothing to do with the meaning of life. On the other hand, the Book of Job and Kierkegaard's philosophy make it quite clear that believing in God need not be tied to views of justice, reward, and punishment. Believing in God gives life meaning even if life isn't fair, but such meaning must be found in a profound and passionate faith, not in a mere factual belief in the existence of some superior being. Such views make it quite clear that believing *in* God, as a matter of great importance to our view of life, is not just a matter of believing that God *exists*. It is also believing in a certain kind of God, a God that somehow matters to us, and a God to whom we in turn matter, too.

GODS AND GODDESSES

This feeling, that the universe is not a mere It to us but a Thou, forced on us we know not whence, that by obstinately believing that there are gods (although not to do so would be so easy both for our logic and our life) we are doing the universe the deepest service we can, seems part of the living essence of the religious hypothesis.

— *William James,* Varieties of
Religious Experience

When someone says he or she does or does not believe in God, we can usually assume that the God in question is some loosely defined Supreme Being drawn from the Old and New Testaments—the Bible. According to this traditional conception, God is a spiritual being, infinitely intelligent and infinitely powerful. He knows everything (including everything that will happen at any time in the future) and He can do anything—change the course of history, make the sun stand still, bring the dead back to life, part the waters of the Red Sea, enter into the human world as a seemingly ordinary person, and so on.

To gain some perspective on our own religious beliefs, it is important to appreciate the variety of beliefs, and the variety of gods and goddesses that have satisfied the religious urge throughout history. There are religions—Buddhism, for example—that do not include a concept of God in anything like our own sense. There are a great many religions that place far more emphasis on ritual and community activity than our sometimes very contemplative and faith-oriented religions. There are religions that distribute the various functions of our God among a large number of gods and goddesses—for example, the gods and goddesses of the ancient Greeks, Romans, and northern European peoples.

In some ancient religions, the question "Which God do you believe in?" had a very specific meaning: It meant, Which gods or goddesses do you particularly pray to and rely upon? This might depend, in turn, on the city you lived in, since each town or city had its own patron deity. It might depend on your family, and what you did for a living. Farmers would tend to worship the goddess of the harvest; a blacksmith would tend to worship the god of metalworking (Vulcan, in Roman mythology). In times of war, the gods and goddesses would typically choose sides; for instance, in the Trojan War, according to Homer, some chose the cause of the Greeks, others the side of the Trojans, and they often intervened in the battle itself, directing an arrow to its mark, or otherwise helping or hindering one side or the other.

In the Judeo-Christian and Islamic traditions, there is only one God, not several. (This is called **monotheism**, as opposed to the **polytheism** of many other cultures.) But our conceptions of the one God have changed significantly over the past two thousand years, and the conception of God displayed in the Bible changed dramatically during the thousand years or so during which its text was written. Our ideas about how a person relates to God have changed even more significantly. To say that a person "believes in God," therefore, is not enough. We must also know which *conception* of God he or she believes in.

GREEK GOD(DESS)	ROMAN GOD(DESS)	NORSE GOD(DESS)	FUNCTION
Zeus	Jupiter	Odin	king
Hera	Juno	Freyja	queen
Ares	Mars	Tyr	war
Athena	Minerva		wisdom
Aphrodite	Venus	Frija	love
Poseidon	Neptune		sea
Hermes	Mercury	Thor	thunder
	Janus	Heimdall	beginnings

OUR TRADITIONAL CONCEPTIONS OF GOD

It is essential to see our own conception(s) of God in social, historical, and cultural perspective. This does not mean that one should no longer believe that his or her God is the "true" God, but it does mean that one should not pretend that his or her conception is the only one possible. Even a religious belief has a particular set of origins, a set of social interests, and a distinct cultural perspective.

In the Judeo-Christian and Islamic traditions, there is but one God (although in Christianity He is sometimes defined as a "Trinity" of "Father, Son, and Holy Spirit"). He is distinctively a male God. And our conception of God is inevitably **anthropomorphic** at least to some extent—that is, we describe God in terms of our own attributes. The Greek and Roman gods and goddesses were almost wholly anthropomorphic, in the sense that they had almost

DOES GOD LOOK HUMAN?

In a recent poll, *People* magazine reported that 55 percent of its readers stated they thought that God looked human, 27 percent said "not at all"; only 18 percent admitted that they "didn't know."

all the usual human characteristics, except that they were more powerful, they were immortal, and they could do some things that most humans wouldn't dream of doing. (Zeus used to change himself into a swan or a bull, for example; all of the gods and goddesses spent at least some of their time turning people into different kinds of plants and animals.) The Greek gods and goddesses often misbehaved—they became jealous and vengeful when their love was thwarted; they sulked and acted childishly.

The God of the Judeo-Christian and Islamic traditions still retains essential anthropomorphic features. As children, we are sometimes taught through illustrations in Sunday school books that God is a kindly old man with a long white beard much like Michaelangelo's famous painting on the ceiling of the Sistine Chapel, in Rome. And even as adults, we are taught to attribute some very human emotions to God—for example, in the Bible, God is sometimes said to be a "jealous God," who wreaks vengeance on those who do not believe in Him or listen to his commandments. Lot's wife, for instance, is turned into a pillar of salt for disobeying the command not to look back at the burning city, and Jonah is devoured by a "big fish" for not obeying God's order to warn an offensive city that it should change its ways. He is also said to be a God of infinite love, compassion, and patience. Throughout the Bible, it is made clear that though God has many human attributes, some of these differ from our own not only in degree but in kind: He feels not just a sense of love and justice but an *infinite* sense of love and justice, which we cannot comprehend. Indeed, one of the features of Christianity as it has developed is the strong emphasis on the **mystery** of God, the fact that it is impossible for us to understand Him or comprehend His ways. And yet, it is also part of our traditional conception of God that He listens to our prayers and cares about us. He is a rational being (in fact, many Christian philosophers have said that God is *reason* itself). But the most blatant evidence of the continuing anthropomorphizing of God is our insistence on using the pronoun "He" to refer to "Him." Why should we think that God has sex (or gender)—as we do? Many men and women are now challenging this traditional "patriarchal" conception of God, charging that thinking of God as male is more a matter of politics than religion. Despite the fact that the central tenet of the Judeo-Christian and Islamic traditions is the existence of *one* God, we must be fully appreciative of the rich variety of conceptions of this one God throughout our long history. From the somewhat childish image of God as a kindly old man who is prone to jealousy and rage and has His "chosen people," we have evolved an enormous variety of complex and abstract philosophical ideas about God, including "God is love" in I John 4:8; the image of God as a continuously active creator in the philosophy of Saint Thomas Aquinas; and the conception of God as merely the first principle of physics in Voltaire, Thomas Jefferson, and some of the eighteenth-century **deists** (see p. 81). Some people conceive of God as a distant mystery, an ideal we long after for much of our lives, but never encounter or know at all. Other people conceive of God as an immediate presence, and they feel Him in their lives virtually every waking moment. For some people, God is known through a personal relationship (for instance, through the person of Jesus); for others, God is merely an abstract force, an impersonal cosmic power, perhaps simply identical to the universe itself. To say that one believes in God, therefore, is not yet to say *which* conception of God.

God as Transcendent

Much of our traditional conception of God emphasizes God as **transcendent**—that is, *beyond* the ordinary world of human experience, outside of ourselves and distinct from the world He created. In the Old Testament, God existed before He created the universe and still exists outside of it. But if God is outside of ordinary human experience, intervening in human affairs only on rare instances, how is it that we are able to know of His existence, and how are we able to relate to Him at all? Some people would not see knowing God as a problem, since they would also see God as present everywhere and all-knowing, revealing Himself to anyone who believes in Him. Others see it as a serious problem, and find the effort to reach out to God one of the monumental tasks of life. Still other people, though believing in God, would say that we cannot know Him at all, but simply must believe on faith. And some people would say that, in general, we cannot know God, but, on rare occasions, we can indeed have a more or less direct experience of Him, and those experiences—**mystical** experiences—are enough to sustain us, even for a lifetime. ("Mystical" does not mean "mysterious"; it refers to an immediate experience of a direct, intimate union with God. [See p. 97])

Relating to God is another question. One view is that we cannot know God personally but that we can know Him and relate to Him through his earthly representations—the church, certain important people (the pope for Catholics, the king in some national conceptions of religion), through the Bible or other scriptures, through the teachings of certain Latter-day saints. Another view is that the knowledge of God and our relationship to Him must be direct and personal. The German churchman **Martin Luther** (1483–1546) initiated the **Reformation** in Christianity, for example, partly because he saw the church as interfering with the direct relationship between the individual and God. The Danish philosopher Søren Kierkegaard, on the other hand, rejected even the influence of Luther's Reformation because, in his mind, the Lutheran church still interfered with what he considered to be the most crucial element in religious belief, the purely *personal* relationship between the individual and God, not based on or helped along by any church or community of believers.

God as Immanent

Other people, however, do not believe that God is transcendent at all. They hold, rather, that He is an **immanent** God, a God *not* outside of us or distinct from the universe. This view has been formulated in many different ways, from the Christian conception of the incarnation of God as a man and the idea of a Holy Spirit that infuses us all, to the elaborate views of some philosophers, according to which God is simply identical to the cosmos as a whole. In the immanent view of God, the problem of our knowledge of God and relation to Him more or less resolves itself, since we do not have to "reach out" to God at all, but simply look within ourselves to find Him. Difficult questions still arise, however. What aspects of our experience are relevant to perceiving God? Loving another person? A deep experience of faith? (But how do you know when it is really faith, as opposed to some nonreligious, but still very powerful, experience?) Feeling a pang of conscience? Feeling awe during a thunderstorm or while gazing at the Grand Canyon?

God as Totally Immanent: Pantheism

There have been a number of conceptions of God as immanent, as within us or as identical to the universe. Perhaps the most simple and powerful of these conceptions is a view called **pantheism**. The most famous defender of pantheism is the seventeenth-century Jewish philosopher **Benedict Spinoza** (1632–1677), who insisted, in a simple phrase, that God is *everything,* identical to the universe itself. Spinoza's aim was to develop a conception of God that would not leave us with that terrible distance between ourselves and the Supreme Being, and that would leave room for any number of different religions and conceptions of God without insisting that any one of them was the only "true" religion. In Spinoza's view, *we* are God, not as individuals, of course, not even as humanity as a whole; we are an integral part of the whole of the universe (or what Spinoza called the "One Substance") and thus an integral part of God as well. (According to Spinoza, God has an infinite number of attributes, of which we know only two—mind and body.) In one of his more striking images, Spinoza suggested that each of us is like a tiny worm in the blood inside the body of some great being. We see only our immediate surroundings and tend to treat that alone as reality, with some vague idea of some greater being "outside of us." But, in fact, we are *part* of that great being, and once we appreciate this, we transcend our limited perceptions and our idea of something outside of us, and, instead, come to see ourselves as part and parcel of that great being. The being, in this case, is the whole of the universe. And believing in God, for Spinoza, is actually coming to realize what we really are, not discovering the existence of something beyond our experience which we ourselves are not part of.

It is worth mentioning, however, that Spinoza's views were not well received, even in his native Holland, the most liberal and religiously tolerant nation in Europe. His insistence on religious tolerance was too extreme, and his own views too unusual. He was exiled from the orthodox religious community in which he had grown up, and his works were banned for Christians and Jews alike until well after his death. And despite his devout beliefs, he was called an "atheist" because, in his view, God could not have created the universe (since He was the universe) and praying to God—as opposed to simply believing in Him—makes no sense. But the lesson to be learned from Spinoza, more than anything else, is that intolerance has greeted virtually all

WHICH SIDE IS GOD ON?

The Divine Law is against communism.

> — *E. F. Landgrebe*

Fascism is God's cause.

> — *Arthur Cardinal Hinsley*

God did not mean for women to vote.

> — *Grover Cleveland*

God loves you. God doesn't want anyone to be hungry and oppressed. He just puts his big arms around everybody and hugs them up against himself.

> — *Norman Vincent Peale*

God ordained the separation of the races.

> — *Reverend Billy James Hargis*

Who says I am not under the special protection of God?

> — *Adolf Hitler*

God has marked the American people as His chosen nation.

> — *Senator Albert Beveridge*

There never was a lawgiver who did not resort to divine authority.

> — *Machiavelli*

None of us is here by accident. Behind the diligence of our staffs, supporters, and our own individual campaign efforts, behind the votes of the people, we recognize divine appointment.

> — *Reverend Richard Halverson, opening the predominantly Republican United States Senate session of 1981*

OTHER RELIGIONS—OTHER ALTERNATIVES

Hinduism does not place the unique emphasis on the one God that we do; in fact some Vedantic (Hindu) sects do not include a conception of God at all. There is simply a conception of ultimate reality (*Brahman*), which is impersonal, with no special concern for human beings. Hinduism is, by Judeo-Christian and Islamic standards, almost devoid of doctrine: Rather, it consists of a variety of myths and methods, with virtually no insistence on "true belief" and therefore no concept of heresy or of orthodoxy. Hinduism is often thought to be a polytheistic religion, but in fact it stresses a singular unit of life that can take many forms. Instead of the all-important emphasis on historical revelation (to Moses, to Saint Paul, to Mohammed), Hinduism stresses revelation and wisdom in each individual, which is the recognition and the feeling of being "one" with the whole of the cosmos (*samadhi*).

Buddhism is a development of Hinduism (Buddha was the son of an Indian king in the sixth century B.C.) which emphasizes suffering as the universal condition of human existence, because of our continuous insistence on self and individuality. Relief from suffering and ultimate peace (*nirvana*) becomes possible when we give up these notions. **Zen Buddhism**, a more recent development (seventh century A.D.), evolved first in China and then moved (with great success) to Japan; it stresses the importance of meditation and direct master-student teaching to achieve *nirvana*. It has become extremely popular in the United States in the past few decades.

changes, throughout history, in the conceptions of God, even those which are undertaken by unquestionably religious people. For most people, it is not just believing in God that counts, but believing in the "right" God—that is, the right conception of God, even if, as Spinoza argued, it is one and the same God for all of us.

Spinoza's pantheism has its parallels in some Eastern religions—in some forms of Buddhism, for example, in which the idea of a God separate from the universe is not intelligible, or, to put it another way, in which it is the universe itself that is divine. In Hinduism, too, *Brahman*-God is everywhere, even in animals and in lower forms of life. But the religious perspective of pantheism renders somewhat confusing our usual question, "Do you believe in God?" If God is identical to the universe as a whole, then what is the difference between believing in God and believing in the existence of the universe? Perhaps an atheist can respond: "I believe in the universe, but I do not see any reason for calling it 'God.'" But the religious attitudes and discipline of Spinoza, the Buddhists, and Hindus show that such a view cannot be suffi-

GOD IN EVERYDAY LIFE

The ordinary believer does not, however, report an awareness of God as existing in isolation from all other objects of experience. His consciousness of the divine does not involve a cessation of his consciousness of a material and social environment. It is not a vision of God in solitary glory, filling the believer's entire mind and blotting out his normal field of perception. . . . The believer meets God not only in moments of worship, but also when through the urgings of conscience he feels the pressure of the divine demand upon his life; when through the gracious actions of his friends he apprehends the divine grace; when through the marvels and beauties of nature he traces the hand of the Creator; and he has increasing knowledge of the divine purpose as he responds to its behest in his own life. In short, it is not apart from the course of mundane life, but in it and through it, that the ordinary religious believer claims to experience, however imperfectly and fragmentarily, the divine presence and activity.

— *John Hick*, Faith
and Knowledge

cient, for there is an enormous difference between an atheist who simply believes in the existence of the universe and a pantheist who believes that the universe is divine. What is this difference? One might say that it is a difference of *attitude*. What they believe in (namely, the existence of the universe) might in a narrow sense be the same, but *the way* they look at it and act in it is entirely different. But this changes religious *belief in something* into a religious

Benedict Spinoza was born in an Orthodox Jewish community in Amsterdam in 1632. His parents had been refugees from the Spanish Inquisition, and Spinoza spent his entire life fighting for religious tolerance. He was thoroughly educated in both Jewish and medieval Christian philosophy, but his unorthodox opinions caused him to be excommunicated from his native Amsterdam, despite the fact that Holland was then the most liberal country in Europe. His books were banned and he spent much of his life working as a lens grinder. The lens dust made him fatally ill and he died in 1677. His whole philosophy is based on the conception that the world and God are a single unity, and all of us are part of that unity (see also Chapter 5).

attitude toward everything, and the idea of believing in God, accordingly, changes radically.

God as Universal Spirit

A related conception of God is the conception defended by Hegel as **Spirit**. But where Spinoza argued that God is identical to the universe in an eternal way, Hegel painted a much more dynamic and complex picture, in which we humans are essentially the primary *expressions* of spirit, which acts *through* us and even *uses* us for its own purposes. But spirit is, at the same time, not to be thought of as different from us. A simple example is this: Think of yourself as being on the football team, or even as one of the loyal fans at the game. You are imbued and inspired by what we call "team spirit." You find yourself caught up by the enthusiasm of the game, as if something has taken hold of you, and indeed it has. What we call "spirit" is not some alien force that invades you, but rather the emotional connection you feel with everyone else in the stadium, the excitement of the game, your shared enthusiasm. Now imagine that picture enlarged to include all of humanity, and a shared "team spirit" of sorts which you share just by being human, a kind of enthusiasm for life; that is what Hegel meant by "Spirit"; it is bigger than any of us, but not something distinct from us. And that, for him, is God.

HEGEL ON SPIRIT

The significance of that absolute commandment; Know thyself— whether we look at it in itself or under the historical circumstances of its first utterance—is not to promote mere self-knowledge in respect of the particular *capacities, character, propensities and foibles of the individual self. The knowledge it commands means that of man's genuine reality—of what is essentially and ultimately true and real—of Spirit as the true and essential being.*

— Encyclopedia of the Philosophical Sciences

The goal, which is absolute Knowledge or Spirit knowing itself as Spirit, finds its pathway in the recollection of spiritual forms as they are in themselves and as they accomplish the organization of their spiritual kingdom.

— Phenomenology of Spirit

God as Process

Hegel's notion of "Spirit" was not only all-expansive with regard to the universe, it was also expansive in the dimension of *time*. One of Hegel's bold suggestions was that God as universal spirit cannot be comprehended just in terms of God's present existence—as a being of a certain sort at a certain time—but must be comprehended through a long period of development, as a **process**. In other words, it is not as if God has always been what He is now, but He is rather in the process of **becoming**. One might say that God is constantly creating Himself—and the universe as well. This means, for example, that the usual battle between "creationists" and "evolutionists" may be a false fight, for God's own existence is an evolutionary process. In recent years this process view of God has been defended in particular by University of Texas philosopher Charles Hartshome, but it is, in some respects, an extremely ancient religious idea. The Egyptian monotheist Akhnaton (1379–1362 B.C.) argued that God was continually self-creating. Buddhism has long argued that the Divine must be understood in terms of process and not in merely static, eternal terms.

God as Transcendent Creator: Deism

The French philosopher Voltaire defended a conception of God as a necessary hypothesis for physics. Although he considered himself an enemy of the church, Voltaire found atheism unthinkable, and he sharply criticized his intellectual friends who did not believe in God. But Voltaire's belief in God was, from most Christian points of view, extremely limited. Not only did he not believe in Christ and most of the doctrines and dogmas of Christianity; he did not even believe that God had any personal or human attributes at all. God could not be said to be just, or wise, or merciful. He could not be said to be loving, or jealous, or concerned with what happens to us. This is why it is so important *not* to insist, if you believe in God, that "we simply can't understand his nature," for if you do, then Voltaire can rush in and say, "See, you agree with me. God is not just, merciful, loving, etc." Perhaps you want to qualify your statements and add, "But God's justice is infinite, and we can't always understand His ways." But to say we cannot understand God at all, that our human word "justice" does not apply to him in any sense, and that "His ways" are beyond our comprehension is to raise the question of how we are to characterize our belief at all. Voltaire insists that we give up the "superstitions" of anthropomorphism, but with this he loses the conception of God as a moral being and as a *personal* God.

Voltaire's view reduced the conception of God to the minimum, and it was not long before another Frenchman, the great scientist Laplace (1749–1827), was heard to say (to the emperor Napoleon), "I have no need of any such hypothesis." For to believe in God simply as an initial creative force is to believe much less than what is required even for the most rudimentary religious belief in our sense. A God who is conceived of as an impersonal force, indifferent to the concerns of human beings, is not a God to be worshiped, not a God who gives meaning to our lives, and in most people's opinion (both theists and atheists) not worth the name "God" at all.

God as the Unknown Object of Faith

As we noted earlier, **Søren Kierkegaard** rejected the idea that the Christian church (or any church) is a necessary intermediary between ourselves and God. He attacked what he sarcastically called "Christendom" and the "Christian hordes" for their hypocrisy. For them, he complained, "being a Christian" just meant that their parents were Christians, that they went to church occasionally, and that they nodded their unthinking assent whenever anyone asked, "Do you believe in God?" But for Kierkegaard, being a Christian, or being "religious" in general, was not *something* in your life; it had to be *everything*. Believing in God was not a matter for intellectual debate; Kierkegaard had nothing but disdain for those theologians who spent their time trying to prove that God exists. In one of his powerful aphorisms, he commented, "To stand on one leg and prove God's existence is a very different thing from going down on one's knees and thanking Him."

For Kierkegaard, being a Christian was a total **commitment**, or what he called a **leap of faith**. One could not know God. One could not know that He existed or anything about Him. But one had to act *as if* one were absolutely certain of His existence, in an intimately personal relationship (like a son and his father or even, he suggested, like two lovers). God is the great unknown, Kierkegaard said, but at the same time one had to believe that He was totally familiar and immediately present. Indeed, Kierkegaard was so vehemently against the idea of *knowing* God (that is, in an abstract, intellectual way) that he rejected the whole of Christian theology and its attempts to de-

---

GOD AS THE UNKNOWN: KIERKEGAARD

But what is this unknown something with which the Reason collides when inspired by its paradoxical passion, with the result of unsettling even man's knowledge of himself? It is the Unknown. It is not a human being, in so far as we know what man is; nor is it any other known thing. So let us call this unknown something: the God. It is nothing more than a name we assign to it. The idea of demonstrating that this unknown something (the God) exists, could scarcely suggest itself to the Reason. For if the God does not exist it would of course be impossible to prove it; and if he does exist it would be folly to attempt it.

— *From* Philosophical Fragments

velop a rational and comprehensible conception of God. Instead, he said that any adequate conception of God is thoroughly incomprehensible and irrational. What is important, therefore, is not our conception of God but the *passion* with which we believe in Him. Again, we can raise the question, "Believe in *what?*" But Kierkegaard would say that such questions are not only irrelevant, they are contrary to religious feeling. He stated, "If anyone succeeded in making Christianity plausible, on that day Christianity would be squashed," and "When faith begins to lose its passion, proof becomes necessary in order to command respect from unbelief." In other words, trying to understand God is antithetical to believing in Him, and rationality only gets in the way of faith. Nevertheless, although Kierkegaard rejected the idea of having a conception of God, he had a distinctive conception of what it is to be religious. So despite his attacks on philosophy, he was very much a philosopher, offering us a radical conception of what it is to believe in God.

God as a Moral Being

Of all the characteristics that have been attributed to God, one set stands out above the rest. Whether or not you believe that God created the universe, that He once entered into human form as Christ, that He once parted the Red Sea, or that He is a transcendent being or an immanent spirit, it is the *moral* features of God, His care for justice and His concern for us, that make religion so important in many people's lives. This is what makes Voltaire's conception of God so unimportant and trivial; it is what makes Kierkegaard's conception so all-important and vital. In terms of the Old Testament, perhaps the single most important lesson, repeated on virtually every page, is that God is a moral being who has given us laws—the Ten Commandments in particular, but thousands of smaller commands, too. In the New Testament, the most important message, again repeated on almost every page, is that God *cares,* that God is the Divine Judge, concerned with virtue and evil on earth, who punishes the wicked and rewards the good. Indeed, even if one doesn't believe in God as primarily a divine Judge who issues rewards and punishments, it is utterly essential to think of God as a moral Being, as a Being who cares, not an indifferent force in the universe. Thus, in all conceptions of God, perhaps the most important questions (apart from whether you believe or not) are, What *moral* characteristics does God have? How much does He care about us? What will He do for us? Will He answer our prayers? (And which ones? Probably not our angry childhood prayer that the kid down the block be struck down by lightning. But what about our prayers for a more peaceful world, or for the strength to carry on through some ordeal, or to be cured of some terrible affliction?) What are God's laws? (He says, "Thou shalt not kill." Does that mean never? Except in war? Except in some ("just") wars? Or except Philistines?) And, perhaps most important of all, what is God's role in controlling the amount of suffering and evil here on earth? Indeed, this problem has struck most philosophers and religious thinkers as so important that an entire field has grown up around it: It is generally known as the **problem of evil**.

THE PROBLEM OF EVIL

The problem of evil begins with the main ingredient in most of our conceptions of God; simply stated, that God is good. But this conception seems to be at odds with one obvious fact about the world—evil and suffering flourish. Now it doesn't much matter how you understand "God is good," whether you think that means that God watches over us every minute and protects us from harm, or that God created us and so cares for us in some general way. The point of the conception is that God does care about us and therefore cares what happens to us. But if this is so, why is there so much evil and suffering in the world, even among the young and innocent children?

The argument can be filled out in the following way. First, we can summarize our conception of God in three statements:

1. God is all-powerful,

2. God is all-knowing, and

3. God is good.

But if there is evil in the world, then so the argument goes, one of three things must be true:

1. He can't do anything about it,

2. He doesn't know about it, *or*

3. He doesn't care about it.

But all of these are contradictory to our conception of God, and so our problem remains unresolved.

Denial of God

There are an enormous number of responses to this argument. One is to conclude that God does not exist, since to deserve the name "God" a Supreme Being must have all three features in the first list. But there are many ways of defending belief in God against this argument, and it is fair to say that every philosopher who has ever written, if he or she believes in God, has felt obliged to respond to the problem of evil in one way or another.

Two Kinds of Evil

The first move for many philosophers has been to distinguish *moral* from *nonmoral* evil, where moral evil is the product of our actions and intentions and nonmoral evil consists of natural disasters and "acts of God." The evil of the Holocaust and the murder of millions of Jews, Gypsies, Catholics, and other minorities was a moral evil. The great earthquake of Lisbon in 1755, in which thousands of innocent people were killed while they sat in church on Sunday morning, is a nonmoral evil. Most attempts to solve the problem of evil tend to be concerned with one or the other of these.

THE DEATH OF GOD: NIETZSCHE

The Madman.—*Have you ever heard of the madman who on a bright morning lighted a lantern and ran to the market-place calling out unceasingly: "I seek God! I seek God!"—As there were many people standing about who did not believe in God, he caused a great deal of amusement. Why! is he lost? said one. Has he strayed away like a child? said another. Or does he keep himself hidden? Is he afraid of us? Has he taken a sea-voyage? Has he emigrated?—the people cried out laughingly, all in a hubbub. The insane man jumped into their midst and transfixed them with his glances. "Where is God gone?" he called out. "I mean to tell you! We have killed him—you and I! We are all his murderers!"*

— *From* The Gay Science

Denial of Evil

One answer to the problem of evil is to say that, contrary to appearances, there is no evil or suffering. And there have always been people who have denied the existence of evil, who have tried to pretend that nothing is wrong. (It is always easier to do this regarding other people's troubles rather than your own, of course.) There have been people who have asserted—despite all evidence to the contrary—that the Nazis did not in fact murder millions of Jews. It has been argued, in turn, that such denials are themselves evil, and cause irreparable harm. There have always been people who have denied war is evil and who have insisted that *everyone* killed or injured in a war—not only soldiers but civilian adults and children—somehow *deserved* it. But this is a solution that becomes more and more implausible and insensitive the more we look at it. Many people who suffer do so because of their own errors, of course (which is, therefore, no reflection on God's goodness). But many do not, especially children who starve to death or are murdered in war. You might say, "They are being punished for their parents' sins," but this would hardly count as justice. Would you think it fair, if one of your parents or grandparents got a reckless driving citation from the police, and they took away *your* driver's license? Justice, whether human or divine, means punishing the person who deserves it, not someone else.

The Least of the Evils

Some people have said that God, in His wisdom, saw all the different ways the world could be; He saw that there had to be a certain amount of evil and suffering in all of them; and He chose the world with the *least* amount of

A FEW OF GOD'S COMMANDMENTS: OLD TESTAMENT AND NEW

OLD TESTAMENT

Honour thy father and thy mother . . .
Thou shalt not kill.
Thou shalt not commit adultery.
Thou shalt not steal.
Thou shalt not bear false witness against thy neighbour.
Thou shalt not covet thy neighbour's house, thou shalt not covet thy neighbour's wife, nor his manservant, nor his maidservant, nor his ox . . . nor any thing that is thy neighbour's.

> — *From the Ten*
> *Commandments,*
> *Exodus 20:12–17*

NEW TESTAMENT

"You have heard that it was said [to the men of old], 'An eye for an eye and a tooth for a tooth.' But I say to you, Do not resist one who is evil. But if any one strikes you on the right cheek, turn to him the other also; and if any one would sue you and take your coat, let him have your cloak, as well."

"You have heard that it was said, 'You shall love your neighbour and hate your enemy.' But I say to you, Love your enemies and pray for those who persecute you, so that you may be sons of your Father who is in heaven; for he makes his sun rise on the evil and on the good, and sends rain on the just and on the unjust. . . . You, therefore, must be perfect, as your heavenly Father is perfect."

"Judge not, that you be not judged."

"So whatever you wish that men would to do you, do so to them; for this is the law and the prophets."

. . . "You shall love the Lord your God with all your heart, and with all your soul, and with all your mind. This is the great and first commandment. And a second is like it. You shall love your neighbour as yourself. On these two commandments depend all the law and the prophets."

> — *Matthew 5:38–40,*
> *43–48; 7:1, 12;*
> *22:37–40*

suffering, or in Leibniz's positive terms, "the best of all possible worlds." This solution requires a good deal of faith on our part, since it is easy to imagine any number of small changes in the world which might make it a better world and not in any way throw off the balance of good and evil. One way of saying this is to agree that there must be *some* evil and suffering in the world, but *why so much?*

The "least of all evils" position is that there is no more evil in the world than is necessary except, perhaps, for the evil that we bring on ourselves—that is, moral evil. (See The Free-Will Solution that follows shortly.) As for nonmoral evil—the catastrophes of nature or the "acts of God" that wreak havoc on so many lives—theologian-philosopher John Hick suggests that such events are "soul-building." They may make our lives less predictable and more tragic, but they also make us better people. This is a common interpretation of the Book of Job, in which a good man is made to suffer in order to "test" his faith. A very different version of the "least of the evils" suggestion has been popularized by Rabbi Harold Kushner, according to which it is God's own limitations that explain, as he puts it, "why bad things happen to good people." But most traditional theists would rather find the explanation in us or in our limited understanding than in God Himself.

The Aesthetic Totality Solution

An elegant variation on the "least of the evils"-type solution—which is sometimes defended by those who argue that God is a process or, in the case of some nineteenth-century Romantics, a kind of cosmic artist—is the vision of a world that is defined by dramatic and aesthetic categories rather than by our rather limited insistence on personal well-being. Once again, this solution urges us to take in "the big picture" in order to see that the beauty and goodness of the whole depend in part on the shadows and tragedies that seem to us to be evil. Looking at God as a process, we can see what we consider evil in the world to be essential steps in God's (and the world's) development. Traditionally such a view has been explored in the history of varied **theodicies**, or theories about the ways of God on earth. If we include the whole of history in our vision instead of simply the particular concerns of the present, we would see, according to this view, that the evil in the world is in some sense necessary and not an argument against God's existence or His goodness at all.

The Free-Will Solution

Another solution, perhaps the most powerful and controversial of all, is the so-called **free-will solution**; the argument is that God created us with free will, the ability to do what we wanted to do. Accordingly, we have created the evil and suffering in the world ourselves, and it is no reflection on God's goodness. But the problems that have been pointed out in this solution are these: First, again, why so much evil and suffering; couldn't God have created us a little bit wiser and less reckless to begin with, still with free will but with a little more intelligence, compassion, and self-control? Second, if God created us with free will does that mean that He *cannot* interfere? If so, then that would seem to mean that He is not all-powerful. If He can interfere, then the question is why He does not (since our suffering often far outweighs our errors). And if he does interfere, then the question, once again, is whether we are really free at all. Third, if God is all-knowing and knew in advance what terrible misfortunes we would bring on ourselves, then why did He give us free will at all? Wouldn't we be much better off without it, preprogrammed by God to be good, kind, and considerate to each other? And fourth, even if one accepts the free-will solution, it still seems most unlikely that all the evil and suffering in the world are due to our own errors and abuse of our freedom. Innocent children have been killed by natural disasters while they sleep or even while they are praying in church. How can this be answered? How could God have allowed (or caused) this to happen?

Justice in the Afterlife

Another solution is the appeal to some further court of justice, not in this life but later on, in which the good are rewarded and the wicked punished. But this raises problems, too: Even if you believe in divine reward and punishment, the question of justice reemerges. Is it fair to allow an innocent man to suffer even if you intend to give him an elaborate reward later on? Is it fair to reward some people who have not had a chance to prove themselves (for example, infants who are killed in war), while other people have to spend a lifetime proving their moral worth? And if you believe that this life is in some sense a "test" for the next one, it is important to ask whether the test is entirely fair (since some people in some societies do not even know that they are being tested) and whether a truly good God would test His believers at all. Consider the story of Job, for example, which is one of the most celebrated case studies in the problem of evil. According to the biblical story, God inflicted all kinds of terrible sufferings on Job, who was a good man and believed in God wholeheartedly. God killed Job's wife and children, ruined his life, and gave him all kinds of painful diseases. And why? Just to test him? Just to win a bet with the devil? Is this justice? And does it make everything all right again if God at the end of the story restores to Job all that he has lost? The story of Job may be one of the great expressions of faith of all time but it does not answer—it only intensifies—the problem of evil.

God's "Mysterious Ways"

Some people have handled the problem of evil by an appeal to God's "mysterious ways." We do not understand why God does as He does, and we should not question Him. But this answer is very much at odds with the need to know something about God in order to have reason to believe in Him at all. Furthermore, is there *any* just interpretation of some of the more brutal stories in the Bible (for instance, the Job story and God's destruction of whole cities, the slaughtering of innocent babies for the sins of their parents)? Sometimes we can understand what it is for a wise person to do something that we do not understand; he or she seems more in command of the situation than we are. But there are limits to how far we can stretch this sort of explanation, and when we cannot even imagine a sense in which a course of action is just, appealing to "mysterious ways" is no longer an answer to the problem, but an admission that we have no idea how to deal with it.

Working Out an Answer

None of these responses is adequate in itself, but none of the above objections is final either. Indeed, the whole history of religion—Judaism and Islam, Buddhism and other Eastern religions as well as Christianity—has been taken up with various attempts at answering this problem. So if your philosophy includes belief in God at all, it is essential that you determine what moral qualities you believe God has and whether these can be made compatible with the existence of evil and suffering in the world. If you do not believe in God, of course, the problem of evil will seem to you to be a final reply, a proof that there cannot be a God who is powerful and all-knowing and just and caring as well. But then you have to face the question of whether there is *any* reason for the evil and suffering in the world, and any way for us to deal with it besides simply accepting it at face value.

FAITH AND REASON: WAYS OF BELIEVING

For many believers, belief in God and knowledge of Him was a matter of pure **reason**. This did not in any way contradict faith, but rather supported it. The eleventh-century theologian **Saint Anselm**, for instance, developed a famous and ingenious "proof" of God's existence (which we shall discuss shortly). The philosopher Saint Thomas Aquinas also developed a number of ways of proving God's existence and nature (which we shall discuss also), and indeed much traditional theology and scholarship is dedicated to this view that knowledge of God is essentially **rational**, and that we can know that He exists by examining our thoughts about Him. On the other hand, there are believers, as we indicated before, who have insisted that God cannot be rationally known at all. And as we have also already mentioned, there are mystics, who believe that we can know God only through a special kind of experience, which most people might never have and in which, if only for a moment, God seems to present Himself to us directly. But how we believe we can relate to God depends, of course, on our conception of Him. If we believe in a largely anthropomorphic, personal conception of God, then relating to Him through prayers and reasonable requests makes perfectly good sense. If, on the other hand, our conception of God is of an all-embracing universal love or a great spirit who watches over the universe, then personal requests may be quite out of line.

DOES IT MATTER WHY IT IS TRUE?

Sophisticated computer calculations indicate that the biblical parting of the Red Sea, said to have allowed Moses and the Israelites to escape from bondage in Egypt, could have happened almost precisely as the Bible describes it in Exodus.

A moderate wind blowing constantly for about ten hours could have caused the sea to recede about a mile and the water level to drop ten feet, leaving dry land in the area where biblical scholars believe the crossing occurred. An abrupt change in the wind would have then allowed the waters to come crashing back in a few brief moments.

Does this support or undermine religious belief in the religious significance of this spectacular event?

From an article from the Los Angeles Times Service, March, 1992 and the Bulletin of the American Meteorological Society

Most of what we have said above applies primarily to those who believe in *some* conception of God, but everything we have said applies just as well to atheists who do not believe in God at all. *Which* conceptions of God do you *not* believe in? If you take the reference to God to be the existence of a wise old man who grants prayers and answers requests somewhat capriciously, your disbelief might well be justifiable by virtue of ordinary common sense. But suppose someone insists, rather, that the proper conception of God is of a vital force that keeps the world in existence, or perhaps the existence of the universe itself; what would it be *not* to believe in God so conceived? To be an atheist, in other words, presupposes a conception of God just as much as to be a believer; it is just as much a question of what one does *not* believe as it is a question of what it is that one *does* believe.

The Cosmological Argument

A good example of a philosopher who believed in God as the most reasonable thing to believe is **Saint Thomas Aquinas**. In the thirteenth century he introduced some of the proofs, or what he called the "Five Ways," which are still standard in rational approaches to religion. (In fact, almost all of these ways had been invented long before Aquinas, some of them by Aristotle, who did not believe in God in our sense at all.) For example, it was Aquinas who defended the proof that you are probably quite familiar with; it is sometimes called the **cosmological argument**. It has many variations, but the simplest one is this: Everything has to be caused by or created from something else. Therefore, there must have been a first cause, or what Aristotle called a

THE COSMOLOGICAL ARGUMENT: SAINT THOMAS AQUINAS

In the world of sensible things we find there is an order of efficient causes. There is no case known (neither is it, indeed, possible) in which a thing is found to be the efficient cause of itself; for so it would be prior to itself, which is impossible. Now in efficient causes it is not possible to go on to infinity, because in all efficient causes following in order, the first is the cause of the intermediate cause, and the intermediate is the cause of the ultimate cause, whether the cause be several, or one only. Now to take away the cause is to take away the effect. Therefore, if there be no first cause among efficient causes, there will be no ultimate, nor any intermediate, cause. But if in efficient causes it is possible to go on to infinity, there will be no first efficient cause, neither will there be an ultimate effect, nor any intermediate efficient causes; all of which is plainly false. Therefore it is necessary to admit a first efficient cause, to which everyone gives the name of God.

— *From* Summa
Theologica

"prime mover," and this is God. Of course, one might object that the universe has always existed and thus does not need to be explained by a "first cause" that supposedly created it. Or one could admit that God created the universe, but then argue (as many deists did) that having set it in motion God lets it exist without any further interference on His part. To answer such objections Aquinas makes it clear that he thinks of God as a first cause in two senses, as both the cause of the universe's coming into existence, and the cause of its being preserved in existence from one instant to the next.

The Argument from Design

A very different argument for rationally believing in God is one that is probably also familiar to you. If we look at the world, we can see that it is intricately designed, everything with its place and its purpose. There are bugs for birds to eat, bark for bugs to eat, rain so trees can grow, clouds to produce rain, and so on. In fact, the universe is so perfectly designed, with the stars in their orbits and our brains in our skulls, that one cannot believe that this all came about by chance. So one must believe that behind the design of the universe is a designer, namely, God. The British philosopher William Paley defended this argument, which is often called the **argument from design**, by drawing the analogy between our finding a watch in a field, and assuming that some person must have been there, and our seeing the intricate design of the world and concluding that some intelligent creator must have made it.

THE ARGUMENT FROM DESIGN: SAINT THOMAS AQUINAS

The fifth way is taken from the governance of the world. We see that things which lack knowledge, such as natural bodies, act for an end, and this is evident from their acting always, or nearly always in the same way, so as to obtain the best result. Hence it is plain that they achieve their end, not fortuitously, but designedly. Now whatever lacks knowledge cannot move towards an end, unless it be directed by some being endowed with knowledge and intelligence; as the arrow is directed by the archer. Therefore some intelligent being exists by whom all natural things are directed to their end; and this being we call God.

— *From* Summa Theologica

A REPLY: DAVID HUME

In a word, Cleanthes, a man who follows your hypothesis is able, perhaps, to assert or conjecture that the universe sometime arose from something like design; but beyond that position he cannot ascertain one single circumstance and is left afterwards to fix every point of his theology by the utmost license of fancy and hypothesis. This world, for aught he knows, is very faulty and imperfect compared to a superior standard and was only the first rude essay of some infant deity who afterwards abandoned it, ashamed of his lame performance; it is the work only of some dependent, inferior deity and is the object of derision to his superiors, it is the production of old age and dotage in some superannuated deity and, ever since his death, has run on at adventures from the first impulse and active force which it received from him. You justly give signs of horror, Demea, at these strange suppositions; but these, and a thousand more of the same kind, are Cleanthes' suppositions, not mine. From the moment the attributes of the Deity are supposed finite, all these have place. And I cannot, for my part, think that so wild and unsettled a system of theology is, in any respect, preferable to none at all.

— *From* Dialogues on Natural Religion

Voltaire, who despised the argument from design, made fun of it in his novel *Candide* with such quips as "Isn't it wise of our creator to give us noses; otherwise we wouldn't have any way of wearing our eyeglasses." But on a more serious note, the argument from design seems to be in serious conflict with Darwin's theory of evolution and natural selection, since the Darwinian theory makes an attempt to explain exactly how a complex world *could* come into existence over time without assuming a divine creator. But Darwin himself believed in God and saw no incompatibility between his theory and his religious beliefs. Here is one of the advantages of the process conception of God, for it makes this conflict entirely avoidable. But the idea of an evolving God-in-process does tend to threaten if not undermine the premise of the argument by design, if only because it shifts the analogy from a fine and finished mechanism (the watch in the field) to a partially completed, still imperfect, and in-process world. The argument from design is a particularly good and dramatic example of the use of *arguments from analogy* in philosophy (see p. 16 in "A Little Logic"). Paley's argument depends upon the similarity between the watch and the world in a great many crucial aspects, whereas the Scottish philosopher David Hume points out that there are many critical points at which the analogy breaks down.

The Ontological Argument

In addition to the cosmological argument and the argument from design, a common philosophical argument for rational belief in God's existence was formulated by an eleventh-century monk named Saint Anselm, and it is called the **ontological argument**. The word "ontological" means having to do with the nature of existence, and the argument, which has been developed in hundreds of variations, is essentially this:

1. We cannot conceive of God except as an infinite and most perfect being.
2. A being who had all perfections (justice, omnipotence, omniscience, and so on) except for the perfection of existence, would not be "most perfect."
3. Therefore, the most perfect being necessarily exists.

So stated, the argument is peculiar and somewhat crude, but the variations on it in recent years have turned it into a logically powerful argument, which has proven acceptable to many logicians. (For some examples, see *The Many-Faced Argument,* by John Hick.) The point behind the argument in all of its variations, however, is to prove by logic alone that, from the very idea we have of God, it is necessary that He exists. And if this is so, then belief in God is rational belief, justifiable on the basis of strict logical considerations.

Needless to say, many philosophers have questioned this logic, even if they themselves devoutly believed in its conclusion. The most famous of these was Immanuel Kant, who argued that the flaw in the argument was its second premise—the idea that existence was a "perfection." Existing, Kant argued, just isn't like being just, being omnipotent and all-knowing. Although a being can exist without being just, it makes no sense to say that a being is just if it doesn't exist. Indeed, it doesn't make sense to say that it is a "being" at all. But new versions of the ontological argument are still being produced today, using all the resources of modern logic.

THE ONTOLOGICAL PROOF: SAINT ANSELM

. . . I began to ask myself whether *one* argument might possibly be found, resting on no other argument for its proof, but sufficient in itself to prove that God truly exists, and that he is the supreme good, needing nothing outside himself, but needful for the being and well-being of all things. . . . And so, O Lord, since thou givest understanding to faith, give me to understanding—as far as thou knowest it to be good for me—that thou dost exist, as we believe, and that thou art what we believe thee to be. Now we believe that thou art a being than which none greater can be thought. Or can it be that there is no such being, since "the fool hath said in his heart, 'There is no God' "? But when this same fool hears what I am saying—"A being than which none greater can be thought"—he understands what he hears, and what he understands is in his understanding, even if he does not understand that it exists. For it is one thing for an object to be in the understanding, and another thing to understand that it exists. When a painter considers beforehand what he is going to paint, he has it in his understanding, but he does not suppose that what he has not yet painted already exists. But when he has painted it, he both has it in his understanding and understands that what he has now produced exists. Even the fool, then, must be convinced that a being than which none greater can be thought exists at least in his understanding, since when he hears this he understands it, and whatever is understood is in the understanding. But clearly that than which a greater cannot be thought cannot exist in the understanding alone. For if it is actually in the understanding alone, it can be thought of as existing also in reality, and this is greater. Therefore, if that than which a greater cannot be thought is in the understanding alone, this same thing than which a greater cannot be thought is that than which a greater can be thought. But obviously this is impossible. Without doubt, therefore, there exists, both in the understanding and in reality, something than which a greater cannot be thought.

St. Anselm, Proslogion, *in* A Scholastic Miscellany, *v. 10 The Library of Christian Classics, ed and trans. Eugene R Fairweather (Philadelphia: Westminster Press, 1956).*

Rational Faith

Some attempts to show that belief in God is rational are of a very different kind. Kant, for example, rejected all three of the above arguments (the cosmological argument, the argument from design, and the ontological argument) and instead tried to show that belief in God is rationally necessary for

FOR THE POPE: ANDY ROONEY

There seems to be a backlash against the Pope, even among Catholics who were originally his most ardent supporters. They don't like what he's telling them. They find him too tough. They can't live by the standards he sets for them, so instead of quitting the Catholic Church, they grumble that he's wrong.

It seems to me that the Pope has done the right thing for Catholics in almost every case. The trouble is, Catholics want their cake and religion, too, and he says they can't have it. I'm for him. Either they're Catholic or they're not, and if they are they have to be willing to accept some of the discomforts of orthodoxy in exchange for the peace of mind they get from their faith. It doesn't seem right that they should have life eternal and everything they want on earth, too. Life eternal would be worth giving up a lot for, I should think, if you really believed in it.

— Chicago Tribune–
N.Y. *News Syndicate,*
Inc., 1980

anyone who would be a morally good person. The result is a *moral proof* for God's existence, the aim being not so much to prove God's existence as a matter of knowledge (on a par, for instance, with our scientific beliefs) but rather as a necessary feature of our moral outlook on the world. The argument is familiar: In order for virtue to be rewarded and vice to be punished, there must be some all-powerful, all-wise judge who can—if not in this life, then in another one—make justice prevail, reward the good, and punish the wicked. Kant called our belief in such a God **faith**. But by this he did not mean an irrational feeling or a belief that we hold despite all evidence to the contrary. Faith in God was, for Kant, every bit as justified as knowledge and not simply a matter of feeling at all, a purely **rational** attitude that can be defended with reasons, with arguments, and with proofs. Without belief in God, Kant argued, our sense of morality and justice would be without foundation.

Pascal's Wager

A different kind of proof is an argument formulated by the French philosopher-scientist Blaise Pascal. Pascal's argument presents us with a kind of betting situation, and the argument is therefore called **Pascal's wager**. It runs like this: Either we believe in God or we do not. If we believe in God and he exists, we will be rewarded with infinite bliss. If we believe in God but He does *not* exist, then the worst that has happened is that we have given up a few sinful pleasures that we might otherwise have enjoyed. But even if God

THE MORAL ARGUMENT FOR BELIEF: KANT

Happiness is the condition of a rational being in the world, in whose whole existence everything goes according to wish and will. It thus rests on the harmony of nature with his entire end and with the essential determining ground of his will. . . . Still, the acting rational being in the world is not at the same time the cause of the world and of nature itself. Hence there is not the slightest ground in the moral law for a necessary connection between the morality and proportionate happiness of a being which belongs to the world as one of its parts and as thus dependent on it. . . . Nevertheless, in the practical task of pure reason, i.e., in the necessary endeavor after the highest good, such a connection is postulated as necessary: we should seek to further the highest good (which therefore must be at least possible). Therefore also the existence is postulated of a cause of the whole of nature, itself distinct from nature, which contains the ground of the exact coincidence of happiness with morality . . . Therefore, the highest good is possible in the world only on the supposition of a supreme cause of nature which has a causality corresponding to the moral intention. . . . Therefore, the supreme cause of nature, in so far as it must be presupposed for the highest good, is a being which is the cause (and consequently the author) of nature through understanding and will, i.e., God. . . . Therefore, it is morally necessary to assume the existence of God.

— *From* Critique of
Practical Reason

PASCAL'S WAGER

Either	Then, if God exists	Then, if God does not exist
We believe	ETERNAL REWARD	We've missed a few pleasures but edified ourselves through prayer.
We do not believe	ETERNAL DAMNATION	We're OK, and we've had some good times.

doesn't exist, the edifying feeling of having faith in Him is rewarding in itself. If we do not believe, however, and God does exist, we may enjoy a few pleasurable sins, but we will be punished with eternal damnation. If we do not believe and God does not exist, then, of course, there is no problem. Now you don't have to be much of a gambler to figure out which alternative is the better bet; it is to believe. Any rational person, therefore, will believe in God: for why risk eternal damnation in return for a few sinful earthly pleasures?

Irrational Faith

But not all arguments for believing in God are rational arguments, and not all belief need be backed up by an argument aimed at convincing anyone else. The most prominent example of a philosopher with this view of religious belief is Kierkegaard, whom we have already discussed. For Kierkegaard, unlike Kant, for instance, *faith* is distinctively **irrational**, and proofs of God's existence are utterly irrelevant. For Kierkegaard, faith in God is an intensely personal, passionate concern, not prone to "proof" by any means. Faith is a kind of *commitment;* it is precisely the fact that one cannot simply *know* that God exists—Kierkegaard calls this an "objective uncertainty"—that requires us to make the "leap of faith." A very different sort of irrationalist approach to religious belief is that ancient tradition called **mysticism**, which says that one can come to believe in God by way of a special experience or vision that cannot be described or communicated to anyone else. (Such experiences are said to be **ineffable**.) A mystic might agree that this experience has proved to him that God exists, but need not say anything at all. In fact, a mystic does not even have to insist that what he has "seen" is *true* at all, but only that it is extremely significant *personally*. Thus there is no argument with a mystic, for he doesn't have to tell you anything, and there is nothing you can say to refute him. And yet, mystical experiences are so powerful, according to those who

MYSTICAL EXPERIENCE

These three dimensions represent three kinds of knowledge. The first is sensual: the eye sees things at a distance. The second is intellectual and is much higher in rank. The third represents [the function of] that aristocratic agent of the soul, which ranks so high that it communes with God, face to face, as he is. This agent has nothing in common with anything else. It is unconscious of yesterday or the day before, and of tomorrow and the day after, for in eternity there is no yesterday nor any tomorrow, but only Now, as it was a thousand years ago and as it will be a thousand years hence, and is at this moment, and as it will be after death.

— *Meister Eckhardt*

MYSTICAL EXPERIENCE

If anyone thinks that mysticism consists in useless dreaming, or in the ideal and selfish enjoyment of wonderful experiences without any practical and valuable effects in life, they have here their answer. It is the universal testimony of those who know that mystical experience transforms human life, and alters character—often from the squalid and mean to the noble and selfless.

I was standing at the recessed window of cell No. 40 and with a piece of iron-spring that I had extracted from the wire mattress, was scratching mathematical formulae on the wall. Mathematics, in particular analytical geometry, had been the favourite hobby of my youth, neglected later on for many years. . . . Now, as I recalled the method and scratched the symbols on the wall, I felt the same enchantment.

And then, for the first time, I suddenly understood the reason for this enchantment: the scribbled symbols on the wall represented one of the rare cases where a meaningful and comprehensive statement about the infinite is arrived at by precise and finite means. The infinite is a mystical mass shrouded in a haze; and yet it was possible to gain some knowledge of it without losing oneself in treacly ambiguities. The significance of this swept over me like a wave. The wave had originated in an articulate verbal insight; but this evaporated at once, leaving in its wake only a wordless essence, a fragrance of eternity, a quiver of the arrow in the blue. I must have stood there for some minutes, entranced, with a wordless awareness that "this is perfect—perfect"; until I noticed some slight mental discomfort nagging at the back of my mind—some trivial circumstance that marred the perfection of the moment. Then I remembered the nature of that irrelevant annoyance: I was, of course, in prison and might be shot. But this was immediately answered by a feeling whose verbal translation would be: "So what? is that all? have you got nothing more serious to worry about?"—an answer so spontaneous, fresh and amused as if the intruding annoyance had been the loss of a collar-stud. Then I was floating on my back in a river of peace, under bridges of silence. It came from nowhere and flowed nowhere. Then there was no river and no I. The I had ceased to exist.

— *Arthur Koestler*

have had them, that doubting God's existence becomes difficult or impossible afterward. Furthermore, the mystical experiences reported by many different people from many different countries at many different times have such similar features that one must wonder whether this in itself is a demonstration of the "truth" of such experiences. But for the mystic, this or any such demonstration is unnecessary, for he or she is not claiming to have "proved" God's existence. It is enough to have experienced God directly, if only for a moment or two; compared with that, what kind of proof would be more convincing?

UNDERSTANDING YOUR BELIEF

Doubt isn't the opposite of faith: it is an element of faith.

— *Paul Tillich*

If God plays any significant role in your philosophy, it is important to come to terms with these various conceptions, attitudes, and arguments. What or who is the God you believe in? What do you expect of Him? What does He expect of you? Why do you believe in Him? Should other people believe in Him, too, or is that none of your business? Can you or should you prove that your belief in God is rational? If not, why would you accept an *irrational* belief? Psychiatrists, beginning with Sigmund Freud, define irrationality not only as believing what cannot reasonably be believed, but also as believing what it is harmful to believe. Freud argued that belief in God is irrational because it is a childish illusion which gives us unwarranted and sometimes destructive attitudes and expectations toward life. Other philosophers—for example, **Karl Marx**—

THE REJECTION OF RELIGION: KARL MARX

The basis of irreligious criticism is this: man makes religion; *religion does not make man. Religion is indeed man's self-consciousness and self-awareness so long as he has not found himself or has lost himself again. But man is not an abstract being, squatting outside the world. Man is* the human world, *the state, society. This state, this society produced religion which is an* inverted world consciousness, *because they are an* inverted world. *Religion is the general theory of this world, its encyclopedic compendium, its logic in popular form, its spiritual* point d'honneur, *its enthusiasm, its moral sanction, its solemn complement, its general basis of consolation and justification. It is* the fantastic realization *of the human being inasmuch as the human being possesses no true reality. The struggle against religion is, therefore, indirectly a struggle against* that world *whose spiritual* aroma *is religion.*

(continued)

Religious *suffering is at the same time an* expression *of real suffering and a* protest *against real suffering. Religion is the sigh of the oppressed creature, the sentiment of a heartless world, and the soul of soulless conditions. It is the* opium *of the people.*

The abolition of religion as the illusory *happiness of men, is a demand for their* real *happiness. The call to abandon their illusions about their condition is a* call to abandon a condition which requires illusions.

— *From* Critique of
Hegel

have argued that belief in God is like a drug, which soothes our suffering but prevents us from seeing the ways in which we could actually improve the world we live in. ("Religion is the opiate of the people," he said.) The emphasis on divine justice and on an afterlife, he charged, is rationalization and compensation for our own injustice here on earth. So one cannot simply say without thought, "I just believe in God on faith, that's all." Faith must have its justification or your beliefs are not your own. Even if you accept the idea of an irrational belief, it is important to show why that belief is something more than mere illusion (as Freud argued) or escapism (as Marx argued).

CLOSING QUESTIONS

1. Give a general description of God, noting those characteristics without which you would not be willing to call Him "God." If you don't believe in God, say with some precision what it is that you don't believe in.

2. If you believe that there is a God and that He is all-powerful, all-knowing and concerned with justice and the well-being of humanity, explain how there can be so much evil and suffering in the world. Pursue as far as you can the responses and objections to *one* of the various attempts to answer the problem of evil. (A good way of doing this is to have a friend act as devil's advocate and try to refute your efforts to defend a solution to the problem.)

THE REJECTION OF RELIGION: FRIEDRICH NIETZSCHE

The deity of decadence, gelded in his most virile virtues and instincts, becomes of necessity the god of the physiologically retrograde, of the weak. Of course, they do not call *themselves the weak; they call themselves "the good."*

• • •

The Christian conception of God—God as god of the sick, God as a spider, God as spirit—is one of the most corrupt conceptions of the divine ever attained on earth. It may even represent the low-water mark in the descending development of divine types. God degenerated into the contradiction *of life, instead of being its transfiguration and eternal Yes! God as the declaration of war against life, against nature, against the will to live! God—the formula for every slander against "this world," for every lie about the "beyond"! God—the deification of nothingness, the will to nothingness pronounced holy!*

— *From* The Antichrist

3. Try to explain to an atheist friend (real or imagined) *why* you believe in God.

If you think there are good reasons for believing, state them.

If you think there are good arguments for, or a *proof* of, God's existence, state the arguments or the proof and defend it against your atheist friend's objections.

If you think that the only way to believe in God is through faith, answer your atheist friend's objections that you are being irrational, that you are simply indulging in "wishful thinking," that you are escaping from your responsibilities to change the world and, instead, accepting a fantasy in which God will take full responsibility.

4. Choose one of the traditional proofs of God's existence and work it out in some detail, answering objections and making the argument as irrefutable as you can. (See Bibliography for further readings.)

5. If you don't believe in God, what would convince you that He does exist? If you do believe in God, what would convince you that He does not exist?

THE REJECTION OF RELIGION: SIGMUND FREUD

. . . if we turn our attention to the psychical origin of religious ideas. These, which are given out as teachings, are not precipitates of experience or end results of thinking: they are illusions, fulfillments of the oldest, strongest and most urgent wishes of mankind. The secret of their strength lies in the strength of those wishes. As we already know, the terrifying impression of helplessness in childhood aroused the need for protection—for protection through love—which was provided by the father, and the recognition that this helplessness lasts throughout life made it necessary to cling to the existence of a father, but this time a more powerful one. Thus the benevolent rule of a divine Providence allays our fear of the dangers of life; the establishment of a moral world-order ensures the fulfillment of the demands of justice, which have so often remained unfulfilled in human civilization; and the prolongation of earthly existence in a future life provides the local and temporal framework in which these wish-fulfillments shall take place. Answers to the riddles that tempt the curiosity of man, such as how the universe began or what the relation is between body and mind, are developed in conformity with the underlying assumptions of this system. It is an enormous relief to the individual psyche if the conflicts of its childhood arising from the father-complex—conflicts which it has never wholly overcome—are removed from it and brought to a solution which is universally accepted.

When I say that these things are all illusions, I must define the meaning of the word. An illusion is not the same thing as an error; nor is it necessarily an error . . . we call a belief an illusion when a wish-fulfillment is a prominent factor in its motivation, and in doing so we disregard its relations to reality just as the illusion itself sets no store by verification.

— *From* Future of
an Illusion

BIBLIOGRAPHY AND SUGGESTED READINGS

William James' *Varieties of Religious Experience* (Longmans, 1902) is probably the best-known work in the philosophy of religion by an American philosopher. The essential text of the Judeo-Christian tradition, of course, is the Bible, although surprisingly few students who proclaim their belief or their interest have actually read it through. Martin Luther's Wittenberg theses, which initiated the Reformation, are available in Luther, *95 Theses,* ed. G. W. Sandt

(Fortress, 1957). Spinoza's pantheism is spelled out in his very difficult book *The Ethics,* trans. R. H. M. Elwes (Doubleday, 1960), but is well explained in Stuart Hampshire's exposition and analysis *Spinoza* (Penguin, 1961). Søren Kierkegaard's works almost all concern themselves with the nature of faith and personal belief in God, but perhaps the best place to start would be a short book called *Philosophical Fragments,* trans. David Swenson (Princeton University Press, 1962), as well as his larger *Concluding Unscientific Postscript,* trans. D. Swenson and W. Lowrie (Princeton University Press, 1941). Kant's discussion of God as a moral being is in his *Critique of Practical Reason,* trans. L. W. Beck (Bobbs-Merrill, 1956). The "problem of evil" is discussed in a book by that name by Nelson Pike, ed., *Good and Evil* (Prentice-Hall, 1964), and the whole range of philosophical problems of religion is discussed in John Hick, ed., *Faith and the Philosophers* (St. Martin's, 1964), and Steven M. Cahn, ed., *Philosophy of Religion* (Harper & Row, 1970). The most blistering attacks on religion in general can be found in David Hume's *Dialogues on Natural Religion* (Bobbs-Merrill, 1947) and Friedrich Nietzche's *The Antichrist,* trans. W. Kaufman in *The Viking Portable Nietzsche* (Viking, 1954). Freud's attack on religion as an illusion is in his *Future of an Illusion* (Doubleday, 1953). Selections of Saint Thomas Aquinas' *Summa Theologica* are available in Vernon Bourke's *The Pocket Aquinas* (WSP) and Mary T. Clark's *An Aquinas Reader* (Doubleday). A classic summary of the teachings of various religions outside of the Judeo-Christian tradition is Huston Smith, *The Religions of Man* (Harper & Row, 1958). An excellent account of African religion and philosophy is found in John S. Mbiti, *African Religions and Philosophy* (Praeger, 1969), and in Jacqueline Thomas, "African Philosophy" in K. Higgins and R. Solomon, eds. *From Africa to Zen* (Rowman & Littlefield, 1994).

The Nature of Reality

Albert Einstein, UPI/Corbis-Bettmann.

THE NATURE OF REALITY

Humankind cannot bear very much reality.
—*T. S. Eliot, "Burnt Norton"*

OPENING QUESTIONS

1. How "real" are the following items? (Rate them on a scale from 1 to 10, where 10 is most real, 1 is least real.)

the person sitting next to you —————

the chair you are sitting in —————

God —————

the planet Uranus —————

Beethoven's music —————

the headache you had last night —————

human rights —————

electrons —————

the woman or man in (not "of") your dreams —————

angels —————

the number seven —————

water —————

ice —————

love —————

beauty —————

genes —————

the theory of relativity —————

Einstein's brain (when he was alive) —————

Einstein's ideas —————

your own mind —————

the color red —————

a red sensation (in your own mind) —————

"unreal numbers" _____

the NFL _____

your own body _____

your soul _____

2. Do you believe that the earth is flat and does not move, while the stars, sun, moon, and planets circle around it in more or less regularly shaped orbits? If not, why not? (If so, why?)

3. If a tree falls in the forest when there's no one around to hear it, does it make a sound? Why or why not? If no one ever sees, hears, or touches the tree itself, what sense does it make to say that the tree is "real"?

4. Does the universe itself have a purpose? If so, what is this purpose? If not, is it, as some modern philosophers have argued, just a universe of "matter in motion"—particles and electromagnetic fields acting according to the laws of physics?

THE REAL WORLD

Much of what we believe about the world we believe on faith. As children, we believed what our parents told us, often without understanding it and only rarely testing their answers for ourselves. Most people most of the time throughout most of history have believed that **reality**—the ultimate nature of the world—was pretty much what their religious leaders told them it was, whether the world was a flat island on the back of a turtle supported by elephants (and from there on, "elephants all the way down," according to one old Indian joke) or an infinite expanse bounded only by God.

Today most of us believe that reality is what our scientists tell us it is. None of us has ever seen or felt an atom; few of us have ever seen the farthest planets in our solar system. Very few of us could even offer any evidence that there is such a thing as our solar system, despite the fact that we have been looking at charts and drawings of it ever since we were children. When I ask my students why they think that the sun doesn't move around the earth (as our very language, with words like "sunrise" and "sunset," would seem to indicate), only a small number of them are capable of giving any half-convincing answers. But even professional scientists will admit that it may be impossible to completely explain reality in scientific terms. Einstein's theory of

SCIENCE AND REALITY

The learned physicist and the man in the street were standing together on the threshold, about to enter a room.

The man in the street moved forward without trouble, planted his foot on a solid unyielding plank at rest before him, and entered.

The physicist was faced with an intricate problem. To make any movement he must shove against the atmosphere, which presses with a force of 14 pounds on every square inch of his body. He must land on a plank travelling at 20 miles per second around the sun—a fraction of a second earlier or later the plank would be miles away. He must do this while hanging from a round planet, head outward into space. . . . He reflects too that the plank itself is not what it appears to be. . . . it is mostly emptiness, very sparsely scattered in that emptiness are myriads of electrical charges dashing about at great speeds. . . . It is like stepping on a swarm of flies.

— *Sir Arthur Eddington*

relativity, for example, may have as one of its primary conclusions the impossibility of our ever knowing what the world is really like, apart from the particular perspective from which we happen to be observing it. If we can't find out the nature of reality from science, where are we to find it?

Before science came to claim complete domination over our picture of reality, during the past three hundred years or so, the ready answer to this question was *God.* According to this view, God is the ultimate reality. The material universe is real only insofar as it is kept in existence by God; in fact, for hundreds of years it was considered heresy to believe that what was ultimately real were the "illusory speculations" of the scientists. What was real were souls, angels, and other spiritual beings, whether or not these could be observed or tested by science. In the modern scientific worldview, which most of us accept without question, on the other hand, what is real is the physical universe; the reality of such nonphysical things as numbers, spirits, minds, souls, angels, and even God is at least questionable—and if they are to be believed in, they must be justified somehow, preferably by appeal to the physical universe. Thus minds are believable because they explain why various bodies behave as they do. And God can be defended, for example, by the so-called argument from design, from the intricacy of the physical universe (see pp. 91–93). So you can see from the start that the answer to the question "What is real?" might have two very different first principles: an appeal to science on the one hand and an appeal to religion on the other. A religious person might still believe in science, of course; philosophers such as Pascal, Leib-

GOD AS REALITY

The perennial Philosophy is primarily concerned with the one, divine reality substantial to the manifold world of things and lives and minds. But the nature of this one Reality is such that it cannot be directly and immediately apprehended except by those who have chosen to fulfill certain conditions, making themselves loving, pure in heart and poor in spirit. Why should this be so? We do not know. It is just one of those facts we have to accept, whether we like them or not and however implausible and unlikely they may seem.

— Aldous Huxley,
*The Perennial
Philosophy*

niz, and Kant were religious men as well as scientists. But for the religious person, the order of the universe is first of all a sign of the infinite wisdom and goodness of God. For the scientist, what is most real is what is most tangible, measurable, testable.

WHAT IS MOST REAL?

In question 1 above, the point of asking you to rank as "real" various **entities** (the more proper philosophical word for "things") was to make some preliminary, crude attempt to get you to order your own sense of reality. This is what philosophers call an **ontology**. An ontology is essentially the study of what is most real. Some people will formulate a commonsense ontology, with the most real entities being chairs, bodies, people; some will take a more scientific viewpoint and say that what is most real are those things discovered by science, like electrons and genes. Other people will take a more spiritual approach and rank God highest, along with soul; some will always take people to be most real. Most people have the most trouble with such peculiar entities as Beethoven's music and the number seven.

There are some people who say that *nothing* is real, and who give a low ranking to virtually every entity on the list. The problem then is to ask, "Compared to what?" For what becomes evident in such an exercise is the fact that "reality" is an **evaluative** term, a way of weighing what is most basic, most real, to our view of the world. To say that nothing is real is to say, in effect, that we don't believe in the world at all, or, for that matter, in the existence of our own minds believing in the world, and you must admit there is something peculiar about this. On the other hand, there are people (including some important philosophers) who have said that *everything* on the list is real. In fact, one might say this: Everything is "real" for the kind of thing that it is. (Thus the number seven is real as a number; Beethoven's music is real as music; angels are real as angels; and the person sitting next to you is real in the way that people in general are real.) But this clever answer tends to miss the point of ontology, which is to discover what is *most* real, what is *most* basic, and what is to be accounted for in terms of what. And if we can't say that Sherlock Holmes or the Loch Ness monster or the pot of gold at the end of the rainbow is not any less real than you, me, and other people, than your own dog, or than the pots and pans in your friend's kitchen, then we seem to have lost our grasp of the notion of "reality" altogether. The whole purpose of thinking about reality is to somehow separate what is most basic and undeniable in the world from what is less so.

The Reality Behind the Appearances

Now, why should this question "What is real?" be so important? Consider this: My dog (and your dog, too) couldn't conceive of such a question. He certainly learns a complex series of causes and effects (when the can opener whirs, he learns to expect dinner). He might also learn to ignore certain experiences as unimportant or untrustworthy. But what he never learns is *explanation*. He never asks, "Why?" He has only expectations, not theories. The

---

APPEARANCE AND REALITY

The distinction that causes the most trouble in philosophy is the distinction between "appearance" and "reality," between what things seem to be and what they are. The painter wants to know what things seem to be, the practical man and the philosopher want to know what they are. . . . but if reality is not what appears, have we any means of knowing whether there is any reality at all?

— Bertrand Russell,
*The Problems of
Philosophy*

Bertrand Russell was one of the great philosophers of our own century. He was born in 1872, into a noble family in England. As a young man, he wrote (with Alfred North Whitehead) a book called *Principia Mathematica* (1903) which set the stage for much of Anglo-American logic and philosophy ever since. Logic was his central tool, and he became extremely controversial on the basis of his logical but unorthodox approach to social and political questions, such as sex before marriage (he was not against it) and refusing to fight in World War I (he was jailed as a pacifist). He died in 1970.

connection between the can opener and dog food is enough for him; his life is a sequence of events, most of them expected, a few of them unexpected, but he has no ability to *understand*. A child, on the other hand, asks "Why?" persistently. "How does a watch work?" for example. We could, if we wished, take it apart and show the child the mechanism. The surface movements are not enough for us; we want to know what is inside. Simply being aware of the sequence of lightning–thunder is not enough for us: we want to know what causes them, whether it is the bad temper of Zeus, of Jehovah, or the collision of convection currents in the atmosphere. And so we begin to postulate a **reality behind the appearances**, an attempt to account for the sequence of events seen in terms of other events unseen. "Primitive" mythologies populate this world behind the scenes with spirits, demons, gods, and goddesses. Science populates it with atoms and electrons and electromagnetic forces. Christianity fills it with God and a spiritual world only dimly perceived by those of us in this one—but it is that eternal world that is far more important than the mere passing appearances of this one. But it is this distinction between what we simply see, what *appears* to be the case, and the "deeper" picture that allows us to explain it, that forces us to introduce the concept of "reality." Reality is the view of the world—or another world altogether—that allows us to understand the world of ordinary appearances, whether the weather or a chemical reaction, whether the seeming injustice of a horrible accident or the meaning of human history. And so we learn to distinguish the ways things appear to us and their "inner" reality. So we learn to explain things to ourselves and make sense of them.

Dreams, Sensations, and Reason: What Is Real?

What counts as "real" obviously varies considerably from ontology to ontology. In our views of reality, for instance, we tend to agree that what we experience in dreams is not real. But some ancient peoples believed that what happened in their dreams was in some sense far more real than what happened to them in their waking hours, and some people still believe that what they "see" in hallucinations caused by drugs or chemical imbalances in their brain is more "real" than the entities of everyday life. We take for granted, for example, that our own sensations are the most dependable source of knowledge, and we say as a matter of course that we will believe something when we see it with our own eyes. But until about three hundred years ago philosophers and scientists trusted their powers of reason more than their senses, which they deeply distrusted. Thus, when Aristotle argued that a large rock would fall faster than a small one, he was simply trusting his reason—and for almost two thousand years everyone else agreed with him. He did not have the measuring equipment to test this belief—as Galileo did in modern times; but even if he had tested it, it is not clear that he would have believed his senses, if the findings had disagreed with his reasoning. We sometimes unfairly criticize Aristotle for slowing down the progress of science; in fact, he just held a different idea about science, a different ontology, in which the objects of

Nietzsche: *Only as creators!*—This has given me the greatest trouble and still does: to realize that what things *are called* is incomparably more important than what they are. The reputation, name, and appearance, the usual measure and weight of a thing, what it counts for—originally almost always wrong and arbitrary, thrown over things like a dress and altogether foreign to their nature and even to their skin—all this grows from generation unto generation, merely because people believe in it, until it gradually grows to be part of the thing and turns into its very body. What at first was appearance becomes in the end, almost invariably, the essence and effective as such. How foolish it would be to suppose that one only needs to point out this origin and this misty shroud of delusion in order to *destroy* the world that counts for real, so-called *"reality."* We can destroy only as creators.—But let us not forget either: it is enough to create new names and estimations and probabilities in order to create in the long run new "things."

From The Gay Science, *trans. W. Kaufman (New York: Vintage, 1974), §58.*

reason seemed far more real and trustworthy to him than the fleeting and undependable experience of the senses.

The Basis of Metaphysics

In what we have said already in this chapter, we have anticipated some of the main themes of what philosophers call **metaphysics**. Metaphysics is the attempt to say what reality is. Ontology is one of the components of metaphysics, the study of what is; another is **cosmology**, or how we think the most real things have come into being. In developing an ontology, as part of our attempt to formulate our metaphysics, we have to evaluate the different entities in the world, picking out those that are most basic. But we have already anticipated two of the tests that are usually imposed on this notion of what is "most real." First, that which is most real is that upon which all else is dependent. For a religious person, God is most real because all else depends on Him; for a scientist, what is most real are the principles and particles on which all of reality can be reasoned to be based. Second, that which is most real is that which itself is not created or destroyed. Thus God created the earth, and He can destroy it, but God Himself was neither created nor can He be destroyed. You can destroy a chair, by burning it up or chopping it to pieces, but you cannot destroy the basic particles and forces out of which the chair is made. When we look back to the very beginnings of philosophy and metaphysics, when people first made the attempt to formulate their view of the world in terms of what was most real and what was not, we find these same two tests being invoked. Indeed, both modern science and modern theology, as well as philosophy itself, are continuations of this same ancient metaphysical tradition.

THE FIRST METAPHYSICIANS

Thales

The disciplines of metaphysics and philosophy, as these are practiced in the Western tradition, began in Greece about twenty-six hundred years ago. The first Western philosopher is generally agreed to have been a man named **Thales**, who lived from about 624 B.C. to 546 B.C. He was said to be somewhat eccentric: He once fell into a well while thinking about philosophy, but he also made a fortune on the olive oil market. His philosophy in a sentence was this: *Water* is the ultimate reality.

This sounds simpleminded, but it is a momentous achievement, and it is not as silly as it might sound. Try to suspend your knowledge of modern science—of the hundred-plus "elements" that have been discovered. Try to look at the world yourself; try to understand it in your own terms. And suppose you have the idea that, in order to make sense of the world, the first thing to do is to discover which element is most basic. (Remember that Greek science identified only four elements—earth, air, fire, and water.) And now try to imagine what the world is *ultimately* made up of.

Now what, you may ask, is so monumentally important about this? Whether the world is really made of water, of course, is not the issue. But what Thales saw, and what we now take for granted, is a difference between the way the world simply *seems* to be and the way it *really* is. The world seems to be made of all kinds of different materials; it took a stroke of genius to suggest that all of these might be made out of a single basic element. Think how difficult life would be, to take but one simple example, if no one had ever noticed that water and ice were actually the same material under different conditions, or if no one had ever discovered that basic food substances could be transformed (through mixing and heating) into an almost infinite variety of different foods. Modern scientific theory, which replaces Thales' initial theory about water with a complex system of elements and subatomic particles, is nevertheless an extension of the same strategy, to distinguish the way the world appears to be from the way it really is, in order to explain why it appears to be as it is. Once we have made this basic distinction, a whole new world opens up to us, a "real world," behind (or above or below) appearances.

The Pre-Socratic Materialists

After Thales, a number of other pre-Socratic philosophers challenged his view of water as the basic reality of the world and suggested theories of their own.

A student of Thales named **Anaximander** went one step further than his teacher and suggested that everything was made of some basic "stuff" (his

OUR OLDEST PHILOSOPHICAL FRAGMENT, FROM ANAXIMANDER

The Non-limited is the original material of existing things; further, the source from which existing things derive their existence is also that to which they return at their destruction, according to necessity; for they give justice and make reparation to one another for their injustice, according to the arrangement of time.

From Kathleen Freeman, Ancilla to the Pre-Socratic Philosophers, *(Cambridge, MA: Harvard, 1948).*

word was *apeiron,* or "indefinite") that we could never experience as such; we could only know its manifestations.

Anaximander had a student named **Anaximenes** who thought that everything was made of *air,* so water was thickened air and earth was thickened even more than that.

A philosopher named **Heraclitus** suggested alternatively that everything was more like *fire* than it was like the other elements—always changing and consuming.

Before the pre-Socratics, wise men in other societies (as well as in Greece) had also made the distinction between the world of appearances and the real world—for example, by appealing to gods and goddesses behind the scenes. But the Greek philosophers made a monumental step forward: They now tried to explain the world, as it normally appeared to them, in a systematic way, not by appeal to the moods and whims of invisible gods and such. And with them, the daily world of appearances, in which different things simply happen one after another, is supplemented by another world, a world in which the world of appearances can be explained.

Now none of us has an ontology as simple as the pre-Socratics'. It is clear to us that there is more to the world than earth, air, fire, water, and the possibility that there is some fifth element, "stuff," which we have never seen. But the pre-Socratics, too, were aware that the world of ultimate reality might be more complex than at first we had imagined. Another pre-Socratic philosopher, **Democritus**, developed a picture of the world that is remarkably close to our current scientific views. He suggested that the world consisted of tiny indestructible elements, which he called **atoms** which combined and recombined in various ways to give us the different elements and all the complex things of this world. These things might change, be created, and be destroyed, but the atoms themselves are eternal. With Democritus, it should be clear to you how much the basic visions of these early philosophers are still the models for what we believe today.

It takes only a little imagination to see that we debate the ultimate nature of reality in much the same terms as these ancient philosophers did. Democri-

> *This world that is the same for all, neither any god nor any man shaped it, but it ever was and is and shall be ever-living Fire that kindles by measures and goes out by measures.*
>
> — *Heraclitus*

tus' view is still very much with us; we no longer believe that atoms themselves are these most basic particles, but we still postulate some such basic elements. A few decades ago, protons, electrons, and neutrons were said to be the basic building blocks of reality. Today, the favorite candidate among physicists are some even more basic building blocks called *quarks.* But if the particles are still smaller, the idea is the same.

So, too, we can understand Heraclitus in modern terms as the view that the nature of ultimate reality is not matter, but *energy.* This view, which became as powerful as it is now only in the late nineteenth century, rejects the traditional emphasis on physical matter (whether tangible matter such as earth or water, or microscopic building blocks such as atoms) and instead declares ultimate reality to be power and forces and energy states, which somehow produce matter as their effects. A still more modern concept would be the view that reality consists of neither matter nor energy as such, but rather of some more basic element—matter-energy—which can manifest itself as either matter *or* energy. This, of course, is much like the view of Anaximander. Laymen often talk as if modern science already knows the ultimate nature of reality, or, in any case, knows much more about it than anyone ever did before. But the basic debate—whether reality should be thought of in terms of basic building blocks or rather, perhaps, in larger, more holistic terms, whether matter or energy should be primary—is still going on. Some people clearly do see the universe as Democritus understood it, consisting of an elaborate order of singular elements that can be understood by taking them apart and analyzing

ANCIENT MATERIALISM

Thales (624–546 B.C.*)—Reality is ultimately water.
Anaximander (610–546 B.C.)—Reality is indefinite "stuff" (*apeiron*).
Anaximenes (585–528 B.C.)—Reality is essentially air.
Heraclitus (536–470 B.C.)—Reality is like fire.
Democritus (460–371 B.C.)—Reality consists of tiny **atoms**.

All dates are approximate.

them. Some people do see the world as Thales did: comprehensible, solid, and substantial, like a pool of water, like the Mediterranean. Some people see the world with Anaximander, as unknowable, mysterious, beyond everyday experiences. And some people see the world as constant energy and change, with excitement and enthusiasm its most important ingredients. Metaphysics, in other words, is not just an ancient, unsophisticated set of views about science. Metaphysics is a basic outlook on the world, and its terms are much the same today as they were twenty-five hundred years ago.

EARLY NONPHYSICAL VIEWS OF REALITY

Now you have no doubt noticed that all five of the thinkers we have named suggested that the basic element of reality was one of the *physical* elements (including "stuff" and "atoms," even though we can't sense them). But there were pre-Socratic philosophers who thought that ultimate reality was not physical at all. One of them was Pythagoras; he believed that the ultimate elements of reality were *numbers.* (If he had answered our opening questions, he would have given the number seven a "10.") For Pythagoras, numbers were eternal and indestructible; the things of this world were in some sense dependent upon numbers for their existence. The heavens, in particular, were divine examples of the mathematical order of the universe. (Pythagoras said that "the whole of heaven is a musical scale and a number.") He and his followers also believed in the immortality of the soul and in reincarnation.

Why did Pythagoras think that numbers were more real than trees and tables? Because numbers were eternal; they never changed, while trees and tables could be chopped up, used for firewood, and destroyed. Reality, according to the view that has been dominant from then until now, is what underlies all change, what does not itself change. Thus another pre-Socratic philosopher, **Parmenides**, went so far as to suggest that the world of our everyday life, because it was so filled with changes and things coming into being and disappearing, could not be real at all. The other pre-Socratics had said that the things of our world were only *less* real and dependent on reality; Parmenides said that our world was actually *un*real.

This principle, that what is real is eternal and unchanging, formed the framework within which most of the pre-Socratics, and almost all modern scientists and religious people, too, developed their view of the universe. But one of the pre-Socratic philosophers challenged this basic principle. He was Heraclitus, whom we have already met as the philosopher who believed that fire was the basic model for reality. But fire is a violent element, always changing and never the same. And so Heraclitus came up with the suggestion that must have upset the early philosophers even more than Parmenides' telling them that the world they lived in wasn't really real. Heraclitus said that *change is real,* thus contradicting the basic principle that reality is what

Pythagoras of Samos (571–497 B.C.) was the leading mathematician of the ancient world, as well as a philosopher who, in southern Italy, led a powerful religious cult whose views were quite at odds with most of the philosophy of pre-Socratic Greece. He believed in the immortality of the soul and in reincarnation, and he established a brotherhood of religious believers in which numbers and mathematics, as the basis of all things, held a special place in the universe. His discoveries in mathematics are still central to the sciences of geometry and acoustics. The Pythagorean theorem is named after him: "The sum of the squares of the two sides of a right triangle is equal to the square of the hypotenuse," or "$a^2 + b^2 = c^2$." He was the first to prove it.

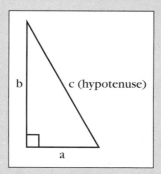

The Pythagoreans also placed great importance on the connections between mathematics and music. They noted, for instance, that if you halve the length of a vibrating string you produce the "same" note at a higher pitch (a discovery you can test for yourselves on a guitar).

doesn't change. (One might say that the only thing that doesn't change is change itself, but this is a good way of tying yourself up in logical knots.) Heraclitus expressed the idea that everything is constantly in flux by saying that you cannot step in the same river twice. Some of his more radical followers claimed that in actual fact you cannot step in the same river once, since there is no moment when the water is not in the process of flowing past. (On the other hand, it has been pointed out by some of his more facetious critics that you *can* step in the same river twice if, having stepped in once, you jump out, run downstream, and jump in again!) It is worth noting, though, that the Heraclitean view of reality is so radical that not even Heraclitus actually held to it. He may have believed that reality was change but he also believed that underlying all change was an eternal principle, **logos**, which did not change. Thus he did believe in eternal reality after all. Heraclitus' view has been defended in our own time by Einstein, who said that, though nature may change

Listen . . . not to me, but to the Logos.

— *Heraclitus*

continuously, the laws of nature stay forever the same. But other philosophers and many scientists now believe that not even the laws stay the same; does this mean that nothing is real? Philosophers have argued about this for twenty-five hundred years.

Now from our abbreviated discussion of the earliest philosophers, we can already see many of the possibilities for a **metaphysics**, an account of ultimate reality, according to which you can express your own view of the world.

First, a metaphysics may consist of purely *physical* or *material* components, whether these are elements such as water or fire or modern components such as atoms, electrons, quarks, and electromagnetic and intranuclear forces. This is called **materialism**.

Second, and opposed to materialism, is the view that the basic components of reality are not physical or material at all—for example, spirits, or minds, or numbers. This is called **immaterialism**.

The whole history of the West, in fact, has tended to be split between these two sets of views. Most scientists, naturally, are materialists, whereas most religions defend immaterialism. But many scientists are also religious, and recognize the importance of immaterialism, too. And most religious thinkers recognize the material nature of the physical world. So one of the most enduring problems of philosophy is the reconciliation of the two.

Ancient Immaterialism

Pythagoras (571–497 B.C.*)—Reality is ultimately numbers.
Parmenides (539–492 B.C.)—Reality is unchanging and unknown to us.
Zeno of Elea (fifth century B.C.)—Reality is unchanging and motion is unreal. ("Zeno's paradoxes" were intended as proofs of this. See, for example, the paradox of the arrow on p. 22.)
Heraclitus (536–470 B.C.)—Reality is change, but with an underlying *logos,* or logic. Thus Heraclitus is sometimes interpreted as saying that reality is *logos.*

All dates are approximate.

PLATO'S FORMS

The ancient philosopher **Plato** tried to have both materialism and immaterialism, but he clearly thought that what was more real were the immaterial entities, which he called **Forms**. The Forms represented Plato's attempt to capture the mathematical insights of Pythagoras and to correlate *being* and *becoming,* following Parmenides and Heraclitus. Like Pythagoras, Plato emphasized the importance of form over material content. Like Parmenides, he emphasized the idea that ultimate reality must be changeless; accordingly our ordinary world of experience cannot be ultimate reality. But like Heraclitus, Plato also appreciated the importance of apparent change, and the need for some underlying *logoi,* or ultimate principle, to make sense of it all. Plato's Forms are his version of the *logos.*

An example of a Form is this: Suppose I draw a triangle on this piece of paper and attempt to prove a theorem of Euclidean geometry about triangles. Now the first thing to notice is that this particular triangle, as I have drawn it, is not even close to being an accurate triangle; but even if I used the most precise instruments in the world, it would still not have exactly straight sides, the lines would still have some thickness (which a true line does not have), and the angles would be slightly in error. In other words, *it is impossible to draw a true triangle.* Second, even if the triangle were much better drawn, how is it possible that by proving something about *this* triangle I have thereby proven something about *all* triangles? Plato's answer is: because what I am really dealing with here is not this triangle at all, which is only a poor material example. I am really dealing with the Form *triangle,* an immaterial perfect triangle that does not exist anywhere in this material world.

Where does the Form *triangle* exist? Today most people would say, "In our minds" or "It doesn't." But Plato thought that it did exist, and in fact it was *more real* than the material triangle drawn on paper. Indeed, his whole philosophy is based on the view that there are *two worlds,* this world of ordinary material existence, in which we spend most of our time and energy, and another world, a world of pure Forms, which is eternal, immaterial, and more real than this one. The first world consists of material things that change, die, and disappear; Plato called it the **World of Becoming**. It is not *un*real but it is *less* real than the other world, the truly real world, which he called the **World of Being**. In his book *The Republic,* Plato gives us a dramatic account of the relationship between these two worlds in terms of a myth, "the myth of

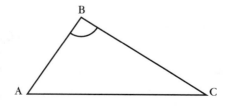

the cave." The cave represents the world of shadows, the World of Becoming, in which we all live. The sunlight represents the truth, the World of Being, which we can know only through *reason,* not through experience.

> SOCRATES: *Here is a parable to illustrate the degrees in which our nature may be enlightened or unenlightened. Imagine the condition of men living in a sort of cavernous chamber underground, with an entrance open to the light and a long passage all down the cave. Here they have been from childhood, chained by the leg and also by the neck, so that they cannot move and can see only what is in front of them, because the chains will not let them turn their heads. At some distance higher up is the light of a fire burning behind them, and between the prisoners and the fire is a track with a parapet built along it, like a screen at a puppet show, which hides the performers while they show the puppets over the top.*
>
> GLAUCON: *I see.*
>
> SOCRATES: *. . . then, such prisoners would recognize as reality nothing but the shadows of objects.*
>
> GLAUCON: *Inevitably.*
>
> SOCRATES: *Now consider what would happen if they were released from the chains. Suppose one of them was set free and forced to stand up, turn his head, and walk with eyes lifted to the light; all these movements would be painful, and he would be too dazzled to make out the objects whose shadows he had been used to seeing. What do you think he would say if someone told him that what he had formerly seen was meaningless illusion, but now, being nearer to reality and turned to the real objects, he was getting a truer view? . . . And suppose someone were to drag him forcibly up the steep and rugged ascent and not let him go until he had hauled himself out into the sunlight . . . and, finally, he would be able to look at the Sun itself and contemplate its nature, not as it appears reflected but in its own domain.*
>
> GLAUCON: *Indeed, Socrates.*

In Plato's view, people who devote all their attention to things in the physical world—the world we experience through our senses—are like people who spend their entire lives watching television. They deal only with images, never with the reality that lies behind those images. To come to know this reality is the work of the intellect and the ultimate task of philosophy.

Now you can see how Plato has saved both sides of his predecessors' philosophical views: He has Heraclitus' constant change, but also his *logos,* which lies in the Forms. He was Parmenides' spectacular claim that the things of our ordinary experience are not truly real, and he has Pythagoras' view that the most real things are the eternal principles of mathematics. Now notice what Plato has done: He has taken the parts of all those views he agrees with and he has integrated them into a single dramatic and compelling picture of the way they fit together in a single worldview. Lesser philosophers might have said, "Well, I believe in material things, of course; I also believe in numbers, and in some eternal principle underlying them." But it is in the working out of a view in which all of this *ties together* that this makes sense. The views themselves, as you have seen, are not particularly original. But almost everyone would agree that Plato is one of the greatest philosophers not only of Greece but of all times, and the reason is the brilliance and imagination with which he has put his views together.

ARISTOTLE'S METAPHYSICS

It is at this point in our history that **Aristotle** enters the scene. Aristotle, who was Plato's student, found Plato's two-world view implausible. Aristotle was far more a common-sense thinker who insisted that reality has to be the everyday world of things, trees, and people, not some other world that we never actually experience. So in effect he brought Plato back down to earth; he rejected Plato's World of Being and the Forms, and insisted, along with what philosophers usually call the "ordinary person" (in other words, you and I, when we are thinking about philosophy), that this world is the real world, and there is no other.

However, although Aristotle insisted that our everyday reality *is* reality, he did not therefore reject the all-important distinction between reality and appearances that had been developing over several centuries. But Aristotle's treatment of that distinction is far more subtle than Plato's; where Plato separated them into two different worlds, Aristotle instead said that the *forms* of things are in the things themselves, and have no separate existence. (Let's use the lower-case letter *f* to show that there is nothing "otherworldly" here.) And in Aristotle, the things of ultimate reality—to which he gave the very important name **substances**—are nothing other than particular things in the world—horses, flowers, people, rocks, and so on. The distinction between reality and appearances stays intact, however, for it is not always true that we understand the essential nature, or what Aristotle called "the essence," of these individual substances. For example, just because we are all familiar with people-substances (that is, people), we don't necessarily understand what it is to be human, what it is to be a person. And, to take a far more dramatic example, just because we are familiar with our small part of the universe in everyday life, it does not follow that we understand the universe as a whole. Indeed, Aristotle's picture of the universe is even more dramatic than Plato's; he envisioned the universe as a gigantic organism, growing and restless, seeking knowledge of itself.

The conflict between their starting points, between Plato's view that reality is something other than our everyday world and Aristotle's view that the ultimate realities are the substances of our daily life, is one that has continued in philosophy until the present day. (In fact, both views became models for Christian thinkers; Plato's view of another, immaterial and eternal world, different from the material world of daily life, became the central thesis of Saint Augustine's philosophy, and the main doctrine of Christian theology for centuries to come. Aristotle's view of a living, growing, self-conscious universe played an important role in the thought of Saint Thomas Aquinas, and is still an important part of Christian theology.)

We can now say quite clearly what we are trying to do. Philosophy—and metaphysics in particular—is an *interpretation of the world*. It is our attempt to make sense of it, our attempt to explain it. Some of our efforts will be directed toward specific issues—for example, what things can we properly consider real? Or, when are a person's actions to be considered as free and as his or her own responsibility? Some of our efforts will be aimed at the whole picture, and we'll ask such questions as "What is the origin of the universe?" and "Why is there a universe at all?" One way to answer such questions is by the pre-Socratic technique: Pick out an essential element or set of elements and show how the world can be explained in terms of the chosen element(s). Another way is the Platonic approach: Postulate and design a world "behind" this one, which explains why things are the way they are. A third way is the Aristotelian way: Assume the commonsense world but then show that there is much in it that we do not yet understand, and that the whole picture cannot be grasped from the details of life alone. The choice largely depends on your views; the pre-Socratic way is initially attractive for its simplicity, but you will find that there is much that cannot be easily accounted for with a single element or set of elements. The Platonic and Aristotelian pictures are much more difficult, but it is for good reason that many philosophers consider virtually all philosophy done in the past twenty-five hundred years to be modeled after Plato or after Aristotle, or after both. Between Plato's imaginative synthesis of the variety of views before him and Aristotle's hardheaded analysis of individuals and their properties, our concept of reality has continued to be formed and re-formed, from generation to generation, and whatever we decide to say about such matters, we can be certain that one or both of them had already anticipated it.

MIND AND METAPHYSICS

Consider this table in front of us, which has hitherto roused but the slightest thought in us. It is full of surprising possibilities. The one thing we know is that it is not what it seems. Beyond this modest result, we have the most complete liberty of conjecture. Leibniz tells us it is a community of souls; Bishop Berkeley tells us it is an idea in the mind of God; sober science, scarcely less wonderful, tells us it is a vast collection of electric charges in violent motion.

> — *Bertrand Russell*, The
> Problems of Philosophy

You may have noticed that one familiar answer to our question of what is real has not been raised. That is the idea that, ultimately, *mind or consciousness* is real. Today most of us would insist that mind be at least part of the answer, and many people—called **idealists**—would insist that it be the whole answer. An idealist believes that the basis of the existence of all things is the mind (whether our own minds or the mind of God). We realize that we know of the existence of material things only through their effects on our minds. Numbers exist because we think them. Beethoven's music exists because we can hear it when it is played, hum it to ourselves, read it from the score if we have had some musical training. According to an idealist, such things are real *only* insofar as they are experienced in the mind; in other words, it is mind that is most real, and other entities are dependent upon mind or minds. Why did none of the Greeks mention this? The fact is, they had no such concept, and so the idea could never have occurred to them. The distinction between entities in the world and ideas in the mind would have made no sense whatsoever to them. This, more than anything else, marks the greatest single difference between their metaphysics and most of ours.

Even if you don't accept the idealists' view that the ultimately real entities are minds, it is still hard to deny the claim that minds are part of reality (although materialism is still alive and well in many quarters, and there are many philosophers and scientists who hope to be able to explain the existence of minds in strictly physical and physiological terms). Others, however, believe minds to have their own kind of existence. Three different views of minds and their place in reality have dominated our thinking for the past several hundred years. All three begin with the idea that mind is a substance (or an aspect of a substance), which is precisely the concept that the Greeks did not have. But in one view, minds are but one *kind* of substance; in another view, minds are but *part* of a substance; and in yet another view, minds are the *only* substances. These three views were represented by three European philosophers from the seventeenth and eighteenth centuries—the French philosopher Descartes, the Dutch philosopher Spinoza, and the German philosopher Leibniz.

Descartes

Descartes was a **pluralist**—a philosopher who believes in more than one substance. He is usually referred to as a **dualist**, who accepts two basic substances—mind and body—but in fact he thought there were three kinds of substances: physical bodies, minds, and God. God created the other two substances, and except by God, they could be neither created nor destroyed. The overriding problem of Descartes' metaphysics was how to connect the various substances—in particular, mind and body. It is obvious that each of us is, in some sense, a complex of both mind and body, mental and physical properties and, therefore, mental and physical substance. But if substances are by definition ultimate and totally independent of anything else, then how can they possibly interact? How is it possible for events happening to my body (a nail in my foot, for instance) to produce an effect in my mind (pain)? How is it possible for events in my mind (deciding to open the door, for instance) to have an effect on my body (I walk over and open the door)? One suggestion might be that the two substances infiltrate one another, as copper and zinc combine (but don't chemically interact) to form brass. Descartes sometimes suggested this. But the interaction between mind and body still seems to go unexplained. In fact, it gets even more complicated when we see that

	DESCARTES	**SPINOZA**	**LEIBNIZ**
Nature of substances	mind body God	the Universe (God)	monads (minds)
Number of substances	three types: many minds, many bodies, one God	one	indefinitely many plus God (the super-monad)
Interaction between substances	causal interaction	Substances do not interact. Mind and body are two of the many attributes of the one substance.	Substances do not interact. Monads only appear to interact, orchestrated by God.

Descartes defined mental substance as that which is not in space (or **unextended** as opposed to physical things, which are **extended** in space). Once we have defined mind and body as two different substances, there seems to be no way of getting them together. And this is even before we begin asking how God as a separate substance can interact with the substances He has created.

Descartes never solved the problem of how substances interact. To solve the problem, there seemed to be only two solutions; either (1) mind and body were not separate substances but parts of the same substance, or (2) they were separate substances alright, but they didn't interact after all. Spinoza chose the first way; Leibniz would choose the second. (We talk about this "mind-body problem" in Chapter 6.)

There are two important points to make about all of this right away. First, don't think that what we are debating are just the complexities of a technical word (that is, "substance"). The word is merely a convenient way of referring to ultimate reality—whatever you think that might be—and the debate between Descartes, Spinoza, and Leibniz is about the nature of reality, not about a word. Second, don't think that these debates about reality are not connected to the more urgent questions about the meaning of life and belief in God: These debates about the nature of reality and "substance" are in fact attempts to answer just those questions, different ways of conceiving of God and His relation to us, and different ways of conceiving of ourselves.

SPINOZA'S METAPHYSICS, FROM HIS ETHICS

Spinoza presented his metaphysical system in the style of Euclid's geometry, with definitions, axioms, and a sequence of "propositions" (theorems) which he proved one at a time. Here are some sample definitions, axioms, propositions, and proofs.

DEFINITIONS

I. By that which is *self-caused,* I mean that of which the essence involves existence, or that of which the nature is only conceivable as existent.

II. A thing is called *finite after its kind,* when it can be limited by another thing of the same nature; for instance, a body is called finite because we always conceive another greater body. So, also, a thought is limited by another thought, but a body is not limited by thought, nor a thought by body.

III. By *substance,* I mean that which is in itself, and is conceived through itself: in other words, that of which a conception can be formed independently of any other conception.

IV. By *attribute,* I mean that which the intellect perceives as constituting the essence of substance.

V. By *mode,* I mean the modifications of substance, or that which exists in, and is conceived through, something other than itself.

VI. By *God,* I mean a being absolutely infinite—that is, a substance consisting in infinite attributes, in which each expresses eternal and infinite essentiality.

AXIOMS

I. Everything which exists, exists either in itself or in something else.

II. That which cannot be conceived through anything else must be conceived through itself.

III. From a given definite cause an effect necessarily follows; and, on the other hand, if no definite cause be granted, it is impossible that an effect can follow.

IV. The knowledge of an effect depends on and involves the knowledge of a cause.

V. Things which have nothing in common cannot be understood, the one by means of the other; the conception of one does not involve the conception of the other.

VI. A true idea must correspond with its ideate or object.

VII. If a thing can be conceived as nonexisting, its essence does not involve existence.

PROPOSITIONS

Prop. I. *Substance is by nature prior to its modifications.*

Proof.—This is clear from Def. III. and V.

Prop. II. *Two substances, whose attributes are different, have nothing in common.*

Proof.—Also evident from Def. III. For each must exist in itself, and be conceived through itself; in other words, the conception of one does not imply the conception of the other.

Prop. III. *Things which have nothing in common cannot be one the cause of the other.*

Proof.—If they have nothing in common, it follows that one cannot be apprehended by means of the other (Ax. V.), and, therefore, one cannot be the cause of the other (Ax. IV.). *Q.E.D.* [Latin, *quod erat demonstrandum,* a phrase used in traditional logic meaning "which was to be demonstrated."]

Prop. IV. *Two or more distinct things are distinguished one from the other either by the difference of the attributes of the substances, or by the difference of their modifications.*

Proof.—Everything which exists either in itself or in something else (Ax. I.),—that is (by Def. III. and V.), nothing is granted in addition to the understanding, except substance and its modifications. Nothing is, therefore, given besides the understanding, by which several things may be distinguished one from the other, except the substances, or, in other words (See Ax. IV.), their attributes and modifications. *Q.E.D.*

Prop. V. *There cannot exist in the universe two or more substances having the same nature or attribute.*

• • •

Prop. VI. *One substance cannot be produced by another substance. . . .*

Spinoza

Spinoza saw that Descartes, having defined mind and body as separate substances, could not explain how they interact. Very well then, he said, I will not treat them as separate substances but as different aspects—or what he called **attributes**—of one and the same substance. Furthermore, if God is a substance separate from the substance of which mind and body are attributes, then God cannot interact with the world, which is nonsense. Therefore, Spinoza concluded, God must be that same substance and in fact, "God" is just another name for that substance. Indeed, the starting point of Spinoza's whole argument is that, since substance is ultimate and totally independent, and since substances cannot interact, there can be only *one* substance. A philosopher such as Spinoza and many of the pre-Socratics, who believes in one substance, is a **monist**.

In Chapter 3 we pointed out that Spinoza was a pantheist, because he believed that God and His universe were the same. Now we can see why that must be so. But Spinoza's metaphysical view has other dramatic results as well: Since mind and body are attributes of the one substance, our everyday division between ourselves as individuals is arbitrary and ultimately unreal. We are in fact all "one," as some Eastern mystics have long taught, too. Individuality is an illusion. So, too, is what we call "freedom." Since we are all an integral part of the one substance, we are wholly *determined* in our thoughts and our behavior by what goes on in the rest of the one substance. So Spinoza's philosophy, which turns on the concept of substance, ultimately presents us with a picture of reality very different from our everyday views; it is a reality in which we are all a unity, in which individuality doesn't count and in which free choice is an illusion. It is a reality in which we are identical to (or part of) God and not to take ourselves as individuals at all seriously.

Leibniz

Gottfried Wilhelm Leibniz, on the other hand, agreed with Descartes that there is a **plurality** of substances—that is, more than one. But Leibniz also agreed with Spinoza that substances cannot interact. Therefore, Leibniz postulated a world in which there are many substances, all of them created by God. These substances are all immaterial, and Leibniz called them **monads**. (God, too, is a monad, but something of a super-monad.) But monads, as substances, do not interact. How then, does it *seem* as if the world is composed of interacting substances?

Leibniz, too, used his metaphysics as a basis for an imaginative and unusual view of the world. But where Spinoza believed that all things are a unity and that there is no individuality. Leibniz was very much an individualist, and it is for that reason that his pluralism of monads is so important to him. And for Leibniz, too, it was important that God is not simply identical to the universe, but separate from it and watching over it, guaranteeing that this is "the best of all possible worlds" (see pp. 86 and 349). Spinoza saw the world as wholly determined and without freedom; Leibniz thought that what is most important—and in fact defines each monad—is its sense of freedom and spontaneity. To prove this, he developed the following view of reality.

Each monad is something like an individual mind. There are no physical substances as such, only appearances of them. Moreover, the monads don't interact; they only appear to do so. Imagine yourself in a room, not merely surrounded by television screens but by the most sophisticated equipment of virtual reality. Television offers visual experiences that are limited to two dimensions and audio experiences that are limited by the placement and range

LEIBNIZ: AN INTRODUCTION TO MONADS

1. *The Monad, of which we will speak here, is nothing else than a simple substance, which goes to make up composites; by simple we mean without parts.*

2. *There must be simple substances because there are composites; for a composite is nothing else than a collection or* aggregatum *of simple substances.*

• • •

8. *Still Monads must have some qualities, otherwise they would not even be existences. And if simple substances did not differ at all in their qualities, there would be no means of perceiving any change in things. Whatever is in a composite can come into it only through its simple elements and the Monads, if they were without qualities, since they do not differ at all in quantity, would be indistinguishable one from another. For instance, if we imagine* a plenum *or completely filled space, where each part receives only the equivalent of its own previous motion, one state of things would not be distinguishable from another.*

9. *Each Monad, indeed, must be different from every other. For there are never in nature two beings which are exactly alike, and in which it is not possible to find a difference either internal or based on an intrinsic property.*

— Monadology

of the speaker system. But a virtual reality room, such as the holodeck in *Star Trek: The Next Generation,* provides holistic experiences. You can travel to distant lands, test your ability to be a good parent, or even indulge in a sexual fantasy that you would never consider in "actual" reality. The equipment does not intrude itself: You see no wires, tubes, or boxes and you can sense no difference between the apparent world and the real world. On the holodeck, you experience the world or, rather, images of the world, and all of us—each in our own little rooms—experience on the holodeck our own perspective on the world. God has programmed all of us to have the right perspective and the right images, so that it seems as if we are all looking at the same world and at each other, but in reality we are not. We never actually see each other, and there is no world as such. There are only our individual perceptions, our individual monads, created and cared for by God in a "preestablished harmony."

IDEALISM

Idealism is the philosophy that says that what is real is mind, that all else—material objects, numbers, ideas—are in the mind or in some essential sense dependent upon minds for their existence.

Descartes himself was not an idealist, but he established the framework for most later idealists when he said, in his *Meditations,* that the only thing one can know directly is one's own ideas. From that, it is a short but spectacular leap to the claim that only ideas are real. Leibniz, for example, was an idealist; he said that physical reality is nothing but "perceptions" in immaterial monads—including the mind of God. According to idealism, however, there is nothing beyond us, except perhaps God. The universe is made up of minds and things dependent on minds, and nothing else. Another early eighteenth-century idealist was the Irish bishop **George Berkeley** (1685–1753). Berkeley held the extreme position of **subjective idealism** which, simply summarized, insisted that "to be is to be perceived" (*esse est percipi*). According to Berkeley, it makes no sense to believe in the existence of anything that we cannot experience. (We will see more of his underlying view, called **empiricism**, in the following chapter.) But all that we can experience, Berkeley argues, are our own ideas. We know that a stone exists because we have ideas (experiences) about it, including the visual appearance, touch, and weight of the stone, as well as the sound it makes when we scrape it, the pain it causes when we kick it, its visible effects on other things (which are also nothing but ideas in our minds). We know that our minds exist, Berkeley argues, because ideas presuppose minds. And we can know that God exists (as an infinite Mind) because, Berkeley argues, our finite minds require God's infinite Mind as a "presupposition." But there is nothing else. No material objects. No world outside of our (and God's) knowledge and ideas.

Idealism in such extreme forms may sound far-fetched and hard to believe, but it is important to emphasize that such positions are not argued

---

Bishop George Berkeley (1685–1753) was a brilliant young Irish philosopher and theologian who is still the leading representative of **subjective idealism**, the view that nothing exists except ideas and minds.

When we do our utmost to conceive the existence of external bodies, we are all the while only contemplating our own ideas. "To be is to be perceived," Berkeley argued, "*esse est percipi.*" All objects exist only in the mind (including the mind of God).

Later in life, Berkeley became an educational missionary, visiting early America. Berkeley, California, is named after him.

There was a young man who said, "God
Must think it exceedingly odd
*   If he finds that this tree*
*   Continues to be*
When there's no one about in the Quad."

REPLY

Dear Sir:
*   Your astonishment's odd:*
*   I am always about in the Quad.*
*   And that's why the tree*
*   Will continue to be.*
Since observed by
    Yours faithfully,

                    GOD

                    — *Ronald Knox,*
                    quoted by Bertrand
                    Russell

lightly. They are based on careful consideration and a large number of sound, hard-hitting arguments. Idealism can be argued, for example, from the seemingly undeniable premise that the only things we can know are based on experience, and that nothing other than experience—for example, material objects existing "outside of us" in the world—can be known. Or, idealism might be argued from the nature of God and His works; if God is infinite Mind, then His creations will be thoughts. Or, idealism might be argued from Platonic considerations about the formal properties of things. But, in any case, idealism is not just the frenzied assertion of a mad person—"Nothing exists but my mind!" It is a philosophical position of long standing for the very reason that it is based on long philosophical tradition and on arguments that many people have found convincing. If idealism seems to contradict common sense, it is nevertheless advanced—by Berkeley, for example—as nothing other than a more adequate account of commonsense experience. The idealist still believes in the reality of rocks and the blueness of the sky. But idealism is an attempt to reason about what these must *really* be like, if we are to know them at all.

The emphasis on argument in the defense of metaphysics cannot be underestimated. Indeed, much of the history of metaphysics since Plato has been based on the idea that reality is ultimately to be discovered not by the senses but by reason—by that abstract and perhaps "godlike" ability we possess to figure things out despite a bewildering confusion of appearances. But idealism has another source of inspiration, too. It is not surprising that many idealists are also devout theists. Both Berkeley and Leibniz invoke God in their idealism as the all-knowing Mind. One reason for this is the necessity of having an all-knowing Mind to perceive things when we do not. But God is not, for them, just a corollary to epistemology (that is, the theory of knowledge and how we have it). They are also devout believers, and idealism suits their religious sensibilities as well as their epistemological theories. Idealism, in general, is a combination of vision and rigorous argument. Like most metaphysical theories, it is a worldview, a **Weltanschauung**, which is supported and structured by careful and often ingenious arguments about why the world *must really be that way.*

Perhaps the most spectacular forms of idealism were developed in the nineteenth century in Germany, by a diverse group of philosophers known, appropriately, as **German Idealists**. The founder and unchallenged leader of this group was the great philosopher from East Prussia, **Immanuel Kant**. Kant, too, began with the epistemological premise that everything we know must be based on experience, but he took this easily agreed-upon premise to astounding lengths. The world, he argued, is essentially *constituted* (like the word "constitution," or "set up") by us, through our concepts and our ideas. There is no space, no time, no objects apart from our experience of them. But the nature of these things is not therefore up to our own individual fancy. Our minds are constructed in such a way that there are certain **a priori** (universal and necessary) rules, so that space *must* be a certain way for us, and, therefore, time and objects must be a certain way, too. What Kant argues, in other words, is that there is a way the world must be, but it is a necessity based on the nature of our minds, not anything in the world itself. We *impose* laws on nature; we do not, like scientists, merely find them.

This radical and exhilarating vision of the world gets coupled in Kant with another, even more dramatic, idealist vision. We live, he says, not just in one world, but in two. When we are involved in knowledge—for example, studying science—we perceive the world through the concepts of our understanding, constituted according to certain rules. But when we are involved in practical matters, for example, or matters of religious belief, those concepts and rules no longer apply. Instead, we use a completely different set of rules. For example, a physician or a physiologist can explain what we do in terms of nerves and muscles, bones and movements. That gives us knowledge. But when we *act* and actually *do* something, we don't see our bodies in terms of

Kant: Two worlds ("standpoints") are equally "real" and rational.

The World of Nature
physical objects
cause and effect
Self as object of knowledge
science, technology,
facts to be known

The World of Action and Belief
rational principles (morality)
freedom to choose
Self as agent
God, immortal soul, faith
duty to be done

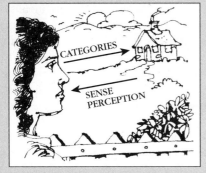

Schopenhauer: The world is illusion, only will is real (but irrational).

(Representations)   *Will* (irrational, without purpose)

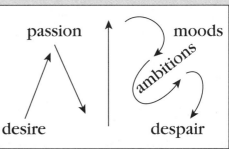

Hegel: The unity of the world and the mind is spirit, discovering itself.

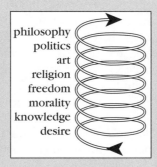

nerves and muscles; our bodies simply become the means by which we carry out our *intentions,* obey certain *principles,* achieve certain *ends.* So, too, when we think about God, we are not thinking of a Being who can be known through the concepts of scientific knowledge; and we already saw (in Chapter 3) that Kant instead defends a *moral* conception of God's necessary existence. Kant once said that he saw his mission in life as being to "limit knowledge to make room for faith." By dividing his idealism into two separate but equal realms, Kant succeeds in giving us an idealist picture of both the world and religion in which science and religion are no longer at odds with one another. His idealism, in other words, is aimed at solving basic problems of life as well as establishing a rigorously argued position in philosophy.

After Kant, a considerable number of young German philosophers followed his lead and became idealists, too. Some preserved his "two world" vision; others rejected it. Arthur Schopenhauer considered himself a dedicated student of Kant, but where Kant tended to perceive the world with hope and considerable respect for humanity, Schopenhauer was a self-proclaimed **pessimist**. He didn't think much of people, and he didn't think much of life. His idealism, accordingly, spelled out his pessimism. But it was also based on a long train of sometimes brilliant arguments, some of them in defense of Kant's idealism, others pointing out where he thought Kant had gone wrong. Kant had divided metaphysics into two worlds—one of nature and knowledge, and one of action, morals, and faith. But both worlds were, in Kant's vision, *rational.* They operated according to necessary laws. Schopenhauer, who was influenced by some of the Eastern mystics, said in effect that both sides of this metaphysical dualism were *irrational,* a fitting conclusion for his pessimism. The world of knowledge was in fact a world of *illusion,* he said. What was real was what was inside of us, making us have desires and other passions, driving us to act. But where Kant, too, believed in the reality of an inner force, which he called the **Will**, this Will was, Kant believed, rational and

Arthur Schopenhauer (1788–1860) was possibly the crankiest philosopher in the history of Western thought. He heaped scorn on most of his contemporaries, purposely announced his lectures at the same time as Hegel's at the University of Berlin in order to steal his students, and was constantly involved in lawsuits, including one for kicking his landlady down the stairs. His philosophy, not surprisingly, is **pessimism**, the view that life in general is no good and has no purpose. Yet he defended his prejudices brilliantly and developed an ambitious system, modeled after Kant, in which "will" becomes the driving force of the universe and of reality itself. It should be said that Schopenhauer himself tended to good living; he lived very well, until the age of seventy-two, enjoying himself considerably.

obeyed the rules of reason. Schopenhauer disagreed. The Will, he said, was irrational. It was not "ours" but rather a violent force operating through us, creating desires and passions and provoking us to act but, ultimately, to no purpose at all. Schopenhauer's answer to this tragic vision of human life was escape from the power of the will—either through aesthetic detachment (the quiet enjoyment of art, literature, and music) or ascetic renunciation (the rejection of desire that characterizes many saints and religious orders).

Kant employed an idealist metaphysics to envision the world as rational and to separate science and religion, because he was devoted to both of them. Schopenhauer used idealist metaphysics to portray his gloomy view of the world in which both science and human passions were pointless. A third German idealist, G. W. F. Hegel (whom we met in the preface), used idealism once again to establish a picture of the world as rational and to reconcile his interests in science and religion. But where Kant's idealism was largely static, a vision of two realms of human life each ruled by *a priori* principles, Hegel envisioned a single cosmos in constant conflict, an all-embracing **Spirit** developing itself through all of us and throughout history. As Spirit, the world is a kind of cosmic consciousness, a universal mind, trying to understand itself. (Hegel borrowed heavily from Aristotle here.) For Hegel, the spheres of science, moral activity, and religion were all ways in which Spirit moved toward self-understanding. Again, Hegel developed this vision through many arguments, some of them defending the general idealist position, some of them attacking the other idealists and saying why his particular vision was preferable to theirs. Other idealists are still doing the same. But idealism always remains this exciting mixture of basic visions and hopes for the world, coupled with hardheaded arguments about why this particular vision is the right one. Whatever else it may be, idealism is the view that our ideas define our world, and that the most essential thing in the world is—the mind.

TELEOLOGY

Hegel's view of the universal Spirit developing through history is a dramatic illustration of another ancient but still modern worldview that we call **teleology** (from the Greek word for purpose, *telos*). A teleological view of the world is one that thinks the world ultimately has a purpose, and is developing toward that purpose. In ancient times, Aristotle defended such a vision of the universe struggling to recognize itself—"thought thinking itself," he called it. So, too, Hegel's vision was universal Spirit struggling through human history to know itself *as* Spirit.

Modern science tends to discourage such thinking in terms of purposes, urging instead explanations in terms of causes. Indeed, since the seventeenth century we have been taught to think of the universe as something of a giant machine, a mechanism that operates according to the causal laws of nature. But this vision of the universe as a machine has always seemed incomplete to a great many thinkers, including even those at the forefront of its formulation.

Hegel: The more conventional opinion gets fixated on the antithesis of truth and falsity, the more it tends to expect a given philosophical system to be either accepted or contradicted; and hence it finds only acceptance or rejection. It does not comprehend the diversity of philosophical systems as the progressive unfolding of truth, but rather sees in it simple disagreements. The bud disappears in the bursting forth of the blossom, and one might say that the former is refuted in the latter; similarly, when the fruit appears, the blossom is shown up in its turn as a false manifestation of the plant, and the fruit now emerges as the truth of it instead. These forms are not just distinguished from one another, they also supplant one another as mutually incompatible. Yet at the same time their fluid nature makes them moments of an organic unity in which they not only do not conflict, but in which each is as necessary as the other; and this mutual necessity alone constitutes the life of the whole.

From Phenomenology of Spirit, *trans. A. V. Miller (Oxford: Oxford University Press, 1977), 2.*

Both Descartes and the great physicist Sir Isaac Newton, for example, defended a mechanistic, causal account of the universe but also insisted that God provided purpose to His creation. So, too, Kant—who was an enthusiastic devotee of Newton—supplemented his causal view of the natural world with a teleological vision of the cosmos, and Leibniz taught that all monads unfolded according to God's purpose.

The idea of the universe as a great machine is relatively new in history, but teleology is almost as old as Western civilization itself. The ancient Greeks were mostly *animists*—that is, they attributed some sort of lifelike activity to all things. Aristotle's teleological metaphysics was just a very sophisticated expression of this, a theory of the purpose *of* nature as well as of purposes *in* nature. So, too, the American Indians have long believed in a vision of the universe that is not mechanical (or "dead") but very much alive. Many Eastern and African religions and philosophies also hold animistic and teleological views of the world, in contrast to our more mechanical, "scientific" models. Today, such process philosophers as Charles Hartshorne and Alfred North Whitehead defend a teleological view of reality as **process** in place of the more static concept of **substance** as a way of once again synthesizing science and teleological metaphysics. Whether or not the purpose of the universe is God's purpose, or the purpose of some other sort of Spirit or spirits, the idea that the universe *means* something and is itself striving for some sort of completion has always been an exhilarating philosophical view. In contemporary

CHARLES HARTSHORNE ON A THEOLOGICAL "MISTAKE"

God Is Absolutely Perfect and Therefore Unchangeable. In Plato's *Republic* one finds the proposition: God, being perfect, cannot change (not for the better, since "perfect" means that there can be no better; not for the worse, since ability to change for the worse, to decay, degenerate, or become corrupt, is a weakness, an imperfection). The argument may seem cogent, but it is so only if two assumptions are valid: that it is possible to conceive of a meaning for "perfect" that excludes change in any and every respect and that we must conceive God as perfect in just *this* sense. Obviously the ordinary meanings of perfect do not entirely exclude change. Thus Wordsworth wrote of his wife that she was a "perfect woman," but he certainly did not mean that she was totally unchangeable. In many places in the Bible human beings are spoken of as perfect; again the entire exclusion of change cannot have been intended. Where in the Bible God is spoken of as perfect, the indications are that even here the exclusion of change in any and every respect was not implied.

ecological context, many people employ the Greek term *Gaia* to refer to a contemporary concept of the earth itself as a living organism.

And yet many people believe that the universe itself does *not* have a purpose, that it is simply "matter in motion" and not here for any particular reason. Einstein thought that the universe had an ultimate purpose. "God does not play dice with the universe," he wrote, thus rejecting the modern tendency to reduce everything to chance occurrences. Indeed, it is in this vision of the purpose of the universe that our question about the meaning of life and our question about the ultimate nature of reality come together as a single problem. Does the universe have a purpose? Is this purpose provided by God? If so, what is it? And if the universe has no purpose, does human life have a purpose? Those are the ultimate questions which we all must ask ourselves at one time or another. For our various answers to them are with us all the time anyway. How we live and what we do, what we can hope for, and even our day-to-day attitudes toward our jobs, ourselves, and each other, ultimately fall within the framework of these ultimate metaphysical questions, and are accordingly affected by them.

But if the word "reality" is an evaluative term for what we consider most basic to our experience, as we mentioned earlier, does reality have to be primarily scientific or religious? Suppose we give up the age-old presupposition that what is real must itself be most durable and eternal. Suppose, for example, one were to suggest—as Hegel suggested—that what is most real is neither the world discovered by science nor the world believed in by religion but our *social* world, and the primary structures of reality are not atoms or electrons or gods and other spirits but other people, tied together in bonds of kinship and community. Knowledge, in this interpretation of reality, becomes those views which are commonly shared and considered provable to anyone—or "objective"; religious belief consists of those doctrines and rituals held in common, which help hold the community together. Or suppose someone else were to say that *passion* is most real, that reality is what you feel when you're in love, or extremely angry, and everything else is but a pale shadow of this. Reality, in other words, is a function of *our* purposes, our passions and our collective social goals.

The possibilities for metaphysics are more expansive than traditional philosophy has tended to suggest. It is a very real question, in other words, whether science and religion have been traditionally overemphasized in our view of ourselves. Are they really what's so important? What about *morality?* Could it be that, when it comes right down to it, we think of being a "good person" as far more important and far more "real" than knowing about the world or even believing in God? What about *art?* Could it be that, for some people, creation of inspirational objects or music or poems is more important than knowledge or religion or morality or even life itself? In other words, we should close this chapter on reality by opening up the subject to new dimensions. Perhaps the stuff of the real world is none of the entities we have been talking about, but rather other people, or art, or music, or whatever—as Paul Tillich said of God—is our "ultimate concern." The question of reality thus turns into the question of the meaning of life, which for some people may be answered in terms of God, for others in terms of science, but for many of us, once we start really to think about it, the answer might lie in an entirely different, perhaps even unexpected, place.

METAPHYSICS AND THE EVERYDAY WORLD

Philosophers frame our everyday experience in a larger vision so that their views about life and its meaning can be used to understand our ordinary experience in a different way. For Spinoza, for example, philosophy was a source of great consolation; it allowed him to see everything that happens as just another mechanical movement of the "One Substance," over which he had no control and in which, in any case, he didn't really matter. For Leibniz, on the other hand, philosophy was a source of optimism and confidence: he saw himself as an individual consciousness developing a view about the whole of the universe, assured from the outset that this view is programmed and guaranteed by God, who is watching over the whole process. It is important to read these eminent writers as engaging in a great imaginative effort. To read them as if they were just solving some technical puzzles or, as some people complain, "just playing with words," is to misunderstand the way that we all see the world. For we all need a vision, a conceptual framework, to give facts and things meaning and make our lives worthwhile. Spinoza and Leibniz were spelling out their vision of the world for themselves, for us to share, or for us to react against. Their success as philosophers depends on whether we do in fact react at all, and whether we try to rethink their visions in our own terms.

You might object that Plato's vision of two worlds or the cosmic visions of Spinoza and Leibniz are poetic metaphors rather than philosophy. The German metaphysical views we briefly explored in earlier chapters—Hegel's grand view of the spirit developing itself through all of us and Schopenhauer's dramatic view of a will in all of us, driving us through our passions for no reason whatever—do indeed seem more like the images of poets than the hardheaded systems of philosophers. But great philosophy is almost always poetry as well as hardheaded thinking, vision as well as argument, imagination as well as intelligence.

In our examinations of philosophers' ontologies and metaphysics, certain basic principles should be becoming clear to you. First, there is a sense in which the underlying assumption is that *what is ultimately real* is that which endures throughout change. A second basic assumption is that reality is somehow a unity. If you believe that there are different ultimate units, or substances (like Descartes) or different worlds (like Plato or Kant), it is necessary to show how they somehow fit together. Thus it is also true that scientists have always preferred that most elegant theory which ties together the most material under the simplest principle, and the ultimate goal of science, from Thales to Newton to Einstein, has been what Einstein called a "unified field theory"—that is, a single theory that would sum up and integrate all the laws of nature. And in religion, too, it is no surprise that some of the most powerful religions in the world, and all of the dominant religions in the West, are monotheistic—believing in one God—since a single deity, like a single explanatory principle, is always more powerful and compelling than a collection of gods or principles fighting among themselves for domination. Again, this assumption can be challenged, but to do so is to oppose the whole intellectual history of the West, and perhaps to be left with a sense of two or more realities which do not tie together in any coherent way.

I repeat these two assumptions not because they are beyond question (nothing in philosophy is beyond question) but because it is important to be aware how powerful they are. The whole history of philosophy, science, and theology has struggled toward eternity and unity, so if you try to defend some other view you'd better have some good arguments for doing so. But these assumptions have been attacked, and brilliantly, for example, by the philosopher Friedrich Nietzsche, who rejected the whole metaphysics of eternity and unity and thus rejected (he thought) the whole of metaphysics as well. If you think reality is to be found in the details of life, however, or in passions or fleeting desires, in short-term relationships with other people, then you might well be forced to reject these time-honored assumptions. But you cannot simply dismiss them. (Nietzsche spent his whole career trying to attack them.) And whatever you do in your philosophy, it is at least important to take account of them. Is it possible that the world in reality is fragmented through and through? Is it possible that life is essential conflict and antagonism—or what philosophers following Hegel and Marx call **dialectic**. Is it possible that there is no single, coherent viewpoint that will make sense of our lives?

Even these are viewpoints to be defended, paradoxically, in a coherent, unified framework. Whatever else it is—visionary, speculative, inspiring—philosophy is also hard thinking, and imagination is its accomplice, not its substitute. Mutual tolerance of opinions is indeed a virtue, but not when it is lazy indifference or simply the insecurity that most of us have about defending our own ideas. When Socrates said that "the unexamined life is not worth living," what he really meant was "know yourself and your ideas; criticize them in order to be confident of them." What you think about reality isn't just "your opinion"; it is also the way you live, the foundation of everything that you do. And a flimsy foundation is no more secure for being unexpressed, unexamined, and unargued.

CLOSING QUESTIONS

1. Choose *one* of the elements defended by the pre-Socratic philosophers (water, fire, numbers, etc.) and argue for it as well as you can, preferably with a friend or a few friends who will try to prove you wrong. For example, if you choose *fire,* an immediate objection would be that fire couldn't possibly be the essential element in cold objects—a block of ice, for example. A reply might be that cold objects simply contain *much less* fire than hot things. You might also argue that not all fire manifests itself as flame, and soon, no doubt, you will find yourself moving into more modern-day talk about energy instead of fire as such. The point of the exercise is to see (1) how very much alive we can still make these ancient theories in our own terms, and (2) to show how any theory, if it has only the slightest initial plausibility, can be defended, at least to some extent, if only you are clever enough to figure out how to answer the various objections presented to you and modify your theory to meet them.

2. Describe the "Form" of some ordinary objects around you, in accordance with Plato's theory. How do you know whether an object is defined by one Form or another? What can you say about the Form of an ordinary object, in the fashion of Plato's discussion of the Form of *triangle?* If an object changes, does it change Forms as well? Can an object have conflicting Forms? Can we understand our recognition of objects without some conception of Forms to explain how it is that we recognize them?

3. Categories in philosophy often seem too rigid or too simpleminded to classify the complexity of our views, but perhaps the following checklist will help you understand your own position in the history of philosophy:

   a. Are you a materialist? An immaterialist?

   Do you believe that ultimate reality can be discovered by science?

   Do you believe that ultimate reality is a matter of religious belief?

   b. What are the basic entities in your ontology? What is most real?

   c. Are you a monist? A pluralist?

   If you are a pluralist, what is the connection between the different entities in your ontology? Rank them in order of their relative reality, or explain their relationship.

   d. Are the basic entities in your ontology eternal? If not, how did they come into being?

   e. Are you an idealist? (Do you believe that the basic entities of your ontology are dependent on the existence of minds?)

   f. How do you explain the existence of (or do you deny the existence of) the following? Minds, numbers, God, tables and chairs, the law of gravity, evil, moral principles, dreams, Santa Claus.

   g. Is the experience of seeing a green flash nothing other than having a certain brain event go on inside your skull? Why would someone want to say that? What problems are there with that suggestion?

h. Could a computer have a sense of humor? What would it have to do to have one? What would it have to do to convince you that it had one? (Would it be enough to print out "Ha Ha" and shake around a bit?)

i. Does the universe have a purpose? (Sometimes, "Why is there something rather than nothing?")

j. What does the word "real" mean to you? Using your definition, run once again through the items in Opening Question 1 and rate them for their "reality" in your view.

k. Do you think *this* world is the real world? Or do you believe that there is an existence more real than our own?

BIBLIOGRAPHY AND SUGGESTED READINGS

A good short introduction to metaphysics is Richard Taylor's *Metaphysics* (Prentice-Hall, 1957). A good introduction to the pre-Socratic philosophers is J. Burnet's *Early Greek Philosophy* (Black, 1958). For a general introduction to Plato and his philosophy, see A. E. Taylor, *Plato, the Man and His Work* (Dial, 1936). An excellent contemporary introduction to Aristotle is Mortimer Adler's *Aristotle for Everyone* (Bantam 1980). The main works of the three philosophers René Descartes, Benedict (Baruch) Spinoza, and Wilhelm Leibniz are included together in *The Rationalists* (Doubleday, 1960). An exciting history of metaphysics is Arthur Lovejoy's *The Great Chain of Being* (Harvard University Press, 1936). Good surveys of the pre-Socratics, Socrates, Plato, Aristotle, Descartes, Leibniz, Spinoza, and other figures mentioned in this chapter are included in Paul Edwards, ed., *The Encyclopedia of Philosophy* (Macmillan, 1967). This is a seminal reference work for all topics for students in beginning philosophy courses. A good discussion of the mind-body problem and the various contemporary solutions is David Rosenthal's *Materialism and the Mind-Body Problem* (Prentice-Hall, 1971). A good short introduction is Jerome Shaffer's *The Philosophy of Mind* (Prentice-Hall, 1968). An account of the German idealists through imaginary interviews is Robert C. Solomon's *Introducing the German Idealists* (Hackett, 1981).

CHAPTER FIVE

THE SEARCH FOR TRUTH

Madame Curie, Brown Brothers.

THE SEARCH FOR TRUTH

*It is now some years since I detected how
many were the false beliefs that I had from my
earliest youth admitted as true, and how
doubtful was everything I had since
constructed on this basis: and from that time I
was convinced that I must for once and for all
seriously undertake to rid myself of all the
opinions which I had formerly accepted and
commence to build anew.*

— *Descartes,* Meditations

OPENING QUESTIONS

1. Some of the information you have been given in your courses in school is, inevitably, not true. How would you start to prove to yourself that *all* of it is not false?

2. Suppose a friend were to challenge you, "How do you *know* that 2 + 2 = 4?" How would you answer?

3. Suppose another friend, in a provocative mood, were to ask you how you know that you are not dreaming right at this moment. What can you say? How would you prove to yourself that this is not true?

4. Is thinking rationally always the best way to think? Is the scientific answer to a question always the most true?

WHAT IS TRUE?

One unerring mark of the love of truth is not entertaining any proposition with greater assurance than the proofs it is built upon will warrant.

> — *John Locke,* Essay on
> Human Understanding

In the previous chapter, you were introduced to a wide variety of views of reality. Which of them do you believe? Which of them is *true?* It won't do to say. "All of them," since some of them contradict the others; nor will it do to say, "It's just a matter of opinion," since you still have to defend the one that you believe to be true. And because these various opinions are all *about* something—namely, the world—it is reasonable to ask whether they do or do not represent the way the world *really* is. But here we run into a more general problem, no matter what particular metaphysical view of the world we support: What is it for a set of beliefs to be true? How will we know when our beliefs are true? Sometimes this seems to be **obvious (self-evident)**: but what if the "obvious" is not always so? These questions are the basis of the discipline called **epistemology** the theory of *knowledge.*

The question "What is it for our beliefs to be true?" has a seductively easy answer: A belief is true if (and only if) it corresponds to the facts. Thus my belief that I have at least 75 cents in my pocket is true if and only if I do *in fact* have 75 cents or more in my pocket. Your belief that the Philadelphia Phillies will win the World Series is true if and only if, *in fact,* the Phillies do win the World Series. The great astronomer Galileo's belief that Jupiter has four moons is true if and only if in fact Jupiter has four moons, and so on. A belief is true if it corresponds to the facts. But that turns out, you will see, not to help us at all.

First, consider the statements "75 × 3 = 225" and "The cube root of 64 is 4." Are these statements true if and only if they correspond to the facts? What facts? Suppose it happens to be the case that there are not, in fact, any actual combinations of three sets of seventy-five things in the world; would that

TRUTH IN PHILOSOPHY

Facts get in the way of truth.

> — *Cervantes,* Don
> Quixote

Facts are only the shadows of truth.

> — *Muhammad Ali*

make the statement "75 × 3 = 225" false, at least for the moment? Of course, you might say that *if* there were three sets of seventy-five things in the world, *then* they would add up all together to 225 things. But it is also true that *if* the Phillies were to win the World Series, then indeed they would win the World Series. But suppose they do not win; the "if" doesn't make it true. But "75 × 3 = 225" seems to be true even if there are no facts in the world for the statement to correspond to. Therefore, presumably, there are true statements that do not (or need not) correspond to any facts.

Second, consider the status of a great many statements of "common sense." For example, going out in cold, damp weather causes us to "lower our resistance" and get sick. Doctors dispute this on the basis of scientific evidence, and yet we hold to such beliefs until they are *conclusively* refuted—some continuing to hold on to them even then. How do we know that what we believe as a matter of common sense is in fact justified and not just a set of plausible falsehoods that have been handed down, uncritically from person to person, generation to generation?

Third, compare such statements as "there is a coffee cup here on the table," which is the report of an immediate and particular perception, and the natural law in science that "there is gravity between any two masses." Both statements claim to be based on experience, but the latter obviously involves a much more complicated process of confirmation than the former. Between the two there are any number of generalizations based on experience—of *hypotheses*—that are formulated and confirmed by inductive argument, such as "water freezes at 32°F" and "cats run away when you wave a German shepherd in front of them." But must all statements in science be confirmed by experience? Could it be that two very general theories might have no observation or experiment that could distinguish between them and verify one while refuting the other? And what about religious truths—not only "God exists" but such claims as "Moses parted the Red Sea with the help of God"? Are these true because they "correspond to the facts"? Because they can in any sense be verified? Or is there a kind of truth that depends on faith and is very different from scientific truth?

Finally, what about very general truths or truisms, such as "all things will pass" and "boys will be boys"? Tautologies are true, even though they don't seem to tell us anything about the world. And what are we to make of those grand statements uttered by the philosophers: "It is the Forms that are most real" and "There is only one substance"? Are they true or not? Are any of them true? How can we tell? What does our knowledge of such matters ultimately depend upon? What is truth, and how will we know it when (or if) we find it?

TWO KINDS OF TRUTH

As far back as the Introduction, it was suggested that true statements (or, simply, truth) might be divided into two separate categories: (1) true because of the facts; and (2) true because of reasoning. Examples of the first would be the true statement that there is no change at all in my pocket, the true statement that Switzerland has not fought in a war in this century, and the true statement that water boils at less than 100°C on the top of a mountain. Examples of the second would be the true statement that $2 + 2 = 4$, the true statement that $A + B = B + A$, and the true statement that no bachelor is married. These "truths of reason" are called **necessary truths** for they could not possibly be false.

Empirical Truth

A statement that is true because of the facts is called an **empirical truth**—that is, true because of experience. (The word "empirical" means having to do with experience.) Empirical truths can only be known to be true once we have actually looked at the world. (Of course, we don't always do this ourselves; most of our empirical knowledge depends upon the observations and experiments carried out by other people. We take their word for it.) But since an empirical truth can be known only by looking at the facts of the world, a statement such as "There are no trees on the University of Texas campus" might—for all we know before we actually go out and look around—be false. Philosophers refer to such a statement (and the circumstances to which it refers) as **contingent** or as a **contingent truth** (if it is true; if it is false, it is a **contingent falsehood**). Thus the statement that there are no trees on the University of Texas campus happens to be false, but it is contingently so. We can *imagine* what it would be like otherwise; if someone were to cut down the few remaining trees, then the statement would become true, but only contingently true, since there might someday once again be trees on the campus. As a general rule in philosophy, all empirical statements are, if true, only contingently true.

Necessary Truth

A statement that is true because of reason, on the other hand, is *necessarily* true; it is a necessary truth. "Necessary" is here the opposite of "contingent": We can always imagine what it would be for a contingent truth not to be true (or a contingent falsehood not to be false). We cannot even make sense out of the suggestion that a necessary truth might not be true (or that a necessary falsehood might not be false). "$2 + 2 = 4$" is a necessary truth, in that we cannot imagine—no matter how imaginative we happen to be—what circumstances might make that statement false. (Suppose I add together two drops of ink, and they combine to form one drop; would this prove the statement to be false? Why not?) For example, the necessary falsehood "$1 + 1 = 1$" cannot be imagined to be true under any circumstances. Necessary truths can be said to be true, accordingly, *prior to* experience or (in Latin) *a priori*. (It is important to note again that *a priori* does not mean "before" in the sense of

Two Kinds of Truth

Empirical, or factual, truth: "There are no rabbits in Antarctica."

Empirical, or factual, truths are true *as a matter of fact*, but it is possible that they might be otherwise and we can imagine what circumstances would make them false. They can be known only on the basis of experience (our own or someone else's).

Necessary truth: "2 + 2 = 4."

Necessary truths cannot possibly be false, nor can we imagine circumstances in which they might be false.

temporally "before any experience"—that is, it does not mean that we know these things before we were born. Some philosophers do believe that there are ideas "born into" us or *innate*. Nevertheless, we must come to recognize these truths after we have learned a language and presumably, acquired considerable intellectual sophistication.)

So long as we restrict ourselves to a limited number of standard examples—the statement that there is so much change in my pocket or the statement that "2 + 2 = 4"—the distinction between empirical, contingent truths, on the one hand, and what some philosophers call "truths of reason," or necessary truth, on the other, seems adequately clear. The distinction becomes extremely problematic, however, when we try to consider the status of the all-important philosophical questions we have been raising in the preceding chapters. Does God exist? What is reality? And, looking ahead, is there a meaning to human life? Are the answers to these questions empirical or necessary truths, and should we appeal to our experience or reason (or both, or neither) to answer them?

Believing in the existence of God, for example, would seem to be a belief in a fact; indeed, many philosophers have argued (by means of the considerations we discussed in Chapter 4) that the existence of God is the ultimate fact. But suppose we imagine an argument between a theist (who believes in the existence of God) and an atheist (who does not). What facts can the theist show the atheist which would compel the atheist to believe in God? The theist can show the atheist one of the many passages in the Bible in which the existence of God is forcefully asserted; but of course the atheist will not accept this as evidence, since an atheist does not believe that most of the Bible is true. A few theists may even be able to claim that they have direct evidence of God's existence, since He has actually talked with or presented Himself to them. But, again, the atheist will not think anything of this alleged evidence either, since he or she will dismiss such experiences as mere delusions. The theist brings up the miracles that have been recorded in history as evidence of God's presence on earth; the atheist dismisses these as accidents or as unexplained (but not unexplainable) occurrences. The theist points to the intricacy of the world (by way of the "argument by design" as evidence that there must be a God to create such a masterpiece; the atheist insists that it is all chance, and, anyway, the world isn't such a "masterpiece" after all; it all depends on how you look at it.

The futility of this debate shows us that believing in God is not simply a matter of accepting the facts, but of something more. What more? "Faith" is one traditional answer, but faith is not so much a claim to know the truth as it is a matter of *hoping* that what one believes is true. It has been argued, however, that believing in the existence of God is perfectly rational and demonstrable, not as a matter of fact but through abstract reasoning. (We saw such reasoning, for instance, in the ontological argument for God's existence in Chapter 4.) If such an argument is successful, then "God exists" is a necessary truth.

Consider in the same way a statement about the meaning of life— whether life is meaningful or not and what that meaning might be. Suppose I insist, without going into details, that human life is meaningful. What facts make this true? I point out the pleasures of love, the joys of knowledge, the thrills of skiing, the delights of a good glass of wine in front of a fireplace. "Life is good," I conclude, as if I've proved it. But you, who think life is absurd, disagree with me. "Love never lasts," you insist; statistically, at least, you are certainly right. You point out the futility of knowledge, the number of broken legs among skiers, the cost of decent wine and firewood. You go through the crudest facts of human history, the atrocities of war, the cruelties and the dead ends, even in those societies that lived under the illusion that life was "getting better all the time." You point out the tragedies in life and, in any

WHAT FACTS WILL PROVE THE EXISTENCE OF GOD?

Theist's Proof	**Atheist's Reply**
Stated in the Bible	Not all statements in the Bible are true.
Experiences God in a vision	Mere hallucination, doesn't prove anything.
Miracle of the Red Sea	Geophysical quirk, not a miracle.
Delicate order of nature	Product of natural selection and chance occurrences.
The existence of the world	Just happened, otherwise, we wouldn't be here to discuss it.
The victory of the good over evil (in World War II, for instance)	Superiority of Allied forces and a few lucky turning points.

case, how short life is. You conclude, "Life is no good." We each have facts on our side. Who is right? Well, once again, it is clear that the facts won't tell us. I can insist that even wars and tragedies serve their purpose, to remind us of the value of life and to give us something to fight for. I can insist that life is intrinsically meaningful no matter how long it lasts or how many misfortunes should befall us. In other words, it is the **interpretation** of the facts that matters, not the facts themselves.

Finally, consider the statement that what is most real are Plato's Forms (from Chapter 4), not the things and facts of everyday experience. If this is true, is it true because it corresponds to the facts? No, since the theory itself says that the facts of everyday life are not the basis of truth. Could you say that this theory in turn does—or does not—correspond to the facts? If you do, then you generate a paradox—namely, that the theory is true because it corresponds to the facts which it denies are the basis of truth. Once again, we can see that this philosophical statement, if it is true, must be true in such a way that the facts are not the central consideration. It, too, perhaps, is defensible through pure thinking and without regard for whether the apparent facts of the world support it. Indeed, most philosophers would say straight out that the facts of ordinary experience (or, for that matter, the facts of extraordinary experience) may have very little to do with philosophical truth. But then are all philosophical truths necessary truths—the product of reasoning? Can reason deliver such an enormous promise? Some philosophers have certainly thought so; others have denied it. But almost all of them (until recently) thought that if there was an answer to any philosophical question (or any other question of knowledge), it would have to be *either* an empirical truth based on experience *or* an *a priori* truth that was both necessary and a product of reason.

It is one thing to say that a statement is true or false and something else to say what *kind* of truth it is and how we would know that it is so. Recent philosophers have argued that knowledge is "justified true belief." Truth is only one of the necessary conditions of knowledge. It is also necessary to be able to *justify* our belief. And it is the attempt to justify philosophical beliefs that has given rise to the single biggest split in modern philosophy.

RATIONALISM AND EMPIRICISM

In the past three hundred years, two schools of philosophy have come to dominate much of the discussion of these questions about the kind of truth to be found in philosophy. They are usually given the names **rationalism** and **empiricism**. The names alone should give you a good indication of the positions they represent.

Rationalism is a broad designation for a variety of theories, all of which have in common the confidence that human *reason* can provide the final answers to the most basic and essential philosophical questions. Furthermore, these answers will all be necessary truths. Great rationalists in modern times include the philosophers Descartes, Spinoza, Leibniz, Kant, and Hegel; in ancient

Rationalism: Knowledge is based on reason

The Continental rationalists:
René Descartes (France)
Benedict Spinoza (Holland)
Gottfried Wilhelm Leibniz (Germany)
Nineteenth century:
Immanuel Kant (Germany)
G. W. F. Hegel (Germany)

Empiricism: Knowledge is based on experience

The British empiricists:
John Locke (England)
Bishop George Berkeley (Ireland)
David Hume (Scotland)
Nineteenth century:
John Stuart Mill (England)
Twentieth century:
Bertrand Russell (England)

and medieval times, most of the great philosophers were rationalists, including Plato, Aristotle (with qualifications), Saint Augustine, and Saint Thomas Aquinas (with qualifications). They all believed—in one way or another—that philosophical reasoning can give us the answers, and that these answers are all necessary truths and are to be found within our thinking processes themselves—whether inspired by God, or radiated by "Forms," or built into the structure of our minds, or "born into" our brains (or "innate"). Experience might provide some of the material for our thinking, as well as some clues and perhaps the trigger to the answer, but experience cannot by itself, according to the rationalists, teach us anything at all. Truth is not subject to the vicissitudes of experience.

Empiricism, on the other hand, is a philosophical method which rejects this conception of "innate ideas" and insists, in the words of John Locke, that "all knowledge comes from experience." According to Locke, the human mind at birth is a "blank tablet" (*tabula rasa*), on which experience writes the general principles as well as the details of all our knowledge. Other empiricists include David Hume, whom we shall discuss further, the nineteenth-century thinker John Stuart Mill, and the twentieth-century philosopher Bertrand Russell.

Empiricists still believe in *reason,* of course, but only in the well-defined activities of calculation and logic—as in mathematics, for example. But they do not believe that reason has anything of importance to say about the big philosophical questions; indeed, the most radical empiricists of this century have even insisted that reason can tell us nothing about the world, but only about the structure of our own language.

The rationalists, on the other hand, do not reject the testimony of the senses either, but they do insist that observation and experiment—in short, *experience*—cannot give us philosophical truths. Both rationalists and empiricists would agree that the question "How much change do you have in your pocket?" is to be answered only by appeal to experience, and that the statement "If *A* is a *B* and all *B*s are *C*s, then *A* is a *C*" is a necessary truth by virtue of reason. What they disagree about is how the fundamental questions of philosophy are to be answered, and whether they can be answered. The rationalists believe that they can be answered, and answered with certainty—that is, as necessary truths. The empiricists generally believe that if they can be answered at all, they will have to be answered either as trivial statements about the meaning of our words (for example, the word "reality" simply *means* "that which is material and sensible") or as generalizations based on extensive experience (for example, the empiricist John Stuart Mill thought that even such statements as "2 + 2 = 4" were in fact very general claims about experience, and not "truths of reason" at all). Since, for the empiricists, all knowledge is based on experience (and inductive arguments), knowledge is (at best) highly probable and not certain. Not surprisingly, many empiricists have argued that some of the big questions of philosophy are not answerable, and much of empiricism has been a reexamination of the questions themselves, an attempt to show that they cannot be answered and, perhaps, that they do not make much sense in the first place.

One of the main points of debate between the rationalists and the empiricists—both in the seventeenth century and today (for instance, in the debate between linguist Noam Chomsky and such contemporary empiricists as Nelson Goodman)—concerns the existence of innate ideas. We have already seen that innate ideas are those "born into" us, but this does not mean (what would be absurd) newborn infants already "know" that 437 multiplied by 73 equals 31,901 (as if he or she just hasn't yet acquired the language to express this). Briefly put, the rationalists generally accept the idea of innate ideas; the empiricists usually reject it. Descartes, a rationalist, tried to begin with such intuitively certain truths as the idea that God is a perfect being, and then tried to deduce from this other truths that would (by virtue of a valid deduction) be equally certain. John Locke, an empiricist, rejected this idea of innate ideas and insisted that the mind is at birth a blank tablet (*tabula rasa*). All of our ideas must therefore be derived from experience, for none of them are innate.

The problem here is that much of our knowledge does not consist of individual perceptions ("Here is a coffee cup.") but rather is made up of universal statements such as "every action has an equal and opposite reaction." How do we get from the individual perceptions and our limited experience to such universal claims? The rationalists insist that it is only by way of some innate ideas or rational intuitions that this is possible—and that the most necessary truths about the world (the statements of mathematics) could not possibly be based on experience, but must be based on innate ideas.

THE PRESUPPOSITIONS OF KNOWLEDGE

Reason already persuades me that I ought no less carefully to withhold my assent from matters which are not entirely certain and indubitable than from those which appear to me manifestly to be false, if I am able to find in each one some reason to doubt.

— *Descartes,* Meditations

We have seen that there are two kinds of truth; we have also seen that it is not at all clear which (if either) kind of truth we will find in philosophy. But at this point in our discussion we should also point out that there are other principles which share this problematic status with such big questions as the existence of God, the meaning of life, and the nature of reality. Unlike the big questions of philosophy, these principles are not usually considered a matter of debate; they are rarely, if ever, suggested to be a matter of mere opinion, or faith, and so they are often not thought of as principles of philosophy at all. But they are. These are philosophical principles that lie at the foundations of virtually all of our knowledge and beliefs. They are the **presuppositions** of our thinking, without which we could believe nothing, know nothing, think nothing else.

For example, the basic philosophical belief that the *world exists* is the presupposition of anything that any scientist wants to say about the world. It is presupposed, too, in our most ordinary statements, such as "We ought to paint the door of the house green instead of red," since that presupposes that there is a door, a house, paint, and the world. Similarly, one of the philosophical principles that has long been discussed and debated is the principle that *everything that happens has a cause* (sometimes called the **principle of universal causality**). We cannot imagine chemistry without this principle, in fact, and we cannot imagine even the most everyday occurrences without it. Consider what you would think of a garage mechanic who told you, when your car wouldn't start, "Nothing's wrong: this is one of those events without a cause." You wouldn't call into question the principle that everything that happens has a cause; you would go to another mechanic.

In moments of uncertainty, most of us wonder whether there is a God or whether life has meaning. Many people wonder from time to time—though only rarely to the extent of the philosophers—what the world is really like. But no one in his or her right mind ever really wonders whether the world exists; indeed, when philosophers debate such curious topics, it is usually only to test out a theory they have about truth or reality, not to see whether in fact the world exists. But however obvious these principles may seem to us, their status as knowledge is in question in much the same way that the status of our big philosophical questions is in question. These statements are not clearly about matters of fact. They are not provable through experience. (That is why we know *before* we go to the garage, or *a priori,* that something must be the cause, though we do not know what.) Neither are they evidently true by virtue of reason. It is not contradictory to think that the outside world might not exist. Yet surely the existence of the world is not a mere matter of

ARE THERE INNATE IDEAS?

THE EMPIRICIST VIEW

It is an established opinion among some men, that there are in the understanding certain innate principles, some primary notions, stamped, as it were, upon the mind of man which the soul receives in its very first being, and brings into the world with it. It would be sufficient to convince unprejudiced readers of the falseness of this supposition, if I should only show how many men obtain to all the knowledge they have, without the help of any such innate impressions. . . . Let us suppose the mind to be a blank tablet; how comes it to be furnished? To this I answer in one word, from experience.

— *Locke,* Essay Concerning Human Understanding

THE RATIONALIST REPLY

Is the soul empty, like a tablet upon which nothing has been written? Does all truth depend on experience, that is to say, on induction? . . . The senses, although necessary for all our actual knowledge, are not sufficient to give us the whole of it, since the senses never give anything but examples. And it would seem that necessary truths, such as are found in pure mathematics and especially in arithmetic and geometry, must have principles the proof of which does not depend on examples, nor, consequently, on the testimony of the senses, although without the senses it never would have occurred to us to think of them.

— *Leibniz,* New Essay on Human Understanding

opinion. So what are we to say about philosophical truth? How can we prove, beyond a doubt, that these obvious truths are indeed true?

SKEPTICISM

Nothing exists. If anything did exist, we couldn't know it. If we could know it we couldn't communicate it.

— *Plato,* Gorgias

It may not be a question we ever ask in real life, but suppose someone were to ask you how you know that you're not dreaming right now. Suppose the

same person—a friend taking his or her first philosophy course, perhaps—
were to ask you how you know that the world even exists or has ever existed,
how you know that everything you have ever experienced, from your
mother's breast to the car you call your own, has not been just ideas in your
own mind. How would you answer? What would you say?

It is important to notice the assumption lying behind these questions, not
necessarily because the assumption is false, but rather because it is indeed the
assumption of most of our metaphysical thinking, as well as our way of talking
about ourselves. The assumption is that there are two distinct realms of reality,
one "outer"—the physical world—and one "inner"—the world of our experience.
The physical world would exist, presumably, even if we were not here to experience it, but the world of our experience might be the same, according to this
assumption, even if we were just dreaming about it, and even if, as Leibniz suggested, each of us were nothing but a mind, programmed by God to have certain experiences at certain times, *as if* there were a physical world "outside" us.

How do we get into this rather odd and troubling assumption? It seems
rather obvious, given the way we have been talking—that each of us knows
the world, from our own perspective, through our own personal experience.
Both the empiricists and the rationalists would agree that what we know
directly (whether through reason or experience) is first of all our own ideas

THE TWO-WORLD ASSUMPTION

causes

The "external world"—objects → the world of experience—representations

events   ideas

states   sensations

and sensations. But these ideas and sensations are "in our minds." The world, obviously, is "outside" of our minds, an "external" world. We assume, naturally, that our ideas or "representations" correspond to the things in the world, but how do we know this? Many empiricists, following John Locke, would argue that the things in the world affect our sense organs in certain ways that cause us to have certain sorts of experiences, and that we infer from the nature of these experiences what the things that caused them must be like. Rationalists, on the other hand, might assume that there is some inherent connection between our ideas and the world—perhaps, as Descartes argued, guaranteed by God. But then, we might wonder, why do the rationalists disagree among themselves?

The two-world assumption, however, leads us into a serious dilemma. We can see the nature of the problem if we restate our assumption in the form of two apparently reasonable claims: (1) there is an "external" world—that is, a world beyond our beliefs and experiences, which is not affected by what we happen to believe about it, and (2) we cannot ever make direct contact with the world itself, but only with the contents of our own minds—with our ideas, our beliefs, our various experiences, and the principles which we find to be necessary truths (such as the principles of logic and arithmetic).

The two statements above have been accepted by a great many thinkers of the past several centuries (though the second would not have been acceptable to most philosophers in ancient times). And they are still accepted by a great many philosophers today. Indeed, we seem to accept both of them, too; the idea that the world actually exists seems so obviously true that, except in a philosophy class, we wouldn't even think of questioning it. And the idea that what we know directly are our own experiences also seems indisputable; don't we often have experiences without knowing whether they are true? And we sometimes have experiences which do not in fact match up (or "correspond") to the world (hallucinations, for example, as well as dreams). Could we know anything whatsoever about the world if we did not first experience it in some way? But however reasonable these two statements may be, together they give rise to an intolerable conclusion: namely, that we can never know—or at least we can never be sure that we know—the world at all.

What we know are our own opinions, ideas, and experiences; what we cannot know is whether those opinions, ideas, and experiences match up to the world as it really is. The world we thought we knew so intimately suddenly seems far away from us, unreachable by either thought or experience.

Now if anything is to be true, it must be true by reference to the facts and objects of the world, or it must be true as a "truth of reason." But according to the two-world assumption, what we know directly are our own ideas and experiences, not the physical world itself. This is why it is possible for us to imagine, without changing anything in our experience, that the world might not exist, or that we are now dreaming. Furthermore, we might raise the question whether the principles we believe *a priori*—our necessary truths— might in fact be true only of our way of thinking, or true of our language, but not true of the world itself—in other words, not true. But now we have raised an embarrassing set of questions, for could it be that the world of our ideas, beliefs, and experiences, no matter how certain we are of them, is not at all like the physical world "outside" of us? This set of doubts that we might not actually know the world at all is generally referred to as **skepticism**. In the sections that follow, we will see how two of the great philosophers of modern times, the rationalist René Descartes and the empiricist David Hume, used this set of doubts as the engine of their entire philosophical enterprise.

Descartes and the "Method of Doubt"

The first rule is to accept nothing as true which I do not clearly recognize to be so; that is to say, carefully to avoid precipitation and prejudice in my judgments, and to accept in them nothing more than what was presented to my mind so clearly and distinctly that I could have no occasion to doubt it.

— *Descartes,* Meditations

The philosopher best known for his deliberations about all of this is the French philosopher **René Descartes** (1596–1650; see p. 29). He wrote a series of essays, the *Meditations,* generally considered to be the foundation of modern philosophy. Descartes accepted both of the statements above; in fact, he considered them both to be obviously true. But Descartes was a rationalist. He insisted on proof. Descartes was so concerned with *proving* his beliefs to be true, in separating his true beliefs from his opinions and false beliefs, that he decided, as a matter of method, to suspend his belief in everything. Doubt everything, Descartes decided; assume that everything one believes is false until one can prove it to be true. Indeed, one of the things Descartes doubted was the very existence of the external world. "Suppose I am now dreaming," we might paraphrase him. "After all, I have found myself dreaming before, when I thought (in the dream) that I was awake. Could I not possibly be dreaming all of the time? In fact, probably not. But if I cannot know this for certain, then I must doubt it, for until I can prove that a belief *must* be true, I do not have the right to believe it at all."

'It's only a rough draft.'

Now you might think that once one has made such a drastic move, there is nothing in the world which cannot be doubted. But this is not the case. It is our second statement, in fact, which provides Descartes with his first absolutely **indubitable** belief (that is, beyond doubt or unquestionable): What we know directly are the contents of our own minds. "Suppose," we might paraphrase him again, "I try to doubt the existence of my own mind. What I find is that I doubt that I am now doubting. But if I doubt that I am doubting, then, as a matter of necessity, I must indeed be doubting." Descartes' conclusion: "I cannot doubt that I'm doubting." More generally he concluded, "I cannot be wrong about the fact that I'm thinking, for the fact that I'm thinking about thinking already proves that I'm thinking." And from this simple logical principle emerges Descartes' most famous statement, "I think, therefore I am" (in Latin "*Cogito ergo sum*"). Here is a statement that cannot be doubted. Here, therefore, is a statement which can be used as a premise with which to prove beyond a doubt the objective truth of other beliefs, too, including our belief in the existence of the external world.

The rest of Descartes' proof remains one of the most heatedly debated arguments in the history of modern philosophy. In brief, it is this: Given the certainty of the statement "I think, therefore I am," Descartes then proved (or tried to prove) the existence of God, by way of one version of the ontological argument. That is, from the fact that I exist and can think and have an idea of God, it must be the case that God exists. So now Descartes had two **certain** statements: "I exist" and "God exists." But God, we know, is by definition a perfect being, who includes within His perfections perfect goodness. And if this is so, God would not allow us to be fooled about the existence of the world. Therefore, since God exists, the world must exist, for otherwise "I do not see how He could be vindicated from the charge of deceit, if in truth (my experiences) proceeded from any other source or were produced by other causes than corporeal things." So, too, Descartes could now argue that all of the beliefs of which I seemed so certain can now be shown to be true, necessarily. "God would not fool me; so I can know that I know the world, after all."

David Hume's Skepticism

A very difficult conclusion emerges from the deliberations of the Scottish empiricist **David Hume**. Hume accepted the two statements—that there is an "external" world existing independently of us, and that each of us is only in direct contact with the contents of our own mind—as obviously true, but he, too, insisted on proof of them. As an empiricist, he accepted John Locke's principle that "all knowledge comes from experience"; so for him the question was whether our belief in the existence of the external world could be proven to be true by appeal to experience. Or, if not, could it be shown to be true as a "truth of reason"? And this would be true of all our other philosophical questions, too, about the principal of universal causality, the existence of God, and the nature of reality. But whereas Descartes emerges from his *Medi-*

David Hume (1711–1776) was, according to many British philosophers, one of the outstanding geniuses in philosophy. He spent most of his life in Edinburgh, Scotland, where he was born, but he traveled frequently to both London and Paris, where he was a celebrity. While still in his twenties (after a vacation in France), he wrote his *A Treatise of Human Nature* (1739) which became one of the great philosophical works in the English language. The book was not well received, however, so Hume wrote two more "popular" books on the same subjects. *An Enquiry Concerning Human Understanding* (1784) and *An Enquiry Concerning Human Morals* (1751). He was also an avid historian, a jovial partygoer, and one of the most popular men in Europe. Because he was also an atheist, however, he was not allowed to teach his philosophy in any university.

tations with the positive conclusion that we *can* know the answers to these questions, and know them with certainty (that is, *a priori,* or as necessary truths), David Hume emerges from his study with the most negative of conclusions—that we cannot know the answers to any of these questions, that the most basic principles of our everyday knowledge as well as the most important guiding principles of our lives are without justification.

Hume's argument was elegantly simple, and philosophers have been trying to refute it ever since. (Bertrand Russell once wrote that in his opinion no one had yet succeeded, and that "Hume's conclusions . . . are equally difficult to refute and to accept.") Hume's position is skepticism, and it amounts to the negative claim that we cannot know the answers to questions to which we once thought the answers were obvious. The argument simply presses home the idea that there are two (and only two) kinds of truth, "matters of fact" and "truths of reason," and any belief which cannot be proved one way or the

HUME'S STRATEGY ("HUME'S FORK")

Every justifiable true statement is either a
"truth of reason" (*a priori*)   or   "matter of fact" (empirical)
    "2 + 2 = 4"   **"There are tigers in India."**

Which are the following philosophical statements?
   "God exists."
   "Life has meaning."
   "Everything that happens has a cause."

other is therefore without justification. So Hume asked, with regard to any belief, "Is this a matter of fact, to be defended by appeal to experience or experiment? Or is this a truth of reason, the truth of which can be demonstrated by an abstract calculation of the kind we find in mathematics or logic?" If the answer is "Neither," then Hume insisted that the judgment in question had no grounds for our continued belief, since it was without rational justification.

Hume's skepticism began, as Descartes' rationalist proofs had begun, by accepting the second of our two statements. He might doubt the existence of the world, but he did not for a moment doubt that our knowledge begins with experience, and that what we know directly are our own ideas and experiences (or what Hume called "impressions"). From this starting point, Hume shows us why we are not justified in believing principles that no sane person would actually doubt (except in philosophical investigations). Let's look first at his argument against the principle of universal causality, then at his argument against our supposed knowledge of the external world.

Is the principle of universal causality a "matter of fact," known through experience? Or is it a "relation of ideas" known through calculation and logic? Let's take the second possibility first: The principle of universal causality essentially says that everything that happens has a cause. Can we imagine a world in which everything that happens does not have a cause? Seemingly so; physicists talk quite frequently about subatomic emissions which have no cause (not simply no *known* cause, but *no* cause). We can imagine a particle in space, significantly isolated from all other particles, simply shooting off in one direction with no cause whatsoever. And regarding all particular causes, this is certainly not a matter of reason. We know, for example, that the collision of one moving billiard ball with another causes the second to move; but this, Hume argued, we learn entirely from experience, not on the basis of reason. The first human being, Hume suggested, could not possibly have figured out that water would drown him, or that fire would burn him, until he actually had the experience of trying (unsuccessfully) to breathe under water, or the painful experience of putting his hand in the fire. Knowledge of causes and effects is a matter of experience, not reason. And so, we presume, is our knowledge that everything that happens has a cause. But this, it turns out, is not the case either.

In our example with the metaphysically perverse garage mechanic, the key to our illustration was the fact that we knew before we entered the garage that something had to be the cause of the car's failure. (In other words, we knew it, or thought we knew it, *a priori*.) But this means that we do not learn the principle of universal causality *from* experience but in some sense carry it *to* experience. No number of unexplained events in the world would ever lead us to give up this principle, and in fact it is only because we already expect a cause that we know how to look for and find one.

One of the presuppositions of knowledge is that there are *causes*. What is a *cause?* We might say that one event causes another if the first event brings

THERE IS NO TRUTH: NIETZSCHE

Ultimate Skepticism.—*But what after all are man's truths?—They are his irrefutable errors.*

— The Gay Science

Truth is the kind of error without which a certain species of life could not live. The value for life is ultimately decisive.

— The Will to Power

about the second. But if you look at the above sentence, we see that it is an utterly trivial statement; "brings about" is just another phrase for "causes," so we have not yet explained what a cause is. Let's take a particular example: the example of the two colliding billiard balls. The movement of the first causes a certain movement in the second. (If we know the speed and direction of the first, we can calculate in advance the speed and direction of the second.) But what we actually see, Hume pointed out, is not the cause at all. What we see are just the two events—(1) the movement of the first ball, and (2) the movement of the second ball. Indeed, the first time (or first several times) we watch, we may have no way of predicting the movement of the second ball at all. We might expect the first ball to come to a complete stop, or bounce backward, or we might expect both balls to break, or explode. This means that knowledge of causes is not a matter of reason. But no matter how many times we watch, all that we ever actually see are the two events—the movement of the first ball, the movement of the second ball—and we never see the connection between them, the actual *cause* of the second event, at all. Hume concluded that we never actually see the cause of events at all, but only that two events are regularly found together, in "constant conjunction." Here, too, Hume's conclusion is skeptical: Something we thought we knew for sure turns out not to be justifiable through experience or reason.

Regarding the existence of the external world, Hume's argument is equally devastating and of much the same form. Can our belief in the external world be shown to be a matter of logic? Clearly not, since we can imagine what it would be for the world not to exist, and we can imagine ourselves simply dreaming, as Descartes suggested. Is it a matter of experience? No, for just the same reason that pinching yourself to see if you are dreaming doesn't tell you if you are dreaming. Any experience is itself a part of that world of experience. So long as we accept the two-world assumption, which seems quite irrefutable, it surely is possible that the world of our experience exists but the physical world does not, and that within that world of experience there is no experience by which we can tell that this is not so.

When we run over libraries, persuaded of these principles, what havoc must we make? If we take in our hand any volume of divinity or school metaphysics, for instance, let us ask. Does it contain any abstract reasoning concerning quantity or number? No. Does it contain any experimental reasoning concerning matter of fact and existence? No. Commit it to the flames, for it can contain nothing but sophistry and illusion.

— *David Hume*, A Treatise of
Human Nature

The Resolution of Skepticism: Kant

Skepticism has been a powerful philosophical position ever since ancient times. It is not an answer to the big questions of philosophy so much as the disturbing reply that there are no answers. Where the basic questions of knowledge are concerned, this does not seem tolerable. Can we really doubt that the world exists or the ordinary presupposition that everything that happens has a cause? For this reason, skepticism has usually been considered more of a problem to be avoided or a challenge to be answered than a philosophical position to be accepted for its own sake. In your own thinking, it is a signal of danger that should keep you on your toes and wary of too easy, dogmatic answers which in fact you can't defend. Indeed, what makes Descartes' method of doubting everything and Hume's skeptical conclusions so valuable to us is, more than anything else, the fact that they make us so aware of how easily we simply presume that the obvious is objectively true. And the point of philosophy, in answering the big questions, is precisely to allow us to go beyond what we first think is obvious, and think things through to the point where we can actually defend what we believe—even against so brilliant a skeptic as Hume. How much of what we believe is merely personal opinion? How many of our beliefs do we share only with our family or our friends but not with the larger community? Which of our beliefs might be generally accepted by everyone in our society but not at all by people in other societies? Which of our beliefs might in fact be built into our language but not into other languages? Are there beliefs which are built into the human mind as such but which may nonetheless be false, beliefs which other intelligent creatures—perhaps highly intelligent beings from another planet— would know to be based on faulty evidence and misleading ideas which for some reason seem to be particularly prevalent on earth? To ask such questions is not to reject any possibility of our knowing the truth, any more than Descartes' method of doubt was an admission on his part that he could never know anything. But it is to make us more sensitive to the limitations of our knowledge, and the need to support our beliefs on more solid footing than the fact that we, personally, find them to be "obvious."

We end our discussion of skepticism, however, not with Hume and the apparent victory of the skeptic, but with Hume's greatest successor, the German idealist Immanuel Kant. Kant read Hume's arguments in defense of skepticism and was deeply shocked—"awakened from his dogmatic slumber," as he put it. He considered Hume's "fork" and realized that so long as one accepted the exclusivity of the "matters of fact"–"relations of ideas" dichotomy and, even more, so long as one accepted the seemingly innocent "two-world assumption," there would be no getting around skepticism—and that meant no way of justifying those basic presuppositions upon which all our knowledge is based. So what Kant does, put simply, is to deny the two-world assumption. We already saw (in Chapter 4) that Kant insisted that we "constitute" or "set up" the world according to *a priori* rules. But then it is not true, he says, that we first of all and "directly" know only our own experiences, and only secondarily or by inference the things of the world. To the contrary, the world *is* just the world of our experience, nothing "beyond" or "external" to it. The mind, Kant suggests, imposes its forms and categories on our experience, and among these forms and categories are those that provide the presuppositions of our knowledge (for example, "causality" and "substance"). These presuppositions, accordingly, are neither empirical truths nor "relations of ideas," but a special and new kind of truth that Kant calls "*synthetic a priori*." The truths are synthetic because they are not mere tautologies, not merely trivially true. They are *a priori* because, like all necessary truths, they are "prior" to experience. What would our experience of the world be like if we didn't impose these forms on it? The answer is that we would not have anything we could really call "experience." We would not be able to identify objects, recognize similarities or differences between our sensations, or even have any sense of self as the subject of different experiences succeeding one another in time. Thus, the presuppositions of our knowledge can be said to be necessarily true because they are the rules according to which any experience at all is possible. And since they are *our* rules, skepticism about them—or whether they "correspond" with the world they constitute—is utterly pointless. Or so Kant argued, and after him Hegel.

KNOWLEDGE, TRUTH, AND SCIENCE

Many people and most philosophers today look for the truth—they look to **science**. For several centuries, science and its methods have been the royal road to finding out how the world really is. Empiricists and rationalists both tended to be scientists or to have great admiration for scientists. Skeptics often tended to defend their skepticism as "scientific." Educated religious critics of science did not usually reject science, but only questioned some particular scientific theory or the intrusion of science into some concern where it was inappropriate. One need not attack science, for example, to reject Darwin's theory of evolution, or to insist that the experience of love is not something that social scientists should try to study. On the other hand, science does presume

a certain worldview that may well be judged to be too limiting or too impersonal for many questions about human life. Nevertheless, this much seems
undeniable: Science is today our touchstone of truth. To say that something is
"scientifically established—whether it is a theory about the surface of the
planet Saturn or the effectiveness of a new, improved brand of toothpaste—is
to say that we have come as close to the truth as we can expect to get.

"Science" has been a word filled with praise for several centuries. The
German equivalent, *Wissenschaft,* was used by such figures as Kant and
Hegel to emphasize the seriousness and thoroughness of their thinking about
all sorts of matters, from physics to metaphysics. Today, however, the term
"science" tends to be limited to those questions that can and must be answered by reference to **experience** and extrapolations from experience.
Thus it might be said that science is an **empirical** discipline—as opposed to
logic and mathematics, for example. Physics, chemistry, geology, and biology—the natural sciences—are the standard examples. Somewhat more controversial are the social sciences—psychology, sociology, anthropology, and
economics—but there is no doubt that, whatever else they may be, they are
also empirical disciplines based on observation and, to a more limited extent
than physics and chemistry, on experiment. (There are no moral restrictions
on chemical compounds, but there are all sorts of ethical limits to the ways in
which one can experiment with people.) To say that a science is empirical is
to insist that its theories and hypotheses must be tested in experience and can
be shown to be true or false by way of experience. Our measure of truth is
largely a matter of whether or not this can be done, and many philosophers—
called **logical positivists**—once argued that any statement that could not be
so tested was simply "meaningless" (unless, of course, it was a trivial truth or
a statement in mathematics or logic).

It would be a mistake, however, to think of science as nothing but the
gathering and testing of facts through experience. It would be a very limited
and boring science indeed that did nothing more than collect large numbers
of facts. Chemistry would be nothing but an enormous laboratory and cata-
logue filled with specimens and names of different substances. Biology would
be nothing but garden-tending and zoo-keeping. But these are not chemistry
or biology, and never were. Chemists since the ancient Babylonians—and
probably long before that—operated not only with observed facts but with
hypotheses and theories. The facts served the theories by *confirming* them—
showing them to be probably true—or by disproving them—showing them to
be probably false. A caveman searching for a mammoth, and trying to avoid a
saber-toothed tiger, is operating with hypotheses about where each of those
creatures should be (behind the bushes, in the swamp, asleep in the cave),
and his experience had better confirm his hypotheses. Modern chemists do
not just collect chemicals but formulate hypotheses about how different
chemicals relate to one another, how one is produced from another, why
some chemicals cannot be further broken down, and so on. To do this, they
need a whole language of chemistry that is not merely descriptive of what we
can see, touch, and pour into bottles. In addition to such a descriptive **obser-**

vational language ("a fine red powder that easily bursts into flame"), chemists also need a **theoretical** language ("atoms," "molecule," "element," "chemical bond," "oxidation"). Strictly speaking, no one has ever seen an electron. Yet electrons are among the most important particles ever discussed by chemists, and it is by talking about electrons (and kindred subatomic particles) that chemists can describe most of what they know about the world.

Science is an empirical discipline, but like metaphysics, it involves speculation, imagination, the specification of things unseen. In addition to the observation of facts and the carrying out of experiments, the scientist or the science student needs to *think* to formulate theories, to go beyond what can be observed and suggest what might explain it. Mathematical models, for example, play a central role in many sciences—physics and economics, for example. Truth in science is not just the truth of facts. It is also the truth of theories. A scientist without a theory and without a hypothesis for guidance would not have anything to do. Like a child with a new chemistry set, of course, a chemist could just throw together one substance after another and see what happens. But in addition to being dangerous, this would be an aimless activity and as unlikely to produce an insight into truth as a monkey at the word processor is to produce a novel.

Hypotheses and theories guide observation and experiment. A scientist might notice something by accident that leads to the formulation of a hypothesis and a sketch of a theory, but this is possible only after the scientist has been thinking about and working with the same subject for some time. A hypothesis tells us what facts to look for. A theory tells us how to understand these facts. The hypothesis that water is a combination of oxygen and hydrogen tells us what kind of experiments to perform (those that combine the two elements, those that divide water molecules into its components). It is atomic theory, however, that tells us how to interpret such results. Indeed, without atomic theory it is not even clear how we would interpret the idea that water is a "combination" of anything—much less the combination of two gases that cannot even be seen.

The importance of hypotheses and theories in science raises enormous problems about truth. We are not very confused about what is meant by "truth" when the claim is observationally straightforward: "The frog is sitting on the stone," for example, or "The powder just changed to blue." But when a large theory is under consideration, its truth, by its very nature, cannot be simply discerned. Darwin's theory is a complex and ingenious scheme for describing an enormously wide variety of observations—many of them not yet made. It is not the only scheme that explains these observations, even within the realm of evolutionary theory. So what does it mean to say that it is "true"? It might be shown that it is the simplest, the most far-reaching, the best-confirmed theory. Nevertheless, we want to say that "truth" means something more than "very well confirmed"; it means "the way the world really is." Are we ever justified in saying this of a theory?

Indeed, are we justified even in saying that a particular fact is true? We have seen how the skeptic tries to throw into doubt *all* our knowledge of the world, except, perhaps, the most basic facts of our senses ("I am seeing green right now"). The importance of theories in science points to a different way in which the truth of science might be doubted. Facts get gathered in order to confirm or disprove a hypothesis; the selection of hypotheses, in other words, determines what we will look for. But observations in general get made in the light of theories. To call something a "sunset" is to see it in the light of a certain astronomical theory—a false theory, in fact. To call a streak of a cloud in a chamber an "electron" is to interpret what we see in the light of a certain theory. One might say, "There are no electrons; they are only postulations of a theory." But so, too, one might object, "There are no sunsets; there is only a certain position of the earth vis-à-vis the sun, with some peculiar refractions of light as the result." Facts get interpreted according to theories. Without a theory, there would not even be certain facts. Some philosophers of science, on the basis of such considerations, have argued that there are no facts as such only facts as viewed in the light of theories. Every observation in science presupposes a theoretical framework, just as every theory presupposes some facts to make it empirically plausible. But suppose, as we look through the history of science, we find that scientists have held very different theories, and interpreted the same facts in very different ways. What, then, are we to say about truth in science? How do we compare theories to tell which, if any, are true?

The question here is whether science really does give us the truth, or perhaps only truth of its own making. For example, many scientific observations are possible only by means of specially invented scientific equipment— a telescope, a microscope, a cloud chamber, or a cyclotron. Could it be that the truth we discover is in fact the creation of the implements we use? Imagine yourself in Galileo's laboratory several hundred years ago, looking through some weird-looking invention called a "telescope." Through this strange tube, you see what look like moons around the planet Jupiter, and you see what look like mountains on the face of the moon. Do you trust your eyes? If you were living at the time, you might well refuse to accept what you saw, on the grounds that the tube distorted your vision, much as a red-colored lens will make the world look red. What would convince you that the tube really had improved your vision rather than distorted it? Or could it be that any implement in science, even while it allows us to learn something, nevertheless interferes with and distorts precisely the subject it seeks to study? (Imagine a traffic cop—in uniform—studying the ordinary behavior of drivers. What the cop sees, for the most part, is not the ordinary behavior of drivers at all, but the behavior of drivers when they are in the presence of a police officer.)

Why do we take science as a paradigm of truth? Isn't it possible that the results of science can be doubted? Isn't it possible that even the facts described by science can be doubted? The answer to both questions is "yes," but nevertheless science has two impressive claims in support of its current status as the road to truth:

1. Science has been highly successful in predicting nature and in giving us the ability to invent instruments to alter nature to our will. One might question whether science has allowed us to understand nature better than ancient religious or Renaissance artists, but one can hardly question the success of science in predicting how hitherto-unknown chemicals will react, or in putting a man on the moon.

2. Science has both empirical and intellectual integrity. Scientific hypotheses can be and must be tested and tested again. No scientific theory is ever simply accepted; it must be supported over and over with new research. It must always stand up to new questions, new challenges. No one ever has the authority to force a theory on science against the evidence, and no opinion is considered influential enough to reject a theory that better explains the evidence. Any scientist will admit that these standards are sometimes violated; scientists are only human, after all. But the ideals remain and are accepted by everyone. Because of the rigor of these ideals, science has earned, and keeps, its place in our philosophy.

Even if we accept all this, however, we can still ask whether science deserves what often looks like an ·*exclusive* right to the honorable word "truth." What about human feelings—are they "true" or not? What about art and beauty—how do they fit into the scientific world? What about human relationships and international politics—are they made better through science? When we pride ourselves on approaching all questions "scientifically," is it possible that we are harming more than helping ourselves?

Consider one of the most controversial debates of our decade: the debate between the theory of evolution (not necessarily Darwin's) and the creationist view of the world based on Genesis. To their discredit, the evolutionists have sometimes dismissed the religious view of creation altogether, not even trying to see how the two views might be fitted together, even if the words in Genesis are taken more or less literally. To their discredit, the creationists have sometimes argued some appallingly bad science in trying to refute the evolutionists, and they, too, have not always been willing to see how the two antagonistic views might be put together. One could interpret evolution as God's means of creation; one can invoke God as the explanation of how the whole process got started. But without entering into the tangled web of emotions and beliefs that make this controversy so intractable, we can make two points in favor of a cease-fire:

1. Whatever the plausibility of creationism as a scientific hypothesis, it must be understood that the thrust behind creationism is not scientific curiosity; it is an attempt to stop science and its exclusive claim to truth from encroaching on territory where it has no business—the domain of religion. The origin of species is the border between the two domains.

2. Whatever one might think of any particular theory of evolution, science is nothing if it is not empirical. A theory must be confirmed by observed

facts, not just based on authority. A theory must be falsifiable by facts; that is, we must at least be able to say what kinds of findings would undermine the theory. On the basis of its importance as a religious viewpoint, creationism may have as convincing grounds for belief as evolutionary theory has. But it is not, and should not claim to be, a *scientific* theory. (If the existence of fossils doesn't undermine it, what could?) Indeed, given the importance of the first point, why would creationism prefer to compete as bad science rather than as solid and established religious doctrine?

THE NATURE OF TRUTH

To say of what is that it is not, or of what is not that it is, is false, while to say of what is that it is, or of what is not that it is not, is true.

—Aristotle

We have already seen that some statements are true whether or not they correspond to the facts. We have also seen that the principles of philosophy are of this sort; they are not "matters of fact," but something else—perhaps (according to the rationalists) "truths of reason," perhaps (according to the skeptics) mere matters of opinion which cannot be justified at all. But in either case, what has become clear to us is that our initial conception of truth is inadequate. Let us give it a name: It is called the **correspondence theory of truth**—that is, a statement is true if and only if it corresponds to the facts. But there are other kinds of truth, as we have seen, such as the true statements of mathematics and logic. We need a more general theory which will include them as well as the true statements (if there are any) in philosophy.

So far we have talked primarily about truth, setting aside the question how we might come to know the truth. But the statement of the correspondence theory of truth, and its presupposed two-world view, forces us to take this secondary question much more seriously. Indeed, what good is a theory of truth if it gives us no indication how—or even whether—we can ever *know* the truth? With that in mind, philosophers have often shifted their attention from a statement or belief *being* true to our *reasons* (or justification) for accepting it *as* true. And what has happened, with this shift in emphasis, is that the search for reasons for accepting a statement or belief as true has come to encroach upon the question of truth itself; in other words, the reasons for believing that something is true have now been suggested to *be* truth.

Consider this. In a detective story, a man is murdered out in the country on a dark and cloudy night. There are no witnesses, only a small scattering of clues (a footprint, some fabric from a raincoat made in Transylvania, some suspicious marks on the neck of the accused). Now, if you are the detective investigating the case, or if you are a member of the jury at the trial, it won't help much to be told that you know that D is the killer if and only if you know that the statement that D is the killer is true. What interests you are the *reasons* for believing that D is the killer—the perfect match of the footprints, the fact that D has recently "lost" his raincoat, the curious toothy smile D occasionally displays in the prisoner's box. But such reasons never add up to a complete picture. They are always no more than evidence, which point to a conclusion but never actually reach it. (This is so even if D confesses; that is sometimes an excellent piece of evidence, but it is not in itself the truth we are looking for.) The truth itself is in the past; all we have now is the evidence.

Now, given the fact that the truth itself seems lost to us, a number of very different conclusions follow from this. Suppose that you, as detective, have developed an airtight case against D. What does this mean? Not that it could not possibly be false (since it is, in any case, a *contingent truth* that D is the killer), but that the alibis that D would need to convince anyone that he was not the killer would seem so ridiculous and so unreasonable that no one would believe them; for example, stories to the effect that he has a twin brother who is always getting him into trouble, or that he is the victim of a collective conspiracy on the part of you, the police, and all the witnesses. The evidence still adds up to less than the truth, but can we say that we *know* that D is the killer, that this is an objective truth instead of a merely subjective opinion? Some people would say, "Yes, of course; all you need to claim that your belief is true is the best available set of reasons; there is nothing else you can have." But others would say, "No, you never actually know what is true; at most, you have the best belief under the circumstances, and you have to make do with that." In the first claim, we still have objective truth, but it now depends not on a property of the object but on the reasons we provide for our beliefs. In the second view, there is no objective truth at all; it is simply a matter of competing opinions, some of which are more persuasive than others.

Now this is even more difficult with philosophical truths. If we are concerned with the existence of God, for example, it is clear that the same problem exists. If He appears directly to us, perhaps that would seem to settle the question. (But even then, how do we know that He is God, as opposed to a delusion, or as opposed to the Devil who is trying to fool us?—only by appeal to the *reasons* for believing one interpretation rather than another.) We claim to have some evidence that God exists (the existence of the Bible, for instance, the existence of the world as a designed masterpiece). But the evidence never adds up to God. To say that one *knows* that God exists is to say that one's belief is both justified and true. But we have already seen that there are serious questions about what should *count* as a justification for belief in God. It seems that one must accept the truth of God's existence not because of, but rather prior to any evidence or argument that would confirm His existence. This is why Kierkegaard holds that all belief in God requires a "leap of faith."

But this apparent need to have the truth *before* one collects adequate evidence and argument is not just a problem with the very special belief in God's existence. It would seem that any claim to know the truth—whether coming

> *But how will you look for something when you don't in the least know what it is? How on earth are you going to set up something you don't know as the object of your search? To put it another way, even if you come right up against it, how will you know that what you have found is the thing you didn't know?*
>
> —*Plato,* Meno, *80d–e*
>
> *From Plato,* Protagoras and Meno, *trans. W. C. K. Guthrie (Harmondsworth, MD: Penguin, 1957).*

from a rationalist or an empiricist—requires that we know the facts *independently* of our claim to know the truth in order to justify our claim to the truth. But this would mean, according to the correspondence theory of truth, that we first need the truth (the facts) in order to justify our claim to the truth. In other words, we can't say that a statement is true without having justifying reasons—but this would seem to suppose (on the correspondence theory) that we can know the world apart from our own knowledge.

And here we meet the skeptic face to face: Is it the case that we can't know the truth because we can never be certain, because there is always a leap from our evidence and our reasons to the "facts"? Or is it even worse, that we can never know the truth because we have to somehow know the truth before we can have any reasons for claiming to know the truth? But perhaps the problem isn't truth but rather this particular, seemingly obvious theory of truth—the correspondence theory. Perhaps there are other conceptions of truth, which have the twin virtues of both accounting for the various kinds of truth we have discussed and of answering the skeptic?

Two such theories have predominated in the past few centuries. They both shift the emphasis away from the "facts" toward the *reasons* for accepting a certain belief. One is called the **coherence theory of truth**, the other is called the **pragmatic theory of truth**.

The Coherence Theory of Truth

The coherence theory begins by rejecting the correspondence theory, insisting that the very notion of correspondence to the facts not only fails to account for truth in mathematics and logic but even fails (as our detective story example showed) to account for ordinary factual truth. All we have are reasons for believing—evidence, arguments, principles, and our various beliefs themselves. But why do we need anything more? Indeed, when we talk about truth, what we mean is simply this: What is true is simply that statement or belief which best *coheres* with, or fits into the overall network of our experience and beliefs. We accept a principle as true because it fits with our other principles. We accept an argument because it follows from what we believe and leads to conclusions we can accept. We agree on the evidence because it fits into our hypotheses, because it fits together, because it adds up to a coherent picture. Nothing else is needed to give us the truth. Of course, our evidence is always incomplete, and the beliefs that we already accept are not always sufficient to allow us to know with certainty whether some new belief should be accepted. In fact, there may be occasions (for instance, a religious conversion) in which the whole network of our beliefs exhibits a significant shift or turnaround or disruption. But this is not to be taken as our inability to ever reach the truth; quite to the contrary, what it means is that the truth is within our grasp, and that with experience we change our beliefs precisely to grasp it more exactly.

The Pragmatic Theory of Truth

Grant an idea or belief to be true, what concrete difference will its being true make in anyone's actual life? . . . What, in short, is the truth's cash-value in experiential terms?

— *William James*, Pragmatism

The pragmatic theory supplements the coherence theory with a practical proviso—namely, that among the reasons for accepting a statement or a belief as true is whether it allows us to function better, whether it suggests fruitful lines of inquiry to be pursued in the future—whether it "works," in the words

James: In the realm of truth-processes facts come independently and determine our beliefs provisionally. But these beliefs make us act, and as fast as they do so, they bring into sight or into existence new facts which re-determine the beliefs accordingly. So the whole coil and ball of truth, as it rolls up, is the product of a double influence. Truths emerge from facts; but they dip forward into facts again and add to them; which facts again create or reveal new truth (the word is indifferent) and so on indefinitely. The 'facts' themselves meanwhile are not *true*. They simply *are*. Truth is the function of the beliefs that start and terminate among them.

The case is like a snowball's growth, due as it is to the distribution of the snow's growth, due as it is to the distribution of the snow on the one hand, and to the successive pushes of the boys on the other, with these factors co-determining each other incessantly.

From Pragmatism *(New York: Longmans, Green, 1907), 225-226.*

of the most famous defender of the theory, the American pragmatist, William James. One hypothesis in science, for instance, may not have any more evidence for it than another, and it may fit into our overall beliefs no better than do a number of others; but it may well be more easily testable, encourage further experimentation in the same field, suggest interesting possibilities not suggested by other hypotheses. To say that a view is true, therefore, is to say that it is the most valuable, the most promising explanation available to us. But the value of a view is not just its scientific promise. It might be its social or spiritual value as well—for example, in our views of morality and religion.

RATIONALITY

With the shift of attention to reasons for believing something to be true, the virtue of having good reasons, or what we call **rationality** has become increasingly important. Throughout most of the history of philosophy, from Plato to the modern rationalists, rationality and the search for truth were considered absolutely identical. But where truth seems to refer only to the "way the world is," without any reference to our ways of knowing it, rationality clearly refers to our activities, to our methods of finding the truth, and so provides us with a much more tangible and less evasive topic of discussion.

Rationality means "thinking and acting in accordance with reason"; rationality is thinking with reasons, good reasons. What is a "good reason"? If thinking is based on "facts," then the facts must be well confirmed, not simply hearsay or wild guesses. (We do not have to say that the facts must be "true" in the correspondence sense; someone might have very good reason to accept them but, by some twist of circumstances, they turn out not to be true.) If thinking is based upon deductive reasoning, then the reasoning must be valid. Of course, a "good reason" must make sense; appeals to mysterious forces or mystical insights will not do in rational argument. And a good reason must be relevant to the case at hand; a brilliant argument and a number of facts do not constitute rationality if they are not directed at the matter under consideration. But this last point is derived from the most important general characteristic of rationality: Rationality depends most of all upon coherence. To be rational is to think of as many reasons, dig up as many facts, and call up as many beliefs as are necessary to provide a comprehensive logical web in support of any given belief.

Since Kant, this ideal of rationality has ruled philosophy in place of the traditional ("correspondence") notion of truth. But what is the relationship between rationality and truth? In one sense, it is important that we insist that rationality does not require that our beliefs be true. For example, you might think that the belief that the earth is flat, or motionless, or made of water, is a false belief, and, in terms of the system of beliefs which we all share today, any of these beliefs certainly is not *rational*. But had you lived in earlier times, in ancient Greece for example, these would not have seemed false at all, but completely rational. And in the context of their system of beliefs, what you now believe would have been utterly irrational. This does not mean that

THEORIES OF TRUTH

Correspondence theory: *True beliefs (or sentences) correspond to the facts.*

"The cat is on the mat."

Coherence theory: *True beliefs (including beliefs about experience) and sentences cohere to each other.*

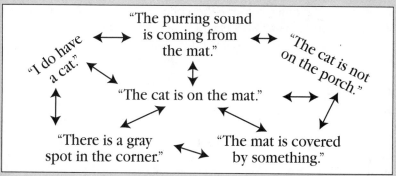

Pragmatic theory: *True beliefs (or sentences) are those that "work."*

it is always rational to believe what everyone around you believes and irrational not to; it *is* possible that everyone's beliefs are irrational, founded on bad reasons, lack of evidence, refusal to think about them clearly or carefully, and unspoken prejudice or superstition. But this is not always or even usually the case. In the above example, we may suppose that the Greeks had the best of reasons for believing what they did about the earth. Rationality, therefore, does not require truth; it requires only that a person make the best possible use of all of the information and "reason" at his or her disposal.

What, then, are we to say about the commonsense idea that truth is "correspondence to the facts"? We don't want to deny this. It is hard to deny that what makes my statement "the cat is on the mat" true is just that the cat is in fact on the mat. But what the preceding considerations and arguments suggest is that we can't simply take this "correspondence" of statement to fact at face value. What lies behind it is the entirety of our language and our ways of conceiving and referring to the world. In isolation, the words (or more properly, the sounds or the scribbles) "the cat is on the mat" mean nothing at all, refer to nothing at all, and are neither true nor false. And what justifies the statement or belief that the cat is on the mat is not "the fact" but the array of evidence, both visual and from the other senses—the coherence of that statement or belief with all manner of other statements and beliefs and the implications for various practical concerns. In other words, even if one wants to insist that what makes the statement true is the relevant fact, we can say that we *know* that the cat is on the mat only because it is the most rational thing to believe. So although we can distinguish between rational thinking and truth in some particular cases, the truth is that which is most rational to believe at a given time and in a given situation, on the basis of the best available evidence and the most careful thinking possible. According to many philosophers, there is no other sense to be given to the words "true" and "truth," unless we are to fall back again into the intolerable and absurd doubts of Hume's skepticism.

Why Be Rational?

By now, you might well ask, why be rational? First, we have to distinguish several conceptions of rationality (just as we distinguished several conceptions of truth). Sometimes, "rational" has a familiar negative connotation, such as when you accuse a friend or lover of "being too rational," meaning insensitive, not in touch with his or her emotions, or abusing thought as a way of escaping from an emotionally charged situation. In this sense, we can quickly agree that there is good reason not to be rational. Similarly, if you think of rationality as "thinking something into the ground" so that you never act upon it at all, or always too late, then we can willingly give up rationality in that sense, too.

The answer to the philosophical question "Why be rational?" is simply this: Rationality is the most efficient way to comprehend the world, and the best guarantee that you know what is going on around you. But if this answer isn't convincing to you, the following should be: It is a mistake to talk about

> Confucius said,
>   To realize that you know something when you do, and to realize that you do not when you do not, this is knowing.

"rationality" as purely a matter of understanding. It is also a matter of action and of living—acting rationally and living rationally. And as soon as we add this pragmatic dimension, the answer to the question "Why be rational?" becomes extremely persuasive. To act rationally is to act in such a way that you are more likely to get what you want (including knowledge as well as enjoyment, satisfaction, and an occasional ego boost). The best way to get something is not always the most "rational" in the narrow sense of "most efficient." In this machine-and-consumer society, it is often more efficient to buy something than to make it with your own hands; that doesn't make it more rational. And it is not necessarily rational to think everything out and plan ahead, for sometimes what we want is novelty and adventure, in which case it may be most rational not to think it all out and plan ahead. But, in any case, rationality, in this sense, is hardly objectionable.

Rationality is trying our knowledge and our lives together in the most coherent and effective way. But here we come back to the dilemma facing philosophy since Kant. If we have separated truth and rationality from the question of the "way the world really is," it is apparent that different societies and even different individuals can tie their experiences and their lives together in very different ways. According to our account of rationality, are we going to be forced to accept any system, no matter how bizarre, as rational and even true, just because it is coherent and satisfies the person or the people who believe in it?

SUBJECTIVE TRUTH: ANY TRUTH AT ALL?

What is Truth but to live for an idea? It is a question of discovering a truth which is truth for me, of finding the idea for which I am willing to live or die.

— *Kierkegaard,* Journals

The objective accent falls on WHAT is said, the subjective accent on HOW it is said.

— *Kierkegaard,* Concluding
Unscientific Postscript

As our conception of truth moves further away from the "way the world really is" and correspondence with the facts, it moves nearer and nearer to the subject, to the person trying to learn the truth. In other words, we move further from **objective truth** (that is, truth independent of our personal opinions) toward what has sometimes been called **subjective truth**, truth *dependent on* *the subject* and his or her beliefs. We might say that the paranoid's view of the world is a subjective truth; true for him, but not objectively true—that is, not true of the world. We might say that an entire society's view of the world is subjectively true for that society, even if we know that its view is objectively false. The problem is that with this conception of subjective truth, we have moved far away from the concept of truth—that is, that there is but one truth, one true set of facts which is true for everybody whether they know it or not. Subjective truth seems to allow for a different truth, a different set of facts, for everyone. But isn't this just saying that *nothing* is true?—that there is no truth but only different perspectives and different ways of looking at the world? In other words, can we call anything "true" if it is true only for one person or one society? Doesn't truth, if it is truth at all, have to be objective?

The most outspoken champion of subjective truth, Søren Kierkegaard, was exceedingly cautious when he defended his notion of a personal truth "for which I am willing to live or die." He insisted that this kind of truth—personal, subjective truth—is the most important kind of truth, the kind of truth that makes life meaningful, the kind of "true commitment" to God or other people that gives life a direction it otherwise would not have. But, at the same time, he did not try to extend his conception of subjective truth to the entire realm of knowledge, only to those areas he called "objective uncertainties." In other words, he also believed in objective truth—in science, for example—and his theory of subjective truth therefore is this: In those areas of human life where science cannot give us the answer, such as in ethics and religion, subjective truth—passionate personal commitment—is necessary. But this still left open the question of the nature of so-called objective truth, which is not denied but simply supplemented by another notion of truth which Kierkegaard thought was more important. (It is worth noting that Kierkegaard also thought that the search for subjective truth is **irrational** that it follows no rules and often requires blind faith rather than careful thinking and planning.) The ultimate question is: Could it be that objective truth is itself subjective?

Where are we to find truth, that is, objective truth? Current thinking on this issue is both confusing and exciting: On the one side, philosophers are generally agreed that subjective truth is, in the realm of science, for example, not sufficient. Truth, if it is truth at all, must be generally believable, confirmable by any number of persons, true not just for someone but true even in spite of what people believe about it. But on the other hand, the arguments of the skeptics and the alternative theories of truth—the coherence theory and the pragmatic theory—have made philosophers (and scientists, too) more humble than they used to be, no longer so sure that they are finding out the facts of the "world as it really is," and wondering just how many of their "discoveries" are indeed the product of an order which they themselves have imposed on nature, through their theories, their concepts, and their experiments. Does this mean that we shall never know the "way the world really is"? Does this mean that two alternative ways of looking at the world might both be *equally* true? However we answer these very difficult questions, our conclusion cannot be, "It's all subjective," which is more often than not a sign of

SUBJECTIVE TRUTH: KIERKEGAARD

When the question of truth is raised in an objective manner, reflection is directed objectively to the truth, as an object to which the knower is related. . . . When the question of the truth is raised subjectively, reflection is directed subjectively to the nature of the individual's relationship; if only the mode of this relationship is in the truth, the individual is in the truth even if he should happen to be thus related to what is not true.

• • •

. . . An objective uncertainty held fast in an appropriation-process of the most passionate inwardness is the truth, *the highest truth attainable for an* existing *individual.*

— *From* Concluding Unscientific Postscript

lazy thinking or of a refusal to answer the hard questions at all. The answer is, rather, that whatever the claims we make for truth, the rules of rationality retain a persistent hold on us. We might have a powerful insight or mystical vision; we might be suddenly inspired or emotionally moved. But what we say and believe nevertheless requires something more: It requires *reasons*. It requires working out. It requires development into a systematic understanding of what this insight, vision, inspiration, or emotion amounts to.

And that's the truth.

CLOSING QUESTIONS

1. Does it make sense to say that a statement or belief is true for a particular person? Can a truth be simply subjective? Give some examples, and explain what significance to give to the above expression "is true for."

2. If a belief makes a person who believes it happier and more secure, in what sense does that make it true?

3. If there were facts, what would they be?

4. Bertrand Russell once wrote, "Better the world should perish than I or any other human being should believe a lie." Discuss. Is truth all *that* important?

5. Are there electrons?

6. Could a scientist give an adequate account of the biblical story of the raising of Lazarus?

BIBLIOGRAPHY AND SUGGESTED READINGS

Bertrand Russell's *The Problems of Philosophy* (Oxford University Press, 1912) is a short classic and an excellent introduction to the problems of "appearance and reality" that have occupied so much of modern philosophy. David Hume's theory of knowledge is summarized in his *Enquiry Concerning Human Understanding* (Oxford University Press, 1955); the more complete argument is his *Treatise on Human Nature,* ed. L. A. Selby-Bigge (Oxford University Press, 1980). The main works of the British empiricists John Locke, Bishop George Berkeley, and David Hume can be found together in *The Empiricists* (Doubleday, 1960). The best general study of the history and strategy of skepticism is Richard Popkin, *A History of Skepticism: From Erasmus to Descartes* (Harper & Row, 1964); and a good study of Descartes and his methods is Anthony Kenny, *Descartes* (Random House, 1968). A short treatment of the various problems of truth is Alan R. White, *Truth* (Doubleday, 1970). Two very good general discussions of the problems of knowledge are Bruce Aune, *Rationalism, Empiricism, Pragmatism* (Random House, 1970) and Adam Morton, *A Guide Through the Theory of Knowledge* (Wadsworth, 1977). A classic study in the philosophy of science is C. G. Hempel, *Philosophy of Natural Science* (Prentice-Hall, 1966). For a modern, though controversial, view of science, see Thomas S. Kuhn, *The Structure of Scientific Revolutions* (University of Chicago Press, 1970). For a detailed study of the creationism-evolution debate, see Philip Kitcher, *The Abuse of Science* (MIT Press, 1983). For a challenging defense of modern skepticism, see Peter Unger, *Ignorance* (Oxford University Press, 1979). A creative approach to these problems can be found in Arthur Danto, *Connections to the World* (New York: Harper & Row, 1989).

CHAPTER SIX
SELF

Frida Kahlo standing next to her self-portrait from 1939 entitled The Two Fridas,
UPI/Corbis-Bettmann.

SELF

*Though man is a unique individual,—he is
equally the whole, the ideal whole, the
subjective existence of society as thought and
experienced. He exists in reality as the
representation and the real mind of social
existence, and as the sum of human
manifestations of life.*

—Karl Marx, *manuscript of 1844*

*I think, therefore I am. . . . But what then am
I? A thing which thinks.*

—*Descartes,* Meditations

OPENING QUESTIONS

1. Describe yourself as a character in a novel. Describe the gestures, postures, revealing habits, characteristic word phrases you use. Try to imitate yourself, by way of parody. What kind of person would you describe yourself as being?

2. Explain who you are to a visitor from another planet.

3. Who are you? Compare the descriptions you would provide

   a. on a job application

   b. on a first date

c. in a talk with your parents, as you are trying to tell them what you have decided to do with your life

d. in a trial with you as the defendant, trying to convince the jury of your "good character"

e. as the "I" in the statement "I think, therefore I am" (Descartes).

4. What is involved in being a "human being"? What (or who) would be included in your characterization? What (or who) would be excluded?

5. Is it ever possible to know—really know—another person? Imagine what it would be like to suspect that you can never know another person's true feelings, that all his or her movements and gestures are intended to fool you and that you can no longer assume that what the individual means (for example, by a smile or a frown) is what you mean by the same outward movement. How do you feel about this?

6. You say to yourself, "I am going to move my arm." You decide to do it, and—lo and behold—your arm moves. How did you do that?

THE ESSENTIAL SELF

With the concept of rationality, we found ourselves moving away from questions about pure reality and back to questions about ourselves and our own activities. Indeed, with the concept of "subjective truth," we found a renewed emphasis on *personal* questions, questions about the self rather than questions about the world. And so we find ourselves raising a new set of issues, questioning what seemed to us so clear and unproblematic before. What is the "self"? What is it to be a person? What do you know when you "know yourself"? What is someone telling you to be when he or she tells you "just to be yourself"?

Our conceptions of self, like our conceptions of God, religion, and the nature of reality, turn out to be extremely varied, different not only for different people and cultures but for each of us from time to time and in different

> Confucius said,
>
> *To discipline oneself through ritual practice is to become authoritatively human. If for the space of one day one were able to accomplish this, the world would appear to be as a model of humanity. However, becoming human emerges out of oneself; how could it emerge out of others?*

contexts. For example, in question 3 above, you probably described yourself on a job application as an industrious worker, with so many years of school and so much experience, with a certain grade point average and a certain amount of ambition. In defending yourself in court, on the other hand, you probably thought very little of your achievements in school; rather, you tried to define yourself in terms of your good deeds, your good intentions, the number of your friends, and the fact that you tend to be gentle with children and animals. To see how bound up with their context such descriptions tend to be, we need only switch them, with shocking results. Imagine yourself giving an employer the information you would more appropriately give to a person on a date. Or consider how you would feel about a supposedly close friend who told you at great length only about his or her achievements in school. What we think of ourselves and what we think of as significant about ourselves—and others—depend to a great extent on the context in which we are trying to explain who we are.

And yet we all have an undeniable sense that, beneath the various descriptions of ourselves that we produce for various occasions, there is within us a "real self," a self that does not vary from context to context. In the Judeo-Christian tradition (and before that, in some ancient religions and in the thinking of the Greeks, for example) this invariant self, our "real self," has been called the **soul**. Philosophers have called the "real self" the **essential self**—that is, the set of characteristics that defines a particular person.

The experience of our real, or essential, self is familiar to us in a great many circumstances. For example, if we are forced to go to a party with people we don't like and do not feel comfortable with, if we are forced to behave in an artificial way, to talk in language that is more vulgar than usual or more sophisticated than usual, to talk about subjects that do not interest us at all, we will very likely describe our experience in phrases such as "I couldn't be myself" or "I felt like a phony." As another example, picture yourself filling out one of those dozens of questionnaires that are forced upon you during every school year; you dutifully list your birthdate, home address, sex, major and perhaps grades, military service, awards, marital status, and so on. A natural reaction to such forms is that they are irrelevant to knowing who you really are. They don't ask the "right" questions, and they leave out any reference to what you and your friends think is most important about you. In

Octavio Paz: Death

The opposition between life and death was not so absolute to the ancient Mexicans as it is to us. Life extended into death, and vice versa. Death was not the natural end of life but one phase of an infinite cycle. Life, death and resurrection were stages of a cosmic process which repeated itself continuously. Life had no higher function than to flow into death, its opposite and complement; and death, in turn, was not an end in itself: man fed the insatiable hunger of life with his death. . . .

Perhaps the most characteristic aspect of this conception is the impersonal nature of the sacrifice. Since their lives did not belong to them, their deaths lacked any personal meaning. The dead—including warriors killed in battle and women dying in childbirth, companions of Huitzilopochtli the sun god—disappeared at the end of a certain period, to return to the undifferentiated country of the shadows, to be melted into the air, the earth, the fire, the animating substance of the universe. Our indigenous ancestors did not believe that their deaths belonged to them, just as they never thought that their lives were really theirs in the Christian sense. Everything was examined to determine, from birth, the life and death of each man: his social class, the year, the place, the day, the hour. The Aztec was as little responsible for his actions as for his death.

— *From* The Labyrinth of Solitude

Octavio Paz, The Labyrinth of Solitude, *trans. Lysander Kempt, Yara Milos, and Rachel Phillips Belash (New York: Grove Press, 1985). Reprinted with the permission of the publisher.*

other words, they don't even begin to get at your essential self, the personal self that is the "real you." This chapter is about the nature of this "real you" and your relationships with other people.

As we have found in other philosophical investigations, the most obvious answer often disappears as soon as we begin to follow our thinking to its consequences, and what once seemed simple turns into a wide variety of answers that sometimes compete with one another. For example, one answer to the question, "Who am I?" or "What is my real, essential self?" is the religious answer; you really are just a soul before God, and all else—your worldly goods and accomplishments, even your physical body and its various pleasures and pains—is insignificant, unimportant. Some people, on the other hand, think of themselves as just another animal, caught up in the process of staying alive and enjoying themselves. A very different answer emerges from Descartes and many other modern philosophers; they say the real self is the conscious self—that is, the thinking self, the self that is aware of itself. There is a powerful contemporary view of the self which insists that there is, ultimately, no set self, that it is a process of creation which goes on as long as we are alive. And there is an Eastern view (in Buddhism, in particular) that teaches us that the self is ultimately unreal, that there is no self at all, only an illusion of one. Finally, and perhaps most important, there is the suggestion that the self is not an individual entity at all, but rather the product of an entire society; your self, in other words, is not really your own, after all.

SELF AS BODY, SELF AS CONSCIOUSNESS

What am I? A thing which thinks. What is a thing which thinks? It is a thing which doubts, understands, affirms, denies, wills, refuses, which also imagines and feels.

— *Descartes,* Meditations

A person's **self-identity** is the way he or she characterizes his or her essential self. This includes both a general characterization—as a human being, as a man or woman, as a creature before God, as an American, as a Christian or Jew, or as a member of any other large organization or group—and a particular description—as the tallest person in the class, as the winner of the Olympic gold medal in pole vaulting in 1990, as the person who is lucky enough to be married to J__, and so on. Sometimes we make these essential characteristics explicit; but even when we don't, they almost always enter into our behavior and our attitudes toward ourselves. Most of us would not think of naming our height as part of our essential self-identity; but, in fact, if we think of the way we stand or walk and if we pay attention to our feelings when we are with people considerably taller or shorter than we are, it becomes evident that such seemingly unimportant characteristics may indeed enter into our conceptions of our essential self. So, too, a person's physical condition is usually a key ingredient in his or her conception of self and his or her self-identity, a fact that becomes obvious, for example, when a person has been ill for an extended period of time.

But although we generally include such physical characteristics in our self-identity, it is also clear that in our whole religious and philosophical tradition we have been taught to play down such physical traits and to emphasize instead the more "spiritual" and "mental" aspects of our existence. Suppose, to choose an extreme example, your best friend turned into a frog. What characteristics would your friend have to retain in order for you to still consider this frog as your friend? The frog would certainly have to display signs of having your friend's mind, most clearly by continuing to talk, if that were possible; then you could recognize that this was indeed your friend, trying to communicate with you and explain what it is that he or she was thinking. We tolerate considerable changes in a person's physical appearance as long as his or her mind seems to remain the same; in fact, we are used to stories, cartoons, and imaginative examples of a person turning into almost anything, from a frog to a cloud to any of a large variety of plants, as long as somehow the person's mind remains intact. On the other hand, it takes very little alteration in a person's mental capacities for us to complain that he or she seems like a different person or that we don't know that person at all anymore.

The theory that the essential self of self-identity is the mind, or self-consciousness, can be traced back to ancient times, but its best-known defender is the philosopher Descartes, who presented a simple but elegant argument that the individual self is the first thing that each of us can know for certain, and that this self, whose existence is indubitable (see pp. 123–124, 157–158) is nothing else but the **thinking self**, the self that is aware of itself. But it was in Descartes, too that we saw the origins of the dilemma that would lead to Hume's skepticism—the possibility that we might, in fact, never know anything but our own ideas and experiences. Now, with reference to the self, a related problem emerges—can we ever know any other self besides ourselves? And we find here, too, an equivalent to Hume's skepticism about knowledge of the world; it is the position called **solipsism**, which says that, indeed, nothing exists but one's own mind. And like skepticism, solipsism is a position that most philosophers find intolerable. The problem is this: If one agrees that one's self should be identified with one's consciousness and that each person can know only his or her consciousness, how is it possible to reach out beyond ourselves to anyone else? Our bodies can touch, even "know" each other in a dubious sense, but our minds cannot.

The theory that the self is consciousness has several ingenious variations. The English philosopher John Locke, for example, argued that the self was not the whole of consciousness, but a specific part of the mind, namely our memory, so that the self is that part of the mind that remembers its past. This explains how it is that we think of ourselves as "the same person" over time, despite even radical changes. Our friend-turned-frog is certainly still our friend if the animal remembers all of the experiences it had as a person before its transformation. On the other hand, we could certainly be suspicious—at the least—if someone who claimed to be our friend could not remember any of the experiences we had shared in the past. (There are, of course, cases of amnesia, or loss of memory; but what is also true of such cases is that the person no longer knows who he or she is; so it is not a question of having a different set of memories but rather of having no self-identifying memories at all.)

The theory that self-identity is determined by memories has its curious difficulties. For example, suppose Mr. Jones has an emergency operation in which his injured brain is replaced by the brain of Mrs. Smith (just deceased). The resulting person has the body, face, and general appearance of Mr. Jones, but the consciousness, memories, and knowledge of Mrs. Smith. Who is the resulting person? It doesn't seem to make sense to say that it is Mrs. Smith, but neither does it make sense to say that it is Mr. Jones. The example becomes even more complicated if you picture yourself in the position of Mrs. Smith,

> **Locke**: *The identity of the same man consists in nothing but a participation of the same continued life, by constantly fleeting particles of matter, in succession vitally united to the same organized body. . . . If the identity of soul alone makes the same man; and if there is nothing in the nature of matter why the individual spirit may not be united to different bodies, it will be possible that those men living in distant ages and of different tempers may have been the same man. . . .*
>
> *But to find wherein person identity consists, we must consider what* person *stands for;—which, I think, is a thinking intelligent being, that has reason and reflection, and consider itself as itself, the same thinking thing, in different times and places; which it does only by that consciousness which is inseparable from thinking, and, as it seems to me, essential to it: it being impossible for anyone to perceive without perceiving that he does perceive. When we see hear, smell, taste, feel, meditate, or will anything, we know that we do so. Thus it is always as to our present sensations and perceptions: and by this every one is to himself that which he calls self. For, since consciousness always accompanies thinking, and it is that which makes every one to be what he calls self, and thereby distinguishes himself from all other thinking things, in this alone consists personal identity, i.e. the sameness of a rational being: and as far as this consciousness can be extended backwards to any past action or thought, so far reaches the identity of that person; it is the same self now it was then; and it is by the same self with this present one that now reflects on it, that the action was done.*
>
> — *John Locke*, Essay on Human Understanding

who awakens after a mysterious lapse in consciousness to find herself with the body of a man; would she know for certain (as the self-consciousness theory would suggest) that she still is, indeed, the same person? Or has self-identity broken down entirely here?

Questions of self-identity give rise to paradoxes of this sort, for what they show us is that our sense of self-identity is far more complex than it seemed at first. If a single characteristic were all there was to the essential self, then self-identity would be that characteristic, no matter what else changed. If memory alone gave us our self-identity, then any being with the same memories, even in a different body, even as a frog, even in two different people, would be the same. But the obvious fact is that we have serious reservations about these cases, and the reason is that we can see that many different aspects of a person enter into our concept of self-identity. "I think, therefore I

What Is It Like, to Be a Bat?

I assume we all believe that bats have experience. After all, they are mammals, and there is no more doubt that they have experience than that mice or pigeons or whales have experience. I have chosen bats instead of wasps or flounders because if one travels too far down the phylogenetic tree, people gradually shed their faith that there is experience there at all. Bats, although more closely related to us than those other species, nevertheless present a range of activity and a sensory apparatus so different from ours that the problem I want to pose is exceptionally vivid (though it certainly could be raised with other species). Even without the benefit of philosophical reflection, anyone who has spent some time in an enclosed space with an excited bat knows what it is to encounter a fundamentally alien form of life.

I have said that the essence of the belief that bats have experience is that there is something that it is like to be a bat. Now we know that most bats . . . perceive the external world primarily by sonar, . . . detecting the reflections, from objects within range, of their own rapid, subtly modulated, high-frequency shrieks. Their brains are designed to correlate the outgoing impulses with the subsequent echoes, and the information thus acquired enables bats to make precise discriminations of distance, size, shape, motion, and texture comparable to those we make by vision. But bat sonar, though clearly a form of perception, is not similar in its operation to any sense that we possess, and there is no reason to suppose that it is subjectively like anything we can experience or imagine. This appears to create difficulties for the notion of what it is like to be a bat . . .

Our own experience provides the basic material for our imagination, whose range is therefore limited. It will not help to try to imagine that one has webbing on one's arms, which enables one to fly around at dusk and dawn catching insects in one's mouth; that one has very poor vision, and perceives the surrounding world by a system of reflected high-frequency sound signals; and that one spends the day hanging upside down by one's feet in an attic. Insofar as I can imagine this (which is not very far), it tells me only what it would be like for me to behave as a bat behaves. But that is not the question. I want to know what it is like for a bat to be a bat . . .

— Thomas Nagel

> Detective-Inspector René "Doubty" Descartes absent-mindedly flicked grey-white ash from the sleeve of his only vicuña jacket and stared moodily across the pigeon-violated rooftops of Whitehall. "I muse," he thought. "Therefore. . . ."
>
> The ginger telephone shrilled its urgent demand. Descartes, rudely awakened from his reverie, snatched the receiver to his ear.
>
> "Descartes here," he posited.
>
> "Sorry to interrupt, sir." The familiar tones of Sergeant Warnock floated down the line. "Sergeant Warnock here."
>
> "How can you be sure?"
>
> "I think I am Sergeant Warnock, therefore I am Sergeant Warnock," replied Sergeant Warnock confidently. Some of Doubty's thinking was beginning to rub off.
>
> — *Monty Python*

ALTERNATIVE CONCEPTIONS OF SELF AS CONSCIOUSNESS

Which is most essential to *you?*

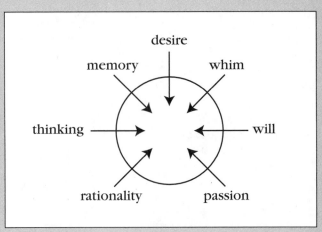

Adapted from F. Bergmann, On Being Free *(Notre Dame, IN: University of Notre Dame Press, 1979).*

KIERKEGAARD: THE PASSIONATE SELF

It is impossible to exist without passion, unless we understand the word "exist" in the loose sense of a so-called existence. . . . Eternity is the winged horse, infinitely fast, and time is a worn-out nag; the existing individual is the driver. That is to say, he is such a driver when his mode of existence is not an existence loosely so called; for then he is no driver, but a drunken peasant who lies asleep in the wagon and lets the horses take care of themselves. To be sure, he also drives and is a driver, and so there are perhaps many who—also exist.

— *From* Concluding
Unscientific
Postscript

am," in all of its variations ("I remember, therefore I am who I am") is too simplistic to capture the whole of our sense of ourselves.

Although the views that the self is defined primarily through thinking and memory have dominated most self-as-consciousness theories, it is important to realize that such theories have pointed to other aspects of consciousness as well. The Danish philosopher Kierkegaard, for example, defined the self as the *passions,* several German philosophers have defined the self primarily as *will.* Dostoevsky defined one of his more perverse characters in terms of *whim,* and many philosophers since Plato have defined the self in terms of *rational thought* (as opposed to mere thinking, which can be rational or irrational). Emphasis on different aspects of consciousness results in very different conceptions of self, and so even if you agree that in some sense the self must be defined through consciousness, it is essential to specify what *part* of consciousness defines the self. What one considers his or her "real self" depends on this.

THE SELF AS A PROBLEM

What existentialists have in common is that they believe that existence comes before essence. . . . man first of all exists, encounters himself, surges up in the world—and defines himself afterwards. . . . to begin with, he is nothing.

— *Jean-Paul Sartre,*
Existentialism as a
Humanism

If self-identity is defined by our answer to the question "Who am I?", one possible answer is "Nothing yet, still in progress." If one sees the self not as an inner soul that is in us from birth (or perhaps from conception), but rather as a *product* of our actions and thoughts, then self-identity is something to be *earned,* not an already existing fact to be discovered. Thus the existentialist **Jean-Paul Sartre** (1905–1980) would say that all of those theories that take the self to be found in consciousness are misconceived. The self is not simply thinking, nor is it memory of the past. The self lies always in the future; it is what we aim toward, as we try to *make* ourselves into something. But this means that as long as we are alive there is no self—at least, no fixed and finished self. The self is an open question.

The first reply to this is usually that it neglects the fact that we are, in fact, a certain person with a fixed identity from the moment we are born, and facts continue to define us all through our lives. Consider, as an example, a person who is born in the year 1959, born female, born blonde, born of a Scandinavian family, born poor; all of these are facts that define this person and have nothing to do with "becoming." At the age of three, the child is injured at play and loses a finger; at the age of eight, the child luckily finds herself in a class with a sympathetic and inspiring teacher, who interests her in science and starts her off on the road to a brilliant career in chemistry. At the age of twenty-seven, she meets by chance a fellow on an airplane; they fall in love and are soon married. He is kidnapped and killed by terrorists. She is hounded by the press, and a popular writer turns her story into a best-selling book. She retreats to her chemistry laboratory, thinks about her life as she runs her experiments, and comes to realize that it all consists of accidental facts—the fact of her birth, her childhood accident, walking into a certain classroom, taking a certain airplane flight, and so on. Those facts are her self. There seems to be nothing else.

Sartre's reply to this portrait is that it leaves out an essential dimension at every turn. What is missing is choice. What is left out is the possibility, at any point in this story, of saying "No" to the facts, or, in Sartre's words, "No matter what is made of one, one is always responsible for what one makes of what is made of one." A person with an injury cannot wish away the injury, but he or she can make of it a badge of courage, a stigma of shame, a cocktail party curiosity, an excuse to keep out of the army, a handicap to be overcome. A person who is born blonde and Scandinavian can be proud of that fact, embarrassed by that fact, indifferent to that fact. One falls in love (which itself has an enormous amount of choice built into it), but one can choose to ignore it, turn it into a tragedy, turn it into a marriage, even turn it into a joke of sorts. Sartre called this dimension of our existence **transcendence** (since we can always **transcend** or go beyond, the facts that are true of us, or what Sartre called our **facticity**). Transcendence means that the self is defined not by the facts about us, but by what we make—and continue to make—of these facts. But since we can change our minds about what to make of the facts true of us for the whole of our lives, the self—which is the outcome of these interpretations and the actions based on them—is an unfinished process until the end of our lives (when both our interpretations and our actions come to a halt).

Consider, for example, a student who had once been extremely ill as a child and now (in college) intends to be a doctor. The facts of his illness are simply true; he cannot now do anything to change them. But he is obviously using those facts to motivate and justify his decision for the future, to become a doctor in order to cure other children who are afflicted as he was. But suppose in his senior year he becomes caught up in local politics, finds that he enjoys this, and, furthermore, that he does quite well at it. He postpones his plans to go to medical school and spends a year campaigning for a political ally. Then he runs for office himself and wins, postponing medical school for another four years. His political career flourishes. Answering reporters when they ask, "How did you get into politics?" he finds himself remembering his childhood talent for negotiating and arguing well. What happened to the fact of his childhood illness? It is still true, of course, but it is no longer of any significance; it no longer fits into the political project he has made for his life. But suppose at the age of forty-three he loses a critical election. His political career is finished, and, not surprisingly, he remembers his old ambition to become a doctor. The fact of his childhood illness is reinstated as the crucial fact of his life, and his projected self is once more a medical self, not because of the facts, but rather because of his renewed intentions.

What this means is that there is no "real self" other than the self that we make for ourselves. Certain facts are true of us, of course, and we cannot make them untrue. But we can make of them what we will, even if what we are able to make of them is also limited by the facts of our circumstances. Even prisoners, Sartre said, are free to make of their imprisonment what they choose; imprisonment can be injustice, or martyrdom, or an excuse for not doing anything, or a challenge to escape, or a symbol to the world, or a way of amusing oneself, or just plain boring. But this also means that there are no "correct" choices; or, in Kierkegaard's language all choices are subjective truths, true for the person who makes them but not necessarily true for anyone else. The self is what each of us chooses *for ourselves,* our projection into our future, our intentions to *become* a particular kind of person. But as we

---

Choosing Oneself

Man simply is. Not that he simply is what he conceives himself to be, but he is what he wills, and as he conceives of himself after already existing—as he wills to be. . . . Man is nothing else but that which he makes of himself. That is the first principle of existentialism.

Man is responsible for himself, not only for his own individuality but for all men.

Man chooses himself, and in choosing for ourselves, we choose for all men.

— *Jean-Paul Sartre,*
Existentialism as a
Humanism

> *These are the voices which we hear in solitude, but they grow faint and inaudible as we enter into the world. Society everywhere is in conspiracy against the manhood of every one of its members. Society is a joint-stock company, in which the members agree, for the better securing of his bread to each shareholder, to surrender the liberty and culture of the eater. The virtue in most request is conformity. Self-reliance is its aversion. It loves not realities and creators, but names and customs.*
>
> *Whoso would be a man, must be a nonconformist. . . . Nothing is at last sacred but the integrity of your own mind.*
>
> — R. W. Emerson,
> "Self-Reliance"

never wholly achieve this—for even when our ambitions are fulfilled we can always change our mind, formulate new ambitions, and so on—the self never really exists in full. It is always at best our image of what we want to be, to which we strive with more or less success and persistency. And this striving, this sense of oneself as always incomplete and responsible for itself, is the **authentic self**.

If the authentic self for Sartre was something created, rather than something found, then the traditional theories which say that the self simply *is* are not only mistaken but, in a very important sense, self-deluding, ways of not recognizing our responsibility for creating the self. This denial of responsibility for one's self Sartre called **bad faith**. Bad faith (*mauvaise foi*) includes try-

Bad Faith: Are You Ever Just What You Are?

Let us take an example: A homosexual frequently has an intolerable feeling of guilt, and his whole existence is determined in relation to this feeling. One will readily see that he is in bad faith. In fact it frequently happens that this man, while recognizing his homosexual inclination, refuses with all his strength to consider himself "a homosexual." His case is always "different," peculiar. He refuses to draw from the facts their obvious conclusion. But then, his friend asks that [he] recognize himself and . . . declare, "I am a homosexual." But we ask, who is in bad faith? The homosexual or the champion of sincerity?

> — Jean-Paul Sartre,
> Being and
> Nothingness

ing to excuse yourself from responsibility for what you are and what you will become by pretending that your life has been defined by the facts (by your facticity) instead of recognizing that you can try to make of those facts what you wish. Bad faith, in other words, is the negative side of having to create your self; it is the rejection of this responsibility—in effect, giving up even before you try.

No Self, Many Selves

In reality, every self is far from being a unity; it is a constellation of selves, a chaos of forms, of states and stages, of inheritances and potentialities. Man is an onion made up of a hundred layers, a texture made up of many threads.

> — *Hermann Hesse,*
> Steppenwolf

There is nothing that can be called a "Self," and there is no such thing as "mine" in all the world.

> — *The Teachings of the*
> *Buddha*

We have assumed throughout the whole of our discussion so far what would seem to be the most indubitable and undeniable thesis, that every person has one, and only one, self. But this assumption, too, can be challenged, and at least one of the major religions of the world—Buddhism—rejects as an "illusion" the very idea of the self.

The rejection of the self can be found in Western philosophy, too. In his *Treatise of Human Nature,* the skeptic David Hume turned his critical attention to Descartes' and Locke's claims to have found the self within consciousness, and he said, with his usual irony, that he found no such self in himself; all he found was a complicated cluster of different experiences and ideas, but nothing that could be called a self.

> *There are some philosophers who imagine that we are every moment intimately conscious of what we call our self; that we feel its existence and its continuance in existence; and we are certain, beyond the evidence of a demonstration, both of its perfect identity and simplicity. . . . But for my part, when I enter most intimately into what I call myself, I always stumble on some particular perception or other of heat or cold, light or shade, love or hatred, pain or pleasure. I never can catch myself at any time without a perception, and never can observe anything but the perception.*

As a consistent empiricist, Hume therefore concluded that we aren't really justified in talking about a "self" since the concept can't be related to something encountered in experience.

Jean-Paul Sartre, too, rejected the idea of the existence of the self in the traditional sense. One way of reinterpreting his philosophy is to say that he, too, denied that we can find any self in ourselves; that for him the self, if it is not an illusion, at least always escapes us, always lies ahead of us in the future.

But let's take these arguments several steps further. Hume's skepticism is essentially a negative thesis: He could not find what most philosophers too confidently refer to as a self. But the negative thesis can be turned into a positive thesis, and this is what happens in Buddhism. For the Buddhist, not being able to find the self is not a philosophical inability; rather, seeing through the illusion of the individual self is the highest act of "enlightenment," our most important single conceptual achievement. The self, in this view, is itself a false idea, a dangerous notion that cuts us off from the rest of life, from the whole picture, which the Buddhists call "Buddha-nature." (If you like, it might be called "the cosmic self," as long as we do not confuse this transpersonal self with the individual, personal self we have been discussing so far.) The idea, then, is that our real self-identity is not individual *self*-identity at all, but rather our unity with the whole of the universe. But this is to say that, in our sense, there is no self, that the self is an idea which has been imposed upon us by a certain kind of society instead of a fact that is true of us or of a soul inside of us.

This rejection of the individual self in favor of an all-embracing cosmic sense of self appears in Western philosophy, too. The nineteenth-century German philosopher Hegel also rejected our emphasis on the personal, individual self. He showed, in his *Phenomenology of Spirit,* that our true self-identity is indeed a universal self-identity—all of us as One—which he called "spirit" (Chapters 2 and 3). For Hegel, too, the individual self is an illusion fostered by a particular kind of society, and our true identity breaks through these limited boundaries to include all of us together.

The rejection of the idea that each person has a self leads to an even more astounding conclusion, found in some of the other philosophies of the East and West as well, which has been defended in the writings of the German author Hermann Hesse. According to this view, there are indeed selves, but not, as we have assumed, one self per person. Each of us is a multitude of selves. We may be a different self in any number of different circumstances, and it is only a philosophical mistake that makes us think that we have to tie

---

THE UNIMPORTANCE OF THE INDIVIDUAL

At a time when spiritual life has become so very much emphasized and strengthened and the mere individual has become correspondingly a matter of indifference, . . . the individual must forget himself; he must simply become and do what he can, but less must be demanded of him and he should expect and ask less for himself.

— *Hegel,*
Phenomenology
of Spirit

all of these selves together into a single coherent package, as a single self. In a striking image, Hesse tells us that "man is an onion," with hundreds of different layers (selves). The traditional view, on the other hand, is that man is a peach, with a solid, single pit in the center (the soul). But if you peel away the layers of an onion, you know that you find more layers; when you reach the last layer, there is nothing more, no pit, no core, no soul. There are only the layers, the many roles we play in different parts of our lives, the many selves, which is to say, no self as such at all.

The rejection of the self in any of these senses is not just a philosophical trick; it quickly becomes a way of life. Most of our plans and our behavior are based on the assumption that we have to *be* somebody, or that we ought to *make* something of ourselves. But according to the views just discussed, an integrated picture of the individual as the unit of selfhood breaks down, and self-realization becomes instead the recognition of ourself as part of something much greater than our (individual) self, or, in Hesse's view, the realization (not just the recognition but the living out) of the multitude of selves that are in us all.

THE MIND-BODY PROBLEM

The identification or the location of the self in consciousness, as opposed to the identification of the self with your physical body, raises a tantalizing and very difficult metaphysical and scientific question: What is the relationship between our minds and our bodies; how do they interact? You remember that Descartes believed that mind and body were two different *substances,* but substances, by their very nature, cannot interact. What's more, Descartes insisted that he could conceive of his mind existing without a body, and it was clear that human bodies could exist (e.g., as corpses) without minds. So what is the relationship between them? Descartes never solved this problem to his satisfaction, and the elaborate metaphysics of Spinoza and Leibniz were, in part, attempts to solve it for him. If substances cannot interact, then it must be that either (a) mind and body do not interact or (b) mind and body are not separate substances. Leibniz defends the first option, arguing that mental events and physical events only *seem* to interact. In fact they stand in "preestablished harmony," like a film and its soundtrack (not his analogy). The two are perfectly coordinated and seem to be causally related, but in fact they are two separate "tracks" on the same type. Spinoza chooses the second option, suggesting that mind and body are not in fact distinct but rather are two different attributes of one and the same substance. His theory, accordingly, is sometimes called "dual aspect theory"—that is, mind and body are two different aspects of one and the same substance (according to him, the only substance).

These metaphysical speculations seem to us somewhat quaint, but they can be readily translated into extremely troubling questions with which contemporary science and philosophy continuously struggle. Mind and body may or may not be two different "substances," but we can all agree that mental events (e.g., a pain) are very different from the physical events occurring in the brain. Moreover, the question of how the one might cause the other seems to be as much a mystery to us as it was to Descartes. Since the seventeenth century, however, there have been some momentous advances in science, and the terms of the question have altered accordingly. First of all, it is only in the twentieth century that we have gained any substantial knowledge about the workings of the brain and the central nervous system. Second, and even more recently, advances in computer technology (only dimly envisioned by Descartes and some of his contemporaries, notably Pascal) have provided a promising analog to the traditional mind-body problem.

These recent discoveries have tended to shift attention to updated versions of Spinoza's solution to the mind-body problem—his idea that mental events and physical (brain) events are not in fact so different but rather intimately related, perhaps even identical. Yet the old questions remain, and it is by no means clear exactly what it means to say that a mental event and a physical event are "identical." Indeed, one can still find defenders of each of the five traditional solutions to the problem, once discussed in the metaphysical language of "substances" but now debated in the contemporary terms of neurology, cognitive science, and computer technology:

1. Mind and body in fact do interact; physical events (a pin in the finger) do cause mental events (a pain) and mental events (deciding to go to the store) do cause physical events (walking toward the store) (Descartes). The question is how they do this.

2. Mind and body don't interact; mental events and physical events occur simultaneously, perhaps coordinated by God in a "pre-established harmony" (Leibniz).

3. There are no mental events (the materialist solution). There are only brain processes, described from the unusual perspective of the person who has the brain.

4. There are no physical events (the idealist solution). Brain processes, too, are only ideas in the mind.

5. Mental events and physical events are in fact the same (Spinoza's solution).

All five solutions are clumsy and obscure. Some seem to be nonsense—for instance, the claim that there are no mental events—but great philosophers (and psychologists), driven to desperate lengths by Descartes' problem, have often chosen this solution as the most palatable alternative. One sophisticated denial that there are any mental events, coupled with the insistence that there are only various patterns of behavior (which we label with mentalistic names such as "belief," "desire," and "anger"), is called **behaviorism**. Both the view that mind and body interact and the view that they do not seem to cause insurmountable paradoxes. There are still a great many **dualists** around—that is, those who continue to argue that mental events and physical events are wholly separate. There are still idealists and there are still some behaviorists who flatly insist that there are no mental events, or at least, no such events that can legitimately function in a scientific theory. But today, even most behaviorists tend to defend the last solution and argue that what we call mental events are really a special category of physical events.

Today, views about the mind-body problem tend to fall into one of three camps, each of them a version of the thesis that mind and body are not really separate substances. Not surprisingly, Spinoza is often invoked as the ancestor of all such solutions. The three types of solution, each to be discussed in turn, are: **behaviorism, identity theory**, and **functionalism**.

Behaviorism

The crude behaviorist might simply deny the existence of mental events, but it is obvious to anyone who thinks that thoughts exist, at least while he or she is thinking them. (Thus Descartes' famous "I think, therefore I am," in which he denies that it is possible to think and intelligibly deny that one is thinking.) The modern behaviorist is more subtle. Of course mental events exist—that is, desires, beliefs, emotions, moods, impulses, and the like are real and undeniable—but they don't exist in the way that most people think they do. They are not "ghosts in the machine" writes philosophical behaviorist Gilbert Ryle, nor are they "occult" or "mysterious" occurrences of any kind. What we call "mental," in fact, is a pattern or a disposition to behave in certain ways. To name a "mental event" is actually to make a prediction about a person's behavior. Thus, to say a man is thirsty is not to name some unseen event in his mind but rather to predict that he will get a drink as soon as he can. To say that a person is in love is not to name a feeling but to predict a familiar sequence of activities, from agitation in the presence of the loved one to writing long letters in the middle of the night. The existence of mental events is not denied; they are relocated, no longer in some mysterious place called "the mind" but in the perfectly tangible body of an acting organism.

For some mental events, behaviorism is perfectly reasonable. For example, a person's intelligence is not anything he or she experiences; it is a tendency to perform well in certain kinds of tests. A person's motives—we know since Freud—might not be known at all, but we can tell what they are by the acts they motivate. Behaviorism runs into more of a problem with such sensations as

Behaviorism: the view that all talk of "mental events" should be translated into talk about tendencies to behave in certain ways.

pain, seeing bright light, hearing a tune in the key of C. We can agree that these sensations may be manifested in dispositions to behave in certain ways—wincing, putting on sunglasses, or starting to whistle—but we will probably insist that there is still something irreducibly mental that lies behind these dispositions, that behaviorism can't be the whole story. Much of what we call "the mind" may indeed be better understood as dispositions to behave in certain ways. But some mental events seem to be *felt,* and with them the mind-body problem emerges once again, as tough as ever.

Identity Theory

For many years, the ever more refined research in neurology has made clear something Descartes and his friends could not have known: that specific mental events are exactly correlated with specific brain events. This picture is made much more complicated by the fact that a single mental event may involve several alternative brain events and, in the case of brain damage, it is even possible for some mental events to be correlated with entirely new brain events. But nevertheless we now know that there is a strict correlation between mental events, from simple pains to raging ambition, and certain processes in the brain. The mind-body problem is: How are these connected?

Correlation is not the same as connection. Two things can be correlated (the mayor of New York eats lunch every day at exactly the same time that the mayor of San Diego eats breakfast) without having any connection. Correlated mental and brain events might be like that, but if they were it would make any scientific understanding of the mind from the physical (as opposed to psychological) standpoint impossible. Perhaps mental events and physical events do cause one another, but then we are still faced with the question of how such different things can do so. The identity theory cuts through all such questions and says that mental events (pains, for example) and brain processes are *the same thing.* They have different properties and deserve different descriptions ("It hurts" versus "The sodium level is back down now") but, nevertheless, they are the same. Here is another case of identity:

Water is H_2O.

Now, it is clear that a description of water—as "wet," as "cold," as "filling the basin"—is quite different from the description of hydrogen and oxygen atoms and the way they combine to form a certain molecule. Nevertheless, it makes perfectly good sense to say that water is H_2O, even if the properties of water—as we normally describe it—and the properties of the molecules—as a scientist would describe them—are different.

Identity theory is still much debated. It solves the mind-body problem, but it raises other questions just as perplexing. For example, it is usually argued that two things are identical only if they have *all* properties in common (a principle propounded by Leibniz and sometimes called "Leibniz's Law").

Gilbert Ryle (1900–1978) was an Oxford don, the author of *The Concept of Mind* (1949), and a leading proponent of **philosophical behaviorism**. According to Ryle, mental-type terms in fact refer to *dispositions to behave,* not to "ghostly private occurrences." A disposition is a tendency, which can be triggered in certain circumstances. "Glass is brittle" refers to a disposition such that glass, when struck, will shatter into tiny pieces. "People fall in love" refers to a disposition such that men and women, when together in certain circumstances (called "romantic"), will begin to act ridiculous, a prelude to spending their lives together.

But it is clear that pains and brain processes do not have most properties in common; for example, we can locate a brain process at a certain place in the brain. There is no such exact localizability for pains. (But then again, if you are in Seattle, it is clear that your headache is not in Portland.) On the basis of such arguments, some theorists have rejected the identity theory. They would say that water and H_2O *can* be described in the same terms, even if they often are not, but that there is no way to describe a pain in the language of brain science, and no way to describe a brain process in the language of sensations. Still other theorists have suggested that the languages we use to talk about pains and brains, respectively, are just curious remnants from the old days, when people knew much less about brains. In the future, they suggest, we will drop the language of sensations and talk comfortably about "having an F-stimulation of my cerebral cortex, process 4.21-B." But whatever form the theory takes, the central claim is this: What we call a "mental event" is not a particular type of event, but just a particular way of describing some brain process.

Identity Theory: the theory that mental states and events are in fact identical to particular brain processes and events, even if viewed from two perspectives and described in two different languages.

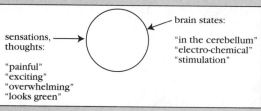

Functionalism

Dissatisfaction with both behaviorism and identity theory as well as the rejection of all the old dualist theories of mind and body, coupled with recent discoveries about the workings of computers and the manufacture of "artificial intelligence" ("AI"), have led to a new solution to the mind-body problem, called **functionalism**. Behaviorism stresses the importance of behavior, but it cannot account for the nature of such sensations as pain and does not talk about the brain and its functions at all. Identity theory emphasizes the sameness of mental events and brain events, but it does not address the question of why this one particular organ should have such remarkable properties. The identity theorist refers to certain processes, but why, one might ask, are they peculiarly *brain* processes? What is so special about the brain? Is it the special material of the brain that makes what we call "mental events" possible? Or is it simply the nature of the processes themselves, without regard for the material in which they occur?

The functionalist answers these questions by insisting that it is the processes themselves that explain the special properties of mental events. The brain is special because it is such a marvelous piece of machinery—or "hardware." But other pieces of hardware not made out of brain material may someday do just as well, and may have minds to match. Ten years ago, skeptics were confidently insisting that no computer could ever play chess; now computers are beating chess masters. Today, skeptics say that no computer will ever feel or think for itself; ten years from now, they may be apologizing to an indignant Apple IXe. Functionalists point out that mental activity is indeed identical to certain processes, but it is the *function* that counts, not the material in which the function takes place. There is no reason to suppose that a computer cannot be built that exactly duplicates the human brain—and the human mind. There is no reason, apart from practicality, why one could not build a brain out of paper clips and rubber bands, so long as it included all the circuits needed to perform all proper functions.

Functionalism, it might be noted, still leaves open some questions. How do pain and other sensations fit in? Does the theory of functions explain how it is that one sees red or hears a melody? And might not a confirmed dualist come back once again and ask, "I agree that there is an impressive correlation between certain functions and mental events, but how does that explain how the one *causes* the other?" Like the identity theorist, the functionalist tries to solve the mind-body problem by asserting that the one thing (in this case a

Functionalism: the theory that mental activity consists of certain functions of the brain—which might well be duplicated in non-brain material. There is nothing necessarily unique about the brain.

function) simply *is* the other. But couldn't it be that pains and great ideas are not identical to anything but themselves, and that their place in a material universe is still a mystery our immaterial minds can't quite grasp?

Functionalism, its advocates argue, is a great advance in the efforts to solve the mind-body problem because it expands our vision to consider increasingly complicated processes of the brain (and its computer analogs) instead of the older, more atomistic image of some comparatively simple event in the brain causing (or being identical to) some discrete mental event. But this same argument can be expanded further, and several philosophers in America and Europe have argued that the whole idea of reducing the mind-body problem to questions about the brain is a step in the wrong direction. We cannot understand human consciousness, the argument goes, apart from the *whole human being*. The dichotomy of "the mind and the body" is already a mistake, given this way of thinking, for what we are is *embodied consciousness*—not a mind *in* a body—and to argue about interaction and identity is already to misunderstand the terms in which human beings must be understood.

This argument against the mind-body problem is also a powerful argument against many of our favorite ideas about the self. To think of the self as an isolated individual consciousness, aware primarily of itself, is, according to similar arguments, a serious misunderstanding of selfhood. The self must be conceived of in terms of the **whole** person. (The position is sometimes called "*holism*," accordingly.) In ancient times, Aristotle argued for such a view of the self as nothing less than the "complete" person; today, too, there are many philosophers who argue that nothing less can give us an adequate understanding of the self. The self is not just consciousness aware of itself but the flesh-and-blood person who is part of a family and a community and a soldier or a shoemaker or a politician. A person is a self not just for one's self, but with and for other people as well.

The Egocentric Predicament

The mind-body problem is just one of several quandaries we get into when we start thinking about the nature of the self. What makes the problem so intractable is that we seen, in some hard-to-define metaphorical sense, to be "inside" of ourselves, in juxtaposition to the "external" world and other people. And so we wonder how the mind is connected to that bit of the physical world closest to us, namely our own bodies. And so, too, we wonder whether we can ever really know if the experiences we have in our minds in fact correspond to the world outside us—the problem of skepticism we discussed in the preceding chapter. This problem also gives rise to the awful possibility of *solipsism,* which we introduced at the beginning of this chapter as the view that only one's own mind exists. What, then, of other people? This odd question has been designated by philosophers as the **egocentric predicament**. "Egocentric" because it begins with the claim that the individual self is at the center of all our experience; "predicament" because it is indeed an intolerable idea that we cannot ever get beyond our own self to know the existence of others. In recent Anglo-American philosophy, the same problem has been called the "problem of other minds," which is, essentially, "How can I ever know of the existence of any mind other than my own?"

This curious problem begins with an assumption we have taken for granted throughout most of this book: We know our own mind directly and beyond any doubt. (There may be—according to Freud, for example—certain aspects of our mind that are "unconscious," or unknown to us, but even Freud accepted the claim that we *generally* know what directly is "in our mind," which is why the idea of "unconscious mental processes" became such a startling discovery.) Descartes' "I think, therefore I am" is essentially a statement of this direct and indubitable knowledge we have of our own consciousness; but even Hume, who rejected the existence of the self, and Sartre, who thought that the self is created, began with this assumption. ("Consciousness is transparent," wrote Sartre. "It has no corners and nothing in it can hide from us.") But if we know our own mind directly and without any doubts, it does not follow that we know other people's minds directly at all. We have to *infer* what other people are thinking or feeling; we have to figure it out. How can we do this?

The standard answer, first formulated as a theory by John Stuart Mill a century ago, is that we know what is going on in other people's minds—indeed, that we can figure out that other people have minds at all—by **analogy**. An analogy is a comparison in which certain similarities are pointed out with the conclusion that there must therefore be other similarities as well. For example, if someone draws an analogy between a college and a business (because, let us say, both need some principles of good management), we may expect other similarities to appear as well: the fact that both produce something which is purchased by consumers, the fact that both are subsidized by our system of taxation and therefore have to answer to the larger community, the fact that both employ a workforce whose responsibility it is to produce the product as efficiently as possible. But, of course, there are **disanalogies**, too, comparisons in which the apparent similarities break down. Knowledge, for example, isn't like most products in that any number of people can "have" the same knowledge, whereas only a limited number of people can share a particular automobile, television set, or toothbrush.

The argument that we can know of other people and their minds by analogy proceeds according to the comparison between our bodies and other people's bodies, our own faces and gestures and other people's faces and gestures. Our bodies, faces, and gestures are quite obviously similar; this similarity is the basis of the analogy. I sometimes frown; you sometimes frown. I sometimes wince in pain; you sometimes wince, too, and in much the same circumstances in which I would wince. Now I know that when I frown it is usually because I disapprove of something, or because I am worried about something. I know, therefore, that my mental state is correlated with certain features and movements of my body: throughout my life I become more and more aware of what these correlations are. I also see that you have similar features and make similar movements with your body, and so I infer from these similarities a further similarity: namely, that you are feeling or thinking as I am when your features and movements are similar to my features and movements. That is, I know that, in my own case, my mental states (M) and my bodily movements (B) are correlated like this:

$$M:B \text{ ("M is related to B")}$$

I also know that your bodily states are similar to mine:

$$M:B::x:B$$

What I must infer, then, is the x, and what I infer, of course, is another M. By analogy, from the similarities between our bodies and the correlation between my mental states and my body, I infer that you have similar mental states. You, too, have a mind.

This argument seems persuasive until we consider the possibility of disanalogies. Is it possible, for example, to imagine a being with human form which does everything that I do, and in the same circumstances, but which does not have any mind at all? Many philosophers have argued that robots are just like this; they can be programmed to behave just as we do, but they have no minds. (Of course, the argument is now turned around the other way, too: since robots can be made to behave as we do in similar circumstances, the argument goes, robots must have the same thoughts and feelings we do.) But at least this much is clear: We can imagine without difficulty that the people who surround us are not in fact human, do not in fact have minds. We cannot doubt, Descartes said, the existence of our own mind. But we can, by this argument, doubt the existence of other minds. Since we can never get into another person's mind, to see if indeed he or she has one, how can we ever check our analogy? How can I ever know that I myself am not the only conscious being, the only mind, the only self, in the universe? On the one hand, this solipsistic conclusion is obviously absurd; on the other hand, the argument that we know of other people and their minds by analogy seems to leave it, at least in theory, an open possibility. What has gone wrong here?

One possibility is that the argument from analogy goes wrong in the very place we most expected it to be unquestionable, in its very first premise, in the idea that we know our own mind directly and beyond any doubt. Let's take another look, therefore, at the assumption we have so far nowhere questioned. Are we indeed "directly" aware of our own minds? Is the existence of our own self indubitable, while the existence of all other selves is an open question? What is the presupposition of this seemingly unquestionable assumption, "I think, therefore I am"?

It has been suggested by a number of philosophers that the proper formulation of Descartes' famous slogan ought to be just "There are thoughts." Descartes was not justified, they have argued, in assuming that if there are thoughts, there must be a thinker. And this, of course, is just what we have been assuming, too, in talking about the individual self. Each of us, the assumption goes, must have a self. Hume, Hesse, and Sartre threw this assumption into disarray, but they did not reject the basis upon which it was formulated. It is still through individual self-awareness that we come to recognize that there is no self, or that each of us may be many selves, or that the individual self must be created. But where do we get this idea of individual self-awareness? Why are we so sure that, for each of us, there are not just thoughts but an "I" as well? In fact, how did we ever learn even to identify "thoughts"?

What has been left out of our account of the self is precisely what we have now come to see as the problem: the existence of other people. In our discussion so far, we first have tried to understand the nature, or essence, of our individual selves. Once we have done this, we ask how it is that we know that there are other selves in the world, too. But if we proceed this way, and if we believe that self has anything to do with consciousness or the way we think of ourselves or the way we project our existence into the future, it looks as if the existence of others will become a problem; and that is absurd.

The Self as Social

Man is by nature a social animal. . . . Anyone who is unable to live a common life or who is so self-sufficient that he has no need to do so is no member of society, which means that he is either a beast or a god.

— *Aristotle,* Politics

It is true, no doubt, that each of us has a conception of our self as an individual self, and we do indeed have some sense of having an "authentic," or "real," self beneath the roles and postures we are taught to adopt in work and society, which sometimes make us feel uncomfortable, "not ourselves." But we have concluded too quickly that our real self is an individual self and that the social roles we play and the conventions we learn in society are distortions and distractions from our true self. Indeed, this is a very old view; it is central to the Christian teaching that the inner soul before God is the real self and that our social position and power are, by comparison, of no real significance. Descartes taught this view when he declared that the real self is oneself as a "thinking thing," as opposed, for instance, to a social being, a son, a father, a daughter, a mother, and so on. The French philosopher Jean-Jacques Rousseau set forth the same thesis again in the mid-eighteenth century when he declared with vehemence that natural, individual human beings are good and innocent until society "corrupts" them, and we in America are still sympathetic to this philosophy, that what is "natural" and "individual" is essentially good.

Paradoxically, the image we have of ourselves as *individuals* is an image that we have been taught collectively, by society, precisely because we are *not* mere individuals. It is one of the premises of our culture, for instance, that the general welfare will best be served by everyone pursuing his or her own interests. This is a premise that is still much debated, of course, but it serves in particular as one of the assumptions of **capitalism** and is certainly central to much of our thinking. But this is a very recent idea; indeed, it would not even have been considered plausible until the middle of the eighteenth century,

Jean-Jacques Rousseau (1712–1778) was a stormy Enlightenment philosopher from Geneva, who fought throughout his life with virtually all his friends and supporters. An extremely troubled and unhappy man, he found in his solitude a conception of humans as basically and naturally good, before the conventions and artificialities of society "corrupted" them. His writings were usually censored and he spent much of his life running away from the law. He died in total poverty, but only a few years later, his ideas became the central theme of the French Revolution.

and the point to be made again is that, though the idea emphasizes the importance of individuals (and individual initiative, individual interests), it is an idea created by a specific kind of society. Our certainty of ourselves as individuals, in other words, is a modern invention though with its roots in early Christianity. And if today we see our own existence as indubitable, that is itself a matter of philosophical curiosity and investigation.

Even in early Christianity, with its emphasis on the individual soul, there was a powerful emphasis on the spiritual community, within which that soul could discover itself and through which it could earn its salvation. Before Christianity, Judaism was far more concerned with the integrity of the Jewish community than with the isolated identity of its members; indeed, Jewish identity was identity in the community, and nothing more. Until modern times our idea of individual identity—as thinker, as existential hero, as Buddhist "Buddha-nature" or as Hesse's onion—would have been unintelligible. And today, too, when we think about the question "Who am I?" we are all too likely to forget that we are something more than our individual characteristics and talents, more than an isolated atom cut off from the community within which our existence, our characteristics, and our talents acquire their significance. What does it mean to be "attractive" or "good-looking," for instance, outside of the context of a particular society? What does it mean to be "smart," "charming," or "fun to be with" except among other people who have similar conceptions of these traits? What does it mean to be "trustworthy" or "generous" except within a community in which these traits make sense and are generally praised? In other words, most of the characteristics we ascribe to

Confucius said,
   The exemplary person seeks harmony rather than agreement; the small person does the opposite.

THE IMPORTANCE OF THE INDIVIDUAL

The view that a society of individuals, each working only with his or her own interests in mind, might collectively serve to improve society as a whole and increase the general welfare was not seriously proposed as a theory of society until 1776, when the Scot **Adam Smith** (1723–1790) published his epoch-making *Wealth of Nations*. Smith is universally considered to be the "father of capitalism" and the first great spokesman for *laissez-faire* ("leave alone") economics. Smith hypothesized that an "invisible hand" would guarantee the overall good of society through the workings of a free and competitive market. But such a market itself was not possible until modern times, when the medieval suspicion of "usury" and profit-seeking was replaced by the recognition of money-making as a legitimate activity and the desires of the individual—by way of supply and demand—would be allowed to determine what was produced and in what quantities.

ourselves as individuals already presuppose the existence of other people and our living with them.

This observation can be repeated at a deeper philosophical level, too; in our presentation of the difficulties of solipsism and the "egocentric predicament," we ended up questioning whether we are indeed directly and indubitably aware of our own self, our own mind, prior to our knowledge of the existence of other people. The first part of that question had started to come out negative; we may be aware of thoughts, but it does not follow that we are aware of ourselves as thinker, aware of the "I." How do we recognize thoughts, however? It can be argued that we recognize thoughts only because we have words and concepts that allow us to. (Ancient peoples, archaeologists tell us, did not have such words and concepts, and so could only refer to what we call "thoughts" as "voices," presumably from the gods.) But where did we get these words and concepts? From our language, which we could have learned only within a community of other people who taught us that language, who gave us that concept, who taught us to say, in effect, "I think, therefore I am"—and not to doubt it.

What this means is that we do not know of our own existence with certainty and that we know of our own existence only because we have been taught by our society to recognize our own existence. But this also means that the existence of other people is not in question; it is not a doubtful belief that needs to be backed up with a problematic and probably inadequate argument from analogy. The existence of others, along with the existence of ourselves, is in fact one of the *premises* of our thinking, not one of its doubtful conclusions. Thus the German existentialist **Martin Heidegger** says that we are originally part of a community, and "nobody" in particular, and that

Martin Heidegger (1889–1976) was a German existentialist who has had a profound influence on many European and American philosophers in this century. His best-known book is *Being and Time* (1927). The concept of "authenticity" (or "authentic self") has become popular largely because of his work.

Everyone is the other, and no one is himself. The "they" *which supplies the answer to the question of the* "who" *. . . is* "nobody."

The Self of everyday [man] is the they-self, *which we distinguish from the* authentic self, *that is, from the self which has been taken hold of in its own way.*

— *Martin Heidegger,*
Being and Time

we learn, within that community, how to be an individual, how to be "authentic" (see box below). Thus Karl Marx tells us that we are essentially social beings and gain our identity only within a society (of a particular kind) and, ultimately, within the whole context of humanity. (He called us "species-beings," beings who live and work not just for ourselves but for the whole.) Hegel wrote that we find our true identity in "spirit." So we all find, as we

Karl Marx (1818–1883) is usually thought of primarily as a social reformer and revolutionary. In fact, he was an accomplished philosopher and one of the leading economic theorists of all times. He was a student of G. W. F. Hegel (though Hegel had died just before Marx started college in Berlin) and borrowed Hegel's concept of "dialectic" as a way of understanding social evolution, through conflict and resolution. But where Hegel's main concept was "spirit," Marx emphasized the more material aspects of human life—the need for food, shelter, and security, for instance. But Marx also stressed the spiritual needs of individuals, especially art and creativity and the appreciation of nature. (He did not include religion among these "spiritual" needs, however.)

As society itself produces man as man, so it too is produced by him. Activity and mind are social in their content as well as in their origin; they are social activity and social mind. . . . The individual is the social being.

— *Karl Marx,*
manuscript of 1844

push our thinking further, that no matter how important our existence as individuals may seem to us, this individual existence gains its significance only through the larger picture of ourselves in a society, and through our relations with other people.

Self and Relationships

The essence of our relations with other people is conflict.

> — *Jean-Paul Sartre*, Being
> and Nothingness

Man is a network of relationships, and these alone matter to him.

> — *Antoine de Saint-Exupéry*

The vision we have of ourselves determines the relations we will have with others. Poets and philosophers have often written that love begins with self-love, and social critics have pointed out that hate often begins with self-hate. But it is a matter for serious reflection that in our self-absorbed, individualistic society, so much is written and said on self-realization and individual self-identity, while somewhat less has been written, at least on the same level of self-conscious philosophical profundity, on the nature of our relations with one another. Of course, we know the reason for this: Our conceptions of self are such that we tend to think that our real or essential or authentic self is ours and ours alone, while relations with other people are secondary to selfhood and, in some sense, "external." We talk about "reaching out to someone;" our poets and psychiatrists tell us about the plight of our loneliness, each of us having been born into the world alone and trying desperately to find refuge with another person through love. But if the self is social, then all of this might very well be untrue: Rather than reaching out to people, we may need to realize the bonds that are already there. And it is simply false that each of us is born into the world alone; it is a matter of biology that even our first grand entrance is staged with at least one other person (our mother), and usually the delivery room is rather crowded. The question then becomes: What is the nature of these bonds between us, with which our conception of selfhood begins?

The bonds between us are of a hundred varieties, of course—love, hate, dependency, fear, admiration, envy, shared joy or suffering, kinship, parenthood, patriotism, competition, sexual attraction, team spirit, being in jail together, running on the same political party ticket, and sitting next to each other in class. Each of these requires its own analysis and understanding. But in general, we can break our conceptions of relationships into two very broad views: "us versus them," (or "me versus them") on the one hand, "we" on the other. The first presumes some basic difference, even antagonism, between us; the second presupposes a shared identity (within which, of course, there can be any number of differences).

The first, "us versus them," view can be illustrated, as an extreme case, by most wars. There are wars, perhaps, in which one or both sides retain some sense of kinship with the other, but even in most civil wars the other side is conceived as "the enemy," and is often depicted as inhuman, barbarian, and uncivilized. On a more personal and less belligerent scale, the "us versus them" view emerges at least temporarily in competition with strangers (for the same job, for the same seat in a bus, or at a track meet). In every case, the emphasis is on the differences between sides; the presumption is usually that one person's gain is very likely another person's loss, and the self-identity of one is defined independently of or in opposition to the other.

The second view, however, takes mutual identity to be primary and differences to be secondary. There is a presumption of cooperation: What helps one will help the other, and self-identity is defined by this mutual identity. A familiar example is the sense of shared identity we have when we are playing on the same team. There are differences between us, of course; we play different positions, we have different skills and different personalities. But what is primary is the team; indeed, we have all seen how a team falls apart when individual players begin to think more of their own performance than of the performance of the team. A second example would be love, whether the love of a mother for her child, the love of a married couple, or the love of a person for a country. Love, too, is the presumption of a shared identity; a person defines self-identity in terms of the relationship (at least in part), and it is assumed that one person's interest is the other's, too. (Even when this is not the case, one person typically takes up the other's interest as his or her own.)

These two views have their roots deep in philosophy. The first can be seen quite clearly, for example, in the "problem of other minds" and the "egocentric predicament" of the solipsist, for whom all other people are literally other, actually unknowable and unreachable. There is more than a hint of solipsism, for example, in those social speakers who urge us to "escape our loneliness" and "reach out to someone." The presupposition of this popular (American) message is that we begin alone and that we desperately try to overcome this aloneness. But imagine telling that to the seventh child in an enormous tribal family. The truth is that our sense of loneliness is not universal or part of the "human condition" but an inevitable consequence of our extremely mobile and individualistic society. And yet, as we have seen, we tend to take the view that the isolated individual self is not only the real self but the only thing of which we can be absolutely certain. Not surprisingly, therefore, our view of relations with other people tends to be that knowing and relating to other people is a problem.

This view was brutally argued, for instance, by Jean-Paul Sartre in his book *Being and Nothingness* (and in many of his novels and plays). Relations with others, Sartre argued, are essentially conflict. But we can see how he must conclude that this is so. He began by defending a conception of self that is strictly individual, in which each of us tries to create ourselves in a certain image and to be authentic to ourselves. Other people, accordingly, tend to be external to this creation of self; or they serve as the instruments or raw materials for the creation of self; or they may become impossible obstacles to the creation of self. For example, other people often restrict our abilities by making their own demands and setting up expectations, and they tend therefore to interfere with our freedom of self-creation. In a relationship between a man and a woman, Sartre argued, this mutual interference and antagonism reach their pinnacle; sex and even love are but weapons in the competition for independent self-realization. Each person tries to force the other to agree with his or her conception of self. Thus all of our relations are essentially conflict, even when they seem to be perfectly pleasant and mutually agreeable. (It is worth noting that Sartre reconsidered these views later in his life, and that he himself had a lifelong and romantic relationship with Simone de Beauvoir.)

This tragic view of relationships, however, is based on a view of the individual self which itself has its problems. If we turn to the second conception of relationships, the "we" view of already existing bonds between us, we solve some of these problems and discover a much less tragic conception of relationships. We refer to this second conception, for example, when we declare that "we were made for each other," in the sense that, before we met, the connection between us had already been established. Similarly, people say "marriages are made in heaven." As a sociological theory, this is seriously challenged by current divorce statistics, but as a philosophical viewpoint, it has much to recommend it. From the moment we are born, we establish and reestablish bonds with others, not just particular people but *types* of people. Thus one adult or one teacher replaces another in our lives; one friend takes the place of another, and one boyfriend or girlfriend seems remarkably like the last. This is not to say, of course, that we are incapable of particular commitments or of sticking with a single friend or spouse, but it is to say that our relations with others are *types* of bonds which we carry from one person to another, some of which we have from infancy. Thus Freud was not being perverse when he insisted that every man falls in love with his mother and every woman falls in love with her father; the bonds and expectations and likes and dislikes that one learns as an infant stay with us through life, usually much modified and even reversed in some significant ways. But, according to this view, we are not isolated individuals searching desperately for other people; we already have networks of relationships, which are fulfilled in different ways at different times by different people. Our conception of ourselves—our self-identity—is determined in turn by these networks, without which we are ultimately nothing.

A marvelous illustration of this second view of relationships, as "made for each other," is a short story told in Plato's dialogue *The Symposium*. Asked to tell his fellow dinner guests about the nature and origins of love, the playwright Aristophanes invents a wonderful fable, in which we were all long ago "double-creatures," with two heads, four arms, four legs, and enormous intelligence and arrogance (or what the Greeks called *hubris*). To teach humans a lesson, Zeus, the king of the gods, struck the creatures down and cleft them in two—"like an apple," Aristophanes says—so that each resulting half-person now had to walk around the world, looking for his or her other half. That is the origin of love, Aristophanes concludes, not the search of one isolated individual for another, but the urge to reunite with someone who is already, as

> ### ARISTOPHANES: HOW TWO BECOME ONE
>
> *And so, when a person meets the half that is his very own, . . . then something wonderful happens: the two are struck from their senses by love, by a sense of belonging to one another, and by desire, and they don't want to be separated from one another, not even for a moment.*
>
> — *From Plato,* The Symposium

we still say, one's "other half." The fable is pure fiction, of course, but the point is profound. Relations with others do not begin when people first meet; they began, in a sense, with the very beginning of our species. The complete self, in other words, is not just the individual person. It is people *together* and, sometimes, in love.

CLOSING QUESTIONS

1. When a person says, "I think such and such . . ." is there necessarily reference to a self there, or is the word "I" simply a function of grammar? Would it make sense to say, as Bertrand Russell once suggested, that "It thinks in me" or "There is a thought here" instead?

2. In his play *No Exit,* Jean-Paul Sartre had one of his characters exclaim, "Hell is other people." What he might have had in mind is that people interfere with each other to such an extent that Hell might simply be people torturing each other forever with their comments and their gestures, just as we torture each other here on earth. Do you agree with this picture of human relationships? Why or why not?

3. If a teenager commits a crime and is sent to reform school for a few years, what justification might the individual have, twenty years later, in explaining, "I am an entirely different person now?"

4. Which aspects of your self (or self-identity) do you attribute directly to your upbringing in a particular family, in a particular society, in a particular

neighborhood or city or other environment? Which do you attribute to "nature" (that is, to instincts and inherited characteristics)? Which aspects of your self (if any) would you say are entirely your own, independent of other people and your biological nature?

5. If you were told (perhaps in a science fiction story) that a certain "person" was a robot, how could you tell?

6. Does your race signify an essential part of your self? Why or why not?

7. Does your sex constitute an essential part of your self? Why or why not?

8. Marriage is sometimes described as a "union" of two people. Sexual coupling aside, what does this mean?

9. Does a newborn baby have a self? What kinds of theories and considerations would you bring to bear on this question?

BIBLIOGRAPHY AND SUGGESTED READINGS

A good general study of the various approaches to self-identity in recent American and British philosophy can be found in John Perry, *Personal Identity* (University of California Press, 1975). An entertaining and useful discussion of the problem in dialogue form is John Perry's *Dialogue on Personal Identity and Immortality* (Hackett, 1978). The existentialist view of selfhood is classically summarized in Jean-Paul Sartre's short lecture, "Existentialism as a Humanism," in Robert C. Solomon, *Existentialism* (Random House, 1974). This anthology also includes relevant selections from Heidegger's *Being and Time* (Harper & Row, 1962). David Hume's skeptical attack on the idea of self appears in his *Treatise of Human Nature*, ed. L. A. Selby-Bigge (Oxford University Press, 1980). Aristophanes' tale is in Plato's *Symposium*, trans. A. Nehamas and P. Woodruff (Hackett, 1989). A good selection of readings on the mind-body question is David Rosenthal, *Materialism and the Mind-Body Problem* (Hackett, 1987). A contemporary account of the self in "cognitive science" is Owen Flanagan, *Self Expressions* (Oxford, 1996).

CHAPTER SEVEN
FREEDOM

John Trumbull, The Declaration of Independence, *detail,* © *Yale University Art Gallery.*

FREEDOM

*In short, the actions of man are never free;
they are always the necessary consequence of
his temperament, of the received ideas, and of
the notions, either true or false, which he has
formed to himself of happiness. . . .*

— *Baron Paul Henri d'Holbach,* System of
Nature

*One's own free unfettered choice, one's own
fancy, however wild it may be, one's own
fancy worked up at times to frenzy. That is the
"most advantageous advantage" which is
always overlooked.*

— *Feodor Dostoevsky,* Notes from the
Underground

OPENING QUESTIONS

1. It is one of the main themes of our literature and folklore that freedom (or liberty) is one of the few things worth fighting for, even dying for. What does this mean? Describe a set of circumstances in which you would accept this as true. Describe a set of circumstances in which you would not accept this as true. What are the important differences between the two cases?

2. Most of what you do and say reflects the influences, training, education, examples, and rules that have affected you all your life. Some of these come from your parents; there were prejudices and preferences taught to you when you were very young, so that you have never even been able to consider the alternatives. Some have been imposed on you by force (through threat of punishment or nonacceptance), while other people have subtly influenced you through television, magazines, and other forms of mass communication. Does all this make your actions and decisions any less "free"? To what extent would you be more free if you

could get outside of all these influences and make decisions without them?

3. Have you ever made a decision that was *entirely* your own? Describe it.

4. We often talk about a person in love being "captive" to that emotion; is this possible? Is a person who acts out of love less free than a person who acts out of deliberate reasoning?

5. If a person commits a serious crime, but is wholly determined or caused to do so by his or her upbringing, by criminal influences, or by drugs, should he or she be held responsible for the crime? Should society be held responsible? Friends? The drug dealer? Should anyone be held responsible? Or is that just "the way things had to happen"?

6. Is freedom necessary for living the good life in a good society? Can you imagine circumstances in which freedom would be undesirable, or at least irrelevant? Is giving people freedom *always* giving them something good?

7. Is a person alone more free than a person bound by obligations to other people? Is it true, as our love songs often say, that breaking up a relationship is "being free again"? Is a person caught up in a web of duties and obligations at work necessarily less free than a person who, by choice, does not work at all?

FREEDOM AND THE GOOD LIFE

"Give me liberty, or give me death," cried the early American patriot Patrick Henry. Most of us, too—whether or not we would go quite so far—believe that freedom is one of the most important things in the world. It is not only an ingredient of but the presupposition of the good life; indeed, it may itself be the good life. It is possible to live our life fighting for freedom, and there are few things that we would say are more important to fight for. And on a deeper philosophical level, freedom seems to be not only the presupposition of the good life; it also seems to be the logical prerequisite for morality and moral responsibility. If we were not free to act as we choose—whether rightly or wrongly—then holding us responsible for what we do would not seem to make any sense, nor would there be much point in imposing upon us those moral rules and principles that tell us what we ought to do. After all, we do not praise or blame a person for obeying the law of gravity, nor do we see any point in telling a person that he or she ought to do so. "Ought implies can," wrote Immanuel Kant in his discussion of moral philosophy and freedom. Without freedom there could be no morality. Without freedom, we often say, life would hardly be worth living at all.

And yet all of this becomes quite perplexing when we start to look beyond the word "freedom." The word itself inspires us to praise and hyperbole. Someone says "liberty" and we stand up and salute. But how important is this freedom, and what is it? These are questions we rarely examine. Furthermore, there is a powerful argument, much of which we have already accepted, that would seem to take as its conclusion the view that there can be no human freedom of choice or action. This view is called **determinism**. The argument, quite simply, follows from the tenet we have called the **principle of universal causality** (see Chapter 4)—namely, the universal necessity that every event must have its explanatory causes. But if human decisions and actions are events, then it follows that they, too, must have their explanatory causes. But if an action or a decision is caused (which is to say, brought about, or determined beforehand, by earlier events or conditions), then how could it possibly be free? What would it mean to say that we have a "choice"?

Before we examine this troublesome matter in some detail, let's first raise two questions too rarely raised in our constant adulation of freedom. Why is freedom so important to us? And what is "freedom"?

Why Is Freedom So Important to Us?

We posit freedom and slavery as opposites. We imagine a polarity and think that liberty represents the one extreme and slavery the other. That makes the case for freedom categorical and simple. Who wants to be a slave? But is the difference between the master and his slave simply that one has freedom which the other lacks? Doesn't the master live in a mansion, and the slave in quarters? Doesn't the slave toil while the other drinks mint julep? Doesn't the master wield the whip that cuts the other's back? A preference for the master's life proves very little about freedom.

— *Frithjof Bergmann,* On Being Free

"Freedom"—the word, that is—excites almost everyone, but it can mean almost anything. We generally define "freedom" as the absence of all (unreasonable) restraint in our movements, our speech, our beliefs, and our activities. But is simply being left alone the same thing as freedom? Is being alone in the desert being free? And what is to count as an "unreasonable" restraint? If we think of almost any controversial social issue—particularly those involving drug-taking, sex, or other personal activities—the vagueness of this question becomes painfully obvious.

In his book *On Being Free,* Frithjof Bergmann outlined what he called our "schizophrenic view of freedom." The first side of this is the familiar view that freedom is "wonderful." It is what gives human beings distinguished status and separates us from nature *and* it is assumed to be the goal of everyone, in every society, even those who do not know the word and have never thought

Do We want the Illusion, Not the Fact, of Freedom?

The Grand Inquisitor is talking to Christ, just returned:

"Didn't you often tell them that You wanted to make them free? Well then," the old man added with a grin, "now you see before you free men. Yes, that business cost us a great deal," he continued, looking sternly at Him. . . . "For fifteen hundred years we were pestered by that notion of freedom, but in the end we succeeded in getting rid of it for good. . . . And I want you to know that on this very day men are convinced that they are freer than they have ever been, although they themselves have brought to us their freedom and put it meekly at our feet."

— *Feodor Dostoevsky,*
The Brothers
Karamazov

about being free. The urge to be free is not to be questioned; the value of freedom is absolute, even more important than life itself. But notice that this view already poses a dilemma: It says both that we are *already* (by nature) free and that we *aspire* to be free. (Rousseau: "Man is born free, and yet everywhere he is in chains.") We might thus distinguish *intrinsic* freedom, or our natural "free will," and *extrinsic* freedom, the freedom for which we must fight. The second view, however, is that freedom is dreadful, and that we want nothing more than to escape from it. It is terrifying to have to make decisions that will affect one's entire life—choosing a college, selecting a marriage partner, deciding whether or not to join the army. And so we feel relieved (or, at least, part of us does) when someone else makes the choice or, better, "fate" steps in and makes it for us. The existentialist Jean-Paul Sartre and the psychiatrist Erich Fromm have both argued, for example, that we all try to "escape from freedom"; we find it too painful. We retreat to the unquestioning obedience of authority; we fall into what Sartre called "bad faith" (see p. 192). The example Bergmann gave is the story of the Grand Inquisitor in Dostoevsky's novel *The Brothers Karamazov*. Jesus finally returns to earth, but he is arrested by the Grand Inquisitor, who is also head of the Christian church. The cause of the arrest is that Jesus offered freedom; the Inquisitor recognizes that what people really want is authority and mystery, and so he has given them the church. The people are left with the *word* "freedom," of course, but what they are taught is obedience and servitude.

Imagine a life in a very happy little village. Everyone is born into a role, which he or she will assume for life, with certain stages appropriate to his or her age. Everyone knows his or her identity; everyone knows what he or she is expected to do. Life is sufficiently full to prevent boredom; it is sufficiently

[In Yoruba philosophy,] *the most important element of personhood is the* ori *or "inner head." . . . The ori determines one's fate, and, contrary to most alternative cultural accounts of the soul, the Yoruba actually* chooses *his ori. In the creation myth* Ajala, *the "potter of heads," provides each body with a head. But before a person arrives on earth, he or she must go to the house of* Ajala *to choose a head. To make matters more complicated,* Ajala *has a reputation for being irresponsible and careless. As a result,* Ajala *molds many bad heads; he sometimes forgets to fire some, misshapes others, and overburns still others. Because it is said that he owes money to many people,* Ajala *commonly hides in the ceiling to avoid creditors and neglects some of the heads he put on the fire, leaving them to burn. When a person gets to* Ajala*'s storehouse of heads, he or she does not know which heads are bad or good—all people choose heads in ignorance. If a person picks a bad head, he or she is doomed to failure in life. Yet, if a person picks a really good head, the person is destined to have a good, prosperous life. With hard work, he or she will surely be successful, since little or no energy need be expended in costly head repairs.*

> — *From Jacqueline Trimier, "African Philosophy"*

luxurious to prevent scarcity and selfish infighting. What would "freedom" mean in such a society? What would be the *value* of freedom in such a situation? And if a ship of European sailors were to land on the island and destroy the structure and the harmony of this little village, force its members to make hard choices and restructure their lives in accordance with what we call "freedom," would this necessarily have to be considered an improvement in their lives? Is freedom necessarily a boon? Or consider a person who has just been fired, whose employer says, "Now you are free to do what you want with your daytime hours." If this is freedom, what is so good about it? Unless the job in question was utterly intolerable, is there any virtue at all in this newfound freedom?

These examples, of course, are biased to present freedom in the worst possible light. But such examples are necessary in order to balance the examples of the other kind, in which people who are generally miserable and oppressed, who are abused by some powerful conquerors, or some insufferable king or queen, revolt in the name of "freedom." The emancipation of the slaves in the southern states in 1865 did not make life immediately better for many ex-slaves. The lack of freedom within many religious communities has not been considered a terrible disadvantage or an inhuman situation—at least, not by those members who conform to their sect's basic beliefs and practices.

Indeed, from this perverse perspective, one might argue that the history of America exhibits the breakdown of family and community values in which obedience and conformity is presupposed; the emergence of "freedom" of personal choice has threatened and sometimes destroyed the peaceful harmony of the conformist community. This argument would seem to us to contradict everything that we in the United States have ever claimed to stand for; but today it is argued persuasively in the name of "American values" and "freedom." And here we have the same dilemma again, hidden by the word "freedom": Do we in fact want freedom above all things? Or is it the case that freedom is often destructive, undesirable, and unwanted? Is it true that the basic value of American life is "freedom"? Or is it rather the case that the basic values of American life are community values and the virtues of moral conformity? Despite familiar rhetoric, these are not the same values—in fact, they seem to be directly opposed to each other. Is it possible, then, for us to want both of them?

What is Freedom?

When people are free to do as they please, they usually imitate each other.

— *Eric Hoffer*

Part of the problem in defining freedom and trying to say what is so good about it is that freedom is so often a negative concept; it is a reaction *against* something, and what that "something" happens to be can be known only in a particular context. When a people are suffering daily under an oppressive and unreasonable government, or when an adolescent suffers through six dreary hours of classes that he or she is forced to attend, the meaning of the word "freedom" is clear: It means "free *from.*" If taxes are imposed and we pay them unwillingly, then relief from taxes would be a form of freedom. If we are prevented by government forces from speaking our opinions or practicing our religion, then our right to speak or our right to worship would be freedom.

What is far more difficult are the cases in which there is no evident oppressor and no obvious suffering, or in which there is no clear context and nothing definite to react against. It is not at all clear, to return to the example above of the little village, that a happy population has been made "free" if we destroyed the life within which its members were most content. Or we may say, if we wish, that people who have just been fired are "free," but the context doesn't really justify this conclusion. The former employees did not want to lose their jobs; there is nothing else they want to do instead. They may be free *from* the demands of that particular job, but it is not at all clear what they are free *to do.* And it simply will not do to say, "They are free to do anything." First, this is obviously false. (None of us has that much freedom.) Second, it is probably true that "free to do anything" is a fraudulent way of talking about not having the faintest idea what to do; or in the words of one popular song, "Freedom's just another word for nothing left to lose."

THREE FREEDOMS

It is by the goodness of God that in our country we have those three unspeakably precious things: freedom of speech, freedom of conscience, and the prudence never to practice either of them.

— *Mark Twain*

The question of context gives rise to the suggestion that freedom cannot be thought of simply as "freedom *from*" some undesirable imposition, power, or rule, but as freedom *to do* or *have* something as well. People seek freedom *from* an oppressive government in order to form a government for themselves. The unhappy adolescent in class wants to be free from school in order to play baseball, or to go fishing, or to just lie around in the sun. These two notions of freedom, freedom *from* and freedom *to do* something, have been called (since the eighteenth century) **negative freedom** and **positive freedom**. They always go together; the one always presupposes the other, even if only one is actually stated. Indeed, it is unthinkable that people would overthrow their government, no matter how intolerable, if they had no idea, however dim, about what they would do to replace it. And it is unimaginable that the adolescent would so desperately want to be free from school if he or she had no idea, however vague, of doing something else instead.

We can see now how it is that such different definitions of freedom have emerged in politics and history; the fascist who claims that freedom is obedience to the state is actually just giving us the positive notion of freedom and

On negative freedom:
The history of liberty is the history of resistance . . . the history of the limitation of governmental power.

— *Woodrow Wilson*

On positive freedom:
Whoever refuses to obey the general will [of the people] shall be constrained to do so by the whole society; this means nothing else than that he shall be forced to be free.

— *Jean-Jacques Rousseau,* The Social Contract

leaving out the negative notion. (If you think of a Catholic in a Protestant country who is not allowed to obey the authority of the Catholic church without being persecuted, for example, you can see how this idea of being free *to* obey can be perfectly acceptable to us.) The civil libertarian, on the other hand, emphasizes the negative notion of freedom—as in the fight to be free from racial or political discrimination—but sometimes fails to mention the positive notion. But leaving out the positive notion of freedom too easily leads to the absurdity of people demanding freedom from everything with no positive idea what they want that freedom for. A person who demands **absolute freedom** of speech, for example, may not be thinking about what restraints may be required on speech. Yelling "Fire!" in a crowded theater may be asserting that person's absolute freedom from any restraint whatsoever, but it is not at all clear that there is any defensible claim for his or her freedom *to do* anything. And if we are looking only at the negative freedom *from* interference by government agencies and other people, this leads us to the absurd conclusion that the person who is most free is the person out in the middle of the desert, who is safely out of range of government interference and any restraints from other people. Of course, we might insist that this person also be free *from want,* but that is saying only that he or she is free *to have* the necessities for human survival, which, for most of us, include human companionship and an orderly society as well as food, water, and shelter.

The force we seek to be free *from* is often more obvious to us than what we want to be free *to do.* It is easy to be so caught up in fighting against something that the alternative, what you are fighting for, becomes neglected, or becomes reduced to a buzzword, like "freedom," whose content has not been thought about at all. What makes this particularly difficult is that most of us feel that, whatever we are fighting against, what we are usually fighting for is in some sense our self, for a chance to improve ourselves, a chance to be what we want to be. But as we saw in an earlier chapter, what counts as our self is not always so obvious either.

If what we mean by "self" is an isolated individual self, then freedom will tend to be freedom *from* other people and society, whatever it is that we want to be free *to do.* Thus we get the idea that freedom to "find yourself" is often obtained by "getting away from it all"—in other words, by a purely negative freedom. On the other hand, if we understand by "self" a social entity that depends for its very existence on our relationships with other people, then what will count as freedom will necessarily involve our relationships with others, and the person who is alone, in this sense, would not be free at all. If, with the Buddhists, we see the "self" as an illusion, freedom will tend to mean freedom *from* this illusion, and a consequent freedom *to* realize ourselves as being a part of "Buddha-nature." If we continue to think of our self as being essentially consciousness, then freedom will tend to mean the development of consciousness—and this indeed is what freedom has tended to mean most often in our Western tradition. But even this is too simple, for there are many aspects of consciousness, not all of them equally our "self."

For example, suppose we identify our self with our feelings about other people, our social attachments, and our sense of ourselves as social beings.

Our concept of freedom, accordingly, will be such that we are most free when we are acting those roles and participating in those relationships. We will be less free if we are prevented from performing those roles, or if we are prevented from being with our friends. People in love will not feel "free" when they are away from their beloved, no matter what else they can do, because what counts as essential to their self-identity is that one relationship. A traveler in a foreign country may be totally free from any expectations or responsibilities, or from interference from other people, but if he or she identifies self with friendship—and no friends are around—it makes no sense to call the individual "free." Freedom, in such a conception of self as social, is the freedom *to* participate in society and the freedom *from* factors that would prevent this. We can call this *social* freedom.

More generally, we can say that freedom depends upon self-identity—namely, those aspects of a person with which he or she identifies and defines the self (see Chapter 6). Consider this alternative view of self, and consequently, of freedom. A person thinks of the true self as the rational self. (Plato would be a good example.) A person acts freely, then, whenever he or she acts in accordance with reason, does what he or she has *decided* to do after careful thought and deliberation. The same person would consider an act less than free, on the other hand, if it were a mere whim or sudden desire, an outburst of emotion or obedience to the urgings of a friend or authorities (assuming, that is, that the person had not already decided that obeying this friend or authority was the rational thing to do). People with such a rational conception of themselves will consider action most free when it has been carefully planned and thoroughly thought out; the less the planning and the thinking, the less free the action and the less it is an expression of the person's true self. This is *rational* freedom.

Yet another example would be of a person who identified most with his or her emotions. People in love would consider themselves most free when acting out of love, even if, on psychological analysis, those actions could be called "compulsive" and even if, according to more rational-minded friends, such obedience to emotion is the very antithesis of freedom. And individuals who so value their emotions will not feel free if forced to suppress violent feelings of anger, but will feel free when they "let it out." For such people, the expression of emotion—whatever emotion—is freedom; being unable, or not being allowed to express emotions, even under the respectable guise of "being reasonable," would seem like being deprived of freedom. This is *emotional* freedom.

Finally, there is the most perplexing example, which Bergmann discusses at great length, based on a most curious character in Dostoevsky's *Notes from the Underground*. The bizarre hero of that short novel considers freedom to be the most important thing in human life. In fact, not only is his notion of freedom based on his sense of self-identity, but his self-identity *is* his conception of his freedom. He is really himself only when he is acting completely freely. But the problem is this: Whenever he acts in accordance with other people's demands, he does not feel free, so he shuns other people and spends much of his time entirely alone. But neither does he believe that acting according to reason is acting freely, since reason is in fact a system of thinking imposed on us by our society. In acting rationally, in other words, we are actually following the demands of other people, and so we are not free. But neither are we free when we act out of emotion, for our emotions do not seem to be products of our reasoning but of forces within us, which are created not only by society and circumstances but by our animal nature. Then what *does* count as a free action? Dostoevsky's perverse answer is, acting entirely on whim, for no reason whatsoever. It is *capricious* freedom. But even acting entirely on whim, how does one know that one is indeed the sole author of one's own action? How does one know that the expectations of society or the hereditary workings of one's brain have not in fact caused this particular whim, which thereby is not one's own at all? One cannot know, and so Dostoevsky's pathetic character becomes in fact totally paralyzed in his actions, since he can never know for certain whether they are truly his own free actions or not.

The philosophical principle here is not unfamiliar to us. It is the idea that there is behind all our more superficial aspects some pure inner self—not our thoughts, emotions, or desires but the self itself. And acting out of this pure self is what constitutes the true nature of freedom. Thus Christianity teaches us that true freedom is giving up the worldly interests we have and focusing wholly on our inner souls. Thus philosophers such as Sartre tell us that consciousness itself is pure freedom, which means not only freedom *to act* in any number of different ways but freedom *from* determination by all other influences—those of other people and those of our own reason, our emotions, and our desires as well. But here we come to our troublesome philosophical argument about the principle that every event has its explanatory causes. If there is a cause for every event, and therefore for every action, what could it mean to say, as Dostoyevsky and Sartre insist, that a truly free action is one that is wholly undetermined by anything but the pure self, which in turn is not determined by anything else? With this question, we enter into one of the most difficult problems in philosophy, the so-called free will problem.

FREE WILL AND DETERMINISM

Correctly conceived, the doctrine called Philosophical Necessity is simply this: that, given the motives which are present to an individual's mind, and given likewise the character and disposition of the individual, the manner in which we will act might be unerringly inferred; that if we knew the person thoroughly, and knew all the inducements which are acting upon him, we could foretell his conduct with as much certainty as we can predict any physical event.

— *John Stuart Mill,* A System of Logic

"The murderer had been raised in a slum. His father abandoned him when he was seven months old; he was beaten by his older siblings and constantly abused by his mother. He never had the chance to attend school; he never could get or hold a job. By the time he robbed the store, he was near starvation, addicted to hard drugs, without friends and without help of any kind. His sister said, 'I've known since he was a child that he would do this some day.' His mother complained, 'I don't understand!' The prosecutor called it a 'cold-blooded, premeditated act.' The defense accused the whole of society, claiming that it had, through its neglect as well as its negative conditioning, made this man an inevitable killer." We know the rest of the arguments: what we don't know is their resolution. Should a man be held responsible for an act for which he has been conditioned the whole of his life? Or must we not hold out that, no matter what the circumstances, he could have resisted, he could have decided not to commit the crime, and therefore he must be held responsible?

DETERMINISM IN THE NEWS

The way lawyer John Badger* saw it, he was giving the judge a chance to "follow the flow into the brotherhood of man" by entertaining the notion that his client's life of crime was ordained by the stars.

But Circuit Judge Ruben Costa, who said he was "inclined to believe there is a certain verity" to astrology, threw out the proposed defense at a pretrial hearing Monday for twenty-three-year-old John Matthew Gopel, who is charged with rape, robbery, and assault.

Badger had planned to argue that Gopel was insane by virtue of his astrological destiny.

Badger said his client, born at 8:14 P.M., on August 8, 1956, was literally "a born loser."

"There is a force in the life of this young man that forced him to go on transmission fluid, sniff gasoline, cocaine, anything he could get his hands on," he said.

Badger said he intended to present testimony from astrologers, scientists, and mental health experts, as well as a bartender who would describe the effects of the full moon on human behavior.

The list of defense evidence included the song "When You Wish Upon a Star," Spiderman comic books, and the plays King Lear *and* Hamlet.

> — *From a news article
> that appeared
> around the nation
> in April 1980*

*All names in this article have been changed to protect the individuals involved.

Are we cogs in the universe? Are we pawns of the fates? People have often thought so. Most of the ancient Greeks believed that our destinies were already decided for us; no matter what our actions, the outcome was settled. Powerful movements in Christianity have taught that God has predetermined or at least knows in advance every action we will perform, as well as our ultimate chances for salvation. And today most people believe that a person's actions and character are the causal result of genes and upbringing, and perhaps also the result of unconscious fears and desires that may never be recognized. Then, too, astrology and other theories of external determination have always been popular, and we can see why they would be. The more our actions are the results of other forces and not our own doing the less we need feel responsible for them, and the less we need worry about deciding what to do. It is already decided, and not by us.

The form of the determinist argument is a syllogism, the premises of which seem beyond doubt:

> Every event has its explanatory cause.
> Every human choice or action is an event.
> Therefore, every human choice or action has its explanatory cause.

Then, by a second syllogism:

> Every human choice or action has its explanatory cause.
> To have explanatory causes is not to be free.
> Therefore, no human choice or action is free.

This also means that there are no choices. If a person can choose only one course of action, and if there are no alternatives that he or she (given the explanatory causes) *can* choose, then it makes no sense to say that the person has a choice. To have a choice means to be able to do either *A* or *B*. To have chosen *A* means that one could have chosen *B*. According to the determinist, even if I (seem to) make a choice between *A* and *B*, what I choose is already determined by causes, including those involved in my character and the process of deliberation. On the other hand, one might want to reply that one could have done otherwise *if* one's character, motives, and deliberations had been different. This retains the determinist's insistence that the choice is caused by antecedent conditions but retains, too, the idea that the person certainly has something to do with the choice. But it would make no sense to suppose that a person could have chosen otherwise if everything else (character, the rest) stayed exactly the same. We sometimes talk of a "free choice," as opposed to a choice made under coercion, but if either is a choice at all, it must be "free" in the sense that one could have chosen otherwise (whatever the cost). If a man holds a gun to my head and forces me to give him my wallet, I have nonetheless freely chosen; I could have chosen to fight and be shot. But this is only to say that some free choices are made under conditions that make some alternatives extremely foolish. It doesn't affect the question of freedom.

But if it is true that every choice or action is fully **determined** (that is, brought about by earlier events and conditions) and fully explainable (if only one knows enough about the earlier events and conditions), then even the most obvious case of a "free choice" would not be free, and would not be a choice at all. It is as if someone said to you, "O.K., here is *A;* there is no *B* or *C.* Now choose." But if the whole of our history, our genetic makeup, our education, the influence of our parents, our "character," and the workings of our brains already predispose us to make choice *A* rather than any other, if our makeup is such that we could not choose any other, then all of our talk about "choice" and "decision"—and therefore "responsibility," too—amounts to just so much nonsense. We may have the *experience* of making a choice, but we never do. Indeed, the experience is just another event in the causal chain, brought about by earlier conditions and just as predictably leading on to other effects in our behavior.

Determinism, therefore, is the theory that every event in the universe, including every human action, has its natural explanatory causes; given certain earlier conditions, then an event will take place necessarily, according to the laws of nature. But we must fill out the determinist's premise by at least one more step. It is not enough to say, "every event has its natural explanatory cause(s)," since this would leave open the possibility that, although every event requires certain earlier events and conditions in order to take place, the event might still be a matter of chance, at least to some extent, or a matter of human choice. In other words, it might be that the earlier events and conditions limit the possibilities, but do not fully determine them. We must say, therefore, that "every event has its *sufficient* natural explanatory cause(s)." *Sufficient* means capable of bringing the event about by itself. Then there is no room for chance, no room for choice and no room for human freedom. Without choice, there can be no freedom, and without freedom, there is no reason to hold a person responsible for his action, no matter how virtuous or how vicious it might be. According to the determinist thesis, we can barely be said to be "acting" at all, for our "actions" are nothing but the result of conditions and laws of nature which leave no room for our "doing something" at all.

Determinism versus Indeterminism

Why should we accept the determinist's premise? Without it, determinism cannot get to first base. Well, in earlier chapters we have already seen the arguments traditionally advanced, even by philosophers who are not themselves determinists. The most general argument is that only by assuming from the outset that every event has its sufficient natural explanatory cause(s) can we ever understand anything. A much stronger argument was made by Kant, who said that the basic rule of determinism, the principle of universal causation, is one of the rules by which we must interpret every experience. But even Hume, who denied that this principle can be justified either through reason or through experience, insisted that it is a "natural habit" or custom that is indispensable to us and that we could not give up even if we wanted to. The consensus, then, has been that the principle itself is inescapable.

Without the assumption that every event has its sufficient natural explanatory cause(s), human knowledge would seem to be without one of its most vital presuppositions. Not only scientific research but even our most ordinary everyday beliefs would be forced to an intolerable skeptical standstill. Our every experience would be unintelligible, and our universe would appear to be nothing but a disconnected stream of incoherent happenings, from which nothing could be predicted and nothing understood. So the answer to the question, "Why should we accept the determinist's premise?" seems to be. "We cannot give it up; how could we possibly do without it?" For no matter how it is rephrased or philosophically altered, the assumption that every event in the universe, including our own actions, can be explained and understood, if only we know enough about it and its earlier events and conditions, is a presupposition of all human thinking that we cannot imagine doing without.

But even if the determinist's premise seems undeniable, it is not yet clear how we are to understand that premise. Many philosophers would defend determinism only as predictability on the basis of probability. To say that every event is determined, according to this view, means only that it is predictable if we know enough about earlier conditions. But it has been objected, against the determinist, that the fact of such predictability is not sufficient to defend determinism. It is one thing to say that all events, including human actions, are actually caused or compelled by physical forces. It is something quite different to say that all events, including human actions, are predictable. They might be predictable, for example, only on the basis of certain statistical probabilities. "Most people in this circumstance would do that." "The odds are for it," in other words. Or, in the case of human actions, the predictability might still be the result of human choices; we can predict each other's actions because we know how we would probably choose in the same circumstances. But there is no need here to talk about "causes" or compulsions. Nor, it has been argued, should we even talk any longer about "determinism," if this is all that we mean by it.

This antideterminist thesis has been called by the name **indeterminism**. Indeterminism is the explicit rejection of determinism, the view that determinism is false, and that not every event has a cause. The advantages of this theory are obvious, for it would seem that, as soon as we allow that there are some events that are uncaused, human actions might be among them. And that means that we can be held properly responsible for our actions and not simply explain them by appealing to certain antecedent conditions. But is the indeterminist thesis plausible?

The indeterminist argument has recently received a boost from physics, the very science that gave rise to the determinist threat in the first place. It was Newtonian physics that gave determinism its strongest claims. The French

Newtonian philosopher Pierre-Simon de Laplace boasted that if he knew the location and motion of every particle in the universe, he could predict every future state of the universe at any time. But it has been shown in recent physics that such knowledge is impossible. One of the most important discoveries of modern physics says that we cannot know both the location and the momentum of a subatomic particle. In coming to know the one, we make it impossible for us to know the other at the same time. From this principle, the British physicist-philosopher Sir Arthur Eddington advanced the indeterminist argument, that determinism is false on physical grounds. Every event in the universe is not predictable. And furthermore, many scientists now agree, on the basis on such considerations, that the concept of "cause" does not apply to certain subatomic particles either. According to the Heisenberg Uncertainty Principle (named after Werner Heisenberg, the German mathematician who discovered it), there is enormous uncertainty in the measurement of anything as tiny as an electron. Although one can ascertain the position of the particle, its motion will be unknown. Or one can measure its motion and not be able to know its position. So this means, on a subatomic level, that it is impossible to predict what the future is. Thus Laplace's bold conjecture that he could predict the entire future of the universe if only he knew the present position and motion of every particle was an empty gesture. He could not know this. But does this refute determinism, or does it simply show that we cannot predict what may in fact be determined? Indeterminists use Heisenberg's principle to argue that the determinist premise, that "every event in the universe has its sufficient explanatory natural cause," is false. Some events, namely those involving some subatomic particles, are not caused, not predictable, and therefore not determined, by any interpretation. And since all events and objects involve subatomic particles as their basic constituents, it can therefore be argued that no event is caused or strictly predictable, or determined. But to be caused and to be predictable are not the same thing. And, of course, the indeterminacy/uncertainty thesis applies only to events with subatomic dimensions. For *macro* events—a person making a decision about whether or not to marry, for example—we can cite the causes and make predictions with a large degree of success, but only, according to these modern physical theories, with a high degree of statistical probability. But if this means that causal explanations are, ultimately, not in order and if not all events are determined, then perhaps human actions are not determined but free.

The object of indeterminism is to deny the determinist position in order to make room for human freedom. But there are, unfortunately, two serious objections to this indeterminist argument.

First, even if we suppose that the conclusions of modern physical ("quantum") theory are correct (a matter still in dispute among physicists), it is clear that determinism is of importance to us primarily as a theory of macroscopic bodies (that is, of visible size—people, trees, cars), not subatomic particles. And no one has ever concluded that quantum theory and modern physics actually refute Newton's theories. It might be true that it is impossible to predict

The Heisenberg Uncertainty Principle:
We can know the position of a particle but not be able to determine its motion.

We can know the motion of a particle but not be able to determine its position.

Therefore, we cannot predict its future states.

what a subatomic particle in our bodies might do. But it does not follow that it is impossible to predict what our bodies will do. Falling out of a plane, we still fall at exactly the same speed as a sack of potatoes. And that is all that determinists need to continue their attack on our conception of freedom.

Second, even if there should be such indeterminism, indeterminism is not the same as freedom. Suppose, all of a sudden, your legs started moving and you found yourself kicking a fire hydrant; surely this is not what we mean by a "free action." Freedom means, at least, that we are free to choose what we shall do and that our decisions are effective. Indeterminism robs us of our freedom; therefore, just as much as determinism. And the argument against determinism, in any case, is not yet sufficiently persuasive to allow for the indeterminist's conclusions.

On the other hand, while indeterminacy in the motion of subatomic particles may not help us understand how freedom of the will is possible, the acceptance of indeterminacy by scientists does have philosophical significance. When the scientific view of things was thoroughly deterministic, those who defended the idea of free will clearly contradicted the scientific attitude; they could, therefore, reasonably be accused of being anti-scientific. But the acceptance of indeterminacy has required scientists to limit their predictions, at least in some spheres, to statements of probability. This kind of probabilistic prediction is much closer to the sort of prediction we can and do make about people without thereby denying the possibility of individual freedom. We can safely predict, for instance, that a higher proportion of people from affluent backgrounds will attend college than will people from economically deprived backgrounds, or that people from this latter category are more likely to spend time in prison. We even quantify such predictions, saying, on the basis of a person's class, race, or sex, what his or her chances are of eventually living past sixty-five, owning a home, having more than three children, committing a crime, or being addicted to cigarettes. This way of describing groups of people resembles probabilistic reasoning in the physical sciences. It is perfectly scientific. But it allows us to maintain in the case of each individual person within a given group that what they do is not determined for them but is, to some extent at least, up to them.

The Role of Consciousness

Determinism is true of us as physical bodies. But, you might insist, we are not just physical bodies, we are also conscious. We can make decisions. We have a will of our own. Whatever we are besides physical bodies, our physical bodies are still subject to all of the laws of Newtonian physics. You can see the problem. If our bodies are just cogs in the universe, what does it matter whether we are conscious or not? Our bodies are composed of bits of matter, various molecules undergoing chemical interactions and acted upon by the various laws of physics. No one can deny that they are subject to all the laws of physical nature. But once all the parts are determined in their various movements and activities, what is left for consciousness to do?

There are two possible replies to this problem, but both seem to support the determinist position and leave us without the freedom we are trying to find room for. Suppose one insists that consciousness, unlike our physical bodies, is not part of the scheme of determinism? Consciousness, unlike our bodies, is free, free to make decisions, free to choose what to do. But if our bodies are determined in their movements, then what can consciousness do, even if it is "free"? Whatever consciousness decides, it cannot have any possible effect on the movements of our bodies; in other words, it cannot affect our actions. Every human action has its sufficient natural explanatory causes apart from consciousness. And so consciousness can make no difference whatsoever. If consciousness could intrude on the physical order of causes and effects, that would seem to violate the most basic physical laws (e.g., the conservation of energy). Here we return to the mind-body problem. What is their relationship? How can the one affect the other?

Most determinists, however, would probably not agree with the idea that any event, even a nonphysical event such as an act of consciousness, could be "outside" the determinism of nature. Most determinists would argue that our thoughts and feelings, even our decisions, are caused by the states of our brains and nervous systems. Our "decisions" are nothing but the conscious effects of complex causal antecedents, most of which we still don't understand, but definitely part of the deterministic scheme of things. Consciousness itself might be a cause of our behavior—including the "decisions" we (seem to) make—but since consciousness itself is caused by earlier events and conditions, this does not make us free. At most, it explains why we might *think* that we are free. (Indeed, the thought that we are free may itself be wholly determined by earlier events and conditions—including the fact that we have always been taught to think of ourselves as free.) Here again, we meet the objection that unless there is a set of (at least two) alternatives from which we can choose, the apparent "choice" is not a choice at all. Deciding to go to the movies is a decision only if it is possible that you choose either to go or not to go. If you are already determined by earlier events and conditions to go, then there is no decision, no matter how long you spend "deliberating" whether to go or not. Thus the determinist concludes, presumably because he himself had no choice but to do so.

> **Determinism**: the position that every event has a cause (including human thoughts and decisions) and is fully governed by the laws of nature. We are neither free nor responsible for our actions.
>
> **Indeterminism**: the position that it is not true that every event has a cause. Some events, possibly human decisions, are free.
>
> **Compatibilism**: determinism is true, but this does not mean that we are not free and responsible for our actions.

"Soft" Determinism

There have been many attempts, needless to say, to slip around determinism and defend the existence of free choices and actions. The basic principle of determinism seems too undeniable to give up, but the need to hold people responsible for their actions is also too important to give up. Thus there has developed a series of views which accept the determinist thesis and try to show that free will and determinism are compatible: These positions are sometimes called **compatibilism**. But in the history of the debate over free will and determinism, a more personal name has evolved for those who accept determinism but refuse to accept its harsh conclusion; such philosophers have come to be called "**soft**" **determinists** (as opposed to the "hard" determinists, who accept both determinism and the implication that we are not free or morally responsible). Soft determinists defend compatibilism in a number of ways. Two of them are worth mentioning in particular:

1. Even if we accept the determinist thesis, it can be argued, we can still believe in freedom. In fact, we *must* believe in freedom, because we can never know all the earlier events and conditions that brought about a particular decision or action. It may be true that *if* we knew everything, we could predict a person's actions with certainty (or at least, a very high probability). But this big "if," which is the heart of the determinist thesis, turns out to be unobtainable in practice; so while in theory we can be determinists, in practice we can continue to believe in free will and hold people responsible for their actions.

2. Even if we accept the determinist thesis, we can still distinguish between those causes that make a person's action free and those that make it unfree. There have been a great many suggestions of this kind. Aristotle long ago claimed that an act would be called "free" if it was not performed (a) from "external compulsion" (the "actor" was pushed or forced) *or* (b) out of ignorance (the "actor" didn't know what he or she was doing). Some philosophers have said that an act is free if it is caused by reason; others have said that it is free if it is caused by consciousness or by the will. David Hume, who was a soft determinist, believed that we could say that an act was free if it followed from a person's "charac-

"SOFT" DETERMINISM: HUME

Men are not blamed for such actions as they perform ignorantly and casually, whatever may be the consequences. Why? but because the principles of these actions are only momentary, and terminate in them alone. Men are less blamed for such actions as they perform hastily and unpremeditatedly than for such as proceed from deliberation. For what reason? but because a hasty temper, though a constant cause or principle in the mind, operates only by intervals, and infects not the whole character. Again, repentance wipes off every crime, if attended with a reformation of life and manners. How is this to be accounted for? but by asserting that actions render a person criminal merely as they are proofs of criminal principles in the mind. . . .

— *From* An Enquiry Concerning Human Understanding

ter." This had the practical advantage of also explaining the purpose of praise and blame—namely, to mold or change a person's character such that he or she would in the future tend to perform more desirable actions. This is still determinism, but it is "soft" in that it carves out an area that can be called "freedom," and thus allows us to talk meaningfully of our actions both as being completely determined *and* as being our own responsibility.

In Defense of Freedom

The demand for freedom and responsibility is not going to be satisfied by these different variations of determinism, no matter how "soft" they pretend to be. A soft determinist may call an act "free" if it is willed by the agent. But either the agent's will is determined or it is not. If it is, then the situation is as the hard determinist describes it. All the soft determinist has done is apply the label "free" to a particular class of actions which are, at bottom, as fully determined as every other action or event. If it is not, then the soft determinist in fact recognizes that what we need is a breach in determinism, a conception of our actions, or at least our decisions, as truly free and not determined in any of the ways discussed previously.

The classic statement of this claim to freedom and responsibility is to be found in the philosophy of Immanuel Kant. We have already seen that Kant (in *Critique of Pure Reason*) gave an unqualified endorsement of determinism, arguing that the principle (of universal causation) upon which it is based is

"SOFT" DETERMINISM: MILL

Correctly conceived, the doctrine called Philosophical Necessity ["determinism"] is simply this: given the motives which are present to an individual's mind, and given likewise the character and disposition of the individual, the manner in which he might act might be unerringly inferred; that if we knew the person thoroughly, and knew all the inducements which are acting upon him, we could foretell his conduct with as much certainty as we can predict any physical event. . . . [But] this does not conflict in the smallest degree with what is called our feeling of freedom. . . . Our actions follow from our characters [but] we are exactly as capable of making our own character, if we will, as others are of making it for us.

The free will doctrine, by keeping in view precisely that portion of the truth which the word "necessity" ["determinism"] puts out of sight, namely the power of the mind to cooperate in the formation of its own character, has given its adherents a practical feeling much nearer to the truth than has generally (I believe) existed in the minds of the [determinists].

— *From* A System
of Logic

nothing less than a necessary rule of all human experience. And this includes human actions:

> *Actions of men are determined in conformity with the order of Nature, by their empirical character and other causes; if we could exhaust all the appearances, there would not be found a single human action which would not be predicted with certainty.*

This is surely a statement of the hardest of "hard" determinism. But Kant also appreciated, as much as any philosopher ever has, the importance of unqualified freedom for human responsibility. (He called freedom, as he had called God, a "postulate" [or presupposition] of practical reason.) But how could he defend both universal determinism and human freedom? Determinism is true of every possible event and object of human knowledge, Kant said, but it does not follow that it is the *only* way of viewing things: Our acts of will can and should sometimes be viewed in a different way. Action is a wholly different matter from knowledge. Kant said that we adopt two different standpoints toward the world, one theoretical, one practical. Insofar as we want to know something, we adopt the standpoint of science and determinism. Within that standpoint every event, including human actions, is determined, brought about by sufficient natural explanatory causes (including the states of our brains and various psychological factors). But when we are ready to do something, we switch to the practical standpoint. And the main point is this: When we are acting or deciding to act, we *must* think of our own acts or will and decisions as the sufficient explanatory causes of our actions, and we cannot continue the causal chain backward to consider whether those acts of will are themselves caused. When we act, in other words, we cannot think of ourselves except as acting freely.

You are about to make a decision: You are finally going to give up smoking. A friend offers you a cigarette on the second day. Yes or no? Do you smoke it? Now it might very well be that, given your personality, your weakness for past habits, and any number of other psychological factors, you are clearly determined to accept the cigarette, and thus to break your resolution. Your friend, who knows you quite well, may even know this. But you can't think of yourself in this deterministic way, for you have to make a decision, you can't simply "find out" what you will do. In other words, you can't simply predict your own behavior, no matter how much you know about the various causes and factors that allow your friend to predict your behavior. If you were to predict, "I'm going to start smoking again anyway," you would not be simply predicting, you would be, in that very act, breaking your resolution, that is, deciding to break it. So, when your own acts and decisions are concerned, you have to act as if you were totally free. This in a way denies determinism. For, as you are the one who has to make the decision, determinism isn't relevant. (Kant said, "And to have to think yourself free is to *be* free.")

Kant's suggestion has been taken up in a very different way in European philosophy, particularly by the existentialists. Like Kant, they accept (or at least do not bother to reject) determinism in sciences. But they insist that, even if determinism is true, we must always view *ourselves as agents* as necessarily free. When we have to decide what to do, all the knowledge of the possible factors determining our decision are not sufficient to cause us to decide. For we cannot predict our own decision without at the same time making it.

Jean-Paul Sartre, the leading existentialist of recent years, defended the Kantian claim for human freedom as far as it can possibly be defended. In *Being and Nothingness,* Sartre argued that we are, always, absolutely free. This means, as Kant had insisted, that insofar as we act (and Sartre said that we are always acting), our decisions and our actions cannot be viewed as having any causes whatsoever. We must make decisions, and no amount of information and no number of causal circumstances can ever replace our need to make them. We can, of course, refuse to make decisions, acting as if they were made for us. But even in these cases, we are making decisions, "choosing not to choose," in a classic Sartrean phrase. We are "condemned to be free," he says. Again, desires may enter into consideration, but only as "consideration." We can always act against a desire, no matter how strong, if only we are sufficiently decided that we shall do so. A starving man may yet refuse food, if, for example, he is taking part in a hunger strike for a political cause to which he is dedicated. A mother may refuse to save her own life if it

ABSOLUTE FREEDOM: SARTRE

We were never more free than during the German occupation. We had lost all our rights, beginning with the right to talk. Every day we were insulted to our faces and had to take it in silence. . . . And because of all this we were free. Because the Nazi venom seeped into our thoughts, every accurate thought was a conquest. Because an all-powerful police tried to force us to hold our tongues, every word took on the value of a declaration of principles. Because we were hunted down, every one of our gestures had the weight of a solemn commitment.

— *From* Situations III

Thus there are no accidents in a life; a community event which suddenly bursts forth and involves me in it does not come from the outside. If I am mobilized in a war, this war is my war; it is in my image and I deserve it. I deserve it first because I could always get out of it by suicide or by desertion; these ultimate possibles are those which must always be present for us when there is a question of envisaging a situation. For lack of getting out of it, I have chosen it. This can be due to inertia, to cowardice in the face of public opinion, or because I prefer certain other values to the values of the refusal to join in the war (the good opinion of my relatives, the honor of my family, etc.). Any way you look at it, it is a matter of choice. This choice will be repeated later on again and again without a break until the end of the war.

— *From* Being and Nothingness

would be at the expense of her children. A student who has resolved to study for tomorrow's test may miss a favorite television show. Whether trivial or grandiose, our every act is a decision, and our every decision is free. And even if we fail to live up to them, or find that we "cannot" make them, we are responsible nevertheless. There is no escape from freedom, or from responsibility. Indeed, for Sartre, freedom is always also an opportunity.

CLOSING QUESTIONS

1. Define "freedom" in your own terms, specifically outlining those aspects of your self that you consider the basis of your own conception of "act-

ing freely." To what extent does your conception include playing roles and interacting with other people? To what extent do other people limit your freedom? To what extent can you be really free only when you are alone?

2. Imagine yourself trying to make a difficult decision (for instance, what job offer to accept, whether to get married, whether to enlist in the army). Now consider yourself a determinist and ask yourself, "What am I going to do in this situation?" What happens to your deliberations?

3. Consider one of the two "compatibilist" ("soft" determinist) positions discussed in this chapter and defend it, or attack it, from the point of view of a "hard" determinist.

4. Aristotle said that we are not free if our action is caused by "external compulsion." What counts as external compulsion, in your opinion? Can compulsions be internal as well? Give some examples, and explain how it is that they interfere with our freedom.

BIBLIOGRAPHY AND SUGGESTED READINGS

A more expanded discussion of the free will and determinism problem is Bernard Berofsky, *Free Will and Determinism* (Harper & Row, 1966) and D. F. Pears, ed., *Freedom and the Will* (St. Martin's, 1963). A good discussion of the link between science, determinism, and free will is found in the variety of essays in Sidney Hook, ed., *Determinism and Freedom in the Age of Modern Science* (Collier, 1961). A good collection of essays on the legal and moral concerns of freedom is Herbert Morris, ed., *Freedom and Responsibility* (Stanford University Press, 1961). Frithjof Bergmann's recent provocative study is *On Being Free* (Notre Dame University Press, 1979). Dostoevsky's *Notes from the Underground* appears in part in Robert C. Solomon, *Existentialism* (Random House, 1974) and Dostoevsky's *Brothers Karamazov* has been translated by Andrew R. MacAndrew (Bantam, 1970). Hume and Mill present their "soft" determinism in their respective books, *An Enquiry Concerning Human Understanding* (Oxford University Press, 1955) and *A System of Logic* (Longmans, 1911). Sartre's view on freedom is found in virtually all of his writings, but in particular in his *Being and Nothingness,* trans. Hazel Barnes (Washington Square Press, 1956).

CHAPTER EIGHT
MORALITY AND
THE GOOD LIFE

Pieter Bruegel the Elder, The Peasant Dance, *Autnahme des Kunsthistorischen Museums.*

MORALITY AND
THE GOOD LIFE

*What I really lack is to be clear in my mind
what I am to do.*
—*Kierkegaard,* Journals

OPENING QUESTIONS

1. We sometimes say that to be a good person, one must be "true to one-self." Do you think this is so? Give examples.

2. Do you believe that a morally good person will, at least in normal circumstances, also be assured of being a happy person? Why or why not?

3. If a sadist were to gain enormous pleasure from torturing his or her victims—in fact, more pleasure than the pain suffered by the victims themselves—would the sadist's cruelty be justified?

4. Is there anything you would find worth dying for? What? (Camus, in his *Myth of Sisyphus,* said, "A reason for dying is also a good reason for living.")

5. Many religious commandments, in sexual and food prohibitions, tell us to abstain from the material, or bodily, enjoyments of life. Is it possible to be a religious person and deny yourself none of the pleasures of life? Or if a religion encourages us to make money, buy fancy cars, and live well, is it thereby corrupting its status as a religion?

6. Do we in fact always act selfishly, even in those instances in which we appear to be "selflessly" helping others?

7. Is it true that the "bottom line" of business is profit and profit alone? Or, even in business itself, are there other, less tangible goals that are intrinsic to and just as important as making money?

8. Do you believe that abortion is justifiable, even in cases in which the life of the mother is not threatened? How do you justify your answer, and how would you defend it against a person who disagreed with you?

9. Assuming that we agree on a list of injunctions that we all *ought* to obey, which we call "morality," why should we be moral?

10. Would it be possible for a person to be perfectly good and yet cause harm to innocent people? Could a person be wicked even if he or she never caused any harm at all?

11. Which is more important to you, success or happiness? What if you are forced to choose between them?

12. We are a nation ruled "by laws, not men." What does this say about our view of "men"?

The discussion of self and of our relationships with others naturally carries us into the realm of what is often called "moral philosophy," which asks such questions as: What should we do? What should we not do? How should we treat other people? How should we ourselves live? These are questions of *value* rather than of truth and reality, the topics we have mostly been discussing so far. Of course, it should already be obvious that our discussions of truth and reality were heavily steeped in values (we frequently referred, for instance, to the meaning of life or the existence of God), and now we find that any discussion of values presupposes a thoughtful and informed view of the world. But **moral philosophy**—the search for the best way to live and the right principles for our actions—nevertheless deserves a chapter of its own.

The moral philosophy of **Immanuel Kant** (1724–1804) is wholly based on the concept of a "good will." To have a good will is to act on moral principles that are wholly justifiable by what he called practical reason, the result of which is *duty*. Kant believed will to be crucial for two reasons. First, he refused to accept the view that our actions are just another set of events in the physical universe, determined by factors beyond our control. *We* are responsible for what we do, he argued; otherwise, the very notion of morality doesn't make any sense, nor does the concept of human dignity, which Kant found all-important. Second, Kant was aware that it makes no sense to blame people for what is beyond their control; the consequences of what we do are often beyond our control, subject to accidents or interruptions that we could not possibly have predicted. Therefore, he said, "The only thing that is good without qualification is a good will"—in other words, our good intentions and attempts to do our duty.

Morality is a set of principles, or rules, that guide us in our actions. Moral rules tell us what to do—for example, "Tell the truth," "Treat others as you would like to be treated yourself"—and what not to do—for instance, "Do not cheat," "Do not kill," and "Do not steal." The Ten Commandments, from the Old Testament, and the injunction to love one another, from the New Testament, form the core of much of our morality, which can therefore appropriately be called Judeo-Christian morality. Moral rules typically take the form of commandments, or orders, often with the words "ought" or "ought not" (or "Thou shalt" or "Thou shalt not"). Morality and moral rules—whether stated as law or not—form the basic structure of every society, defining the limits of what is permitted, and defining what is expected, too. The key to morality, according to the German philosopher Immanuel Kant, is **duty**—doing what you *ought* to do.

But morality is part of a much larger quest, which gives morality its importance. Why shouldn't we kill each other? Why should we help each other? What reasons can we give to defend one sexual ethic rather than another? And, in general, why should we be moral? The answer to this last question must be larger than morality itself, for it must supply us with the reasons for accepting moral principles and rules. That answer is called **the good life**. It is a phrase without precise meaning, but we all know quite well what it signifies. How should we live? What do we want? And what should we want? What do we most enjoy? What should we most enjoy? What is worth working for? And what is not worth the effort? What should we accept? And what should we try to change? These are questions for which we all have answers before we enter philosophy, but philosophy sometimes has surprising results in changing them, or at least in giving us better arguments to support them.

The goal of moral philosophy is to develop a set of principles and a view of our aims in life that will allow us to live with clarity and confidence. This general quest, which includes morality as well as the search for the good life, is usually called **ethics**. In what follows, we begin with a discussion of various suggestions about what it is to live well. We then return to the more specific matter of morality and the role of morals in society.

THE GOOD LIFE

Hedonism

In Plato's dialogues in which Socrates is the leading character, the recurrent theme is the search for the good life. And from Socrates' discussions with his fellow Greeks, it is evident that this was not at all a new question, but one about which virtually everyone had very strong opinions. And almost all of these opinions are still defended today. Most prominent among them is the philosophy called **hedonism**, the view that says the good life involves getting as much pleasure out of life as you possibly can.

Hedonism is an attractive candidate for the good life, but Socrates and people ever since have seen that it has certain limitations. You might notice that people talk a lot more about hedonism than they actually practice it. Students often talk about hedonism, but their ambitions and worries about school and careers show that they want something more than just pleasure—success, security, social standing, respect, power, money, freedom. This is not to deny that they also want pleasures, but more as distractions, entertainments, and enjoyments than as the goal of life. Compared with the average cat, for example, we are masters in self-denial. We put off meals when we are

---

Perhaps the most famous philosophical hedonist in history was the Greek **Epicurus** (342[?]–270 B.C.). He argued that the good life was the love of pleasure, and we still refer to a person who spends his or her life living for pleasure (good food, enjoyable vacations, etc.) as an *epicurean*. In fact, however, Epicurus taught that not all pleasures are good; he encouraged simple pleasures, peace and quiet, and pleasures of the mind, and fellowship with friends.

The pleasant life is not the product of one drinking party after another or of sexual intercourse with women and boys or of the seafood and other delicacies afforded by a luxurious table. On the contrary, it is the result of sober thinking.

— *Epicurus,* Letter to Menoeceus

hungry, because we have work to do, or because we are on diets. We suppress our sexual impulses because it would be awkward or embarrassing to act on them in the middle of class or at the dinner table; we want much more than "just sex." Many people argue that the reason they deny themselves pleasures now is in order to get more pleasure later. But, if that is so, then most people are surely fooling themselves, for we all know that work and responsibility breed more work and more responsibility. Social respect and manners constantly require more respectable behavior and more manners, and the idea that we are simply delaying our pleasure is usually disproved by our own actions. People also argue that the work itself, or the respect, or the success, is what gives them pleasure, but here philosophers have pointed out a crucial distinction—between acting for the sake of pleasure and acting for some other goal whose achievement gives pleasure. Hedonism is the first, not the second.

The classic argument against hedonism as the good life was formulated by Aristotle twenty-five hundred years ago. He argued, as we have suggested above, that pleasure is not an activity in itself but rather something that accompanies satisfying activities. Thus the key to the good life is to be found in the notion of "satisfying activities," not in the pleasure itself. Our goal is not the pleasure but the activity, and the pleasure is more like a bonus, or what Aristotle called the "completion" of the activity. Forbidden activities or vulgar pastimes may be pleasurable, but the pleasure is more than balanced by the amount of pain and discomfort (for example, guilt) they eventually produce. An activity may be extremely painful, on the other hand—running long distances or enduring a rigorous test—but, because the activity itself is admirable or challenging, it may nevertheless produce pleasure of a meaningful variety. But this means that pleasure itself, even if it is an essential component of the good life, cannot be the good life itself.

There are actually very few hedonists among us. In Chapter 9 we will discuss a certain imaginary invention (based upon the research of a Cornell psychologist, James Olds). It is a box, fixed with electrodes and medical equipment. A person is strapped in, the electricity is turned on, and he or she experiences continuing waves of pleasurable sensations. The box is equipped to take care of all a person's biological needs, and a person will live in the

> *One might think that all men desire pleasure because they all aim at life, but life is activity. Pleasure completes the activities and therefore life. It is with good reason then that they aim at pleasure too, since it completes life, which is desirable. . . . Without activity pleasure does not arise, and every activity is completed by the attendant pleasure.*
>
> — *Aristotle,* Ethics

box at least as long as he or she would outside of it. The only hitch is this: Once you get into the box, you will never want to or have to get out of it. Here is the life of absolute pleasure, but in return for it, you will give up your ambitions and your friends, sports, reading, sex, food, and television. Of course, after only a few months in the box you will become grotesquely out of shape, pale and not much more interesting than a prepackaged hamburger bun, which by this time you will strongly resemble. But you won't care about any of this—you will be leading the life of total pleasure. Would you do it? In my years of teaching several thousand students, I have found only a dozen or so who would. Most of us desire other satisfactions over and above sensory pleasures.

Success

The exclusive worship of the bitch-goddess Success is our national disease.

— *William James*

Success is counted sweetest/By those who ne'er succeed.

— *Emily Dickinson*

In our society, the good life is often equated with success. Success may mean money, but it does not mean only this. It involves social status and respectability as well (although these often go together). There are curious twists: For example, gangsters are sometimes admired as eminently successful, no matter how they acquired their wealth and status. Some creative people and hermits may be admired and idolized as successful despite the fact that they are, by any customary measure, total failures. But once again, we must be careful not to confuse what people say they take to be the good life with the way they actually live. Many people who work very hard for success will say that they are working toward their retirement, or in order to have enough security to enjoy themselves, or in order to have enough money to buy themselves lavish pleasures. But, again, their lives often demonstrate the opposite, as people work themselves into exhaustion long after they have "made it," to such an extent that they are no longer capable of enjoying the simplest pleasures. You might say that they are success addicts, just as people become money addicts, working at first in order to get something else, but ultimately working simply for the thing itself. Money addicts start earning money like everyone else, to buy homes, cars, TV sets, but they end up needing the money itself so much that they work only for it. Success addicts work hard for security, social status, or wealth, but end up working just for the success itself.

The life of seeking success has its problems. There is always the real possibility of failure, of course, but this is equally an argument against almost every lifestyle. In any case, the threat of failure is not a good reason to reject a lifestyle—the problem is rather the threat of success. We all know stories of

> Confucius said,
>   Having three kinds of friends will bring personal improvement; three kinds will bring injury. To have friends who are straight, who are true to their word, and who are well-informed is to be improved; to have friends who are ingratiating, foppish, and foolish is to be injured.

successful people in their mid-forties or fifties committing suicide, just when it would seem that they have achieved what they have been working for most of their lives. Why? Because, once earned, their success proved not to be what they wanted after all. If a certain conception of the good life fails us, that doesn't mean that there is no good life, much less that life isn't really worth living. It does not even mean that success is not worth having, or that success is wrong. It only means that success, by itself, does not seem to give us the good life.

Asceticism

In recent decades in our society, dissatisfied with this success conception of the good life, the "success ethic," has given rise to a reaction in precisely the opposite direction. In place of success, many people demand simplicity and even poverty—freedom from the burden of possessions. At the extremes, this manifests itself in our choice of folk heroes, off in the wilderness as pioneers or rebels. More moderately, it manifests itself in the return to the country, life on the farm or in a small commune, largely by people who have been brought up in big cities and nurtured on the success ethic. It is worth noting that this is not at all a new philosophy. It was in reaction to the decadent success ethic of the Roman Empire, for example, that simple Christian asceticism began. (**Asceticism** is the proper word for this life of simplicity and self-denial.) And even before Christianity, around the time of Socrates, a group of philosophers who called themselves *Cynics* defended a similar lifestyle. (The word *cynic* comes from the Greek word for dog.) The most famous of them was Diogenes, who lived in a bathtub and owned nothing but a single lantern, with which he is said to have searched the faces of everyone, "looking for even one honest man." When Alexander the Great came to his city, he asked to see Diogenes, of whom he had heard much. On their meeting, Alexander asked Diogenes, "What can I do for you?" Diogenes turned to the ruler of most of the known world and said, "Move over, you're blocking the sunlight."

Many people have accepted the ascetic life as the means to the good life, but not as the good life itself. A great many religious people, for example, have accepted asceticism as a way to salvation or "purification." It is not the self-denial itself that they praise, but self-denial as a means to the holy life. Some artists adopt the ascetic life, but only because it seems to them the best way to achieve what they really consider the good life, namely, creativity. And it is important not to confuse asceticism, with its extremes of self-denial, with that familiar belief that the "simplest" pleasures in life are not only the best but the easiest to obtain. Many try to "simplify" their lives, just because society makes life so bureaucratically and socially complicated. But they do this "in order to enjoy life more," not for purely ascetic reasons. But here, too, asceticism is a corrective and a means, not an end in itself.

Freedom

Freedom can be singled out as a separate conception of the good life. Usually, freedom is considered a means, the freedom to do what one wants: to satisfy pleasures or ambitions, create or worship, retreat from society or live as one wishes. But, like other means, freedom may become an end in itself. The person who throws over a promising career and takes to the open road might be said to value freedom more than any pleasures or successes. Freedom from ties and responsibilities may be preferable to an intimate relationship or marriage, just because it is more "free." The life of freedom need not be any particular way of life, since one might, within it, be religious, hedonistic, or ambitious. The question is ultimately, which is more important—the freedom itself or these other concerns? The extreme of this conception is the peculiar and extravagant conception of freedom portrayed in Dostoevsky's "underground man." He was willing to give up everything, not only success and pleasure but even his health, just in order to realize his "most advantageous advantage," his freedom.

Power and Creativity

There are many other conceptions of the good life. Indeed, there are as many possible conceptions as there are human goals. Some of the other most common conceptions of the good life are very close to those we have discussed so far: For example, the life in pursuit of great wealth or political power is very much like the life of the success ethic. But then there is another sense of "power" that is not political but personal. It is the power to grow as a person, to "expand one's consciousness," to develop one's talents and to create. Friedrich Nietzsche, for instance, defended such a conception of the good life under the phrase the "will to power." Arguing against those many philosophers, particularly the British moralists, who argued that humans act only for pleasure, Nietzsche sarcastically quipped: "Man does not desire pleasure; only the Englishman does." What all people ultimately want, Nietzsche argued in his *Will to Power,* is power:

> *Not need, nor desire—no, the love of power is the demon of man. One may give them everything—health, nourishment, quarters, they remain unhappy; for the*

demon insists on being satisfied. One may take away everything from them and satisfy this demon: they then are almost happy.

All other seeming conceptions of the good life, Nietzsche added, are in fact different ways of seeking power. Even religion, as well as the contemporary scramble for wealth. But the highest sense of power, Nietzsche argued, is reserved for those people who live autonomously and creatively, as artists, philosophers, or saints. The composer Mozart, for example, probably considered the good life to be the life of artistic creativity, which is not to deny that he enjoyed a great many of the pleasures of life along the way. The good life for Socrates was a life in accordance with the moral principles he had defended in his philosophizing, though he, too, had more than his share of pleasure and success as well. For him, the good life was the life of wisdom, the life of principles and creative thinking. And these were worth holding onto even when they meant his death.

Religion

Religion is our ultimate concern.

— *Paul Tillich,* Dynamics
of Faith

The religious conception of the good life also deserves special consideration, not when it is simply intermingled with the other goals and ambitions of life and squeezed into Sunday mornings, but when it is truly the goal of life to which all other goals are subordinated. But it is never altogether clear how many people have completely endorsed this conception of the good life. There are millions of people who have said that they do, but whether their lives bear out their statements is something that we must always view, particularly in our own case, with a cautious eye. The religious life is a life of devotion: In the Christian tradition, it is sometimes said to be "living with the fear of God in one's heart." The religious life need not be based on "fear," but the point is that the truly religious person lives with an emotional attachment to his or her religion that permeates and dominates everything else. This is not to say that the religious person doesn't perform any but religious acts, but religious behavior must have the primary place in his or her life. In practice the religious life is often in conflict with other conceptions of the good life.

Each of these conceptions of the good life is fairly specific; it singles out one goal or type of goal among the many that we desire, and it claims that one goal as the mark of the good life. But, once we have begun thinking about it, all of these seem one-sided. Who wants pleasure if it means giving up all friends and social ties? Who wants power or success if it makes us miserable? Who would even want to be creative if nothing but misery came from it? Wouldn't it be better to be both creative and enjoy life? Or be creative and successful as well? Wouldn't religious people have a better life if they did not devote themselves to God exclusively but also enjoyed the blessings of the secular world, without diminishing religious faith? The good life, in other words, seems to be something more general than any single goal, no matter how grand that single goal may seem to many people. Yet we should not conclude that the good life is simply "the best of everything," without further qualification. Even if we reject these one-sided views, we may still find that the good life has but a single goal.

Happiness

In the ancient world, Aristotle examined the different one-sided conceptions of the good life and rejected them in favor of a single conception with which most of us are probably in agreement—happiness. Happiness is the good life, although happiness itself is not a single activity but the result of a great many activities. Aristotle took personal development or self-realization as his goal. In his *Ethics,* Aristotle examined two one-sided conceptions of the good life, pleasure and success (which meant political success for him) and rejected them; yet he also insisted that one cannot possibly lead the good life without them. But they themselves are not the good life, only necessary conditions for it. The good life is *happiness,* which he defined as that which is wanted "for its own sake" and not "for the sake of anything else." As it turns out, happiness included a large number of advantages and virtues, including wealth, power, and community status as well as military courage, the ability to drink wine without getting too obnoxious, a sense of justice, good friends, and a good sense of humor. "Happiness," in other words, was not just a sense of well-being, as it is for us; "happiness" for Aristotle meant the good life as a whole, an integrated life with all the virtues and good fortune and the philosophical wisdom to appreciate it. Happiness is nothing less than an entirely good life, with all of its parts in balance. Indeed, he tells us, it makes no sense at all to say that a person is happy for a few hours or days or even months or years. A person can be called happy only on the basis of his or her entire lifetime. Aristotle even suggested, at one point, that a person can be made unhappy after death—for example, if an individual's children dishonor the family name.

This indicates an important difference between Aristotle's society and moral philosophy and our own. It seems to make perfectly good sense for us

> *In view of the fact that all knowledge and every pursuit aims at some good, what is the highest of all goods achievable by action? Verbally there is very general agreement; for both the general run of men and people of superior refinement it is happiness; they identify living well and doing well with being happy.*
>
> — *Aristotle,* Ethics

to say that a person could be happy for even ten minutes: for example, you can imagine waking one fine spring morning to the sun and the chirping of birds, feeling quite happy, only to find out ten minutes later that you have just been kicked out of school. But for Aristotle, "happiness" requires a lifetime of good living. Part of this might be attributed to a difference in language; Aristotle's word (**eudaimonia**) more accurately means "doing well" or "well-being." But the difference in language reflects a profound difference in moral philosophy as well; we tend to think of the good life primarily in terms of inner satisfaction and a sense of well-being. Aristotle's Greeks would not have understood this at all (indeed, they would have considered a man who could keep a sense of well-being in the midst of misfortune to be insane, not happy). The good life for the Greeks was a public, social, objective life of achievement and good fortune; it had little to do with one's inner feelings. We, on the other hand, tend to believe a person to be happy if he or she is satisfied with what life has provided, whatever others may think—indeed, even if others think he or she is most unfortunate. So the ideal of "happiness," which we would all agree is the key to the good life, nevertheless leaves a great many questions open. How important is inner satisfaction? How essential is our place in the community and are our actual accomplishments? Is happiness available to everyone (as we like to think)? Or is happiness instead the privilege of the very powerful and very rich or very lucky, as the Greeks used to think? Would it be possible—in our sense—to be happy and to still not live the good life?

Of the various conceptions of the good life as pleasure, success, asceticism, freedom, power, creativity, religion, and happiness, some are available to virtually everyone (for example, the life of simple pleasures) and others are available only to a lucky few (the life of creativity). But it must have struck you by now that all of these conceptions of the good life have left something out. However radical the differences between hedonism and the religious life, the success ethic and the ascetic life, the life of seeking wealth and the life of freedom, creativity, or happiness in general, there is something that they all share in common. They are all self-centered; they make no mention of other people. They are all, in one form or another, varieties of *egoism*. This will not be true of Aristotle's philosophy as he developed it, we shall see; nor is it true of Socrates' moral life. One might hesitate to include the religious life of an isolated monk or an ascetic as "selfish" in any sense, but the monkish life takes too little account of our relations with other people, and places its emphasis on the good life for a single person.

EGOISM VERSUS ALTRUISM

Egoism is the thesis that everyone always acts for his or her own advantage, that the only reason why people act respectfully or kindly toward each other is that courtesy and generosity, too, for one reason or another, are to their advantage. It might be fear of punishment that makes them act "correctly"; some have "ulterior motives"—that is, they expect other things later on, perhaps a

EGOISM AND ALTRUISM	
Psychological egoism	**Psychological altruism**
"All acts are basically selfish."	"Some of our acts are 'naturally' altruistic."
Ethical egoism	**Ethical altruism**
"You ought to act selfishly."	"You ought to act for the good of others."

favor in return, or reward in heaven after they die, or they are trying to avoid guilt, or are after a feeling of self-satisfaction. In popular language, the egoist position is often called "selfishness."

One of the most widely read contemporary egoists, Ayn Rand, has written of the "virtue of selfishness." According to her, we all should act for our own interests. At this point, we must distinguish two very different forms of egoism, although people often confuse them. First, there is the position that everyone in fact acts according to his or her own interests, that our psychology is such that we cannot help but act in this way. Accordingly, this position is called **psychological egoism**. The second position must be defended or attacked independently of the first: It is the thesis that people *ought* to act to satisfy their own interests, and this presupposes that they have a choice whether to act that way or not. This position is **ethical egoism**.

Both egoist positions are contrasted with what is usually called **altruism**—that is, acting for the sake of other people's interests. There are degrees of altruism. One may be altruistic because one acts morally, because one recognizes an obligation to other people. Or one may be altruistic in actually making another person's interests as important as or even more important than one's own interests; this can be found between lovers or brothers and sisters. Altruism can also be divided into two distinct theses, although these are not so often distinguished. There is **psychological altruism**, which says that people "naturally" act for each other's sakes. **Ethical altruism**, on the other hand, says that people *ought* to act with each other's interests in mind. This is, of course, a basic statement of morality, best summarized in the so-called Golden Rule: "Do unto others as you would have them do unto you." Altruism need not mean self-sacrifice, however. Altruism means acting for the (intended) benefit of others—but not necessarily *against* one's own interests. So, too, acting in one's own self-interest is not necessarily *selfish*—that is, acting contrary to or without regard for other people's interests.

The most familiar and most difficult question is about psychological egoism: Is it true that people only act for their own self-interest? A famous story

Tzu-Kung asked, "Is there one expression that one can act on to the end of his days?" The Master replied, "There is deference: do not impose on other people what you yourself do not desire."

about Abraham Lincoln is an apt illustration of the thesis. As he was arguing the psychological egoist position with a friend, his carriage was passing a mudslide, where a mother pig was squealing as her piglets were drowning. Lincoln stopped the carriage, saved the piglets, and then moved on. His friend asked him whether that wasn't a clear case of altruism. Lincoln replied: "Why, that was the very essence of selfishness. I should have had no peace of mind all day had I gone on and left that suffering old sow worrying over those piglets. I did it to get peace of mind, don't you see?"

Many actions are based on self-interest and are "selfish" without any question. But are there any actions that are not based on self-interest? Lincoln's response is an excellent example because it would seem as if his action is not for selfish reasons at all. Yet according to him, there was a selfish reason behind his actions—his own sense of satisfaction and "peace of mind." Could this be true of all our actions?

Among the many arguments that have been put forward against the view that all actions are essentially selfish, three in particular have been much repeated since they were formulated several hundred years ago by an English clergyman, Bishop Joseph Butler.

1. Many of our actions are motivated by desires which themselves are aimed at the good of others, whether or not they are of benefit to ourselves. Lincoln may have reflected beforehand and thought, "If I don't save those little pigs, I will be miserable all day." But it is unlikely that he did. At somewhat minimal inconvenience to himself, he acted out of a motive common to (almost) all of us, the urge to help another creature or person in trouble, or what we usually call **compassion**. In friendship and with those we love, in particular, we are often moved to act in such a way that it would be absurd to say that we acted for our own satisfaction or to avoid guilt. Of course, in every case in which we act out of desire, we satisfy a desire of ours to act. But this is not the same as being selfish or egoistic, which means not just satisfying my desire but satisfying my desire *with an eye to my interests alone*.

2. Many of our desires in life have to do with obtaining the approval and recognition of other people. Therefore, in acting to get what we want—namely, their approval—we act on their behalf and in accordance with their desires and needs as well. It is a tricky question, on occasion impossible to answer, to what extent we are moved by the urge for approval alone and to what extent we are truly motivated by the desire to serve others. But it is certainly not plausible to suggest that we *always* act just

to get approval and not at all to help others. Indeed, one of the things most of us want most in life is self-respect, a sense of being a "good person," and this is utterly impossible unless we not only help others but help them for their sake alone, even if, afterward, we may enjoy the self-satisfaction of having helped them.

3. There is in all of us a sense of right and wrong, or what we sometimes call "conscience." It does not matter, for purposes of this argument, whether conscience is simply the voice of our parents within us (as Freud argued, calling this the "superego") or the voice of God, as many religious people believe, or simply the fear of punishment, as many psychologists have argued. The point is that we do have such a conscience, and to act in accordance with its demands is not to act in our own interests alone, even if we know that not obeying our consciences will very likely be followed by the pain of guilt. Further, it must be asked, why is this guilt so painful, except for reason of conscience and the fact that we do want to, or feel the need to, act on others' behalf without regard to (and sometimes even against) our own needs and desires? And even if, on rare occasions, some of us obey our consciences only with an eye to avoiding future self-punishment, it is surely not the case that we all do this all the time. But this is what the psychological egoist argues, and this, we can see, is plainly false.

The argument against the psychological egoist, in a single statement, is this: Merely acting in accordance with our own desires—assuming that we always do this—does not make an action selfish; for all actions are, in some sense, based on our desires, but at least some of those desires are desires to serve someone else's interests. Thus the "object" of desire is what makes an act selfish or unselfish, not merely the fact that one's own desire is acted upon. The satisfaction that accompanies good acts is itself not the motivation of the act. Here is the answer to Lincoln. His act was, despite his philosophical claims, an altruistic one; his satisfaction was not the motive of the act but only its consequence. And, if psychological egoism is not always true, then altruism is at least possible.

But even if altruism is possible, whether it is desirable is still an open question. An ethical egoist, for example, would admit that altruism is possible, but would attack it all the same. Ayn Rand, in her polemics on the "virtue of selfishness," argued that the strict definition of this word is "concern with one's own interest." She then launched into a diatribe against altruism.

> *If it is true that what I mean by "selfishness" is not what is meant conventionally, then* this *is one of the worse indictments of altruism: it means that altruism permits no concept of a self-respecting, self-supporting man—a man who supports his life by his own effort and neither sacrifices himself nor others. It means that altruism permits no view of men except as sacrificial animals and profiteers-on-sacrifice, as victims and parasites—that it permits no concept of a benevolent coexistence among men—that it permits no concept of justice.*

> — The Virtue of Selfishness

Ayn Rand (1905–1982) was a popular American novelist, a Russian immigrant, whose defense of what she called "the virtue of selfishness" earned her an enormous following. She is the author of *The Fountainhead* (1943) and *Atlas Shrugged* (1957), among other novels.

The argument here is extreme and utilizes the same kind of fallacy that the psychological egoist employs. The argument contrasts the notion of "acting in one's own interest" (that is, selfishness) with self-sacrificing and lack of self-respect. That is, if an act is for the benefit of others, then it cannot be to one's own benefit as well. Similarly, if an act is not in one's own interests, it is an act that denies one's self-respect. You can see how unjust this extreme contrast is, treating all human situations as if they must be either black or white. Our every action and intention is aimed at a larger number of goals: Some are immediate, others are long range, some are means, others are ends. But to pretend that every action and intention can be simply defined by a single goal—either self-interest or other people's interest—is to treat human action as we might treat the actions of rats or bees, as utterly simpleminded.

It is true that people who follow the rules of morality without any exceptions may hurt themselves and other people as well. A person who refuses to tell a lie under any circumstances may well be self-sacrificing in just this way. However, from the fact that unnecessary self-sacrifice is undesirable it does not follow that acting for the benefit of others is equally undesirable. Even the paragon of self-sacrifice, the martyr, sees himself or herself as gaining at least self-respect. And the paragon of action in one's own interest, according to Rand's own ethic, the businessperson who dedicates everything to personal achievement, may end up "sacrificing" self *and* self-respect most of all.

To act strictly according to "your own self-interest" is to rob yourself of the richness of goals for both self and others that gives human action its complex social and personal textures. This is not to say that we should always—or even ever—act against our self-interests. It is rather to say that any philosophy of human life will have to begin with a far richer conception of morality and human motivation than this limited ethical egoism. This is the main thrust of Bishop Butler's arguments.

In order to make her thesis more palatable, Rand argued that acting in one's own self-interest, in an enlightened way, will result in the mutual benefit of us all. Now, in one sense, this is an extremely respectable philosophy, and we shall discuss it at length under the name *utilitarianism* later in this chapter. But it is important to distinguish the two theses, for the utilitarian is perfectly aware that the general welfare may require the sacrifice of personal self-interest in a great many cases. Rand refused to acknowledge this. And to suppose that acting in our exclusive self-interest without sacrifice or attention to the welfare of others will in fact turn out to be to our mutual benefit is so contrary to our very experience that it cannot be made into a convincing thesis, even in fiction. Psychological egoism is a problem; if it is true then we have to teach people to consider other people's interests to be their own. But ethical egoism is more than a problem; as an ideology, telling us all to be even more selfish than we usually are, it may be a social disaster.

Psychological altruism in a universal sense has never had much of a following as such. The view that people always act for other people's benefit has never even been defended. At most, it is argued that we have the psychological capacity for altruism, that we at least sometimes feel pangs of sympathy for the other person, and, if certain misunderstandings and unnecessary social pressures are corrected, then people will act altruistically. But we must distinguish the claim that we *can* act altruistically from the claim that we *ought* to do so.

Among the various possibilities of altruism, one stands out above all others—morality. Morality is not, strictly speaking, action for the sake of others, although that is typically a part of it. Morality is action for the sake of principle. And since moral principles are those we recognize as overriding our own interests, it makes little sense to suppose that morality itself is selfish. Of course, it may still be that people are moral only because of selfish reasons— out of fear of being punished, for example, or because they believe it will bring them reward in heaven. And we all know people who use morality to further their self-interests. But whether or not this is so, morality must be discussed in its own terms, even if there may be egoistic or selfish motivation behind it as well.

MORALITY AND THEORIES OF MORALITY

An action done from duty derives its moral worth, not from the purpose which is to be attained by it, but from the maxim by which it is to be determined, and therefore does not depend on the realization of the object of the action, but merely on the principle of volition by which the action has taken place, without regard to any object of desire.

> — *Immanuel Kant,*
> Grounding of the
> Metaphysics of Morals

Morality gives us the rules by which we live with other people. It sets limits to our desires and our actions. It tells us what is permitted and what is not. It gives us guiding principles for making decisions. It tells us what we ought and what we ought not to do. But what is this "morality" that sounds so impersonal and "above" us? It is important to begin with an appreciation for the metaphor that so well characterizes moral rules. Nietzsche described it this way: "A tablet of virtues hangs over every people."

This "tablet of virtues" is morality. Morality consists of the most basic values and rules of behavior. The prototypes of morality, in this sense, are those ancient codes, carved in stone, with commands that are eternal and absolute. We know best the two tablets allegedly inscribed by God and given to Moses, which we call the Ten Commandments. And they are indeed *commandments.* They are absolute rules that tell us what we must do or not do, no matter who we are, no matter what we want, and regardless of whether our interests will be served by the command or not. "Thou shalt not kill" means, even if you want to, even if you have the power to, and even if you can escape all punishment, you are absolutely forbidden to kill.

The image of morality as coming "from above" is appropriate. First, moral laws are often said, and not only in our society, to come from God. Second, we learn these laws from our parents, who do indeed stand over us and indoctrinate us with them through their shouts, commands, examples, threats, and gestures. Finally, and most important, morality itself is above any given individual or individuals, whether it is canonized in the laws of society or not. Morality is not just another aid in getting us what we want; it is entirely concerned with right and wrong. And these considerations are above tampering by any individual, no matter how powerful, as if they have a life of their own.

This characteristic of morality as independent of individual desires and ambitions has led many people to characterize morality simply in terms of some absolute and independent agency. Most often, this absolute and independent agency is God.

But whether or not you believe in God, it is clear that something further is needed to help us define morality. Even assuming that there is a God, we need a way of determining what His moral commands must be. One might say that He has given these commands to various individuals, but the fact is that different people seem to have very different ideas about the morality that God has given them. Some, for example, would say that it explicitly rules out abortion and infanticide. Others would argue that God does not rule these out, but makes it clear that they are, like other forms of killing (a "holy war," for example), justifiable only in certain circumstances. And in view of such disagreements, we cannot simply appeal to God but must, with reasons that we can formulate and defend, define our morality for ourselves. There is the further question of whether we should follow God's laws just because they are His or rather, whether God is good because His laws are good. If the latter, then we have to decide what is good in order to know that God is good. If the former, then we have to decide whether or not to believe in God precisely on the basis of whether we can accept those laws. Either way, we have to decide for ourselves what laws of morality we are willing to accept.

Similar considerations hold true of that familiar appeal to conscience in determining what we ought to do or not do. Even if one believes that conscience is God-given, the same problems emerge again. Should we follow our

> *Imagine that you are creating the fabric of human destiny with the object of making men happy in the end . . . but that it was essential and inevitable to torture to death only one tiny creature . . . and to found that edifice on its unavenged tears; would you consent to be the architect of those conditions?* Tell me, and tell the truth!
>
> — *Feodor Dostoevsky,*
> The Brothers
> Karamazov

conscience just because "conscience tells us to"? Or do we follow our conscience just because we know that what our conscience commands is good? And if we believe that conscience is simply the internalization of the moral teachings of our parents and society, then the question takes an extra dimension: Should we accept or reject what we have been taught? Since our consciences often disagree, we must still decide which rules of conscience one ought to obey. Conscience doesn't determine what we ought to do, it only reminds us of rules we have already accepted.

We have talked about morality thus far as if it is always to be defined in terms of rules and principles, but there is another conception of ethics and of "morals" that places its primary emphasis not on rules and principles but on questions of *character*—that is, the ethics and personality of the individual (and, perhaps, of an entire culture). Of course, one aspect of having a good moral character is obeying the rules of one's society, but there are several virtues of character that seem not to be governed by rules at all—for example, courage and kindness. A general rule to the effect "be courageous" or "be generous" seems not only uninformative and unnecessary, but the rule seems to contradict the spirit of the virtues themselves, which are best displayed through spontaneous action and not following deliberation and obedience. One of the questions that has become prominent in modern moral philosophy is how distinct and how important are such questions of character and virtue as opposed to the concern with rules and principles in morality.

But whether it is a matter of principles or virtue, the basis of morality is an attempt to get straight about how we should lead our lives. How do we want to live? How *ought* we to live? But here we confront a problem that, since the days of Plato and Aristotle, has challenged moralists and morality alike—namely, why should one be moral? It is clear that moral principles—(e.g. do not lie) sometimes go against our self-interests. Why, then, should we obey them? (So, too, a virtue such as courage may, in certain circumstances, place one in severe danger. Why, then, should we be virtuous?) When moral rules and virtues serve our self-interests there is, of course, an easy answer to such questions: One acts morally because it is (perhaps "in the long run") in one's own best interests to do so. But what of those cases in which such self-interest is not even plausible (e.g., when one is morally required to sacrifice one's life or career)?

What, in other words, is the justification of morality? What rules count as *moral* rules and what sort of people should we be? These are the questions that define the work of moral philosophy. At the core of our concern, of course, are those central principles of Judeo-Christian morality—"don't kill," "don't steal," "honor your parents," and so on. We might disagree about what counts as killing, of course (or more precisely, what counts as *murder*—that is, intentional, wrongful killing). But what we might also disagree about is the reason behind the principle in the first place. Should we not kill because, ultimately, not killing is in our own best interests? Should we not kill because morality or being moral is desirable for its own sake, whether or not it is in our interests? Could it be that this principle is just one of the curiosities of our own society, a rule that we consider extremely important but which other societies may not?

Theories of morality are formulated in order to answer these questions of interpretation and justification. What is it for a principle to be a *moral* commandment in the first place? Is it in order to make us happier and healthier? In order to guarantee a more orderly society? In order to please God and not have our city destroyed, like Sodom or Gomorrah? For example, if the commandment not to kill is interpreted according to the theory that morality is a set of principles imposed upon us by God, then the interpretation of that principle is to be filled out, presumably, by looking for further information about God's intentions, whether in the Scriptures or by appealing to the current authorities in whom such opinions are vested (the Pope, the church in general). If, on the other hand, moral principles are taken to be efficient guides to promoting human happiness and the general welfare, then the law against killing has to be interpreted and defended by showing that obedience to such a law does indeed make more people happier and fewer people miserable than they would be if there were no such law. Abstract moral theories, therefore, and the substantial principles and activities of morality are intimately connected. We often talk as if moral principles appear from nowhere. But in fact, all of our moral principles are embedded in an enormous network of theory and practical observations, and that network allows us to interpret and make sense of what otherwise would be empty commands that might be interpreted any way anyone wanted to interpret them. (It was more or less clear to the Hebrews, for example, how the Ten Commandments were to be interpreted, since those were the key principles of a morality which they had more or less been following for centuries already.)

In the twenty-five hundred years or so in which scholars, preachers, and philosophers of all kinds have been formulating their moral theories, it has become evident that theories of morality tend to fall into a number of precise but overlapping categories. For our purposes here, we might classify moral theories into three groups: duty-defined moralities, consequentialist theories, and virtue ethics.

DUTY-DEFINED MORALITY

The least complicated example of a duty-defined morality would be the Ten Commandments, which simply give us a list of our duties. Such orders were called by Immanuel Kant **categorical imperatives**—an "imperative" simply being an order or a commandment, "categorical" meaning "without qualification." They are categorical, or without qualification, because they offer no reasons or conditions; they just tell us what it is that we must do or not do. It is the authority of the principle itself—or the authority by which it is given to us—that is the sole reason needed to obey it. In addition, of course, obeying the principle might in fact be good for us; indeed, it might even be the precondition for the stability of our society. But a duty-defined morality insists that it is the status of the principle itself, whatever its consequences and whatever personal reasons we might find in addition for obeying it, that is its justification for us.

Duty-defined morality may appeal to a number of authorities, and these authorities may be either within us or outside of us. The traditional Judeo-Christian moral theory makes the authority and the source of morality (God) wholly outside of us (although there may be some inner reminder as well, such as conscience). But duty-defined morality may be secular as well as religious, and the king, the president, the state in general, or the local oracle or prophet may serve as source and authority of moral principles. When people say, "You must obey; it's the law," they are appealing to the state (or the "law") as an authority to be obeyed, even if the consequences of the law in question are such that we might all be better off if there were no such law. And within the family, it is often the case that, without understanding the purpose or the consequences of an order, young children are expected to obey the authority of their parents, just because they are, in that small context, the authorities who define the rules for their children, presumably in accordance with the established rules and values of their society.

Kant and the Authority of Reason

The most complex and sophisticated theories of moralities of principles, however, are the ones that make the authority *internal* to us. According to such theories, moral rules and principles are not imposed upon us by God or by society but rather are to be found within us, as *conscience,* for example, or as the voice of *reason*. Kant insisted that morality, whatever else it might be, is first of all a matter of reason and rationality, and that the source and justification of moral principles—however we might learn them as children—are ultimately in ourselves. He called this **autonomy**, which means that every one of us is capable of figuring out what is right or wrong on his or her own, without appeal to external authority, just by using the faculty of reason. But this does not mean that morality is whatever each of us decides it to be, a mere matter of personal or "subjective" opinion. Reason is an authority that is "in" us but yet transcends us. It is "objective" and prescribes universal and

Nothing can possibly be conceived in the world, or even out of it, which can be called good without qualification, except a good will.

• • •

To secure one's own happiness is a duty, at least indirectly; for discontent with one's condition, under a pressure of many anxieties and amidst unsatisfied wants, might easily become a great temptation to transgression of duty.

• • •

Kant's formulations of the categorical imperative:

1. *Act only on that maxim [intention] whereby you can at the same time will that it should become a universal law.*

2. *Act as if the maxim of your action were to become by your will a universal law of nature.*

3. *Always act so as to treat humanity, whether in yourself or in others, as an end in itself, never merely as a means.*

4. *Always act as if to bring about, and as a member of, a Kingdom of Ends [that is, an ideal community in which everyone is always moral].*

— *Kant,* Grounding of
the Metaphysics of
Morals

necessary laws and duties. It is the authority of reason that justifies moral principles. Kant added the intriguing suggestion that the laws of God are justified because they, too, are clearly rational, whereas the traditional view is that the laws of God are justified just because they are from God. (Kant believed devoutly in God but he also believed that morality has to be a matter of autonomy for us, which means that God cannot give us laws; He can only tell us what our reason is already capable of justifying.)

Kant's morality of principles theory begins with the insistence that it is always the rationality of the principles, not the consequences of our actions, that is morally relevant. Accordingly, he said, it is not so much our actions themselves which are of moral interest (since any number of circumstances or events can interfere with them) but rather our *intentions,* which are completely within our control. (Someone who has good intentions is described by Kant as having a "good will.") A person is moral insofar as he or she tries to be moral, tries to obey moral principles, tries to do his or her duty. And though obeying these moral principles and trying to do our duty will, in most cases, benefit both us and other people, this is in no way relevant to their justification. The justification for being moral is simply that it is the rational thing to do. Nothing else.

If, as Kant maintained, consequences themselves are irrelevant, how are we to decide what the moral thing to do *is?* First of all, Kant didn't say that consequences are in no way to be considered; what he said was that our acts are to be judged on the basis of our intentions (which includes a concern for the *intended* and *expected* consequences) and not on the basis of the *actual* consequences of our action, which in the case of an unpredictable accident may have nothing to do with the rightness of our intentions. Moreover, Kant's conception of a moral principle is such that it is always the *type* of action that is in question (e.g., "a case of cheating") rather than the particular action as such. For example, suppose we want to know whether it would be moral to tell a lie in certain circumstances. Suppose I need fifteen dollars immediately, but I know that I cannot pay it back. I now consider, "Should I lie to you and tell you that I will pay you back when I know very well that I won't?" But since what concerns us here is the rationality of such action, rather than the consequences of this particular transaction, what I must ask myself, according to Kant, is whether such action could be carried out *generally,* by everyone in similar circumstances. Thus I ask myself, "What if everyone were to borrow money under false pretenses, by lying about being able to pay it back?" Kant's answer is clear; if everyone were to lie about paying back money, it would be a very short time until no one would believe anyone else who promised to pay back money. If someone said to you, "Could you lend me five dollars? I'll pay you back tomorrow," you would simply laugh and consider it some kind of joke. This, Kant argued, is enough to show that the intended action is immoral and irrational. If it's not possible for everyone to act similarly, then the action in question is immoral and should not be taken. (Some of Kant's examples can be found on pp. 338–339.)

Now we get a clear view of what is perhaps the most important feature of Kant's morality of principles theory. The test of a moral principle's rationality is its **universalizability**—that is, its capacity to be generalized for everyone, everywhere. What this also means is that one and the same *set* of moral principles will apply to every person, in every society, at every time in history, regardless of the particular circumstances and interests of individuals or different societies. Of course, this is also sometimes said to be true of God-given moralities (though not, usually, of moralities whose authority resides within a particular society). Customs may differ, of course, but morality must be the same everywhere. Thus the authority of reason, for Kant, was as powerful and as universal as the authority of God in his giving us the Ten Commandments. Indeed, Kant said, they ultimately are one and the same authority.

CONSEQUENTIALIST THEORIES

"The road to Hell," we are told, "is paved with good intentions." What good is a "good will," we might ask, if it does not produce good consequences—that is, if it does not make people (in general) happy or, at least, protect them from pain and suffering? Of course, because people usually do what they intend to do, even allowing for mistakes and the usual amount of stupidity in the world, good intentions usually lead to good consequences. But are the intentions good because of the consequences, or do the consequences count as good because (at least in part) of the goodness of the intentions? Kant insists on the priority of the good intentions. Consequentialist moral theorists, however, insist that it is what actually happens that makes an act (and its consequences) good or bad. A good act, whatever its intentions, is one that has the happiest (or at least the least miserable) results.

Utilitarianism: Bentham and Mill

The clearest case of a consequentialist moral theory in modern times is a still dominant view called **utilitarianism**, which was formulated in the eighteenth and nineteenth centuries by a number of British philosophers and social thinkers, including **Jeremy Bentham** (1748–1832) and **John Stuart Mill** (1806–1873). Utilitarianism is clearly a goal-oriented moral theory because it places all of its emphasis on the actual consequences of moral rules and principles, and insists that they be justified only by appeal to how happy they make us. The duty-defined morality theorists, on the other hand, do not ask whether being moral will make us happier; they insist that we ought to be moral for the sake of being moral. Of course, duty-defined morality theorists also want to be happy and want us all to be happy, too, but they separate, as the utilitarians do not, moral questions of what is *right* from merely practical questions of what will benefit or harm us.

For the utilitarian, however, questions of what will benefit or harm us count for everything; as Mill said succinctly, "The sole evidence it is possible to produce that anything is desirable is that people actually do desire it." The goal of morality, according to Mill, Bentham, and almost all other utilitarians, is to make people happy, to give them pleasure and spare them pain. Indeed, Bentham developed a "happiness calculus" precisely in order to calculate, for any action or law, what the consequences in terms of pleasure and pain would be. Thus, in the previous section, if we wanted to evaluate the action that Kant rejected as "immoral" and "irrational," we would not ask, "What if everyone were to lie?" but rather, "What would be the actual consequences of my lying in this situation?" Bentham would essentially add up the benefits of the action, using a quantitative point system, subtract the painful consequences from this, and see whether the action was therefore desirable or not.

The utility principle. Always act for the greatest good for the greatest number of people.

John Stuart Mill was born in London in 1806. His father was also a famous philosopher, and the young man was subjected to a rigorous education in virtually every field of knowledge. He became the leading logician, social scientist, and moral theorist of nineteenth-century England. His view of individual liberty (as the right not to be interfered with so long as you do not harm others) is still the basis of much of our own thinking about civil liberties, and his theory of morals—utilitarianism—is still taken to be the dominant moral theory, according to many contemporary philosophers. He died in 1873.

John Stuart Mill qualified Bentham's calculus in at least one important way. Mill insisted that there were different *qualities* of pleasure and pain as well as differences in *quantity*. It is better to be only slightly satisfied with a "higher" pleasure than to be very satisfied with a lower pleasure—or, as Mill put it in his work *Utilitarianism,*

> *It is better to be a human being dissatisfied than a pig satisfied; better to be Socrates dissatisfied than a fool satisfied.*

Mill's qualification makes purely quantitative calculation virtually impossible, but the basic principle is still the same: the greatest good for the greatest number of people, the most happiness and the least pain for as many people as possible, for every act and every law or principle.

Why is Mill's alteration of Bentham's utility principle so important? Doesn't it unnecessarily complicate the question and make the elegant simplicity of

JOHN STUART MILL: WHY BE NOBLE?

The utilitarian standard is the greatest amount of happiness altogether; and if it may possibly be doubted whether a noble character is always happier for its nobleness, there can be no doubt that it makes other people happier, and that the world in general is immensely a gainer by it. Utilitarianism, therefore, could only attain its end by the general cultivation of nobleness of character, even if each individual were only benefited by the nobleness of others, and his own, so far as happiness is concerned, were a sheer deduction from the benefit. But the bare enunciation of such an absurdity as this last renders refutation superfluous.

John Stuart Mill, Utilitarianism *(Indianapolis, IN: Bobbs-Merrill, 1957), 15–16.*

Bentham's "happiness calculus" unworkable? Bentham himself said that "pushpin [a "simpleminded" game of the time, sort of like shuffleboard] is as good as poetry," indicating that one activity was as good as any other if it provided as much pleasure (or as little pain). But Mill's qualification is not just a matter of defending his love of fine literature and philosophy against philistines who would just as soon drink beer and wallow in the mud. There is a much more serious objection to Bentham's purely quantitative calculus than its refusal to give adequate respect to the "finer things in life."

Morality, as we have noted, sometimes goes against our interests. Morality sometimes prohibits pleasures, and being moral sometimes causes pain. But if morality is not just a set of "rules of thumb" for making people happy (and Kant, for one, certainly denied that morality had this ultimate purpose), then we can expect that there will be some cases, at least, in which the principle of utility will contradict even the most basic moral values. For example, suppose that a sadistic dictator derives so much pleasure out of torturing his subjects that his pleasure outweighs their collective pain. Or suppose a group of rich people in a community devise a way to get even richer by legally depriving a great many poor and middle-class people of just a small amount of their income—and get more pleasure from their considerable gains than the others suffer from their modest losses. (They might not even know about the losses.) Surely in such cases we all agree that the principle of utility should be abandoned in favor of considerations of morality and fairness. The greatest good of the greatest number is not the only important consideration. There are also those moral concerns Kant defended that constrain utility and provide rules that shouldn't be violated *even if* more people suffer than prosper because of them. Mill's qualification of the utility principle allows us to build such notions as justice, morality, and virtue into the notion of "quality"—even if this means that we must give up the simplicity of Bentham's quantitative calculus.

ARISTOTLE AND THE ETHICS OF VIRTUE

The function of man is a certain kind of life, and this is an activity of the soul embodying a rational principle, and the function of the good man is the good and noble performance of these.

— *Aristotle*, Ethics

We have already mentioned (in our discussion of "The Good Life") Aristotle's view that "happiness" (or *eudaimonia*) is the ultimate good in human life. Aristotle, like Bentham and Mill, thought that what is good and right in human activity are those actions which aim at happiness. But Aristotle, unlike Bentham and Mill, did not equate happiness with pleasure; he insisted that the happy life is the life of *virtuous action,* filled with pleasure too, perhaps, but it was not the pleasure which makes life good. For Aristotle the aim of happiness would always be the well-being of the entire community. Bentham calculated the greatest good for the greatest number of people by adding up the individual advantages and disadvantages of an action or rule. But what this seems to leave out entirely are the intentions and the character of the actor. Kant, on the other hand, gives generous attention to the intentions but little attention to the consequences, and says little about the community in which these actions take place. Aristotle simply assumed that the ultimate advantage of the individual would be identical to the well-being of the community in which he or she lived. In fact, if one looks over Aristotle's list of "virtues," it becomes clear that every one of them is aimed at strengthening and protecting the community as well as adding to the status and happiness of the individual.

The most essential virtue of all, not named on the list but rather presupposed by all the other virtues, was *honor.* We still use the word, but what we mean by it is a much-watered-down version of what was for the Greek philosophy the most important thing in life, even more important than life itself. Honor was the fusion between the individual citizen and the community. Since honor was bestowed upon the individual by the whole of the community—and we must be careful to distinguish this general sense of honor from the occasional honors (medals, citations, commendations) that a person might receive—and since honor was the most important ingredient in the good life, it followed that it was wholly in the interest of every individual to maintain his

ARISTOTLE'S LIST OF VIRTUES

Courage—particularly courage in battle.

Temperance—which includes the enjoyment of pleasure as well as moderation; a man who abstained from sex, food, and drinking would not be considered virtuous by the Greeks, as he might be by some people today.

Liberality—what we would call charity

Magnificence—spending lavishly and entertaining well

Pride

Good temper—but it is important to get angry when appropriate

Friendliness—a very important virtue for the Greeks, not just a personal pleasure or necessity

Truthfulness

Wittiness—People who can't tell or take a joke aren't virtuous. Aristotle would not equate "seriousness" with being moral, as some people do.

Shame—being sensitive to one's honor and feeling appropriately bad when it is besmirched. "Feeling guilty," on the other hand, did not even seem to be worth talking about.

Justice—the sense of fair treatment of others

or her honor. Individual interests and society's interests were therefore impossible to separate.

Aristotle was clearly concerned with consequences, but he included within his theory elements that might rightly be considered part of a duty-defined theory. For example, like Kant, he considered reason and rationality essential to morality and the good life, and rationality, for him, included the understanding and contemplation of principles. Moreover, these principles have authority (both the authority of reason and the authority of society as a whole), which is their justification. Indeed, Aristotle defended one further virtue, which he sometimes described as the good life as such, the "life of contemplation." From this view, the good life is essentially the life of the philosopher, and its main ingredient (as in Kant) consists of the wisdom of thinking about, as well as acting upon, the general principles of virtue.

MORALITY — RELATIVE OR ABSOLUTE?

The content of ethics and "morality" seems to mean different things to different philosophers. Kant strictly defines morality when he equates it with duty and "the dictates of practical reason," whereas utilitarians tend to focus instead on the consequences of action. Aristotle did not even have a conception of "morality" as we know it, but he certainly believed both that reason played a major role in ethics and that the consequences of our actions were just as important as our good intentions. Other cultures—even more different from ours than ancient Greece—display even greater differences in their conceptions of morality, and many do not have a concept anything like our "morality" at all. But does this mean that there is no single set of **absolute** values, certain fundamental values that are essential to every system of ethics? Does this mean that all values are **relative** to a particular society or people?

Traveling around the world—reading novels and books on anthropology— it is evident that people do believe and have believed in very different moral and ethical systems. One culture believes an action is right that another believes is wrong. A society suffering from a severe food shortage and overpopulation believes it permissible to abandon newborn babies, who will almost certainly die; another, like our own, finds this practice horrible and condemns it in the strongest moral terms. Are we right and they wrong, or are they "right," too? Who is to judge? (If we call in a third party, an "impartial" judge, wouldn't that just make it a three-way rather than a two-way disagreement?)

Many of the differences between us, of course, are merely superficial, for instance, differences in custom or etiquette (dress, table manners). Some are profound—such as differences in religion and philosophy—but yet most cultures manage to coexist with others whose beliefs are startlingly different. Where the differences become something more than ethnic peculiarities and matters of tolerance, however, is where they become serious disagreements over basic ethical questions—questions about life and death, questions about the very nature of society. But even there we can ask whether the differences are in fact rock-bottom disagreements or still based on some more basic,

Moral Relativism: the thesis that there *are no* universal and essential moral values, that morality is "relative" to particular societies or peoples.

Moral Absolutism: the thesis that there *are* universal and essential moral values. If some society or people do not accept these values, then they are not moral.

shared value. For example, the overpopulated culture that abandons newborns presumably does so for the well-being of the already mature or maturing members of society. And this—the well-being of the society—is a value that we share with them even if we are horrified by their practice of abandoning babies.

If there are fundamental differences between our society and its morality and others, does this mean that morality must be relative? Let us distinguish two very different theses. **Cultural relativism** is the thesis that different people around the world (and even in the same society) in fact hold different values and believe in different moral codes. But this leaves open the question as to which (if any) is correct. **Ethical relativism** is the thesis that whatever a culture or a society holds to be right *is* therefore right or, at least, "right for them." From an extreme individualist view, this could be interpreted as meaning that you are right if you sincerely think you are (which is different from saying that sincerity itself is what ultimately makes a moral belief right). It is this view—ethical relativism—that raises deep questions for philosophers. Cultural relativism—the thesis that different people have different moral beliefs—can be accepted as true without concluding from it that different people are right in their different beliefs. It could still be that every society but one is wrong, or even that every society is wrong.

One immediate problem with ethical relativism is that it renders meaningless any moral judgments about another culture's behavior. If morality were truly relative, how could we continue to condemn the horrors committed against innocent civilians in Nazi Germany, or how could we condemn apartheid in South Africa today? We need some standard or standpoint from which we can affirm one morality and reject another, whether or not it is the

Cultural Relativism: the thesis that different people *in fact* have different values. This leaves open the question as to which (if any) is correct.

Ethical Relativism: the thesis that whatever a culture or a society holds to be right *is* therefore right or, at least, "right for them."

generally accepted morality of the other society. Naturally, it never is. The Jews, Catholics, and Gypsies who were herded into the Nazi death camps did not share their persecutors' moral values; nor does the large majority of blacks and coloreds in South Africa share the government's view of racial separation and privilege.

To defend moral absolutism, we should add, is not to affirm one culture-bound set of moral rules as applicable to everyone else on earth (which is sometimes called "moral imperialism") but rather to affirm one set of standards that transcends any one culture and applies equally to all cultures. It is at least possible, accordingly, that our shared sense of morality is inadequate or less moral than the values of some other people. To be a moral absolutist is not necessarily to be a moral imperialist (although the temptation to take one's own deeply felt moral values as absolute is almost unavoidable).

Tolerance is one of the central values of our multiracial, multiethnic, polydimensional society. Ours is a **pluralistic** society, which means that we are not so much a "melting pot" as a "mixed salad" of a society in which different groups have very different values, different religions, and different customs, and in order for us to get along together it is essential that we tolerate these differences. We force ourselves to tolerate—which means that we must accept—behavior very different from our own and very different from what we think is right. Sometimes, though, we may feel that to be tolerant would be to abdicate our responsibilities. Consider issues such as abortion, pot smoking, or racially exclusive clubs. At some point most people will start to argue that a certain practice is so reprehensible that the good of suppressing it overrides the imperative to be tolerant. The question of moral relativism asks whether there is a limit to this tolerance, an end point to these differences. Or is it the case that even the most basic moral values will inevitably be points of contention and conflict? It is important to note that even advocating tolerance is to defend at least one value as absolute (e.g., the value of "getting along" with one another), and so to reject strict relativism.

NIETZSCHE AND THE ATTACK ON MORALITY

> *By morality the individual is taught to become a function of the herd, and to ascribe to himself value only as a function. . . . Morality is the herd instinct in the individual.*

> — *Nietzsche,* The Gay Science

The theories of morality that take morality to be primarily a matter of duties and the consequentialist theories that take moral rules to be mainly guidelines to human happiness have in common most of their substantial moral principles. Indeed, John Stuart Mill and Immanuel Kant would probably have agreed on most major issues, though their reasons may have been quite different. Even Aristotle would have agreed with most of their recommendations.

But there is a further step that may be taken in moral theorizing, which is far more skeptical and far less respectful of our ordinary moral sentiments than any of the theories we have discussed thus far. Suppose we were to return to our initial question of this section and ask, once again, why an individual should act against his or her own self-interests and obey a moral principle. According to duty-defined moralities, the answer would be something like "Because of the authority vested in the principle" (whether by God, by society, or by reason). The answer of consequentialist moralities would be something like "Because it will be best for most of us in the long run." But suppose a philosopher comes along who asks why he or she *should* personally respect the authority of God, or society, or reason. What would happen if it turned out in the long run that what is best for a single individual is not best for more of us? Why, then, should that person be moral?

Friedrich Nietzsche led an attack on morality—more precisely. Judeo-Christian morality—from which our society has never fully recovered. Nietzsche attacked the authority of the Ten Commandments; in fact, he declared that "God is dead," thus leaving His morality devoid of its divine justification, source, and sanctions. Nietzsche pointed out that societies of modern times were "decadent," falling apart, and that their moral authority need no longer be binding on a creative individual who rejected that decadence and disintegration. And as for reason, he pointed out, there are other things of importance in human life besides reason—passion, the love of adventure, artistic creativity, the effort to go beyond the rational principles that most people tend to accept. Mere pleasure and happiness are not of ultimate importance either, he argued, but rather, our primary goal in life is, in every case, what he called "power" but what might better be understood as "self-expression." The meaning of human life, according to Nietzsche, is creativity; the good life is the artist's life. But this, he argued, was incompatible with what is now called morality, which dampens creativity, which tries to make all of us the same, which prevents us from being daring and inventive.

There are two completely different ways of interpreting Nietzsche, but both are probably correct. On the one hand, Nietzsche talked in the most belligerent language imaginable, sounding very much like an ancient barbarian out to destroy everything in modern civilized life, with all its comforts and conveniences, in order to return to a world in which the strongest, most creative creatures survived and flourished and the weak tended to perish. This is the Nietzsche who outraged his contemporaries and has terrified some undergraduates and most Sunday school teachers ever since. But Nietzsche himself, according to all reports, was a perfectly civilized, shy, witty gentleman. The other Nietzsche, accordingly, was a mild-mannered but outspoken defender of creative ideas, a critic of those who hid behind moral principles as an excuse for doing nothing and making nothing of themselves, an enemy of hypocrisy, laziness, and cowardice but not of civilization and sanity. In fact, what Nietzsche envisioned was a society more exciting and more civilized than our own, a society of a dynamic individuals rather than (according to his favorite metaphor) a herd of sheep. He called the members of this future society übermenschen, or "supermen." But to clear the way for this superior

"MASTER" AND "SLAVE" MORALITY: NIETZSCHE

Wandering through the many subtler and coarser moralities which have so far been prevalent on earth, I found that certain features recurred regularly together and were closely associated—until I finally discovered two basic types. . . . Master morality and slave morality. . . . The noble human being separates from himself those in whom the opposite of such exalted, proud states finds expression: he despises them. It should be noted immediately that in this first type of morality the opposition of "good" and "bad" means approximately the same as "noble" and "contemptible." (The opposition of "good" and "evil" has a different origin.) . . .

It is different with the second type of morality, slave morality. Suppose the violated, oppressed, suffering, unfree, who are uncertain of themselves and weary, moralize: what will their moral valuations have in common? Probably, a pessimistic suspicion about the whole condition of man will find expression, perhaps a condemnation of man along with his condition. . . . Conversely, those qualities are brought out and flooded with light which serve to ease existence for those who suffer: here pity, the complaisant and obliging hand, the warm heart, patience, industry, humility, and friendliness are honored—for here these are the most useful qualities and almost the only means for enduring the pressure of existence. Slave morality is essentially a morality of utility.

Here is the place for the origin of that famous opposition of "good" and "evil": into evil one's feelings project power and dangerousness, a certain terribleness, subtlety, and strength that does not permit contempt to develop. According to slave morality, those who are "evil" thus inspire fear; according to master morality it is precisely those who are "good" that inspire, and wish to inspire, fear, while the "bad" are felt to be contemptible.

— *From* Beyond Good and Evil

civilization it would first be necessary to remove the false justifications of the reigning morality, Judeo-Christian morality.

Nietzsche's moral theory, therefore, is an attempt to undermine morality, to get rid of it, to show it to be fraudulent. One part of his attempt is his rejection of God as dead, by which Nietzsche meant, essentially, that people no longer really believe in God; they go to church and say a few prayers, but they don't believe in God's ability or willingness actually to enforce morality. Morality, according to Nietzsche, is a kind of trick; it is a trick to gain power, a trick not needed by strong, creative souls (for they already have power), but rather a trick perpetuated by the weak, as a way of protecting themselves against the strong. If we consider once again the various rules of morality—for example. "Don't kill," "Don't steal," "Don't cheat"—we might notice that a significant proportion of such rules are *prohibitions*—that is, rules forbidding us to do something. Why is this? Suppose we change our approach to these questions and ask, "Who benefits from these prohibitions?" The answer is not, "Everyone," but rather, "Those who cannot protect themselves"—in other words, the weak. Now we can see why so many of the rules are prohibitions rather than positive virtues (as in Aristotle): The rules benefit the weaker members of society by preventing the stronger members from taking advantage of their strength. The strong can take care of themselves; morality is the protection of the weak.

We can understand, too, according to Nietzsche's view, why the idea that moral rules must be universal becomes so important. Moral rules would not protect anyone if those people against whom the rules were formulated did not obey them, or if they thought that the rules did not apply to them. But once this has been pointed out, Nietzsche said, those who are strong and creative will realize that, contrary to the utilitarian promises, obedience to the rules may not be advantageous to everyone—namely, not to them. And with this argument, Nietzsche believed that he could undermine morality. And yet, Nietzsche did not enjoy the idea that civilization as we know it might soon break down and give way to an orgy of violence and political chaos. In fact, he predicted such a future (that is, the twentieth century) with considerable horror. Indeed, Nietzsche even said that the strong have a "duty" to help the weak—very Kantian language—and the idea seems to be that the creative hero for whom Nietzsche's philosophy is intended should be concerned primarily not with being a "good man" and being moral but rather with living the good and exciting life. And this is the problem that Nietzsche has left for us: How can we justify the rules of morality for all of us without quashing the individual creativity that is in the best of us? "Why should we be moral?" is no longer an immoral question to ask. In fact, it has become an essential part of the moral life itself.

CLOSING QUESTIONS

1. What is your conception of the good life? What goals or principles are primary? What are the roles of success, wealth, freedom, and friendship? Are they ends or means? If they are means, how do they lead to the end in question?

2. What qualities do you consider to be the most important virtues a person can possess? What are the qualities most valued by our society?

3. In our sense, is it always the case that everyone strives for happiness? Are there other goals or principles that might be more important?

4. What considerations do you use to tell whether someone's action is "self-ish"? Is selfishness always wrong? Sometimes wrong? When? Be specific.

5. Under what circumstances, if any, is it permissible to lie? What does your answer indicate about the justification of the principle that one ought not to lie?

6. How would you apply the first formulation of Kant's categorical imperative to a specific circumstance? Imagine, for instance, that you are considering stealing a book when no one is looking. How would you decide, according to Kant, that this act is immoral?

7. The British philosopher Alfred North Whitehead once wrote, "What is morality in any given time and place? It is what the majority then and there happen to like and immorality is what they dislike." Do you agree?

8. A hungry cannibal chieftain looks you over and declares that you will indeed make a fine dinner. What can you say to him to convince him that cooking you would be *wrong?* (Convincing him that you won't taste good is not enough.)

BIBLIOGRAPHY AND SUGGESTED READINGS

A brief but comprehensive history of ethics is Alasdair MacIntyre's *A Short History of Ethics* (Macmillan, 1966), which can be followed by MacIntyre's more recent and very exciting book on contemporary morality, *After Virtue* (University of Notre Dame Press, 1981). A schematic discussion of the various theories of ethics is Robert C. Solomon, *A Handbook For Ethics* (Harcourt Brace, 1996). The classic argument against egoism is in Joseph Butler, *Fifteen Sermons upon Human Nature* (Macmillan, 1900); a more recent set of arguments is Thomas Nagel's *The Possibility of Altruism* (Oxford University Press, 1970). Aristotle's ethics are mainly to be found in his *Nicomachean Ethics,* trans. W. D. Ross (Oxford University Press, 1925). Kant's best summary of his moral philosophy is his *Foundations of the Metaphysics of Morals,* trans. L. W. Beck (Bobbs-Merrill, 1959). John Stuart Mill summarizes his utilitarian moral philosophy in his short book *Utilitarianism* (Bobbs-Merrill, 1957). Nietzsche's most systematic study of morality is in his *Genealogy of Morals,* trans. W. Kaufman (Random House, 1967).

CHAPTER NINE

JUSTICE AND
THE GOOD SOCIETY

Corbis-Bettmann.

JUSTICE AND THE GOOD SOCIETY

"Justice is that which is most primitive in the human soul, most fundamental in society, most sacred among ideas, and what the masses demand today with most ardour. It is the essence of religions and at the same time the form of reason, the secret object of faith, and the beginning, middle and end of knowledge. What can be imagined more universal, more strong, more complete than justice?"

—*Pierre-Joseph Proudhon*

OPENING QUESTIONS

1. In what kind of society would you prefer to live? A large urban society; a small rural society; some safe suburb; a bustling commercial city; a quiet, more or less homogeneous town in which people more or less share the same values; a multiethnic neighborhood with many different peoples?

2. Do you believe in the death penalty for the most heinous crimes? Why or why not?

3. Should a president of the United States be impeached if his (her) subordinates break the law?

4. Should shelter for the homeless be provided at government (i.e., taxpayer) expenses? Should this be undertaken at the federal, state, or local level? If you say "none of the above," what do you think should be done about the problem?

5. Is political power ultimately nothing but the rule of the strongest, the most powerful, the most persuasive on TV? Is a government anything more than the power of those who run it? Why are there governments at all?

6. Does the government have the right (rather than merely the power) to demand a percentage of your paycheck as taxes? Why or why not?

7. What is justice? What aspects of our society make it a just society? What aspects of our society are unjust?

8. Are there any reasons for paying one person less than another for the same measurable productivity?

9. Is there a "human right" to an education? Who has the obligation to make sure that you get one—your parents, the government, you yourself?

10. Do you believe that "all men [and women] are created equal"? What does this mean? In what respects are they equal?

MORALS AND SOCIETY

The Greeks had a saying: "To live a good life one must live in a great city." What counts as a "great city," of course, is always a matter of considerable dispute: New York or Omaha, Los Angeles or Austin, Texas? But what the Greeks had in mind, of course, was the idea that, to live a good life one had to live in a good community—one in which people respected one another and obeyed the rules, one that flourished and was not overwhelmed with problems of crime and poverty, one in which the happiness of one person was not to be gained at the expense of others. Aristotle's *Ethics* described the ideal citizen of such a community, and Bentham and Mill's utilitarianism provided one description of the ultimate goal of such a community—the greatest happiness of the greatest number of people. Indeed, even Kant, in his final formulation of the categorical imperative, suggests that one should always act in such a way as to bring about a "Kingdom of Ends," an ideal community. There seems to be no doubt about it: for almost all of us the good life presupposes living in a good place to live with other people, and our ability to be a good person depends at least in part upon those with whom we share our world and the society in which we live.

But although we can perhaps imagine a society in which everyone is wealthy and healthy, in which everyone at least respects everyone else and there is no crime and no poverty and plenty of everything for everyone, the world we live in is just not like that. It is worth noting that the imaginary perfect societies that some of the great philosophers and social thinkers have dreamed of and written about have been called **Utopia**—which means both "good place" and "nowhere." Human life as we know it is burdened with misfortune and tragedy. There is not plenty for everyone, and sometimes there is not even enough to go around. People are born in poverty while others are born into riches. Some people are born crippled or retarded, and most of us become seriously ill at some time or another. People of one race or religion look down on people of other races and religions, and crime runs rampant, not just in the streets of the city but all over the country, and not only because of poverty or need. So the question of living in an ideal society remains but a dream; meanwhile, we have to figure out how best to live in the world we actually do inhabit. Given the fact that people are born into very different circumstances and enjoy or suffer very different fates during their lives, how should society take this into account? What should we do with those who break the law and intentionally or irresponsibly harm others? How should we organize society, and who should have the power to run things? Just as we asked in Chapter 8 how we ought to live as individuals, we must now ask how we ought to live as a society. Of course, the questions can never be kept wholly apart.

The Nature of Society

People have always lived in groups, in large families or tribes that evolved into great cities and nations. "Man is a social animal," wrote Aristotle 2,500 years ago, and if some caveman 25,000 years ago had been asked his opinion he probably would have said pretty much the same thing. Apart from an occasional (usually fictional) hero alone in the wilderness, we are mutually dependent creatures. We need to live together. And with the exception of that one noisy neighbor, we usually *like* to live together. But any group of people, no matter how large or small, needs some form of organization, and organizations of people have not implausibly been compared to living organisms, in which a collection of individuals happen to live in one place. Every society has its own structures, its own "culture," its history, its mode of organization, its rules. The question is what kind of structures and rules these ought to be, and what kind of people we are such that we need these structures and rules.

The nature of the societies people have built and grown up in vary enormously, from the peasant and family-based agrarian cultures we still find in many parts of the world to the bewilderingly mobile and fast-paced cities of

SOME KEY CONTRASTS IN SOCIAL PHILOSOPHY

Person as a social function ⟷ Individual free to define
him/herself

Social status/privileges ⟷ Equality
(by virtue of birth, power,
talent, skill, achievement)

Obligations to society ⟷ Rights (demanded of society)

New York, Paris, New Delhi, and Beijing. In some of these societies, a person is viewed strictly in terms of his or her place in the society—as a member of a certain family, as a member of a certain class, as one who will be trained to be a soldier or a shoemaker or a farmer or a diplomat. In others, the concept of "the individual" is all-important, and a person's self-identity is to be distinguished from all of these "accidents" of birth and functions. In some societies, it is taken for granted that some people are "better" than others, by virtue of their birth or their abilities or their accomplishments; in others, it is said that everyone is equal and due equal respect and consideration.

The nature of society and the role of the person in society are essential considerations in social philosophy. It is not surprising that, as one reads the different philosophers who have written about the nature of society, that philosophers tend to reflect or project the perceptions, preferences, and dissatisfactions with their own societies. Plato's imaginary Republic is easily recognizable as a variation on Greek society, and the philosophers of the late Middle Ages who lived under monarchies defended the "divine right of kings." The philosophers of eighteenth-century England—living during the industrial revolution and the boisterous birth of capitalism—not unnaturally defended the right to private property that capitalism presupposed. And most contemporary social philosophers in America defend first and foremost the rights of the individual, such as freedom of speech and religion. This is not necessarily because of any cowardice or lack of imagination on their part but rather because we are, no matter how free-thinking and imaginative, a part of the society in which we were raised. Our conception of the good society and its structure is usually based on values we digested along with our mothers' milk. There will always be the occasional conversion—the repentant communist who turns into a vehement anticommunist and the successful capitalist who devotes the rest of his life to advocating socialism—but these are special stories just because they are so rare. Sometimes an entire society may undergo such a conversion—China rebelling against its Confucian heritage and embracing communism in the 1940s—but the enormous difficulties that such societies face in carrying out their conversion just goes to show how deep-set the old ideas will always be.

WHO SHOULD RULE?— THE QUESTION OF LEGITIMACY

What kind of a society do we want? Who should run things? Since prehistoric times, it seems that someone—usually the strongest or the wisest of the group—has taken charge, given orders to the others and taken on certain privileges and status himself or herself. Looking beyond ourselves to the rest of nature, we can see why this should be so. A wolf pack is led by the strongest, smartest wolf, and without such a leader the pack usually perishes. A hive of bees or a nest of ants each has its queen, without which there could be no hive or nest. And so it is easy to presume that the emergence of a leader in human society is just as "natural," and that he or she will be the strongest or wisest of the society. Who that is, of course, will depend on the nature of the society. In a warrior society, it will probably be the best soldier; in an intellectual society, it will probably be the wisest scholar. In a society where money is power, the rule will be by the rich (a **plutocracy**). In a society that depends on certain specialized skills (e.g., intimate knowledge of computers), power will depend on merit and ability (a **meritocracy**). In some societies, religion rules and those who hold power are the most powerful religious people (a **theocracy**; literally, "rule by God"). In some societies, those who rule come from the highest caste or class in society—whether one is born into this position or comes to adopt it by virtue of certain credentials, such as a sufficiently prestigious university degree (an **aristocracy**; literally, "rule by the best"). In some societies, the ruler will be one person (a **monarchy**); in others it will be a few (an **oligarchy**); in others, like our own, rule is shared, at least in theory, by everyone (a **democracy**).

But we are not, we keep telling ourselves, just animals. We are rational as well as social animals; we can figure things out while most animals cannot. Perhaps it is true that every society needs some authority and organization, but why should such power and direction be in the hands of one man or woman? Why not a group? Why not everyone, working and thinking together? And if there is to be some governing body, why should we simply let nature "take its course" rather than design it ourselves?

Plutocracy: rule by the rich.
Meritocracy: rule by virtue of merit and ability.
Theocracy: rule by religion, or "by God."
Aristocracy: rule by "the best."
Monarchy: rule by one person.
Oligarchy: rule by the few.
Democracy: rule by "the people."

Even in ancient times, the idea that the strongest deserve to rule was hard to swallow. To be sure, one had to accept such a leader if one wanted to survive oneself. But the idea that such power was **legitimate**, that such power was justified—that was a different matter. And throughout history, when those who have the power abuse it ("**tyranny**" is the ancient Greek word for such abuse of power), some people have banded together (the ruler's own inner circle, a popular uprising) to "throw the bums out" (in our distinctively American political vocabulary). Legitimate power—or **authority**—is not just a matter of strength or cleverness. It is a matter of justified power. That is why, for many centuries, monarchs claimed to rule by "divine power." In a religious society, who could provide a more powerful, more unassailable justification?

We reject the idea of the "divine right of kings," of course, because we know that kings and queens, like all of us, are "only human" and make mistakes and sometimes occupy positions for which they are ill-suited or incompetent. Kings and queens, like anyone else, rule according to the "will of the people." But notice that we haven't entirely gotten rid of the old idea of "divine right." We just don't give it to monarchs any more. We give it instead to "the people," which some scholars insist is a very modern concept and holds a place in our philosophy very much like the old idea of "divine right." Of course, some societies today manage to retain their nostalgia for old-fashioned monarchies and traditions in combination with parliamentary democracy. But even then it is usually understood that the legitimacy of the monarchy lies with the "will of the people" and not with the rights inherent in tradition alone.

What makes a government legitimate? It used to be thought that rulers were justified by God. But while our own politicians may often invoke God in

---

The best rulers are those with a shadowy presence to the people. Next comes the ruler they love and praise. Next comes one they fear. The next are those they despise.

Therefore the sage says: I take no action and the people of themselves are transformed. I engage in no activities and the people of themselves become prosperous.

Act without action. Do without ado.

Therefore the sage never strives for the great.

> — *From the* Tao Te Ching *(Lao-Tze) (5th Cent. B.C.)*

That gov't is best which governs least.

> — *Thomas Jefferson (1776)*

Political **power** is one thing, but **legitimate** power is **justified** power, or **authority**. A legitimate government has a **right** to rule. The extreme abuse of political power is **tyranny**.

support of their own positions (see box on p. 77, Chapter 3), we no longer think that God alone justifies a government and, in any case, one has to prove God's support by winning an election or two. So, too, it may have once been the case that **might makes right**—that those who were strongest or otherwise most superior would rule—but we do not accept the idea that the fact that one has and can hold power gives one the right to power, that is, legitimate power or authority. We believe, in short, that governments are supposed to serve the people, and the legitimacy of a government depends upon this. But even here, there are hard questions. Does serving the people mean making them prosperous? Is a rich society therefore a good society? And is the ruler who makes people rich therefore a legitimate ruler? Or is there another consideration here, that it is not the overall wealth or well-being of a society that counts first and foremost but rather the prevalence of *justice* in society (an important concept that we shall discuss shortly)? Is a legitimate government one that protects not only the rich but the very poor as well? Or is a legitimate government one that defends justice in a different sense, by enforcing the various rules and customs of the society, by punishing wrongdoers and thus protecting the values of the culture? Or is the legitimacy of a government not at all dependent on what the government does *for* the people but rather how the government is formed *by* the people. Thus a legitimate government, in our eyes, is first and foremost one that has been properly elected in a fair political contest.

ANARCHISM, THE FREE MARKET, AND THE NEED FOR GOVERNMENT

One possible, and in one sense not unappealing, suggestion is that no one should run things. We all know that governments typically make a botch of things, often take too much power and privilege, and provide too little in return. Perhaps we should just let everyone do what they want, government from the state of affairs more pejoratively called "**anarchy**"—a state of confusion and social disorder. Not having a government would create certain obvious problems of organization (e.g., establishing rules for safe driving and ensuring that essential goods and services are provided). But it is not at all obvious that a reasonably sized group of intelligent planners could not design an organization (for instance, a set of traffic rules and regulations, a system of supermarkets and service stations) that would be agreeable to everyone in the

THE BENEFITS OF CAPITALISM: ADAM SMITH

If we examine, I say, all those things . . . we shall be sensible that with-out the assistance and cooperation of many thousands, the very meanest person in a civilized country could not be provided, even ac-cording to what we very falsely imagine, the easy and simple manner in which he is commonly accommodated. Compared indeed with the more extravagant luxury of the great, his accommodation must no doubt appear extremely simple and easy; and yet it may be true, per-haps, that the accommodation of a European prince does not always so much exceed that of an industrious and frugal peasant, as the ac-commodation of the latter exceeds that of many an African king, the absolute master of the lives and liberties of ten thousand naked savages.

— *Adam Smith,*
Wealth of Nations

society. We agree to drive (in this country) on the right-hand side of the road not because the government forces us to but because we all agree that we must agree to drive on one side or the other, to drive safely, to drive sober. And given that most people are right-handed and shift gears with that hand, the agreement makes even more sense. To be sure, there will always be those who refuse to comply with such agreements, but do we really need a govern-ment (a highway patrol, traffic courts, judges) to enforce such mutually agreed-upon rules? And, to be sure, the absence of any higher power to dele-gate responsibilities might cause certain temporary shortages of goods—if it happens that no one at the moment is producing such goods—but must we assume that governmental authority is the only correction to such shortages?

One of the most powerful arguments of our times insists that, indeed, we do not need government to organize society. In a sense, we can just let every-one do what they want. It is the idea of the "**free market**"—that people will do what they need to do without being forced to do so by any law or govern-ment. If essential goods and services are needed, enterprising people will provide them—at a profit to themselves, motivated by self-interest. And if there are mutual agreements that must be made to make society better or safer, we will accomplish this ourselves, in our own interest, without the in-terference or the authority of anyone else. Of course, there may still need to be rules and restrictions (e.g., regulations to ensure "fair play")—but there need be and should be no government interference or organization where freedom of the market is concerned.

On the other hand, free markets have not shown themselves capable of solving some very pressing social problems. We need not question the value

The Invisible Hand: Adam Smith

As every individual, therefore, endeavours as much as he can both to employ his capital in the support of domestic industry, and so to direct that industry that its produce may be of the greatest value; every individual necessarily labours to render the annual revenue of the society as great as he can. He generally, indeed; neither intends to promote the public interest, nor knows how much he is promoting it. By preferring the support of domestic to that of foreign industry, he intends only his own security; and by directing that industry in such a manner as its produce may be of the greatest value, he intends only his own gain, and he is in this, as in many other cases, led by an invisible hand to promote an end which was no part of his intention. Nor is it always the worse for the society that it was no part of his intention. By pursuing his own interest he frequently promotes that of the society more effectually than when he really intends to promote it.

— *Adam Smith,*
Wealth of Nations

of individual freedom or the efficiency of the free market to satisfy at least some of our needs and desires in order to argue that certain basic needs are not well served by such a market. Health care is one example much in the news today. The demand for health care is simply not like the demand for most consumer goods. When a person becomes acutely ill, he or she is in no position to "shop around" or to consider whether the services in question are affordable. And with the advances in medical science, the cost of effective care is now prohibitively expensive for even the reasonably well-to-do. Moreover, since illness is often a consequence of other deprivations—malnutrition or lack of adequate shelter—illness often strikes hardest at those who can least afford it.

The free market has also shown too little ability to care for the poor. There is an old bit of market wisdom: the rich get richer and the poor get poorer. There seems to be no correction built into the market to handle such increasing inequality, and so there is a need for some "countervailing force"— notably government—to ensure that the very poor are adequately protected and provided for. Some people get extraordinarily rich, and some people sink into a cycle of poverty from which there seems to be no escape without considerable outside assistance. There is always charity, perhaps, but what if it isn't adequate? What we are discussing here, of course, is that enormous political concept called **justice**. Insofar as the purpose and the legitimacy of governments is to promote justice, we want to know—as Plato asked long ago in his great book *The Republic*—"what is justice?"

"ALIENATED LABOR": KARL MARX

What constitutes the alienation of labour? First, that the work is external *to the worker, that it is not part of his nature; and that, consequently, he does not fulfill himself in his work but denies himself, has
a feeling of misery rather than well-being, does not develop freely his
mental and physical energies but is physically exhausted and men-
tally debased. The worker, therefore, feels himself at home only during
his leisure time, whereas at work he feels homeless. His work is not voluntary but imposed,* forced labour. *It is not the satisfaction of a need,
but only a* means *for satisfying other needs. Its alien character is
clearly shown by the fact that as soon as there is no physical or other
compulsion it is avoided like the plague. External labour, labour in
which man alienates himself, is a labour of self-sacrifice, of mortifica-
tion. Finally the external character of work for the worker is shown by
the fact that it is not his own work but work for someone else, that in
work he does not belong to himself but to another person. . . .*

*We arrive at the result that man (the worker) feels himself to be
freely active only in his animal functions—eating, drinking and pro-
creating, or at most also in his dwelling and in personal adornment—
while in his human functions he is reduced to an animal. The animal
becomes human and the human becomes animal.*

— *Karl Marx, from his
manuscript of 1844*

WHAT IS JUSTICE?

Justice is the first virtue of social institutions, as truth is of systems of thought.

— *John Rawls,* A Theory
of Justice

Life is not fair, and it is a good thing for most of us that it is not.

— *Oscar Wilde*

In a good society there will be something more than prosperity; there will
also be justice. For example, one might insist that people who are good will
be rewarded, while those who are bad will be punished. One might insist that
people who work hard will be held in esteem and paid well for their work.
One might insist that people will get to keep what they have, without fear that
it will be taken away, and that those in need are taken care of. The problem
of justice arises when *all* these various demands cannot be satisfied, when

> **Retributive justice**: making sure that the wicked and wrongdoers get theirs.
> **Distributive justice**: the fair arrangement of the goods, benefits, and responsibilities of a society.

there is not enough to go around, or when the demands simply contradict one another. How can we make sure that the needy are taken care of if there are no taxes on the rich? How can we make sure that innocent people are protected without letting go some of the guilty? Justice, accordingly, is concerned with the priority of these various concerns and their implementation in a society that is, we admit, something less than perfect.

Justice is often divided into two parts, one concerned with punishment, the other with the distribution of goods and responsibilities. The first is called **retributive justice**, coming from the word "retribution"; criminal courts and prisons are society's instruments of retributive justice, and in a just society criminals are caught and sentenced fairly. A harsh sentence for a minor crime is an injustice, but so is a light or a suspended sentence for a heinous crime. If the guilty party "gets off easy" because he or she is rich and powerful, justice is particularly ill-served, for one of the presuppositions of justice is the fact that it is "blind" to particular individuals, their status, and their power. (That is why the depiction of justice traditionally shows a woman with scales, *blindfolded*.)

The other kind of justice is **distributive justice**—the distribution of goods—which includes salaries and bonuses for well-done work and education and medical care for the public. Distributive justice continues to be a source of deep controversy in contemporary life. For example, there is vehement disagreement, to say the obvious, over Karl Marx's famous suggestion: "From each according to his abilities; to each according to his needs." This is a summary of one theory of justice, but notice that it says nothing about what people *earn* or about their right to what they already have. It does not suggest that people might ever deserve more than they need. On the other hand, a great many people are outraged that some shiftless playboy can lead a life of luxury just because his father worked himself to death, leaving his fortune to this wastrel. And yet most Americans would say that the young man is *entitled* to the money, if only because his father was entitled to do what he liked with his earnings. But such entitlement plays no role in the Marxist conception of justice, where serving people's needs is the main concern of justice. The American sense of justice, on the other hand, is more concerned with making sure that people get and keep what is theirs. In a Marxist society, justice would demand that the playboy be disinherited and sent out to work for a living. His unearned fortune would be distributed among the needy. In our society, the young man gets to keep his money, even though we think he

FOUR KINDS OF EQUALITY

- Every person has the same abilities, talents, and advantages (implausible).
- Every person has the same status before the law (fundamental to the American conception of justice).
- Every person deserves to be given the same goods, benefits, and responsibilities in our society (unworkable, and contrary to our notions of merit and entitlement).
- Every person should have the same opportunities for achievement and advancement in our society (a necessary ideal but difficult to achieve).

doesn't deserve it, because justice demands that a person get to keep what he or she is entitled to.

Of course, matters of justice are not so simple. Marxist societies find it necessary to reward people for their work, if only to give them *incentives* to work harder. In our society, the shiftless young man may get to keep a substantial part of his fortune, but we can be sure that the government will take a good chunk of it for its own redistribution purposes. Indeed, every line on a tax return is, in effect, a miniature theory of justice—stating what people deserve and what activities are considered particularly worthy. Having children is rewarded with tax deductions; gambling losses are ignored. Return on investments may be rewarded with a low tax rate, lower than taxes on salaries. (What does this say about the concept of justice?) Distributive justice is an all-pervasive concern in our society: in every salary negotiation, in every commercial transaction, and in every grade assigned by a professor.

Our concern for justice, however, is a never-ending balancing act among a number of very different and sometimes antagonistic factors. We agree with Marx that people should work up to their abilities and have their needs served, but we do not put these two considerations at the forefront of our

FOUR CONCERNS OF JUSTICE

- People should get what they need.
- People should give what they can.
- People should be allowed to keep what they have (**entitlement**).
- People should get what they deserve (**merit**).

sense of justice. We are also concerned that people get what they earn (just as, in criminal cases, we think they should get what they deserve). We also think that taking risks and shouldering considerable responsibilities should be highly rewarded. And we think—a thought worth pondering—that it is perfectly just that the highest paid, most honored, and celebrated members of our society are those who entertain us—in sports or on the stage, for example.

But our sense of justice also insists, above all, on that sense of entitlement—that people deserve to keep what they have, no matter how little they have done to earn it, no matter what we may think of them. This makes our sense of justice largely conservative, as opposed to the radical redistribution of wealth urged in revolutionary countries. Indeed, many prominent social theorists have argued that, whatever our emphasis on hard work and merit, our capitalist system of justice depends first of all on this conservative sense of entitlement (the inviolability of private property, for example) and only afterward on these other concerns.

THE MEANING OF EQUALITY

The law, in its majestic equality, forbids the rich as well as the poor to sleep under bridges, to beg in the streets, and to steal bread.

> — *Anatole France*

What is most important for justice, however, in both Marxist society and our own, is the concept of **equality**. On the one hand, it is obvious to everyone that all people are *not* equal in one sense. Some are born healthy, wealthy, and smart; others are born wretched, impoverished, and handicapped. People have different talents, different looks, different capacities. Nevertheless, justice insists that they are all equal. What does this mean?

It means, first of all, that they are all equal *before the law*. Again, the blindfolded figure of justice signifies the fact that justice does not recognize individual differences in rank and privilege; justice sees everyone as equal. In theory, at least, the same laws apply to everyone and in the same way. A judge is obliged to hand out the same sentence to a rich man as to a poor man, an ugly bum as to a movie star, if they have committed the same crime. Two people doing the same job deserve the same salary, and it does not matter if one is male and the other female, if one is black and the other white, if one is tall and the other is short. Indeed, this sense of "same job, same pay" is written into law, because it is so important to our sense of justice and the good society.

But many writers have argued equality cannot mean that everyone should be made equal in a more general sense. In a story by Kurt Vonnegut, the author talks about a society in which everyone is made equal by handicapping the advantaged. Strong people are made weak by being forced to carry heavy weights all the time; smart people are made dumb by wearing noisemakers

A PRINCIPLE OF JUSTICE

Inequalities are arbitrary unless it is reasonable to expect that they will work out to everyone's advantage and provided that the positions to which they attach are open to all.

— *John Rawls,*
Harvard University

that distract them from thinking; graceful people wear lopsided weights to keep them off balance. But the outrageousness of the story is an argument that *inequality* is inevitable in any society. Some inequalities reflect real differences in accomplishment and make our whole society richer. People who work hard ought to live better, and people who can but refuse to work shouldn't have those same advantages given to them. And so the argument is that—above a certain subsistence level necessary for human existence—inequality should be tolerated as inevitable and, in certain ways, as desirable and advantageous to everyone. But should there be *so much* inequality? And even though we can understand why virtue and productiveness should be rewarded, why should we therefore accept the very different thesis that mediocrity and failure—or just plain bad luck and misfortune—should be punished? Could we not have incentives for hard work and productivity that nevertheless coexisted with material equality?

What equality means, many writers say, is **equal opportunity**. But here too there are problems. When we try to insist that everyone should be equal, we run up against the unavoidable fact that people are from birth unequal in abilities and advantages, and even the most radical and topsy-turvy restructuring of the society would leave this largely so. Besides that, our feeling that people ought to be rewarded (and punished) for what they do and our sense that people should get to keep what they have are both in conflict with that sense of equality. And so we retreat to the idea of equal opportunity. But here again the brutal facts of life are before us. There is no equality of opportunity, since the same circumstances that give some people ample advantage over others give them much greater opportunities too. "It takes money to make money" goes an old piece of wisdom, and no one can doubt that even a mediocre, lazy child who goes to a first-rate prep school has a better chance at opportunities for the future than bright, energetic children in an inner-city school. Equal opportunity seems as evasive as equality.

One might think that such complications would be enough to render an ideal impractical, but that is to miss the point of moral ideals in society. There has probably never been a perfectly just society; perhaps there never will be. But what our ideals of justice and equality do for us is to remind us, all the time, what we believe in and what we stand for. An overall scheme for assuring

TWO PRINCIPLES OF JUSTICE: JOHN RAWLS

We may think of a human society as a more or less self-sufficient association regulated by a common conception of justice and aimed at advancing the good of its members. As a co-operative venture for mutual advantage, it is characterized by a conflict as well as an identity of interests. There is an identity of interests since social cooperation makes possible a better life for all than any would have if everyone were to try to live by his own efforts; yet at the same time men are not indifferent as to how the greater benefits produced by their joint labours are distributed, for in order to further their own aims each prefers a larger to a lesser share. A conception of justice is a set of principles for choosing between the social arrangements which determine this division and for underwriting a consensus as to the proper distributive shares.

The two principles of justice . . . may be formulated as follows:

First, each person engaged in an institution or affected by it has an equal right to the most extensive liberty compatible with a like liberty for all; and

Second, inequalities as defined by the institutional structure or fostered by it are arbitrary unless it is reasonable to expect that they will work out to everyone's advantage and provided that the positions and offices to which they attach or from which they may be gained are open to all.

These principles regulate the distributive aspects of institutions by controlling the assignment of rights and duties throughout the whole social structure, beginning with the adoption of a political constitution in accordance with which they are then to be applied to legislation. It is upon a correct choice of a basic structure of society, its fundamental system of rights and duties, that the justice of distributive shares depends.

— *Peter Laslett and W. G. Runciman, eds.,* Philosophy, Politics and Society

equality or equal opportunity might escape us, but we can, by virtue of our insistence on equality, be aware of *in*equalities that exist around us, and correct them. It is "natural," one might argue, for people to associate with people of their own age, race, religion, and political persuasion; nevertheless, when this "natural" inclination interferes with fairness—for example, when an employer is hiring, firing, or promoting, or when some workers are forming a union, or when a club is being formed—our sense of justice intervenes and reminds us (perhaps with the help of the law) that such discrimination is not fair. It is inevitable, one might similarly argue, that in a complex corporation different people doing the same job with the same title will find that they have different salaries; but our concept of equality comes once again to the rescue, for it is under the power of that concept that we feel compelled—and the corporation will too—to make sure that people doing the same job are paid the same salary. However difficult and controversial our concepts of justice and equality may be, they serve an invaluable purpose in our society. We may argue for another two centuries on exactly what they mean and how they apply, but in the meantime they will be the instruments we use to improve our society.

There is one notion of equality, however, that should stand in front of all these other notions. It precedes equality before the law and is more important than equality of incomes and even opportunities. And that is the notion of *equality of respect*—the presumption that we will view everyone we meet with the vague but immensely meaningful idea that he or she, like ourselves, is a human being with feelings and thoughts, hopes and worries, affections and concerns. It is not a political or even a social sense of equality so much as a deeply felt personal one, taught to most of us from childhood as an essential part of being a citizen of a "classless" society, whatever the inequalities in income, wealth, and power among us. But if we appreciate the importance of such mutual respect, perhaps some of the other inequalities in our social lives will gradually be corrected.

THE ORIGINS OF JUSTICE AND THE SOCIAL CONTRACT

Outside of civil states, there is always a war of all against all.

— *Thomas Hobbes*

Man is born free, and everywhere he is in chains.

— *Jean-Jacques Rousseau*

Where does justice come from? And why should considerations of justice have any binding authority over us? Why do we have states and governments, and why (apart from fear of punishment) should we obey them? The most popular modern answer to these questions—which has come down to us primarily from the great social thinkers of the seventeenth and eighteenth centuries (especially Hobbes, Locke, and Rousseau) is that justice and the whole of society as well have been produced by a general social agreement, a **social contract**. We are obliged to obey the rules of justice—and the governments that enforce them—because we (in some sense) *agreed to do so*. It is as if we made a contract with the state—or, more properly, with everyone else in (what is now) our society—to live together according to certain rules that, according to our best calculations, are in everyone's interest, including our own. In return for our obedience of the rules, everyone else will obey them too (or be threatened and forced to do so). Just think of traffic rules alone to see how well this idea works as an account of both why there should be such general rules and how it is in our interest to obey them (most of the time) ourselves. And in return for our agreement to be fair and to support and participate in fair institutions—in particular the justice system but also the tax system (by willingly paying our "fair share"), the market system, and the system of contracts and ownership—others will participate as well. Society will be orderly and more or less peaceful; property will be safe and secured, and our personal lives protected. Justice thus results from a mutual agreement according to which we all agree to abide by certain rules and principles.

We ourselves have signed no such contract, of course; although one can argue (as even Socrates did in the *Crito,* almost 3,000 years ago) that one has made an implicit agreement with the society in which one lives simply by "choosing" to (continuing to) live there. And in the United States, in particular, there actually is something like a "social contract," an actual written document signed by representatives from the various then-existing states in order to "set up" a government and a set of general laws—our Constitution. But the appeal of the social contract view, whether or not one believes that there ever actually was or is such a contract, is that it makes government conditional on our (collective) interests and dependent on our (collective) decisions. (Jean-Jacques Rousseau, one of the leading defenders of this theory, referred to our collective demands as **the General Will** of the people.) Governments, on this view, don't just appear "by nature" and impose themselves upon us. We, in effect, are the ultimate source of their rules and laws, and it is our "will" that becomes the law of the land. As Rousseau profoundly put it, we ultimately impose the laws on ourselves.

What was there before people got together to form society? Why did they get together? The most famous theory of the prior "state of nature" (that is, before the formation of society) is that of Thomas Hobbes, who argued that human life before society and justice was "a war of all against all" and, consequently, "nasty, brutish, and short." He suggested that people are naturally selfish and, in a world with too scarce resources, we would literally kill one another if there were no laws and governments to force us to behave ourselves. So why would we join a society and agree to such laws? Because each of us would be quite afraid of being hurt or killed by the others. And in return for our promise not to harm them, they agree in return not to harm us. Not a bad deal. The implication, of course, is that human nature is still much the same and, without laws and governments, we too might return to that same brutal, mutually murderous situation. Writing at the time of the English Civil War, Hobbes regarded civil discord as the worst evil that could befall a society. The only way to avoid it, he argued, was for power to be given to a strong central authority, which could be either an individual or a collective body. On this view, the members of society voluntarily give up their rights to

The **social contract** was a concept that became enormously popular and powerful in the eighteenth century as a theory of the nature of society, although it was typically presented instead as a view about the origins of society, which was most implausible. The social contract theory views society as based upon the shared agreement of all individuals who are its citizens; as citizens, they give up certain rights and privileges in return for the protection and the mutual advantages of the state. The best single example of a historical manifestation of such a contract is the United States Constitution, in which representatives of the various states and commonwealths got together and composed a contract setting up the federal government and its limitations. Moreover, the idea of a social contract was one of the basic justifications of the French Revolution (1789) and, a few years earlier, the justification used by the American colonies to break away from Britain. ("When in the course of human events it becomes necessary for one people to dissolve the political bands which have connected them with another. . . . Governments are instituted among Men, deriving their just powers from the consent of the governed. . . ."—The Declaration of Independence, July 4, 1776.)

The idea of a social contract was influenced by three authors in particular:

Thomas Hobbes (1588–1679) was an English philosopher who also defended the theory of **materialism** ("Everything is matter in motion"), which influenced Sir Isaac Newton.

John Locke (1632–1704) was an English physician and philosopher who became known as the father of British empiricism (see Chapter 5). He defended the idea of the social contract in his *Essays on Civil Government* in 1690, just after the English Revolution (1688).

Jean-Jacques Rousseau (1712–1778) was a French philosopher; in 1762 he wrote the influential book entitled *The Social Contract*.

the sovereign power; but Hobbes believed this was a price worth paying in order to ensure peace.

A somewhat more benign theory of the social contract was defended by Hobbes' successor, John Locke. Locke suggested that in the state of nature we were basically hard-working creatures who tried to build things and cultivate the soil, and by doing so claimed ownership of that property with which we had "mixed our labor." But ownership in the state of nature would be a tenuous business. For although one had earned the right of ownership through one's work, protecting what one owned was quite a different matter. We got together to form societies with laws and governments, therefore, in order to protect our hard-earned property. Locke's theory, needless to say, places a high premium on the importance of private property both in justice and in the workings of society.

An even more benign theory was defended by Jean-Jacques Rousseau, who saw society and justice (as we mentioned earlier) as the expression of the General Will of the people. But Rousseau did not see the state of nature as a brutal war, as Hobbes did, nor did he see it primarily as a world of hard-working individuals. Rousseau instead imagined a world of plenty, in which our presocietal ancestors could easily survive picking berries off the trees and sleeping in natural shelters. They left one another alone, and even felt pity for others in need. "Natural man," Rousseau argues, was happier and healthier than most of us. Why, then, did people in the state of nature ever decide to form societies? Well, much of the evolution of society, Rousseau tells us, is something of a tragedy, a product of our inventiveness but also our gullibility. Whereas nature finds us naturally good and happy, society, he says, "corrupts" us. But, nevertheless, society properly conceived will not only restore something of our natural vitality and utilize our inventiveness but will actually make us into something more than merely "natural." Society will make us moral. Society will change a mere man or woman into a **citizen**.

These three views of human nature differ considerably, but they all point to the same conclusion. For whatever reason, we got together and formed society, with laws and justice as its central feature. It is an exciting vision. And whether or not one gives any credence to its historical claims—either the theories of human nature presupposed or the story of the social contract itself—the vision exemplifies many of our most treasured demands about ourselves and the society we live in.

RIGHTS AND THE NOTION OF THE SELF

One of the most important ingredients in most contemporary theories of justice—some authors would insist it is the definitive ingredient in justice—is the notion of **rights**. A right, essentially, is a kind of claim. Employees have a right to their salaries, for example, by virtue of a prior agreement with the company. Students have a right to an A if they have done excellent work in a course. To say that a person has a right is to say that someone else (perhaps the whole society) has a duty or an obligation to that person. For example, if a child has a right to a decent education, society has an obligation to make such an education available. Needless to say, there may be considerable disagreement about who should be responsible for this and how it will be paid for. Nevertheless, the right exists, with the corresponding obligation. To be a self in a society is to have such rights, as well as the corresponding obligation (for example, to help see to it that others get an education, by paying taxes, by sending your children to school, perhaps by teaching school).

There are different kinds of rights and duties signifying different levels of self. For example, some are **contractual**—the right to be paid for one's work, the obligation to pay for what you buy, the duty to keep one's promises. Some are **legal**—such as the right to drive (with certain reasonable restrictions) and the duty to drive (more or less) under the speed limit. Other rights and duties are **civil**, defining the self whether or not they are written into law—such as the right and the duty to vote, the right and the duty to speak one's mind about topics of political concern. Finally, there is the general category of **human** (or "*natural*") rights, which apply to every human being on earth, no matter what the society or the circumstances—for instance, the right not to be tortured and not to be imprisoned without reason, the duty not to torture and not to imprison without reason.

This conception of the self as having rights and duties, however, gives rise to some notorious political problems about the scope and nature of these rights and duties. For example, we can all agree that the right not to be tortured is a global human right, but what about the right to free medical care? Or the right to keep what one has earned, however one has earned it? How much power should society (through government or "the state") have over individual citizens? Indeed, how much of one's self is defined by citizenship? How much is one a self quite apart from one's membership in society?

A broad spectrum of answers to these difficult questions has emerged over the past several hundred years, as concern for the individual has increased and as the size and power of societies has increased too. We may mention, for instance, three possibilities: **libertarianism**, **liberalism**, and **communitarianism**.

Libertarianism

This is the view that people are defined as selves by a strong set of natural rights as individuals, including the right to be left alone and not to be interfered with, the right to keep what one has or has earned, and the right to be free from government interference in all things except when absolutely necessary to the general good. Libertarians tend to be strongly against taxes and big government, and strongly for individual freedoms of all kinds. For the libertarian, the self is largely independent, and people establish themselves as selves by what they do with this freedom.

Liberalism

This view also holds that people are defined as selves by a strong set of natural rights, but the set of rights is quite different from the rights defended by the libertarian. Where the libertarian emphasizes the right not to be interfered with, the liberal emphasizes people's rights to the benefits of society (decent housing, education, food, health care, security). Where libertarians stress minimal and local government ("That government is best that governs least") liberals tend to support a strong centralized government to administer social programs. For the liberal, the self is the bearer of rights to a decent life, which become the obligation of society.

Communitarianism

This view rejects the one-sided liberal and libertarian emphasis on rights and stresses the concept of duty instead. What defines a citizen is not his or her rights but rather his or her duties ("Ask not what your country can do for you, but what you can do for your country"). In the communitarian view, the self sometimes becomes a function of society rather than an independent entity. G. W. F. Hegel, for example, attacked the very idea of a social contract theory because such a theory claims that there are individual selves who are capable of entering into a contractual agreement before the origins of society in which such agreements are possible. This, he insists, is nonsense. The self must be defined by society; there is no self outside of society. At its extreme, this view sometimes leads to totalitarianism (or fascism), which holds that the individual self is literally nothing, that the whole self is defined by—and is the property of—the state. (Hegel himself rejected this conclusion.) But for all three positions on the spectrum, the self is (at least in part) a product of society, a *citizen* as well as a particular individual.

CLOSING QUESTIONS

1. What does it mean to say that "might makes right"? In your opinion, what makes a government "legitimate"?

2. In your opinion, what is the single most important feature of justice? Is it serving the needs of the worst off? Ensuring that people are paid fairly for what they do? Ensuring that people may keep what they earn? Protecting people's rights? Making sure that everyone is treated equally?

3. What do you think human beings were like before the formation of societies as we know them? What would we be like if we were raised (and somehow survived) outside of any social or societal context? Do you think that such questions are relevant?

4. If you and several hundred other people were about to form a new society (let's say, as you plunged into space, to populate a newly discovered planet), what principles of justice would you propose to your peers? What sort of principles (if any) do you think would gain general agreement? (Examples: "finders keepers, losers weepers," "everyone shares what they've got equally with others," "no one should be punished under

any circumstances," "anyone who breaks even the smallest law is exiled to space.")

5. If an already rich person makes another fortune on a lucky stock market investment, does he or she have the right (entitlement) to the entire gain—or should this be subject to taxation? What does your answer suggest about your sense of justice?

6. Would it be fair to hire or fire a female TV news anchor on the basis of her age or appearance? Why or why not?

7. Is it just that people should receive better schooling, better health care, and better legal aid just because they have more money? If you think it is just, explain why; if you think it is unjust, say what you think should be done to remedy the situation.

8. In what sense is it fair and in what sense is it not fair to treat everyone equally—for example, in the distribution of salaries and payment for services? Should someone who works hard make more than someone who does not? Why do we believe that "hard work" should be rewarded? Should a twenty-year employee make no more than a novice? Why should "time on the job" make a difference? Should the owner of a company keep no more in profits than she pays her employees? Why should ownership make a difference? Should a person who desperately needs a good deal of money for a life-saving heart operation be given more than another person who is in perfect health and has no particular need for the money? Do we in fact consider such need an important measure of "just desert"? Finally, why should a person make more because he or she is particularly talented or skilled? After all, he or she was lucky enough to be born with talent or into a family where talent could be cultivated. So why should we treat people unequally just because of luck?

BIBLIOGRAPHY AND SUGGESTED READINGS

For a general selection of views on social philosophy, see Joel Feinberg, *Social Philosophy* (Prentice-Hall, 1973). The first text for any study of justice and society is Plato's *Republic*, trans. Grube (Indianapolis: Hackett, 1974). Two classic statements of the social contract are Thomas Hobbes, *Leviathan* (New York: Hafner, 1926) and Jean-Jacques Rousseau, *Discourse on the Origins of Inequality* and *The Social Contract* (Indianapolis: Hackett, 1981). For a selection of modern theorists on justice, see James P. Sterba, *Justice: Alternative Political Perspectives* (Wadsworth, 1979). For a complete (and somewhat overwhelming) look at the leading modern theory today, see John Rawls, *A Theory of Justice* (Cambridge: Harvard University Press, 1971). A very different sort of theory is Robert Nozick, *Anarchy, State and Utopia* (New York: Basic Books, 1974). For a fascinating discussion of the nature of the disagreement between Rawls and Nozick, see Alasdair MacIntyre, *After Virtue* (South Bend: University of Notre Dame Press, 1981), esp. ch. 17; I have discussed these issues in my own *A Passion for Justice* (Reading: Addison-Wesley, 1990). The outstanding defense of "rights" in contemporary thinking about justice is Ronald Dworkin, *Taking Rights Seriously* (Cambridge: Harvard University Press, 1977). On equality, see Bernard Williams, "The Idea of Equality" in *Problems of the Self* (New York: Cambridge University Press, 1973) and Thomas Nagel, "Equality" in *Mortal Questions* (New York: Cambridge University Press, 1979).

CHAPTER TEN

PHILOSOPHY, SEX, RACE, AND CULTURE

Martin Luther King, Jr., UPI/Corbis-Bettmann.

PHILOSOPHY, SEX, RACE, AND CULTURE

Remember all men would be tyrants if they could. If particular care and attention is not paid to the ladies we are determined to foment a rebellion, and will not hold ourselves bound by any laws in which we have no voice or representation.

—*Abigail Adams, letter to John Adams (1776)*

[I]t doesn't mean that we're anti-white, but it does mean that we're anti-exploitation, we're anti-degradation, we're anti-oppression. And if the white man doesn't want us to be anti-him, let him stop oppressing and exploiting and degrading us. . . .

—*Malcolm X, "The Ballot or the Bullet" (1964)*

Better to be fond of something than merely to know it. Better to be happy with something than merely fond of it.

—*Confucius,* The Analects

OPENING QUESTIONS

1. Do you believe that men and women think differently? How do you know? If so, to what do you attribute the difference—nature, education, or choice?

2. Do you believe that members of different races think differently? How do you know? If so, to what do you attribute this difference—nature, education, or choice?

3. When you describe yourself (notably, to yourself), with what do you most closely identify—your nationality, your neighborhood, your social class, your sex, the people you love, your race, your beliefs, your achievements or ambitions, or still something else? Of what importance to your self-identity are the features you chose *not* to mention?

4. What makes one "culture" different from another? How is it possible to "translate" a practice or a belief from one culture into another? Do you believe that all cultures could understand one another, if only they learned to "speak the same language"?

5. Why do you think it is that white males have so dominated the cultural life of "the West"?

6. Before the legal abolition of slavery, was it morally legitimate to own slaves? Why or why not?

7. In India, some wives have been expected to share the funeral pyre with their just-departed husbands. In what terms is it possible for us to criticize or object to such a practice? In some parts of Africa, until very recently, young women were expected to undergo the painful operation of clitorectomy. In what terms is it possible for us to criticize or object to such a practice? In most countries today, infant boys (or, sometimes, young men) are expected to undergo the painful operation of circumcision. In what terms would you criticize or defend such a practice?

EXPANDING THE
PHILOSOPHICAL "CANON"

Looking back over the other chapters in this book and the philosophers mentioned in them, you have probably noticed that virtually all of the authors cited are white males. (Saint Augustine and Confucius are the very few exceptions, but Augustine's African origins are rarely explored in most philosophical discussions.) What most of these men have in common—in addition to their caucasian maleness—is that they all share a philosophical tradition that begins in ancient Greece and develops through Judeo-Christian theology and the rise of science in Europe. In this book so far, although we have primarily focused on philosophical problems rather than figures as such, we have mainly traced this tradition and stayed within its bounds. But there is much more to philosophy and the story of human thinking than this one "Western" tradition.

There is an ancient tradition—or rather several traditions—in India and southern Asia that are at least as old as the Western tradition, and there is a philosophical tradition in China that also stretches back thousands of years. Moreover, there is persuasive evidence that there were thriving schools of philosophy in the Americas and in North Africa before the arrival of the Europeans. There are living oral traditions in Africa and many South Pacific islands that have been passed down from generation to generation, and virtually every civilization we have ever heard of has some articulated conception of its origins and its place in the universe. It is important, therefore, that we should not be so arrogant or provincial as to define "philosophy" to include only the ideas of ancient Greece and medieval and modern Europe.

Then, too, within the Western tradition, we should ask: Where are all of the women? We know of female students in Plato's Academy and throughout the Middle Ages, but why are they not part of the official "canon" of philosophy? The short answer, perhaps, is that most of them never got the opportunity to run their own schools, found it hard to have their ideas preserved in writing and have been, for whatever reason, "written out" of the official history of the tradition.

According to recent critics, there has been an effort among philosophers and scholars to create and preserve an exclusively male, white, Greco-European Western intellectual tradition, which has marginalized or ignored the contributions of thinkers who were not male, white, and of European descent. Throughout the years of development of the current university curriculum in Europe and the United States, according to these critics of the university "canon," the political interests of Europe—essentially, a mixture of colonialism and industrialized capitalism—have influenced and distorted intellectual life throughout the world as well as in the university curriculum. They have argued that the traditional canon is propaganda for the industrialized world and its particular ideas of culture and philosophy. Thus the great ideas of philosophy and the great philosophers tend to be found only in a well preserved written, argumentative and more or less scientific or at any rate literalist tradition, that is, one that demands literal truth in philosophy and does not rest content with mere metaphor or allegory. Philosophers who did not make their way into print (or who were not lucky enough to have Plato as a student or Aristotle as an admiring commentator) disappeared from the tradition. Thinkers who did not engage in active argument with the tradition were often ignored. (Thus the mystical and "esoteric" tradition in the West is often confined to footnotes.) And nonliteral, nonscientific explanations of life and the universe through myth, heroic legends, and nonmonotheistic religions were simply dismissed as, at best, primitive or prephilosophical. The result is the rather well-defined list of problems and sequence of philosophers that we

Thinking about how the facts of "race" and the demand for justice may be accommodated to each other and to the realities of our various identifications and identities: nothing could be a more recognizably philosophical project. And what [W.E.B.] Du Bois called the "social heritage of slavery; the discrimination and insult" as well as the contemporary meaning of "racial difference" need always to be borne in mind if these discussions are to hew to reality.

• • •

These issues, which are crucial for questions of race in public life quite generally, intersect with a more narrowly academic range of questions in what I suppose we could call not so much the philosophy of education as the philosophy of the academy, questions about how racial identities and racist histories have shaped our disciplinary heritages. Philosophers (like others) have not always been good at seeing clearly the historical formation of their own discipline.

• • •

Feminist philosophers have argued that the structure of philosophical discourse reflects the longstanding exclusion of most women and women's concerns, first from the life of intellectuals, then, as it developed, from the university; and their lesson is not simply that here, as elsewhere, sexism has damaged women and men but that it has clouded our understanding. There has not been an equally extensive exploration of the question how racism has misguided our more abstract reflections; of how the absence of black voices has shaped our philosophical discourse. . . . [I]t seems simply astonishing how little of the political philosophy of the philosophers explicitly acknowledges the distinctive and different significances of race and other kinds of collective identity as well as of gender to the questions that arise at the intersection of the state with morality.

K. Anthony Appiah, The Philosophical Forum: A Quarterly *V (xxiv, nos. 1–3, Fall-Spring 1992–3: 30–31.*

have discussed in this book. It is an admirable and noble tradition, but it is not the only one.

In this final chapter, we cannot hope to become even casually acquainted with the main different philosophical traditions of the world. Rather, what we can do is to become aware of the peculiarities and limitations of our own ways of thinking and, especially, see how that thinking has been shaped and perhaps distorted by the particular features of our tradition. Throughout the chapter, we will take a peek at authors and perspectives not usually included in standard philosophy courses. In some instances, we may discover familiarities and contributions that we may not have expected—for example, some similarities between Confucian ethics in China and Aristotelian ethics in ancient Greece. There is also the enormous debt that European philosophy owes to medieval Arabic, Jewish, and Persian philosophers for interpreting and keeping many ancient Greek and Roman philosophies alive during that long period during which they were proscribed in that same Western tradition that would later claim them as exclusively their own. In many instances, however, what we will notice are the enormous differences between our own thinking and the thoughts of others. Often these differences are such that we cannot even explain exactly what they are. Chinese logic, for example, is so different from the logic we discussed at the beginning of this book (which is mainly derived from Aristotle) that an attempt simply to "translate" from one logic into the other is bound to failure or misunderstanding. Chinese philosophy is largely concerned with analogies and analogical thinking, what we would call metaphorical comparisons rather than a logic of evidence and inference as such.

BEYOND THE "WESTERN TRADITION"

It would seem, perhaps, as if all that would be necessary to revise and expand the "canon" of philosophy would be to assign more books in our classes and expand our reading lists—with books by African Americans, third world philosophers, Native Americans, women, and other neglected philosophers. We could add some Indian philosophy, some Chinese philosophy, some Arabic or ancient Egyptian philosophy, and that, of course, is exactly what many of the current philosophical reformers are doing. But many of the texts that define entire traditions are inaccessible because war and disease wiped out the entire culture, or because the texts themselves were destroyed, or because there never were any written texts, only oral traditions that have been grotesquely distorted or disappeared. Moreover, the charge made by many critics is that the influence of the tradition we have been discussing has been so great that it has pervaded or transformed every other tradition that we might try to read, so that an "authentic" voice from another tradition is impossible to find. Thus several advocates of a distinctive female philosophical style insist that there is no guarantee that a woman author will advocate women's issues or express a woman's perspective, and some advocates of an African-American philosophy rightly complain that every attempt at such philosophy is already contaminated by the harsh history of colonialism and slavery and that an "authentic" African perspective is no longer available to us.

A very different kind of problem is presented to us by Chinese philosophy. China has energetically protected its own traditions, several times sealing itself off from the West, precisely in order to avoid that sort of compromise and "contamination" that has destroyed the original cultures and ideas in other parts of the world. But the Chinese have thus remained so distinctive—"inscrutable" is not an appropriate description of this distinctiveness—that, even if we read the Chinese texts, we have great difficulty entering into the context within which those texts are comprehensible. Furthermore, the language is so different that it frustrates any attempt at mere translation. Chinese is wonderfully ambiguous, a feature of the language beloved and admired by Chinese scholars and philosophers but frowned upon by Western thinkers and frustrating to Western translators. In a sense, therefore, the texts are available to us and can be easily added to any reading list, but this does not mean that we will understand them or the world of which they are such an important part.

One of the most important and challenging projects for today's philosophers and philosophy students is to expand the number of contexts in which they feel comfortable and familiar. But it has also become more important to understand one's own texts and traditions in a different way, to understand the relation between a text—even in mathematics or epistemology or religious philosophy—and its social and cultural context, and perhaps also the social and political position of it author and its initial readers. As we have seen, much of philosophy consists of a kind of self-reflection, an attempt to understand oneself and one's place in the world. But it may do one little good—and perhaps a great deal of harm—to be forced to understand oneself in *another culture*'s categories. Thus some women philosophers object that they have been forced to think of themselves in philosophy in male terms and, therefore, as inferior or inadequate males, and third world philosophers similarly object that they have been forced to view themselves philosophically in Western terms and, therefore, as philosophically naive, primitive, or merely as "developing" societies. The groundswell of "feminist" and "multicultural" philosophy today, accordingly, consists largely of a rejection of the categories of "the other" and an attempt at genuine self-reflection, figuring out just what it means to be female or feminist, African American, Asian, Chinese, Vietnamese or Korean, or to be racist or nonracist, "Western" or "non-Western." Are there perhaps some concepts in philosophy that are inherently racist or sexist? So it has been charged. Is our conception of philosophy itself somehow racist, sexist, or otherwise exclusionary? So it has been alleged. Answering these complex and sometimes subtle questions about how thinking and writing carry political implications is itself a philosophical enterprise.

OTHER CULTURES, OTHER PHILOSOPHIES

It is no easy task to understand the philosophy of another culture. If some of the concepts of "Western" philosophy seem a bit strange to the average American student, at least the ways of thought and thinking of which they are a part are quite familiar. The examples (usually) strike home. The questions sufficiently resemble those with which we have grown up to make sense, even if they sometimes seem extreme or strange. (For example, "is my mind

> *Would the world seem entirely different if it were pictured, felt, described, studied, and thought about from the point of view of women? A great deal looks altogether different when we notice the realities of class brought to our attention by Marx and others. Not only do economic activity, government, law, and foreign policies take on a very different appearance. "Knowledge" itself can be seen as quite a different enterprise when subject to the scrutiny of the sociology of knowledge. When connections are drawn between intellectual enterprise and class interests, social sciences claiming to be "value-free" can be seen to lend support to a capitalist status quo, and we can recognize how normative theories presented as impartial can be used to mystify reality rather than to contribute to needed change.*
>
> *Gender is an even more pervasive and fundamental aspect of reality than class. If feminists can succeed not only in making visible but also in keeping within our awareness the aspects of "mankind" that have been so obscured and misrepresented by taking the "human" to be the masculine, virtually all existing thought may be turned on its head . . . a revolution is occurring that is as important as those that took place when the views of Copernicus, Darwin, and Freud changed so radically man's view of man. Some feminists think this latest revolution will be even more profound.*
>
> — *From Virginia Held, "Feminism and Epistemology"*

or soul distinct and separable from my body?" or "How can God allow evil in the world?") But to understand another culture's philosophy, we would really have to submerge ourselves in that culture as well. Philosophy is never a completely detached, timeless or placeless set of ideas. It always has its roots in the people who ask the questions and seek the answers. The styles as well as the subjects of philosophy vary from society to society, and while we can be confident of always finding some familiar similarities—after all, we are all human beings and face some of the same basic problems in life—we will always be struck and sometimes stopped by the differences.

Just as much of Western philosophy gets its background and impetus from our religious traditions, so the source of culturally diverse philosophies is often found in different religious traditions. In India, for example, philosophy is much more difficult to distinguish from religious thought than it is in the modern, more secular traditions of the West. In many cultures, in Africa and China and many islands of the South Pacific and Southeast Asia, for example, religion is itself much less abstract, much more human. This does not mean that its deities are anthropocentric but, much more important, that the

From time to time I began to feel an awkwardness arising from the difference between my ways of thinking and feeling and those of my hosts (That is Americans). For example, not long after my arrival in America I visited the house of someone to whom I have been introduced by a Japanese acquaintance, and was talking to him when he asked me, "Are you hungry? We have some ice cream if you'd like it." As I remember, I was rather hungry, but finding myself asked point-blank if I was hungry by someone whom I was visiting for the first time, I could not bring myself to admit it, and ended by denying the suggestion. I probably cherished a mild hope that he would press me again; but my host, disappointingly, said "I see" with no further ado, leaving me regretting that I had not replied more honestly. And I found myself thinking that a Japanese would almost never ask a stranger unceremoniously if he was hungry, but would produce something to give him without asking.

— Takeo Doi

most important ingredient in their religion and philosophy is one which plays a very small role at best in Judaism, Islam, and Christianity, and that is the notion of the **ancestor**. In many cultures, one's ancestors are considered, with varying degrees of literalness, to still be present and influential in on-going life. In New Guinea, for example, ancestors form an essential part of and define every community. In China, an overwhelming emphasis is placed on the ancestral family and the community. Confucius and the Buddha, the figureheads of two of the great religions of the world, are not deified in the way that Christianity, for example, views Jesus, and it is often pointed out (as we pointed out in Chapter 3) that some of the great religions of the world should not be classified as "theism." So, too, some of the great philosophies of the world begin with a very different set of concepts than those which have defined Western philosophy since Plato and before.

In what follows, we present a brief introduction to the various famous and influential philosophical traditions from some of the world's great cultures. But, before we begin, consider the short statement at the top of this page by the well-known Japanese philosopher-psychologist Takeo Doi, who finds himself puzzled by one of the most ordinary gestures in American life. So, too, we should find ourselves feeling "out of place" in our initial exploration of other philosophical traditions.

South Asian Philosophy

The oldest philosophical text (even older than the Old Testament) was written in India, possibly as early as 1500 B.C.. It is the *Rg Veda,* a book of

THE ṚG VEDA

HYMN OF CREATION

1. Non-being then existed not nor being:
   There was no air, nor sky that is beyond it.
   What was concealed? Wherein? In whose protection?
   And was there deep unfathomable water?

2. Death then existed not nor life immortal;
   Of neither night nor day was any token.
   By its inherent force the One breathed windless:
   No other thing than that beyond existed.

3. Darkness there was at first by darkness hidden;
   Without distinctive marks, this all was water.
   That which, becoming, by the void was covered,
   That One by force of heat came into being.

4. Desire entered the One in the beginning:
   It was the earliest seed, of thought the product.
   The sages searching in their hearts with wisdom,
   Found out the bond of being in non-being.

5. Their ray extended light across the darkness:
   But was the One above or was it under?
   Creative force was there, and fertile power:
   Below was energy, above was impulse.

6. Who knows for certain? Who shall here declare it?

A. A. Macdonell, ed. and trans. Hymns from the Ṛg Veda *(London: Oxford University Press, 1911).*

reflection on the origins and ultimate nature of the world and the personality of the gods and goddesses. It was one of many "Vedas," or holy books. The philosophy of ancient India is bound up with "Hinduism," but, strictly speaking, there is no single set of philosophies—or, for that matter, no single religion—called "Hinduism." (*Hindu* is an Arabic word, referring not to a religion but a place, "east of the Indus River.") *Hinduism* refers to an enormous variety of beliefs based on the Vedas. Hinduism also refers to a particular social system, the caste system, which was rationalized by the philosophy of the Vedas.

Traditional Hinduism is populated with fantastic creatures and divinities. A central trinity of gods is fundamental to classical Hindu mythology: Brahma (the creator god), Vishnu (the god who maintains the universe), and Shiva (the god of destruction). But these are, we are told, the faces of one God, one reality rather than many (a view sometimes called *henotheism*). The familiar depictions of Shiva point to a tradition in which the gods routinely take on various forms and manifestations, adopt different personae, serve very different functions, and accordingly have many different names as well. Throughout ancient Hindu thought, however, we find the enduring themes of renewal and the continuity of life, the oneness of the universe, however many its manifestations or appearances may be. Later commentaries on the Vedas, the *Upanishads* or Vedanta, further focus on that oneness of ultimate reality, whose name is Brahman (to be distinguished from the god with a similar name). The theory of Brahman, like the rich mythology of earlier India, is the idea is that there is one substance underlying infinitely many manifestations. The idea that there are many gods, all of whom are manifestations of the same God, is no doubt bewildering to monotheists and polytheists alike, if they think of being godlike as an inherently stable quality. Indian philosophy will also seem bewildering or incoherent to those who insist on not only the singularity but the ultimate rationality of reality and on its unchanging existence. Brahman is unchanging only in the sense that it is always changing.

Hinduism gave rise to two other great religions, roughly around the sixth century B.C. The first was **Buddhism** which was founded by Siddhartha Gautama ("the Buddha," 566–486 B.C.E.). The other was **Jainism**, a religion thoroughly committed to the sanctity of life and nonviolence, which was founded by the Buddha's contemporary, Mahivira. Both rejected the caste system, and both focused their attention on the problem of suffering in the world and how to escape or "liberate" oneself from it. Buddhists refer to this escape as enlightenment, as ***nirvana***, Hindus refer to it as ***mukti***, a state of bliss. For all three philosophies, this liberation is achieved through proper living, through ritual practice (for example, "yoga") and through meditation. Central to all three religions is the profound experience of **mysticism**. It would be an enormous mistake to think of Indian philosophy, even in its most ancient forms, as *nothing but* mysticism, the favorite excuse of many Western philosophers for ignoring Indian philosophy altogether. But the skeptical doubts expressed in the oldest Vedas continue to haunt the discipline, suggesting that Brahman can be comprehended through reason or reflection alone. Knowledge of Brahman may come through an all-embracing, unifying mystical experience.

Buddhism split early in its history into a southern version, mainly in and near India, which focused attention on personal enlightenment, and a northern version, which quickly spread to Tibet, Nepal, then China, Korea, Vietnam and Japan, where it became popular among the samurai warriors as Zen. The northern Buddhists insisted on the primacy of compassion and regard for the less fortunate. Those people who are already enlightened should "stay back" to help others. Such a person is a ***Bodhisattva***. Bodhisattvas do not enter the state of nirvana when they reach enlightenment. Instead, they remain active in the world, as the Buddha did, to help others extinguish suffering by sharing their insights with others.

A concern for the nature of the Self pervades Indian philosophy. On the one hand, there is the conception of the individual soul, *jiva,* which distinguishes each individual as a unique being. Whether or not this *jiva* is

ZEN BUDDHISM: DŌGEN

... In such an unpredictable world, it is extremely foolish to waste time worrying about various ways of earning a living in order to postpone one's death—uncertain as it is—to say nothing of plotting evil against others.

Precisely because this is reality, the Buddha preached it to all living beings, the patriarchs taught only this truth in their sermons and writings ... Impermanence is swift; life-and-death is the great matter. Reflect on this reality again and again in your heart without forgetting it, and without wasting a moment. Put your whole mind into the practice of the Way. Remember that you are alive only today in this moment. Other than that, [practice of the Way] is truly easy. You needn't discuss whether you are superior or inferior, brilliant or dull.

genuine, however, or in any way sufficiently substantial to survive the death of the body, is a matter of fascinating debate. On the other hand, the self is also referred to as *atman,* which might be understood as the principle of life that exists in every human being. Thus one might see each and every individual as a *jiva* vitalized by an *atman,* or, quite differently, one might come to see *jiva* as a false self and *atman* as the true self. The Vedas make clear that we are not to think of *jiva* and *atman* as two selves fighting for superiority within a person.

Buddhists ultimately reject the idea of the self altogether. They believe that all of life is impermanent, that reality amounts to a series of momentary existences, that there are no enduring substances. It is only delusion that leads us to believe that our selves have an enduring reality. In fact, there is no permanent self or soul. A human being is just a temporary composite of body, feeling, thoughts, dispositions, and consciousness. There is no underlying substance, a self or soul in addition to this composite. There is no larger eternal self, what the Vedantists call atman. There is only *anatman,* "no atman," no self. Recognition of the impermanence of both self and all objects of desire is a step toward insight and the end of misery. Jains, by contrast, hold onto the belief in an individual self or soul, not only in human beings but in every living thing. That is why their respect for all life is so uncompromising, since they believe—like many Hindus—that human souls may be reborn in animals. Jains take as their primary principle "do no harm," and they practice respect for life—all life—even to the point of taking care that they do not crush the insects on the ground beneath them or accidentally inhale those flying in the air.

Since both Buddhism and Jainism pay special attention to the nature of suffering and liberation from suffering, their philosophies are centrally con-

FROM THE *DHAMMAPADA*

Let each man first direct himself to what is proper, then let him teach others; thus a wise man will not suffer.

If a man make himself as he teaches others to be, then, being himself well-subdued, he may subdue others; for one's own self is difficult to subdue.

Self is the lord of self, who else could be the lord? With self well-subdued, a man finds a lord such as few can find.

The evil done by one's self, born of one's self, begotten by one's self, crushes the foolish, as a diamond breaks even a precious stone. . . .

The foolish man who scorns the instruction of the saintly, of the elect [ariya], of the virtuous, and follows a false doctrine—he bears fruit to his own destruction, like the fruits of the Katthaka *reed.*

By one's self the evil is done, by one's self one suffers; by one's self evil is left undone; by one's self one is purified. The pure and the impure stand and fall by themselves; no one can purify another.

Let no one forget his own duty for the sake of another's, however great; let a man after he has discerned his own duty, be faithful to his duty.

All forms are unreal—he who knows and sees this is at peace though in a world of pain; this is the way that leads to purity.

He who does not rouse himself when it is time to rise, who, though young and strong, is full of sloth, whose will and thought are weak, that lazy and idle man never finds the way to wisdom.

Watching his speech, well-restrained in mind, let a man never commit any wrong with his body! Let a man but keep these three roads of action clear, and he will achieve the way which is taught by the wise.

cerned with this problem. The Buddha denounced the caste system because it increased human suffering, for example. The Buddha's basic philosophy, however, is concerned primarily with the individual's *inner* transformation, achieved by means of insight into the "Four Noble Truths" of Buddhism:

1. Life is suffering.
2. Suffering arises from selfish craving.
3. Selfish craving can be eliminated.
4. One can eliminate selfish craving by following the right way.

This right way to liberation or enlightenment is called the *Eightfold Path* of Buddhism, which consists of (1) the right way of seeing, (2) right thinking,

THE FOUR NOBLE TRUTHS (IN BUDDHISM)

1. *All is suffering (and transitory).*
2. *The root of suffering is desire, attachment, and personal clinging.*
3. *There is a way to eliminate desire, and thereby eliminate suffering, namely* nibbana.
4. *The way to this supreme good is The Eightfold Noble Path:*
    1. *right thought,*
    2. *right resolve,*
    3. *right speech,*
    4. *right conduct,*
    5. *right livelihood,*
    6. *right effort,*
    7. *right mindfulness, and*
    8. *right concentration or meditation.*

(3) right speech, (4) right action, (5) right effort, (6) the right way of living, (7) right mindfulness, and (8) right meditation. The aim of Buddhism is to free oneself from deluded belief in the ego and all that goes with it, desire and frustration, ambition and disappointment, pride and humiliation, and to gain enlightenment and the end of misery, the condition that the Indian philosopher Nāgārjuna calls "emptiness."

Seeing, hearing, smelling, tasting, touching, and mind are the six faculties. Their spheres consist of the object of seeing, etc.

Seeing does not perceive itself, its own form. How can that which does not perceive itself, see others?

When an analysis is made in terms of emptiness, whosoever were to address a refutation, all that is left unrefuted by him will be equal to what is yet to be proved.

When an explanation in terms of emptiness is given, whosoever were to address a censure, all that is left uncensured by him will be equal to what is yet to be proved.

— *Nāgārjuna*, The
Philosophy of the
Middle

East Asian Philosophy

The great Chinese philosopher Confucius (551–479 B.C.) was active about the same time as the Buddha and Mahivira and the earliest Greek philosophers. In the sixth century B.C.E. China was already a highly advanced political culture. It was also a society in turmoil. Confucius' philosophy, accordingly, was concerned with harmonious social and political relationships, good leadership and getting along with others, and personal virtue. The central aim of

TAO (THE WAY) (LAO-TZE)

The Way that can be spoken of is not the eternal Way;
The name that can be named is not the eternal name,
The nameless is the origin of Heaven and Earth;
The named is the mother of all things.

These two are the same,
But diverge in name as they issue forth.
Being the same they are called mysteries,
Mystery upon mystery, the gateway to all subtleties,

My mind is that of a fool—how blank and how muddled.
Vulgar people have clear ideas. They see clear-cut distinctions. I alone
make no distinctions. They all have a purpose. I drift like a high wind
and the ocean. They are alert and smart. I am uncouth and rustic.

The highest good is like water. Water is good; it benefits all things
and does not compete with them. It dwells in lowly places that all
disdain. This is why it is so near to the Way.

Human beings are supple and weak when living, but hard and stiff
when dead. Grass and trees are pliant and fragile when living, but
dried and shriveled when dead. Thus the hard and the strong are the
comrades of death; the supple and the weak are the comrades of life.

Therefore a weapon that is strong will not vanquish;
A tree that is strong will suffer the ax.
The strong and the big fall to the lower positions,
The supple and the weak take the higher positions.

— Tao Te Ching,
translated by
Thomas Seung

Favor and disfavor have been called equal worries,
Success and failure have been called equal ailments.
How can favor and disfavor be called equal worries?
Because winning favor burdens a man
With the fear of losing it.
How can success and failure be called equal ailments?
Because a man thinks of the personal body as self.
When he no longer thinks of the personal body as self,
Neither failure nor success can ail him.
One who knows his lot to be the lot of all other men
Is a safe man to guide them.
One who recognizes all men as members of his own body
Is a sound man to guard them.
What we look for beyond seeing
And call the unseen
Listen for beyond hearing.
And call the unheard,
Grasp for beyond reaching
And call the withheld,
Merge beyond understanding
In a oneness. . . .

— *From the* Tao Te Ching

TAOISM: CHUANG-TZE

Now, speaking is not simply discharging air. Speaking has that which it says, only that about which is spoken is never fixed. In effect, do we say something or have we never said anything? It is considered to be different from the chirping of young birds, yet is there really any distinction or not? How is the dynamic pattern of things [tao] so obscured that there is such a thing as "genuine" and "counterfeit"? . . . The dynamic pattern of things [tao] is obscured by small contrivances, and what is said about it is obscured by embellishments on them. Thus we have the right and wrong of the Confucians and Mohists who contradict each other. If we really want to contradict them both, nothing can compare with enlightenment.

Eight Chinese Thinkers

Confucius (5th c.)	virtue, harmony in relationships
Lao-Tze (5th c.)	the importance of harmony with nature
Mo-Tze (5th c.)	people need love (and a good army)
Sun-Tze (5th c.)	the art of war
The Legalists (5th c.)	people need rules
Chuang-Tze (4th c.)	(Taoist) emphasis on natural harmony
Mencius (4th c.)	(Confucian) people are good (by nature compassionate)
Hsun-Tze (3rd c.)	(Confucian) people are bad (culture makes them good)

Confucianism was to define and cultivate the Way (*Tao*) to a harmonious society. Unlike his contemporary the Buddha, Confucius had no intention of founding a religion, but Confucianism—often along with Buddhism—is now the religion of one third of the world.

Around the same time, a sage called Lao-Tze argued a very different vision of "the Way" (*Tao*) to peace and enlightenment. Lao-Tze attributed great importance to nature and less to human society. Confucius thought certain passions "unnatural," for example, which meant, essentially, that they should play no part in the proper life of a gentleman. Lao-Tze, by contrast, had much more faith in nature and much more trust, accordingly, in the passions of un-educated, uncultivated men. For Confucius, the way to the good life is to follow the traditions of honor and respect set down by one's ancestors. For Lao-Tze,

Five Key Terms in Chinese Philosophy

Tao	"the Way," the process of living well.
jen	to be human/humanity/virtue
li	ritual
he	harmony
yi	appropriateness

the Way is more mysterious. It cannot be spoken. It cannot be spelled out. It cannot be explained in a recipe or guidebook or a philosophy. (According to Lao-Tze's *Tao Te Ching,* "The Tao that can be followed is not the true Tao; the name that can be named is not the true name.") But that does not mean that one cannot find and try to live according to it, and Taoist teachings are intended to guide us on our way.

Between them, Confucius and Lao-Tze defined Chinese philosophy. They agreed on their overall emphasis on harmony as the ideal state of both society and the individual, and they insisted on an all-encompassing or "holistic" conception of human life that emphasizes a person's place in a larger context. For both Confucianism and Taoism, the development of personal character was the main goal in life, but the personal was not to be defined in individualistic terms. For the Confucian, the personal was the social. For the Taoist, the personal was living in accordance with nature. Whatever their disagreements about the relative importance of nature and society, the Chinese thinkers were in considerable agreement concerning the necessity of harmony in human life and a larger sense of the "person" than merely individual. Accordingly, Buddhism found a natural home—where it intermingled with Confucianism and Taoism—in China, when it arrived early in the first century B.C.

The Middle East

The Middle East was one of the "cradles" of civilization and, so, too, the birthplace of not only the three most influential "Western" religions (all of them from what was known as the "Orient" or the East) but some of the first great philosophies as well. The ancient capitals of Babylon, Assyria, and Persia, for example, nurtured systems of ideas which eventually gave rise to many of our own concepts in philosophy and religion. The ancient Persian religion of Zoroastrianism, for example, is generally recognized as the precursor of the other great religions and of many of our central philosophical conceptions as well (for example, the basic opposition between good and evil). The Middle East was also responsible, during medieval times, for keeping many of the great ideas of ancient Greece and Rome alive when they were proscribed in Europe, and at the height of the medieval period the interchange between Christian, Jewish, and Islamic philosophers was so intense that it is often hard to separate the various innovations and influences.

Islam, the third and latest of the three great Western religions, developed a theology and an accompanying philosophy that were in every way as profound and detailed as their contemporaries in Europe. But although we often tend to collapse the various cultures of the Muslim world into the single concept of "Arabic," there were and still are vital differences between the very different cultures, some of them not "Arab" at all. In Persia, for example, there is an active tradition of theology and philosophy that goes back to Zoroaster. With the spread of Islam in the seventh century, Persia turned to theology and questions which were also being asked by the Christians in Europe, about revelation and "proof," about the ability of the intellect to grasp the concept of God. In what follows, the sixteenth century Shi'ite thinker Mulla Sadra reflects on these questions in the *Qur'an,* the scriptures of Islam (from his *Wisdom of the Throne*):

PHILOSOPHY FROM PERSIA (IRAN)

Know that to attain the true inner divine knowledge one must follow a proof or "unveiling" by immediate vision, just as He—May He be exalted!—said Say: "Bring your proof, if you are among those who speak truthfully!" *(2:111); and He—May He be exalted!—said:* Whoever calls upon another god together with God has no proof for that *(23:117).* *This proof is a Light that God casts on the Heart of the man of true faith, a Light that illuminates his inner vision so that he "sees things as they really are," as it was stated in the prayer of the Prophet—May God's blessings and peace be with him!—for himself and the elect among his community and his close disciples: "O my God, cause us to see things as they really are!"*

Know, too, that those questions concerning which the commonality of the philosophers have disagreed with the prophets—May God bless them!—are not matters that can easily be grasped and attained; nor can they be acquired by rejecting our rational, logical intellects, with their (intrinsic) measures and their contemplative activities of learning and investigating. If this were so, then there would never have been any disagreement (with the prophets) concerning these questions on the part of those intelligent men who were busy all their lives using the tool of thought and reflection to acquire a (true) conception of things; those (philosophers) would never have fallen into error in these questions and there would have been no need for the sending of the prophets (if these metaphysical realities were so easy to grasp). So it should be known that these questions can only be comprehended by taking over Lights from the Lamp-niche of Prophecy, and by earnestly seeking Them. For these are the Secrets which are the true inner meaning of Discipleship and Sainthood.

— *Mulla Sadra*

The passages in roman are from the Qur'an, or Islamic scripture. In parentheses are their chapter and verse citations. This and all following passages are from The Wisdom of the Throne: An Introduction to the Philosophy of Mulla Sadra, *trans. by James Winston Morris (Princeton: Princeton University Press, 1981).*

Native American and African Philosophy

Unknown to the Greeks and Romans (as much as they traveled), unknown to the Indians and the Chinese, were flourishing civilizations in the Americas, later to be known as "the New World."

The problem for philosophers and historians interested in the cultures of the Americas is the absence of records. In many cases, they existed but were destroyed, often along with the civilizations themselves. For example, the Aztecs of Mexico had a thriving school of philosophers called *tlamatinime* (which means "knowers of things"). But all we have left are fragments of their teachings, largely because their Spanish conquerors deliberately burned most of their books.

At the core of American philosophy (in what is now Mexico and central South America) was a belief in three levels of time and reality—ordinary, mythical, and divine. The mythic and divine levels of reality exerted tangible influences on the ordinary plane of human experience, and they did so at predictable times. This belief motivated detailed attention to the construction of calendars and to astronomical observation. The balance between the different orders of reality was sufficiently fragile that human beings had to assume responsibility for maintaining the cosmic order. They believed that the continued existence of the universe itself depended on human actions and rituals, and, in particular, the willingness of humans to sacrifice themselves. The Mayans and the Aztecs believed that blood was the fundamental life force.

Such beliefs, taken together, suggest the logic behind the best-known and most horrifying of ancient Aztec rituals, bloody human sacrifice on an enormous scale. Similarly, the Mayan kings and queens regularly pierced themselves and lost enough blood to cause them to have religious visions. They understood such relatively modest sacrifice as repayment to the gods, who had sacrificed themselves to create the world. For the Aztecs, the sacrifice was far less modest, involving wholesale killing of the best youths of their society along with captured enemies. It has been suggested that one of the reasons the warrior Aztecs lost so badly to the Spanish invaders was that, in desperation, they sacrificed so many of their best young warriors to the gods who had seemingly turned against them. Thus philosophy can be the undoing as well as the strength of a great civilization.

In North America and in Africa a major problem was the fact that cultures that had literary traditions were entirely oral (as was Greece, before the philosophers, in the time of Homer). But this meant that when the cultures died out or were overwhelmed by colonial conquerors, philosophy usually died with them. Consequently, we do not know how long civilizations existed in Africa or the Americas or when or how they developed. We do not know how ancient are the abandoned ancient cities of the central African rain forest, how long the Navaho, the Hopi, the Ojibwa, the Apache, the Seminoles, the Iroquois, and hundreds of other American Indian tribes lived in the northern Americas. There is archaeological evidence that North America was populated thousands of years ago; and it is quite clear that Africa was populated top to bottom tens of thousands of years ago. The fact that these cultures seem to lack a history reflects the lack of written records rather than evidence that they had no philosophy.

What we are learning, however tentatively, about these various world cultures is, nevertheless, increasingly rich and fascinating. We can only indicate this growing awareness with a few general points here. With regard to Africa, of course, there are hundreds of different cultures, indeed, hundreds of different languages, but a good deal of precolonial African philosophy can be characterized by means of the twin notions of *tribalism* and a special sense of *identity with nature.*

Tribalism establishes an individual's identity and significance as a person only in the context of his or her family and community. This idea may sound striking to those in the contemporary West who have relinquished such familial and communitarian sensibilities in favor of a radical individualism. But for those who live such a philosophy (and this would include the Confucian cultures of Asia as well as the many tribal societies of the Americas and the South Pacific), an isolated individual lacking the concrete presence and intangible ties of kinship would be understood as hopelessly lost or effectively dead.

Traditional African tribes tend to see personhood as something achieved over time, by means of becoming a part of one's community. As in China, ritual plays a particularly important role in this. To become a person is an

OUT OF AFRICA

Give me back
my black dolls
so that I can play the games of my instincts

I become myself once more
myself again
out of what I used to be
  once upon a time
    once without complexity
      once upon a time
when the hour of uprooting came

Will they never know the rancor in my heart
opened to the eye of my distrust too late
they did away with what was mine

> — *From the poem*
> *"Limbé" by Léon*
> *Damas*

achievement. Birth and death do not mark the person's beginning and end. A newly born baby is not yet a person, while a deceased person who lives in the memory of his or her descendents is a person still, despite physical death. Initiation rites are crucial to achieving full membership in most tribal communities and thus becoming a full person. Similarly, throughout a person's life span, rites and ceremonies keep the individual's life in rhythm with that of the community.

The Western conception of an individual, atomic soul for each person is alien to the thinking of most traditional Africans. In some tribes, such as the Yoruba (now mostly in Nigeria) and the Lugbara (now mostly in Uganda), the communal basis for personhood is reflected in a conception of the human being as composed of multiple spiritual elements, all of which are essential to the person's life. In the Yoruba tribe, for instance, ancestors' souls can return in their descendents, sometimes over and over again. So far are the Yoruba from believing in an isolated individual soul that they believe that even immediate descendents may be reincarnations of souls of their mothers or fathers, *even while the latter are still living.*

In light of this sense of identity, members of African tribes typically emphasize the worship of ancestors, who are considered living inhabitants of the spirit world, capable of assisting their descendents. As for the African attitude toward nature (and this would apply to many of the tribes of North America and the South Pacific, too), we need only point out that for thousands of years many have accepted a philosophical perspective that we in the West are just now beginning to appreciate. On this view, human beings have not been placed here on earth to "have dominion" over all other creatures and things, as promised in Genesis and reiterated by Frances Bacon. We are a part of the earth, dependent on it, and it is dependent on us. We have ecological responsibilities, and the world around us, "nature," is not just a resource or a source of aesthetic fascination.

African and American Indian tribal societies often embraced **animism**, the belief that entities throughout nature are endowed with souls, often thought to be souls of ancestors who are no longer individually remembered. Nature, for most traditional Africans, is full of living forces. Spirits dwell within it, and human beings can interact with them to some extent, utilizing these spirits' powers or driving them elsewhere. The African conviction that human beings are intimately connected to nature is part and parcel of the traditional belief that nature is essentially spiritual.

The hunting tribes among the North American Indians acknowledged the debt that they had to the creatures that provided their food. In their view, killing other creatures is not a right but a necessity that demands gratitude and reverence. Saying prayers and thanking one's quarry may strike most supermarket shoppers as a bit odd, but the consciousness of the fact that another creature has been killed for one's benefit might better be seen as an essential gesture of humanity. The gesture of prayer in thanksgiving reflects a feature common to most American Indian traditions—the tendency to see everyday life as sacred, as part of a great spiritual circle.

You know, it always makes me laugh when I hear young white kids speak of some people as "squares" or "straights"—old people, hardened in their ways, in their minds, in their hearts. They don't even have to be old. You can be an "old square" at eighteen. Anyway, calling these people "squares"—an Indian could have thought it up. To our way of thinking the Indians' symbol is the circle, the hoop. Nature wants things to be round. The bodies of human beings and animals have no corners. With us the circle stands for the togetherness of people who sit with one another around the campfire, relatives and friends united in peace while the pipe passes from hand to hand. The camp in which every tipi had its place was also a ring. The tipi was a ring in which people sat in a circle and all the families in the village were in turn circles within a larger circle, part of the larger hoop which was the seven campfires of the Sioux, representing one nation. The nation was only a part of the universe, in itself circular and made of the earth, which is round, of the sun, which is round, of the stars, which are round. The moon, the horizon, the rainbow—circles within circles within circles, with no beginning and no end.

To us this is beautiful and fitting, symbol and reality at the same time, expressing the harmony of life and nature. Our circle is timeless, flowing; it is new life emerging from death—life winning out over death.

The white man's symbol is the square. Square is his house, his office buildings with walls that separate people from one another. Square is the door which keeps strangers out, the dollar bill, the jail. Square are the white man's gadgets—boxes, boxes, boxes and more boxes—TV sets, radios, washing machines, computers, cars. These all have corners and sharp edges—points in time, white man's time, with appointments, time clocks and rush hours—that's what the corners mean to me. You become a prisoner inside all these boxes.

More and more young white people want to stop being "straight" and "square" and try to become round, join our circle. That is good. . . .

John (Fire) Lame Deer and Richard Erdoes, Lame Deer: Seeker of Visions *(New York: Pocket Books, 1976).*

SEXUAL POLITICS: THE RISE OF FEMINIST PHILOSOPHY

Women have been largely excluded from philosophy. With only a few exceptions, they were long deprived of the chance to study, the opportunity to participate in philosophical discussions and to publish their ideas. They and their ideas were not taken seriously, or they functioned, as the queen of Sweden functioned for Descartes, as a good student might, to sharpen *his* philosophy and provide an easy foil for *his* ideas. But since politics and inferior social status kept women out of philosophy, it is natural and understandable that feminist philosophy should first of all be social and political philosophy.

Since the 1960s and even since the early suffragettes, feminists have sought first and foremost political equality for women. But political equality presupposes philosophical equality, and a turning point in modern feminist political philosophy was Simone de Beauvoir's *The Second Sex* (1953). De Beauvoir's work was a groundbreaking analysis of the experience of women in our society, and it motivated women worldwide to reflect upon their social and political position and to work to improve it.

> *There have always been women. They are women in virtue of their anatomy and physiology. Throughout history they have always been subordinated to men, and hence, their dependency is not the result of a historical event or a social change. It was not something that occurred, . . . but it might seem that a natural condition is beyond the possibility of change. In truth, however, the nature of things is no more immutably given, once for all, than is historical reality. If woman seems to be the inessential which never becomes essential, it is because she herself fails to bring about this change. . . . [W]omen do not say "We," except at some congress of feminists or similar formal demonstration; men say "women," and women use the same word referring to themselves. They do not automatically assume a subjective attitude. . . .*

> — *Simone de Beauvoir,* The Second Sex[1]

Following de Beauvoir, Kate Millett claimed in her *Sexual Politics* that the political domination of women by men was evident in every institution, every economic relationship, every work of literature, every personal relationship, of our society, both now and throughout history. Millett called this pervasive system of male domination "*patriarchy,*" and gave analyses of how patriarchy was the norm in every arena of our lives.

> *A disinterested examination of the situation between the sexes now, and throughout history, is . . . a relationship of dominance and subordination. What goes largely unexamined, often even unacknowledged (yet is institutionalized nonetheless) in our social order is the birthright priority whereby males rule females. Through this system a most ingenious form of "interior colonization" has been achieved. . . . Sexual domination obtains nevertheless as perhaps the most pervasive ideology of our culture and provides its most fundamental concept of power.*

> *This is so because our society, like all other historical civilizations, is a patriarchy. The fact is evident at once if one recalls that the military, industry, technol-*

---

[1]*Translated by H.M. Parshley, (New York: Knopf, 1953), introduction.*

ogy, universities, science, political office, and finance—in short, every avenue of power within the society, including the coercive power of the police, is in male hands.

— *Kate Millett,* Sexual Politics[1]

One of the most controversial arenas of the current debate has to do with the question of whether femininity and masculinity (as opposed to the physiological categories "male" and "female") is one of biology or upbringing, "nature or nurture." Many feminists hold that the categories of gender (that is "feminine" and "masculine"), unlike the categories of sex ("male" and "female"), are created and defined by culture. They are not "natural," much less obligatory. Our culture creates these categories and the social and political status that goes along with them, and our culture can change those categories and their status. Feminist philosopher Sherry Ortner has argued that the distinction between nature and culture is not itself a natural distinction, but rather a distinction made in language, and therefore, within culture. (But within human culture, nevertheless, Ortner claims that women are and have always been represented as "closer" to nature, as the caretakers of children, the cookers of food, the domesticators of households, while culture is mainly the domain of men.) Other feminists, however, have celebrated the difference between feminine and masculine characteristics and argued that the feminine virtues of nurturing and caring are far preferable and more conducive to a caring, peaceful civilization than are the abstract, more warrior-like virtues of masculine thinking. They do not deny the differences but rather insist that women should have more say in society—and perhaps more say than men.

Women and Nature

The idea that women are more often represented as part of nature comes in part from the idea that women are more identified with their bodies than men. Culture is then defined as the domain of men. In earlier chapters, we studied the philosophical problem of "mind and body." Ever since Plato, philosophers have found it important to distinguish the mind—as that with which we think and reason—from the body—as that with which we feel and move and take up space in the world. It is also the body, of course, that is so easily injured, gets sick, disintegrates with age, and eventually dies, so it is not surprising that so many philosophers have tried to separate and protect the mind from similar calamities. In particular, the modern philosopher Descartes claimed that the mind was a separate substance from the body and that only the mind can be known for certain to exist. The body, according to Descartes, is a separate substance, known by way of inference. But in several recent articles and books various feminist philosophers—notably Susan Bordo and

[1]*New York, Avon, © 1969, 70, by Kate Millett, pp. 44-45.*

Genevieve Lloyd—have taken philosophers such as Descartes and Plato to task on feminist grounds. Since, claim these feminists, the mind or reasoning faculty is dubiously associated primarily with masculinity and the body with femininity. Descartes and Plato can be understood on one level to be justifying male authority over women. Not only in Descartes' metaphysics, but in his theory of the passions as well, he puts mind or reason in authority over everything having to do with the body. Since Descartes and Plato are crucially important philosophers in the Western tradition, these feminists attribute some responsibility to them for the bias against women and the celebration of the supposedly more masculine virtues of pure thinking.

In sexuality in particular, the roles of men and women seem to some extent to be biologically defined. But how the obvious differences between men and women and their biological roles are understood, particularly in the act of procreation, makes all the differences. In his *Generation of Animals,* Aristotle argued:

> *For there must needs be that which generates and that from which it generates. . . and in those animals that have these powers separate in two sexes the body and nature of the active and the passive sex must also differ. If, then, the male stands for the effective and active; and the female, considered as female, for the passive, it follows that what the female would contribute to the semen of the male would not be semen, but material for the semen to work upon.*

> — *Aristotle,* Generation of Animals[1]

Thus Aristotle suggests that by nature women are more passive and men more potent, that the essence of reproduction comes from the male while the female provides mere matter. A blob of clay has the potential to be a statue, but it is the mere matter. For the statue to be created, the inert matter must be acted upon by the sculptor. Aristotle believed that in the creation of a human being the inert matter that is acted upon is the female contribution to the creation, and the activity that brings about the change is the male contribution. In his ethical theory, as well, Aristotle seems to corroborate this claim, implying there that the male is more able to actualize fully his potential as a human being than is the female.

This association of masculinity with action and femininity with passivity did not end with Aristotle. It is evident in many doctrines of the Christian church and in many religions. We find it also in Sigmund Freud's theories about men and women, and in many other theories of human nature, for example, in the ancient Chinese Confucian tradition. Many feminists have taken issue with it—and in philosophy Aristotle comes under particular scrutiny. Since Aristotle's worldview set the tone for both Christian theology and modern metaphysics, it must be considered a profound problem if he held a mis-

---

[1]Generation of Animals, *1:20. 25–30, translated by Arthur Platt, in* The Basic Works of Aristotle. *ed. by Richard McKeon (New York: Random House, 1941).*

taken belief about women and femininity. There, as elsewhere, his views held sway for nearly two thousand years, and many of them persist today.

Plato: Patriarch or Early Feminist?

While Aristotle's view of women and femininity were fairly clear, those of his teacher Plato are much disputed among feminists and among philosophers in general. In some ways, Plato seems to have been radically egalitarian for his time, particularly regarding women. In the *Republic* for instance, Plato has Socrates argue for the complete equality of women in the ideal city. The important "guardian class," which is composed of both soldiers and police, ought to be composed, argued Socrates, of women as well as men. And he further claimed any two people who do the same job, whatever their sex, ought to be educated, brought up, and treated in the same way. In Plato's *Republic,* Socrates argues:

> *There is therefore no pursuit connected with city management which belongs to a woman because she is a woman, or to a man because he is a man, but various natures are scattered in the same way among both kinds of persons. Woman by nature shares all pursuits . . . All things . . . should be done in common.*
>
> — *Socrates, in Plato's* Republic[1]

These and similar claims in Plato's dialogues have led some feminists to the conclusion that Plato was sympathetic to their cause. One noted scholar of ancient philosophy, Martha Nussbaum, for instance, calls Plato "the first feminist."

Other feminists, however, have taken these claims of Plato's to be only minor gestures in an otherwise typically "masculinist" Platonic philosophy, Plato's repeated claim, for instance, that reason ought to rule over the passions in the healthy soul indicates to many Plato's accession to the gender-imposed opposition between mind and body. Since reason, as these feminists see it, is arrogantly associated with masculinity, and passion with femininity, Plato's concept of the harmonious soul is basically that of a male soul.

Reason Versus Passion in Ethics: The Ethics of Care

One important realm for the philosophical discussion of gender is moral philosophy. If reason is associated with masculinity, then rationalist ethical theories, such as those of Kant, are degrading to women, at least according to some feminists, because they imply that men are better able to make moral decisions than women.

A particularly important feminist claim to this effect was launched in the early 1980s by Harvard psychologist Carol Gilligan against the well-known psychologist of moral development, Lawrence Kohlberg. Kohlberg had studied

---

[1]*Republic 445d–451e, translated by G.M.A. Grube (Indianapolis, IN: Hackett, 1974).*

the development of moral reasoning in children, and had concluded that as people mature, their method of moral decision making goes through certain stages. Moral thinking, he claimed, develops from the self-absorbed, purely personal, or "egocentric" framework of infants and very young children to become the completely abstract and principled framework of the mature adult. This last stage, as Kohlberg described it, is very much akin to Kant's version of moral reasoning, and to the philosopher, it sounds as though Kohlberg is claiming that we develop from pure egoists to Aristotelians to utilitarians and finally to Kantians (see Chapter 8).

Few people, according to Kohlberg, matured fully in their moral reasoning to this Kantian level, but women hardly ever did so. According to Kohlberg's findings, most women got "stuck" at the "fourth" stage, in which they made moral decisions according to social or familial norms. In her groundbreaking book, *In a Different Voice*, Gilligan takes a stand against Kohlberg (and so, indirectly, against Kant). She suggests that women make moral decisions according to different but equally mature and morally upright reasoning. Gilligan conducted her own studies, using many more women as subjects, and concluded that mature women, on the whole, understood moral problems in a different way than men, and in a different way than that described by Kohlberg and Kant.

Rather than thinking of ethics in terms of impersonal, abstract, moral principles of right and wrong, claimed Gilligan, women tend to think of ethics in terms of personal moral responsibility. While men understood a moral dilemma posed by the experimenter as a problem having a right or wrong answer, women understood such a dilemma as the result of an interpersonal conflict in need of resolution, not a right-versus-wrong answer. Gilligan hypothesized that in addition to the moral reasoning grounded in abstract principles of right and wrong described by Kant and Kohlberg, there is also a more "feminine" but equally valid type of moral reasoning that is grounded in maintaining the stability of interpersonal relationships.

Gilligan claimed that both types of moral reasoning were important to a fully developed person and society, but some of her followers have gone further, claiming that the feminine "ethics of care" is a superior, more mature type of moral reasoning than that which appeals to abstract principles. In their cause, they cite the supposed failure, both of instances of "masculine" moral reasoning and of the moral theories which advocate it, to solve moral dilemmas. Recently, some feminists have drawn a comparison between this "ethics of care" and the "virtue ethics" of Aristotle and his contemporary advocate Alasdair MacIntyre (see Chapter 8). Some detractors, on the other hand, claim that Gilligan's data and her interpretations are dubious and that she cannot justify her claim to such a difference between the sexes.

> *As we have listened for centuries to the voices of men and the theories of development that their experience informs, so we have come more recently to notice, not only the silence of women, but the difficulty in hearing what they say when they*

speak. Yet in the different voice of women lies the truth of an ethic of care, the tie between relationship and responsibility. . . .

To understand how the tension between responsibilities and rights sustains the dialectic of human development is to see the integrity of two disparate modes of experience that are in the end connected. . . .

— *Carol Gilligan,* In a
Different Voice[1]

Feminist Epistemology and Feminist Science

Finally, some feminists are asking whether the very notion of knowledge is sex- or gender-biased and whether women view reality and think in the same way as men. In the same vein as Gilligan, de Beauvoir, and Millett, some feminist thinkers have claimed that scientific methodology and standards for knowledge have employed masculine models throughout their Western history. Some of them believe that a feminist model of scientific method would yield a very different body of scientific knowledge as well.

One might imagine how this could be so. We often anthropomorphize (i.e., personify, or understand in overly human terms) scientific concepts in order to understand them. You may have had a chemistry teacher who described a molecule as "thinking" that it needed to find another hydrogen atom, for example. But sometimes such anthropomorphisms make their way into scientific hypotheses. For example, a biologist talks about "dominant" and "recessive" genes, and these descriptions have been made to carry the same gender connotations of "activity" and "passivity" that some feminists have opposed in more general Aristotelian discussions of reproduction. There are also, of course, "male" and "female" fittings in electrical circuits, and various other oppositions used in modern science which lend themselves to feminist interpretations. Evelyn Fox Keller argues in her "Feminism and Science":

To see the emphasis on power and control so prevalent in the rhetoric of Western science as a projection of a specifically male consciousness requires no great leap of the imagination. Indeed, that perception has become a commonplace. Above all, it is invited by the rhetoric that conjoins the domination of nature with the insistent image of nature as female, nowhere more familiar than in the writings of Francis Bacon. For Bacon, knowledge and power are one, and the promise of science is expressed as "leading you to nature with all her children to bind her to your service and make her your slave. . ."

— *Evelyn Fox Keller,*
"Feminism and Science"[2]

---

[1]*Cambridge: Harvard University Press, 1982, pp. 173–174.* © *Carol Gilligan.*

[2]*Reprinted in* The Signs Reader *(University of Chicago Press, 1982), pp. 109–122 (p. 118). Ms. Fox Keller's quotation is taken from B. Farrington,* "Temporis Partus Masculus: *An Untranslated Writing of Francis Bacon"Centaurus I (1951): 193–205, esp. 197.*

THE REVIVAL OF AFRICAN-AMERICAN PHILOSOPHY

In the United States, one of the most important marginalized groups is African Americans. The race problem has been of crisis proportions in this country ever since the drafting of the Declaration of Independence in 1776, and even before, when the first slaves were brought over from Africa to toil in the fields of Virginia and the Caribbean islands. The question of race has become, over the last thirty years, an inescapable question that threatens the very moral integrity as well as the social harmony of life in America. How are we to understand racial differences? Do we, in fact, even acknowledge such differences? The fact that African-American writers have traditionally been left unread and out of the curricula in American universities has been challenged as a continuation of "cultural slavery," the marginalization of one people's ideas by another.

Martin Luther King, Jr., and Malcolm X

We do not have the space here to go into all the various contributions of African-American thinkers over our country's history. But two African-American thinkers from the 1960s have become extremely influential—**Martin Luther King, Jr.,** and **Malcolm X**—and so it may be helpful to devote our attention to them. The two men—who knew each other and both worked throughout their lives to enhance the position of blacks both in America and in the world—held widely different political philosophies.

Martin Luther King, Jr., advocated "civil disobedience" in the tradition of Gandhi and Thoreau. In other words, he sought to advance the position of African Americans in this country through peaceful political protest. Such protest included breaking unjust laws and suffering the consequences of doing so; but never violence. He was also an "integrationist," meaning that he believed that equality of the races required mixed neighborhoods, workplaces, and schools. His goal was full integration and the equal recognition of civil rights for black and white Americans, to be achieved through peaceful and ultimately "color-blind" means.

Malcolm X, on the other hand, advocated "Black Nationalism," and he was generally taken to be a revolutionary. Black Nationalism was a separatist movement, not an integrationist one. The black nationalists sought a unification of African-descended people all over the world into a separate society. Malcolm X is somewhat notorious for his claim that the interests of blacks throughout the world should be advanced "by any means necessary," meaning that violence was appropriate where peaceful means failed. And in general, Malcolm X believed that peaceful means had failed during the hundreds of years of white oppression of blacks. During much of his active life, Malcolm X was a Black Muslim, a member of an American-based sect of Islam. The Islamic religion, the Black Muslims believed, lent itself particularly well to

You may well ask: "Why direct action? Why sit-ins, marches and so forth? Isn't negotiation a better path? . . ." The United States Negro is moving . . . toward the promised land of racial justice. If one recognizes this vital urge that has engulfed the Negro community, one should readily understand why public demonstrations are taking place. . . . If his repressed emotions are not released in non-violent ways, they will seek expression through violence; this is not a threat but a fact of history.

Martin Luther King, Jr., "Letter from Birmingham Jail," reprinted as chapter 5 of Why We Can't Wait *(New York: New American Library, 1988 [reprint]).*

No, since the federal government has shown that it isn't going to do anything about [the Klan] *but talk, then it is your and my duty as men; as human beings, . . . to organize ourselves and let the government know that if they don't stop that Klan, we'll stop it ourselves. Then you'll see the government start doing something about it. But don't ever think that they're going to do it just on some kind of morality basis. No. So I don't believe in violence—that's why I want to stop it. And you can't stop it with love, . . . No! So, we only mean vigorous action in self-defense, and that vigorous action we feel we're justified in initiating by any means necessary.*

Now, for saying something like that, the press calls us racist and people who are "violent in reverse." This is how they psycho you. They make you think that if you try to stop the Klan from lynching you, you're practicing violence in reverse. . . . Well, if a criminal comes around your house with his gun, brother, just because he's got a gun and he's robbing your house, and he's a robber, it doesn't make you a robber because you grab your gun and run him out. No, the man is using some tricky logic on you. . . . With skillful manipulating of the press they're able to make the victim look like the criminal and the criminal look like the victim.

— Malcolm X[1]

[1]Speech at the Afro-American Broadcasting Co., Detroit, February 14, 1965, reprinted in Malcolm X Speaks *(New York: Grove Press, 1965), © Merit Publications and Betty Shabazz.*

the project of worldwide unification for blacks. Although Malcolm X later qualified his strong views about violence and separatism, he defended them in much of his writing, and since he died early in his life, he is largely remembered for them.

Although Malcolm X and Martin Luther King, Jr. disagreed in their political orientations and analyses, they were agreed in their resolution to press the cause of African Americans. Both, however, made enemies, some of whom were not content to continue the conversation through words and symbolic actions. Malcolm X was assassinated in 1965, and Martin Luther King, Jr., in 1968. Blacks have proceeded from a premise that equality means what it says, and have taken white Americans at their word when they talked of it as an objective; but most whites in America in 1967, including many persons of good will, proceeded from the premise that equality was a loose expression for improvement. White America is not even psychologically organized to close the gap—essentially it seeks only to make the situation less painful and obvious but in most aspects to retain it.

CLOSING QUESTIONS

1. Do you think that there are universal truths that underlie all religious belief? Do you think that the different religious traditions and their different views are incompatible? Why or why not?

2. Do you think that patriarchy (rule by men) and racism are institutionalized in Western philosophy and culture? Why do you think so, or not?

3. In what sense are philosophies products of their culture? How or how not, or to what extent?

4. Do you agree that the various binary oppositions in our language are always or basically gender-related? Why do you think so, or not?

5. Do you think that African Americans have made significant progress in their struggle for equality? Do you think that integration could be effective in bettering race relations in this country? Do you think that voluntary segregation could be as effective? Why or why not?

BIBLIOGRAPHY AND SUGGESTED READINGS

For an introductory survey of world philosophy, see K. Higgins and R. Solomon, *From Africa to Zen* (Lanham, MD: Rowman and Littlefield, 1993). A parallel volume of original texts in translation is Higgins and Solomon, *World Philosophy* (McGraw-Hill, 1995). See also R. Ames, D. Hall, *Thinking Through Confucius* (Albany: State University of New York, 1987). An easy-to-read classic in the field is D. T. Suzuki, *Zen Buddhism* (New York: Doubleday, 1956). Carol Gilligan's *In a Different Voice* is now the established statement of the new gender-specific moral theory, but for a spectrum of views, see *Woman, Culture, and Society,* edited by M. Z. Rosaldo and L. Lamphere, (Stanford, Stanford University Press, 1974). On feminist epistemology, metaphysics, and philosophy of science, see Ann Garry and Marilyn Pearsoll, *Women, Knowledge and Reality* (Boston: Unwin and Hyman, 1989). For an excellent and very readable book on the new feminism, see Linda Nicholson, *Feminism/ Postmodernism* (New York: Routledge, 1990). Several of Martin Luther King's most famous and influential speeches are collected in *Testament of Hope* (New York: Harper & Row, 1986). *The Autobiography of Malcolm X* (with Alex Haley) has been republished (New York: Ballentine, 1987), with an excellent film version by Spike Lee (1992). A recent excellent commentary on race in America is Cornell West, *Race Matters* (Beacon, 1993).

APPENDIX I
WRITING PHILOSOPHY

*The true form in which truth exists can only
be the scientific system of it; philosophy must
be systematic.*

—Hegel

*The will to a system is a lack of integrity . . . a
subtle corruption, a philosopher trying to appear more stupid than he really is.*

—Nietzsche

OPENING QUESTIONS

1. By now you should know fairly well which ideas form the basis of your philosophy. The question at this point is what to do with them. Write down in a short list (no more than ten lines) the ideas that you want to present and defend. Rank them according to their importance to you, and rewrite the list in order of this ranking with the most important ideas first.

2. Imagine yourself with a particular reader. (It might be a friend; it might well be your instructor. It might be a wholly imaginary reader, such as one of the great philosophers in history.) Take your list again and rank your ideas, this time in order of their probable appeal to this reader. Which ideas may be wholly agreeable? Which ones may be disagreeable? In other words, which can you present rather matter-of-factly and which ones will you have to argue for?

3. Take these two lists together and plan a strategy of presentation. Decide which idea or ideas to begin with, presumably on the basis of their initial agreeability and sketch out a series of arguments from idea to idea. Be sure you make it clear which ideas you consider most important, which

are merely preliminary, and which you consider to be consequences of your main idea.

4. Write a one-page *abstract*—that is, a summary of your intentions—in which you describe to your imaginary reader what you ultimately intend to prove, and how and why. (This will be the first of several such abstracts before you actually sit down to write a final version.)

THE RULES OF GOOD WRITING IN PHILOSOPHY

Philosophers sometimes feel more strongly about the *form* of philosophy than they do about its *content*—in other words, the particular view of the philosopher. And this is for good reason, since we have already said that most people in a society will have most of their views in common, and therefore it is the form, the style, the personality of the writing that gives a philosophy its distinctive character. And since by this time you are probably getting ready to begin your own writing, or wondering how to begin, this appendix is devoted to the various forms in which a philosophical viewpoint can be expressed. At the same time, it will give you a chance to see a bit more of the variety of actual styles of some of the great philosophers in history. But the main idea is to provide you with some models for your own work.

We can distinguish two basic categories of philosophical presentation, which we call simply "standard" and "indirect." In the standard presentation, you simply present your main ideas at the very beginning, and then proceed to argue for them, give examples that support them, and show how they tie together. Indirect writing can take a number of forms, from the still rather straightforward but more subtle technique of saving your more controversial ideas until later, building up to them from viewpoints that are less controversial or even apparently trivial, to the much more difficult and complex styles of dialogue and aphoristic presentation. The distinction between the two styles—like most distinctions—is somewhat dogmatic; most philosophies combine the two. But, at least to begin, let's look at philosophical presentation which is as straightforward as possible.

The rules of good philosophical presentation are the rules of good essay writing in general.

Organize

Organize your thoughts *before* you begin to write. Be clear about your main points, answer the primary questions (such as "What is the meaning of life?," "Do you believe in God?," and "What is real?") and arrange these, not necessarily in order of importance to you but rather in the order in which you feel most prepared to argue for them. In a straightforward presentation, your essay itself should show this organization.

An outstanding example of straightforward, point-by-point organization is found in Ludwig Wittgenstein's book *Tractatus Logico-Philosophicus.* (You will probably want a simpler title for your own work.) Wittgenstein organized his entire work around seven points, numbered them from 1 to 7, and numbered the arguments and qualifications by decimals, such as, 1.1, 1.2, 1.21, 1.22. His philosophy is rather technical, but it might be worthwhile to show some of his basic outline.

1. The world is everything that is the case.

1.1 The world is the totality of facts, not things.

2. What is the case—a fact—is the existence of a state of affairs.

2.1 We picture facts to ourselves.

2.2 A picture has a form in common with what it depicts.

3. A logical picture of facts is a thought.

4. A proposition is a thought with a meaning.

4.1 Propositions represent the existence or nonexistence of states of affairs.

• • •

7. What we cannot speak of we must pass over in silence.

Wittgenstein was a writer who was heavily analytic—and he tried to avoid grand metaphors. Most of these claims seem rather obvious, but what Wittgenstein derives from them is not obvious and becomes dramatically inspirational. But you can see how straightforwardly the outline (and therefore the work) moves from one point to the next, beginning with a statement that seems totally unobjectionable and arguing from point to point.

A much longer and more imaginative work in which the organization is made obvious in its structure is Spinoza's *Ethics* (see pp. 125–126). Spinoza's outrageous conclusions—that individuality is an illusion, that there is no freedom, and that God is nothing but the universe itself—are embodied in a long technical work that begins with a number of statements that are so obvious that no one would think of questioning them. In fact, Spinoza designed his whole philosophy along lines of geometry, and the proof of theorems from axioms and definitions, from which we can then prove further theorems, and so on, just as you did with triangles, lines, and points in high school. But Spinoza was talking about nothing less than the meaning of life, the existence of God, and the nature of reality. All of this, however, begins (as we have seen) with the definition of a technical word, "substance."

You may find the geometrical rigor a bit too cold for your own tastes, but this is to be balanced against the drama of Spinoza's images and is an excellent illustration of how well-organized the best philosophies tend to be. In any case, even if you are not so explicit in your writing, it is a good idea to write down an outline of the main ideas you want to establish, the order in which you want to establish them, and a sketch of the kinds of arguments, examples, and considerations you want to use.

Write Simply

Many students seem to feel that because they are doing philosophy and writing about such "profound" topics as the meaning of life, they ought to be particularly pompous and obscure. (Nietzsche once commented on some of his colleagues that "they muddy the water to make it look deep.") Good philosophy is like good journalism or good short story writing; it consists of simple, straightforward sentences. Except for a few specialized terms, it uses 25-cent words, not $3.00 words that are to be found only in a thesaurus. Say clearly what you want to say, so that your readers don't have to spend their time trying to figure out what you mean. (Nietzsche also said, "It is one of the virtues of a theory that it is refutable.") Let your reader know what you think, so that he or she knows right away how to discuss things with you. For example, consider this beginning statement in Kant's theory of morality:

> Nothing in the world—indeed nothing even beyond the world—can possibly be conceived which could be called good without qualification except a good will. Intelligence, wit, judgment, and the other talents of the mind, however they may be named, or courage, resoluteness, and perseverance as qualities of temperament, are doubtless in many respects good and desirable. But they can become extremely bad and harmful if the will, which is to make use of these gifts of nature and which in its special constitution is called character, is not good. It is the same with the gifts of fortune. Power, riches, honor, even health, general well-being, and the contentment with one's condition which is called happiness, make for pride and even arrogance if there is not a good will to correct their influence on the mind and on its principles of action so as to make it universally conformable to its end. It need hardly be mentioned that the sight of a being adorned with no feature of a pure and good will, yet enjoying uninterrupted prosperity, can never give pleasure to a rational impartial observer. Thus the good will seems to constitute the indispensable condition even of worthiness to be happy.

> — *Foundations of the
> Metaphysics of Morals*

Be Clear

The philosopher Wittgenstein said, "Whatever can be said can be said clearly." There are some notable exceptions among the great philosophers, but for every obscure philosopher who for some reason becomes idolized by his students, hundreds are quite properly ignored. Reading them is not worth the time. Why hack a path through a jungle when there is a clear road in the same direction?

A good example of what your philosophy should *not* look like is this:

> Individual Being of every kind is, to speak quite generally, *"accidental."* It is so-and-so, but essentially it could be other than it is. . . . But the import of this contingency, which is there called matter-of-factness, is limited in this respect that the contingency is correlative to a *necessity* which does not carry the mere actuality-status of a valid rule of connexion obtaining between temporo-spatial facts, but has the character of *essential necessity,* and therewith a relation to *essential universality.* Now when we stated that every fact could be "essentially" other than it is, we were already expressing thereby *that it belongs to the meaning of everything, contingent that it should have essential being and therewith an Eidos to be apprehended in all its purity;* and this Eidos comes under essential truths of varying degrees of universality.

There is no need for so much technical jargon, without examples or clarification. There is no need for a foreign word (*Eidos* is the word Plato used for "Form") when a good English word is available. There is no need for quotation marks when their only function is to undermine the significance of the word they enclose.

It happens that this passage is from a very important twentieth-century philosopher (Edmund Husserl, *Ideas*), but it must also be said that no one would possibly take the time to read it if it had not been written by someone already known to be profound and important. Most of us are not so lucky. If we don't write clearly, we have no right to expect to be read or understood or—more immediately—well graded.

Be Human

Remember you are trying to court the attention of your readers and make your views attractive and appealing. That means that they first have to feel that you really believe what you say and that they are sharing your thoughts rather than being attacked by them. Personal anecdotes and examples can help a great deal. Consider this famous opening of Descartes' *Meditations:*

> It is now some years since I detected how many were the false beliefs that I had from my earliest youth admitted as true, and how doubtful was everything I had since constructed on this basis; and from that time I was convinced that I must once for all seriously undertake to rid myself of all the opinions which I had formerly accepted, and commence to build anew from the foundation, if I wanted to establish any firm and permanent structure in the sciences. But as this enterprise appeared to be a very great one, I waited until I had attained an age so mature that I could not hope that at any later date I should be better fitted to execute my design. This reason caused me to delay so long that I should feel that I was doing wrong were I to occupy in deliberation the time that yet remains to me for action. To-day, then, since very opportunely for the plan I have in view I have delivered

my mind from every care (and am happily agitated by no passions) and since I have procured for myself an assured leisure in a peaceable retirement. I shall at last seriously and freely address myself to the general upheaval of all my former opinions.

And this well-known passage from David Hume's *Treatise of Human Nature:*

> Most fortunately it happens, that since reason is incapable of dispelling these clouds, nature herself suffices to that purpose, and cures me of this philosophical melancholy and delirium, either by relaxing this bent of mind, or by some avocation, and lively impression of my senses, which obliterate all these chimeras. I dine, I play a game of back-gammon, I converse, and am merry with my friends; and when after three or four hours' amusement, I would return to these speculations, they appear so cold, and strain'd, and ridiculous, that I cannot find in my heart to enter into them any farther.

Use Examples

It is no good starting a string of abstractions that never touch earth. If you are discussing the possibility of God's entering into earthly affairs, use an example or two from the Bible. If you are discussing the meaning of life, don't be afraid to talk about life. If you are talking about explanations in science, don't be afraid to use some examples from science. Consider, for example, the following use of examples by Immanuel Kant. He has just finished arguing, in a very abstract way, that a moral action is one which would make sense if everyone were to act similarly (see Chapter 8). And so he presents us with a series of examples in which this thesis is demonstrated:

> 1. A man who is reduced to despair by a series of evils feels a weariness with life but is still in possession of his reason sufficiently to ask whether it would not be contrary to his duty to himself to take his own life. Now he asks whether the maxim of his action could become a universal law of nature. His maxim, however, is: For love of myself, I make it my principle to shorten my life when by a longer duration it threatens more evil than satisfaction. But it is questionable whether this principle of self-love could become a universal law of nature. One immediately sees a contradiction in a system of nature whose law would be to destroy life by the feeling whose special office is to impel the improvement of life. In this case it would not exist as nature; hence that maxim cannot obtain as a law of nature, and thus it wholly contradicts the supreme principle of all duty.
>
> 2. Another man finds himself forced by need to borrow money. He well knows that he will not be able to repay it, but he also sees that nothing will be loaned him if he does not firmly promise to repay it at a certain time. He desires to make such a promise, but he has enough conscience to ask himself whether it is not improper and opposed to duty to relieve his distress in such a way. Now, assuming he does decide to do so, the maxim of his action would be as follows. When I believe myself to be in need of money, I will borrow money and promise to repay it, although I know I shall never do so. Now this principle of self-love or

of his own benefit may very well be compatible with his whole future welfare, but the question is whether it is right. He changes the pretension of self-love into a universal law and then puts the question: How would it be if my maxim became a universal law? He immediately sees that it could never hold as a universal law of nature and be consistent with itself; rather it must necessarily contradict itself. For the universality of a law which says that anyone who believes himself to be in need could promise what he pleased with the intention of not fulfilling it would make the promise itself and the end to be accomplished by it impossible; no one would believe what was promised to him but would only laugh at any such assertion as rain pretense.

3. A third finds in himself a talent which could, by means of some cultivation, make him in many respects a useful man. But he finds himself in comfortable circumstances and prefers indulgence in pleasure to troubling himself with broadening and improving his fortunate natural gifts. Now, however, let him ask whether his maxim of neglecting his gifts, besides agreeing with his propensity to idle amusement, agrees also with what is called duty. He sees that a system of nature could indeed exist in accordance with such a law, even though man (like the inhabitants of the South Sea Islands) should let his talents rust and resolve to devote his life merely to idleness, indulgence, and propagation—in a word, to pleasure. But he cannot possibly will that this should become a universal law of nature or that it should be implanted in us by a natural instinct. For, as a rational being, be necessarily wills that all his faculties should be developed, inasmuch as they are given to him for all sorts of possible purposes.

4. A fourth man, for whom things are going well, sees that others (whom he could help) have to struggle with great hardships, and he asks, "What concern of mine is it? Let each one be as happy as heaven wills, or as he can make himself. I will not take anything from him or even envy him; but to his welfare or to his assistance in time of need I have no desire to contribute." If such a way of thinking were a universal law of nature, certainly the human race could exist, and without doubt even better than in a state where everyone talks of sympathy and good will, or even exerts himself occasionally to practice them while, on the other hand, he cheats when he can and betrays or otherwise violates the rights of man. Now although it is possible that a universal law of nature according to that maxim could exist, it is nevertheless impossible to will that such a principle should hold everywhere as a law of nature. For a will which resolved this would conflict with itself, since instances can often arise in which he would need the love and sympathy of others, and in which he would have rubbed himself, by such a law of nature springing from his own will, of all hope of the aid he desires.

— *Foundations of the*
Metaphysics of Morals

One author who is particularly well-known for his examples is the French existentialist Jean-Paul Sartre. Sartre, as you may well know, was also a novelist, playwright, and journalist. His abstract statements are often extremely abstruse, such as, "Being for itself [consciousness] is what it is not and is not what it is." But his examples, befitting a novelist, are almost always insightful, and he used them to break up his abstract prose and at every turn to get the reader to see his point. As an illustration of his conception of "bad faith," for example (see p. 192), he gives us the illustration of an anti-Semite (though any racist or extremely prejudiced person would do). And with this example, what otherwise might be an abstract philosophical concept becomes a very real flesh-and-blood problem.

> The anti-Semite has created the Jew from his need. Prejudice is not uninformed opinion. It is an attitude totally and freely chosen. . . . The anti-Semite is a man who is afraid, not of the Jews, of course, but of himself, of his conscience, his in-stincts, of his responsibilities, of solitude, of change, of society, and the world; of everything except the Jews. He is a coward who does not wish to admit his cow-ardice to himself, . . . a malcontent who dares not revolt for fear of the conse-quences of his rebellion. By adhering to his anti-Semitism, he is not only adopting an opinion, he is choosing himself as a person. . . . He is choosing the total irre-sponsibility of the warrior who obeys his leaders—and he has no leader. . . . The Jew is only a pretext; elsewhere it will be the Negro, the yellow race. . . . Anti-Semitism, in a word, is fear. . . .
>
> — *Portrait of the Anti-Semite*

A third use of examples can be found in another existentialist, Søren Kierkegaard (whom we discussed in Chapter 3). Kierkegaard was concerned about the relationship between what he called the *ethical* life ("Do not kill," "Do not steal," and so on) and what he called the *religious* life, which is a life of devotion to God. Most people assume that these are the same, but Kierkegaard wondered whether they can sometimes conflict. He found that they do, and he showed us how in an example drawn from the Bible, which is much more powerful than any long-winded, abstract discourse could be. The story, from Genesis, is the one in which God commands Abraham to prove his devotion by killing his son Isaac. What could be a more immoral act than to murder your own son? But what would be more irreligious than to disobey a direct command from God? In the example, Kierkegaard proves his point, though in the end, he argued, the two views of life can still be under-stood as compatible. Elsewhere, in a book called *Either/Or,* Kierkegaard made a similar point about the antagonism between the ethical life and what he calls the aesthetic life of pleasure. His example is marriage, and with this ex-ample he captures all the differences between the moral life of duty and obligation and the irresponsible life of just enjoying oneself, whatever the cost to others. But again, it is the example that makes his distinctions and argu-ments work; otherwise his discourse would just be a string of abstractions.

Argue Your Point

Arguing doesn't have to be belligerent or nasty; in philosophy, to argue is to establish your viewpoint, give reasons why you accept it and why others ought to accept it, too. An argument begins with a statement that you can assume your reader already accepts and proceeds to some other views that your reader may not accept at all. Thus Spinoza starts out with some innocent and noncontroversial definitions of words such as "substance" and "God" and "freedom" and a few axioms that no one could possibly disagree with and then goes on to prove some extremely controversial views about life and God and ourselves.

There are many kinds of arguments, but in every case what makes a good argument is that it is *convincing*. Many students seem to think that, once they have accepted a position themselves, any argument will do. But remember that a bad argument, even surrounded by several good ones, is more likely to turn your readers against your view than convince your readers. "If the writer uses such bad arguments to support this position, the position itself can't be worth very much," is a common reaction. An ideal argument is sufficiently succinct and complete so that the reader is locked into it, with nowhere to go but to agree with you. Consider the tight argument from the Scottish philosopher David Hume, which we discussed in Chapter 5. First, Hume distinguished two ways in which a statement can be demonstrated:

1. If it is a mathematical statement or a "truth of reason," then it can be demonstrated by calculation (as in arithmetic) or by defining the meanings of the words involved (as "dogs are animals" can be proven to be true by showing that the word "dog" means, in part, being an animal).

2. If it is a "matter of fact," then it can be proven through experience. The statement "There are dogs in Australia," for instance, can be shown to be true by going to Australia and finding some dogs.

These are the *only* ways to demonstrate the truth of a statement, Hume said, and this sets up the argument (in fact a whole series of arguments) to come. (If you want to attack Hume because you don't agree with his conclusions—which will probably be the case—this is the place to start. Are these two kinds of arguments the only kinds of arguments there are?)

Now Hume takes up the question of whether we are justified in believing that there really is an "external world," a world outside our minds—or whether it could be the case that we are just dreaming right now, that the world is a dream and not outside of us at all. You might say, "That's ridiculous!" But according to Hume, if our statement that "there is an external world" is justifiable, then we have to be able to *prove* it to be true. How can we do that? Only in two ways, Hume tells us:

1. Is the statement that there is an external world to be proven like a mathematical statement? Is it just a matter of the words involved? Some philosophers would in fact say that the word "world" already means "external," but it is still an open question whether the external world actually exists. Hume says "No"; the existence of the external world can't be a matter of "reason" alone; it is not a matter of definition or of logic, either, for we can at least imagine (we already have) what it would mean for there not to be an external world, for us to be dreaming, for instance.

2. Could the statement that there is an external world be proven by appeal to experience? Your first response might be to say "Yes," but then you have to ask yourself, "What experience?" Are there any experiences that you have when you're awake that you couldn't possibly have in your dreams? Is there any test you could apply to yourself to tell the difference? Some people think that you can tell whether or not you're dreaming by pinching yourself, but, of course, you could also dream that you are pinching yourself, and you could dream that it hurts. (You can even dream that you wake up, while you are still, in fact, dreaming.) So our statement that there is an external world can't be justified from experience.

Hume's conclusion is that we can't know whether we're dreaming or not, whether there is in fact an external world. You might think this is absurd. He does, too (see the brief quote on pp. 337–338). But his arguments are so persuasive and tight that even the great philosopher Bertrand Russell, almost two hundred years later, could still say,

> Hume's skeptical conclusions . . . are equally difficult to refute and to accept. The result was a challenge to philosophers which, in my opinion, has still not been adequately met.
>
> — *History of Western Philosophy*

A good argument should be succinct—short and to the point. Afterward, you can qualify your comments and further support your claims, but the power lies in the precision. Consider the following three arguments for God's existence in Saint Thomas Aquinas (we saw the second in Chapter 3, as the *cosmological argument*):

> The first and more manifest way is the argument from motion. It is certain, and evident to our senses, that in the world some things are in motion. Now whatever is moved is moved by another, for nothing can be moved except it is in potentiality to that towards which it is moved whereas a thing moves inasmuch as it is in act. For motion is nothing else than the reduction of something for potentiality to actuality. But nothing can be reduced from potentiality to actuality, except by something in a state of actuality. Thus that which is actually hot, as fire, makes wood, which is potentially hot, to be actually hot, and thereby moves and changes it. Now it is not possible that the same thing should be at once in actuality and potentiality in the same respect, but only in different respects. For what is actually hot cannot simultaneously be potentially hot; but it is simultaneously potentially cold. It is therefore impossible that in the same respect and in the same way a thing should be both mover and moved, i.e., that it should more itself. Therefore, whatever is moved must be moved by another. If that by which it is moved be itself moved, then this also must needs be moved by another, and that by another again. But this cannot go on to infinity, because then there would be no first mover, and consequently, no other mover, seeing that subsequent movers

move only inasmuch as they are moved by the first mover, as the staff moves only because it is moved by the hand. Therefore, it is necessary to arrive at a first mover, moved by no other, and this everyone understands to be God.

The second way is from the nature of efficient cause. In the world of sensible things we find there is an order of efficient causes. There is no case known (neither is it, indeed, possible) in which a thing is found to be the efficient cause of itself; for so it would be prior to itself, which is impossible. Now in efficient causes it is not possible to go on to infinity, because in all efficient causes following in order, the first is the cause of the intermediate cause, and the intermediate is the cause of the ultimate cause, whether the intermediate cause be several, or one only. Now to take away the cause is to take away the effect. Therefore, if there be no first cause among efficient causes, there will be no ultimate, nor any intermediate, cause. But if in efficient causes it is possible to go on to infinity, there will be no first efficient cause, neither will there be an ultimate effect, nor any intermediate efficient causes; all of which is plainly false. Therefore it is necessary to admit a first efficient cause, to which everyone gives the name of God.

The third way is taken from possibility and necessity, and runs thus. We find in nature things that are possible to be and not to be, since they are found to be generated, and to be corrupted, and consequently, it is possible for them to be and not to be. But it is impossible for these always to exist, for that which can not-be at some time is not. Therefore, if everything can not-be, then at one time there was nothing in existence. Now if this were true, even now there would be nothing in existence, because that which does not exist begins to exist only through something already existing. Therefore, if at one time nothing was in existence, it would have been impossible for anything to have begun to exist; and thus even now nothing would be in existence—which is absurd. Therefore, not all beings are merely possible, but there must exist something the existence of which is necessary. But every necessary thing either has its necessity caused by another, or not. Now it is impossible to go on to infinity in necessary things which have their necessity caused by another, as has been already proved in regard to efficient causes. Therefore we cannot but admit the existence of some being having of itself its own necessity, and not receiving it from another, but rather causing in others their necessity. This all men speak of as God.

— *Summa Theologica*

Consider the Objections and Alternatives

Philosophy is not just the presentation of a viewpoint; it is also a dialogue and part of a discussion, whether or not it takes the form of a dialogue or a discussion. This means that you will always be anticipating some critic (it helps to have someone specific in mind as you write) who will respond to your views and your arguments with objections and examples designed to show that you are wrong. One argument is almost never enough. Consider the following passage from Bishop Berkeley's *Principles,* which in effect includes an imaginary dialogue with an opponent (the opponent he has in mind is John Locke):

> But, say you, though the ideas themselves do not exist without the mind, yet there may be things *like* them, whereof they are copies or resemblances, which things exist without the mind in an unthinking substance. I answer, an idea can be like nothing but an idea; a color or figure can be like nothing but another color or figure. If we look but never so little into our thoughts, we shall find it impossible for us to conceive a likeness except only between our ideas. Again, I ask whether those supposed originals or external things, of which our ideas are the pictures or representations, be themselves perceivable or no? If they are, then they are ideas and we have gained our point; but if you say they are not, I appeal to anyone whether it be sense to assert a color is like something which is invisible, hard or soft, like something which is intangible; and so of the rest.

Define Your Specialized Terms

If you introduce a technical term that is not part of ordinary speech, or if you use an ordinary word in some special way, tell the reader what you mean, and *stick to that meaning.* If you use the word "substance" to refer to the ultimate units of reality, say clearly (as many great philosophers have not) what will count as a substance and how you know whether something is or is not a substance; do not at any point slip into our ordinary talk about "substance" (gum on your shoe, the unknown stuff in the pot in the garage). Do *not* feel compelled, though, to define your terms at every turn of the argument. Language doesn't work that way, and you can take it for granted that your readers understand ordinary English, as long as you *use* ordinary English.

A straightforward but somewhat clumsy way of introducing your specialized terms is to define them right at the beginning, in a series of specialized definitions, as we saw in Spinoza's *Ethics* (pp. 125–126). A more graceful way of doing so is to introduce them as they appear in your essay, building the definition right into your discussion. For example, Immanuel Kant introduced the technical terms "empirical" and "*a priori*" into his discussion in this way:

> Is there any knowledge that is independent of experience and even of all the impressions of the senses? Such knowledge is called *"a priori"* and distinguished from the *empirical,* which has its sources in experience.
>
> — *Critique of Pure Reason*

Whenever you use words such as "subjective" and "objective," which have been defined in a variety of different ways (see Chapter 5), it is particularly important to be clear which definition you are using and *stick to it.* It is also important not to define words in ordinary English in ways that are at odds with that ordinary usage, for this is sure to cause confusion. For example, Ayn Rand defined the ordinary word "selfishness" as simply "acting for one's own benefit," whereas the ordinary word means "acting for one's own benefit and *against the interest of others.*" Not surprisingly, then, Rand later had to defend herself by insisting, "If it is true that what I mean by 'selfishness' is not what is meant conventionally, then *this* is one of the worst indictments of altruism: it means that altruism permits no view of a self-respecting, self-supporting man." But, of course, Rand herself had defined the terms this way and the problem she raised is primarily of her own creation.

Use the History of Philosophy

After all, you are now part of it. Don't be afraid to bring in the opinions of other philosophers you have read to support you. You can repeat their arguments (with an acknowledgment that you are doing so); you can quote them. You can use a particularly appealing phrase or description they use to amplify your own views. You can begin by quoting or representing other philosophers' views, to which you are directly opposed. And as you argue your position, it is always a good idea to think of those philosophers who would certainly disagree with you and what they might say (or have already said) in reply. Of course, you can't know the whole history of philosophy when you're just beginning, but the more you know, the better. The more clearly you see yourself as part of that long tradition and other people's terms and ideas as influencing your own, the more confident you'll feel about what you say. The idea that each of us is supposed to have an "original" philosophy is utter nonsense; indeed, a humbling exercise I sometimes do with my students is to reduce the thoughts of the great philosophers down to slogans your grandmother might have said to you—such as reducing Kant's whole moral philosophy (see Chapter 8) down to the question "What if everyone else were to do that?" It is doubtful that there are any new ideas. Even Einstein's views can be traced back to those of the early Greek scientists. What makes philosophy worthwhile is not total newness but its sense of being a part of a long tradition and the individual style and personality you yourself contribute to it.

The rules for using other philosophers are simple enough: When you represent them, be sure that you do so accurately. If you offer an interpretation of a philosopher which is unusual or controversial, say so. ("I am aware that this is not the usual view of Socrates, but I think I can justify it on the grounds that. . . .") If you follow some other commentator, it is usually a good idea to say so. ("According to the noted Spinoza scholar S. H., . . .") And whenever you borrow ideas or phrases and especially longer quotations, *name your sources.* A footnote will do, or you can do it more informally in the text. For instance, you could say "As Hegel argued in his *Phenomenology,* . . ." or "In the more dramatic expression suggested by Hegel, . . . !'" Don't make allusions to famous philosophers unless the references are so obvious to your readers that no one will be left in the dark. For example, in his *Phenomenology of Spirit,* Hegel freely alluded to "the philosopher of the One Substance" without naming him, but everyone would know he meant Spinoza. In other places, however, Hegel alluded to philosophers whose identities were not so readily known, and the result was confusion and wasteful scholarly controversy over whom he really meant.

INDIRECT STYLES

Indirect styles are *much more difficult* to bring off than straightforward presentations, and you are *well advised to check with your instructor* before trying the indirect approach for your own project. **They are not, in general, recommended for introductory philosophy students, except, perhaps, as a personal experiment**. One form of indirect style, however, is safe enough and we have already treated it as "standard"—namely, that seductive approach (as in Spinoza) in which you save your most important conclusions for last and begin with a far less controversial set of statements, designed to lead readers from what they will certainly agree with to what they most likely will not. The problem with this method, and the problem many students have reading an author like Spinoza, is that readers get bored long before they get to the best part. As if you were writing a mystery novel, therefore, you have to attract the reader's interest right from the beginning, by presenting certain problems that will keep everyone puzzled, by making a personal appeal that will convince everyone that this is a worthwhile project to pursue. What usually does not work is continually promising the reader great things to come. ("Later on, we will see the exciting consequences of this.") Most readers (especially instructors who are reading dozens of papers) will get restless long before then, and will probably be disappointed when they get there.

Dialogue Style

The first and most famous style of indirect presentation is the dialogue style, which is the style of Plato's transcriptions of Socrates' discussions with his friends—thus called "Socratic dialogues." (In fact, as we have already pointed out, Plato made up many of these dialogues, and Socrates probably never had any such discussions at all.) The strategy of the dialogue is to get someone else to make a philosophical statement, in order to refute it. The sequence of statements and refutations is such that, by the end, Socrates (Plato) emerges with his own view, which has already been demonstrated to be better than all of the rest. The following excerpt is from Plato's *Theaetetus*.

> *SOCRATES: To start all over again, then: what is one to say that knowledge is? For surely we are not going to give up yet.*
> *THEAETETUS: Not unless you do so.*
> *SOCR.: Then tell me: what definition can we give with the least risk of contradicting ourselves?*
> *THEAET.: The one we tried before, Socrates. I have nothing else to suggest.*
> *SOCR.: What was that?*
> *THEAET.: That true belief is knowledge. Surely there can at least be no mistake in believing what is true and the consequences are always satisfactory.*

SOCR.: *Try, and you will see, Theaetetus, as the man said when he was asked if the river was too deep to ford. So here, if we go forward on our search, we may stumble upon something that will reveal the thing we are looking for. We shall make nothing out, if we stay where we are.*

THEAET.: *True; let us go forward and see.*

SOCR.: *Well, we need not go far to see this much: you will find a whole profession to prove that true belief is not knowledge.*

THEAET.: *How so? What profession?*

SOCR.: *The profession of those paragons of intellect known as orators and lawyers. There you have men who use their skill to produce conviction, not by instruction, but by making people believe whatever they want them to believe. You can hardly imagine teachers so clever as to be able, in the short time allowed by the clock, to instruct their bearers thoroughly in the true facts of a case of robbery or other violence which those bearers had not witnessed.*

THEAET.: *No, I cannot imagine that; but they can convince them.*

SOCR.: *And by convincing you mean making them believe something.*

THEAET.: *Of course.*

SOCR.: *And when a jury is rightly convinced of facts which can be known only by an eye-witness, then, judging by hearsay and accepting a true belief, they are judging without knowledge, although, if they find the right verdict, their conviction is correct?*

THEAET.: *Certainly.*

SOCR.: *But if true belief and knowledge were the same thing the best of jurymen could never have a correct belief without knowledge. It now appears that they must be different things.*

A more modern example is Bishop George Berkeley's dialogue on idealism and materialism in "Three Dialogues":

PHILONOUS: *Either, Hylas, you are jesting, or have a very bad memory. Though indeed we went through all the qualities by name one after another; yet my arguments, or rather your concessions no where tended to prove, that the secondary qualities did not subsist each alone by itself: but that they were not at all without the mind. Indeed in treating of figure and motion, we concluded they could not exist without the mind, because it was impossible even in thought to separate them from all secondary qualities, so as to conceive them existing by themselves. But then this was not the only argument made use of upon that occasion. But (to pass by all that hath been hitherto said, and reckon it for nothing, if you will have it so) I am content to put the whole upon this issue. If you can conceive it possible for any mixture or combination of qualities, or any sensible object whatever, to exist without the mind, then I will grant it actually to be so.*

HYLAS: *If it comes to that, the point will soon be decided. What more easy than to conceive a tree or house existing by itself, independent of, and unperceived by any mind whatsoever? I do at this present time conceive them existing after that manner.*

PHIL.: *How say you, Hylas, can you see a thing which is at the same time unseen?*

HYL.: *No, that were a contradiction.*

PHIL.: *Is it not as great a contradiction to talk of* conceiving *a thing which is* unconceived?

HYL.: *It is.*

PHIL.: *The tree or house therefore which you think of, is conceived by you.*

HYL.: *How should it be otherwise?*

PHIL.: *And what is conceived is surely in the mind.*

HYL.: *Without question, that which is conceived is in the mind.*

PHIL.: *How then came you to say, you conceived a house or tree existing indepen-dent and out of all minds whatsoever?*

HYL.: *That was, I own, an oversight; but stay, let me consider what led me into it.—It is a pleasant mistake enough. As I was thinking of a tree in a solitary place, where no one was present to see it, methought that was to conceive a tree as existing unperceived or unthought of, not considering that I myself con-ceived it all the while. But now I plainly see, that all I can do is to frame ideas in my own mind. I may indeed conceive in my own thoughts the idea of a tree, or a house, or a mountain, but that is all. And this is far from proving, that I can conceive them existing out of the minds of all spirits.*

PHIL.: *You acknowledge then that you cannot possibly conceive how any one cor-poreal sensible thing should exist otherwise than in a mind.*

HYL.: *I do.*

PHIL.: *And yet you will earnestly contend for the truth of that which you cannot so much as conceive.*

HYL.: *I profess I know not what to think, but still there are some scruples remain with me. Is it not certain I see things at a distance? Do we not perceive the stars and moon, for example, to be a great way off? Is not this, I say, manifest to the senses?*

PHIL.: *Do you not in a dream too perceive those or the like objects?*

HYL.: *I do.*

PHIL.: *And have they not then the same appearance of being distant?*

HYL.: *They have.*

PHIL.: *But you do not thence conclude the apparitions in a dream to be without the mind?*

HYL.: *By no means.*

PHIL.: *You ought not therefore to conclude that sensible objects are without the mind, from their appearance or manner wherein they are perceived.*

HYL.: *I acknowledge it. But doth not my sense deceive me in those cases?*

PHIL.: *By no means. The idea or thing which you immediately perceive, neither sense nor reason inform you that it actually exists without the mind. By sense you only know that you are affected with such certain sensations of light and colours, etc. And these you will not say are without the mind.*

HYL.: *True: but beside all that, do you not think the sight suggests something of* outness *or* distance?

PHIL.: *Upon approaching a distant object, do the visible size and figure change perpetually, or do they appear the same at all distances?*

HYL.: *They are in a continual change.*

PHIL.: *Sight therefore doth not suggest or in any way inform you, that the visible object you immediately perceive, exists at a distance, or will be perceived when you advance further onward, there being a continued series of visible objects succeeding each other, during the whole time of your approach.*

HYL.: *It doth not; but still I know, upon seeing an object, what object I shall per-ceive after having passed over a certain distance: no matter whether it be ex-actly the same or no: there is still something of distance suggested in the case.*

PHIL.: *Good Hylas, do but reflect a little on the point, and then tell me whether there be any more in it than this. From the ideas you actually perceive by sight, you have by experience learned to collect what other ideas you will (according to the standing order of nature) be affected with, after such a certain succession of time and motion.*

HYL.: *Upon the whole, I take it to be nothing else.*

PHIL.: *Now is it not plain, that if we suppose a man born blind was on a sudden made to see, he could at first have no experience of what may be suggested by sight.*

HYL.: *It is.*

PHIL.: *He would not then, according to you, have any notion of distance annexed to the things he saw, but would take them for a new set of sensations existing only in his mind.*

HYL.: *It is undeniable.*

PHIL.: *But to make it still more plain; is not* distance *a line turned endurise to the eye?*

HYL.: *It is.*

PHIL.: *And can a line so situated be perceived by sight?*

HYL.: *It cannot.*

PHIL.: *Doth it not therefore follow that distance is not properly and immediately perceived by sight?*

HYL.: *It should seem so.*

PHIL.: *Again, is it your opinion that colours are at a distance?*

HYL.: *It must be acknowledged, they are only in the mind.*

PHIL.: *But do not colours appear to the eye as co-existing in the same place with extension and figures?*

HYL.: *They do.*

PHIL.: *How can you then conclude from sight, that figures exist without, when you acknowledge colours do not; the sensible appearance being the very same with regard to both?*

HYL.: *I know not what to answer.*

PHIL.: *But allowing that distance was truly and immediately perceived by the mind, yet it would not thence follow it existed out of the mind. For whatever is immediately perceived is an idea: and can any* idea *exist out of the mind?*

Ironic Style

The second strategy is even more difficult than the first; it is the style of **irony**, in which one attacks a view by stating it in such a way that it becomes ridiculous. Consider the following parody from Voltaire's *Candide,* in which Voltaire makes fun of Leibniz's view that this is the "best of all possible worlds":

STORM, SHIPWRECK, EARTHQUAKE,

AND WHAT HAPPENED TO

DR. PANGLOSS, TO CANDIDE AND

THE ANABAPTIST JACQUES

Half the enfeebled passengers, suffering from that inconceivable anguish which the rolling of a ship causes in the nerves and in all the humors of bodies shaken in contrary directions, did not retain strength enough even to trouble about the danger. The other half screamed and prayed; the sails were torn, the masts broken, the vessel leaking. Those worked who could, no one cooperated, no one commanded. The Anabaptist tried to help the crew a little; he was on the main deck; a furious sailor struck him violently and stretched him on the deck; but the blow he delivered gave him so violent a shock that he fell head-first out of the ship. He remained hanging and clinging to part of the broken mast. The good Jacques ran to his aid, helped him to climb back, and from the effort be made was flung into the sea in full view of the sailor, who allowed him to drown without condescending even to look at him. Candide came up, saw his benefactor reappear for a moment and then be engulfed for ever. He tried to throw himself after him into the sea: he was prevented by the philosopher Pangloss, who proved to him that the Lisbon roads had been expressly created for the Anabaptist to be drowned in them. While he was proving this *a priori,* the vessel sank, and every one perished except Pangloss, Candide and the brutal sailor who had drowned the virtuous Anabaptist: the blackguard swam successfully to the shore and Pangloss and Candide were carried there on a plank.

When they had recovered a little, they walked toward Lisbon; they had a little money by the help of which they hoped to be saved from hunger after having escaped the storm. Weeping the death of their benefactor, they had scarcely set foot in the town when they felt the earth tremble under their feet; the sea rose in foaming masses in the port and smashed the ships which rode at anchor. Whirlwinds of flame and ashes covered the streets and squares; the houses collapsed, the roofs were thrown upon the foundations, and the foundations were scattered; thirty thousand inhabitants of every age and both sexes were crushed under the ruins. Whistling and swearing, the sailor said: "There'll be something to pick up here."

"What can be the sufficient reason for this phenomenon?" said Pangloss.

"It is the last day!" cried Candide.

The sailor immediately ran among the debris, dared death to find money, found it, seized it, got drunk, and having slept off his wine, purchased the favors of the first woman of good will be met on the ruins of the houses and among the dead and dying. Pangloss, however, pulled him by the sleeve. "My friend," said he, "this is not well, you are disregarding universal reason, you choose the wrong time."

"Blood and 'ounds!" he retorted. "I am a sailor and I was born in Balavia; four times have I stamped on the crucifix during four voyages to Japan; you have found the right man for your universal reason!"

Candide had been hurt by some falling stones; he lay in the street covered with debris. He said to Pangloss: "Alas! Get me a little wine and oil; I am dying."

"This earthquake is not a new thing," replied Pangloss. "The town of Lima felt the same shocks in America last year; similar causes produce similar effects; there must certainly be a train of sulphur underground from Lima to Lisbon."

"Nothing is more probable," replied Candide; "but, for God's sake, a little oil and wine."

"What do you mean, probable?" replied the philosopher; "I maintain that it is proved."

Candide lost consciousness, and Pangloss brought him a little water from a neighboring fountain.

Next day they found a little food as they wandered among the ruins and regained a little strength. Afterwards they worked like others to help the inhabitants who had escaped the death. Some citizens they had assisted gave them as good a dinner as could be expected in such a disaster, true, it was a dreary meal; the hosts watered their bread with their tears, but Pangloss consoled them by assuring them that things could not be otherwise. "For," said be, "all this is for the best, for, if there is a volcano at Lisbon, it cannot be anywhere else; for it is impossible that things should not be where they are; for all is well."

Aphoristic Style

The most difficult style of all is the aphoristic. Like acupuncture, it hits all the vital points, but it is, figuratively, like dozens or hundreds of little pinpricks in a body of views that are already well established. What is essential, therefore, is that it be extremely clear to your reader what the point of these pricks is supposed to be. And it is equally important that the pricks be sharp and *to the point*. A dull aphorism is like a dull needle; it either doesn't get through at all or else it is very painful. You might try your hand at a few of these, but it is not advisable that you make this the style of your overall project.

Two simple aphorisms that we can use as examples are the German aphorist Lichtenberg's remark—aimed directly at the argument from design—that it is lucky that God made slits in the cat's skin right where his eyes are and Nietzsche's comment on the phony obscurity of his contemporaries: "They muddy the waters to make them look deep." A good aphorism is very short—rarely more than a sentence; it is usually extremely clever and must go right to the heart of the matter. And it must be clear what "the matter" is. For instance, Kierkegaard's aphorism, "It is one thing to stand on one leg and prove God's existence and quite another to go down on one's knees and pray to him" strikes at the heart of the whole history of theology. Another of Kierkegaard's aphorisms, from his *Journal*.

> The two ways: One is to suffer; the other is to become a professor of the fact that another suffered

is an indictment of abstract learning as opposed to passionate participation. He makes the same point, too, against abstraction in this aphorism, also from his *Journal:*

> Like Leporello, learned literary men keep a list; while Don Juan seduces girls and enjoys himself, Leporello notes down the time, the place and the description of the girl.

or this one:

> People hardly ever make use of the freedom they do have, for example, freedom of thought; instead they demand freedom of speech as compensation.

Nietzsche was one of the great aphoristic philosophers of all times, but even he admitted that behind all of his aphorisms, he was much clearer about what he hated than what he was aiming for. Some of his aphorisms were a cutting sentence—for example, a whole theory of truth in a single line, "What after all are man's truths but his *irrefutable* errors?" Others were a full paragraph. A short set of selections follows:

[97]

One becomes moral—not because one is moral. Submission to morality can be slavish or vain or selfish or resigned or obtusely enthusiastic or thoughtless or an act of desperation, like submission to a prince: in itself it is nothing moral.

• • •

[297]

Corruption. The surest way to corrupt a youth is to instruct him to hold in higher esteem those who think alike than those who think differently.

— *The Dawn of Day*

[126]

A people is nature's detour to arrive at six or seven great men—and then to get around them.

— *Beyond Good and Evil*

[290]

One thing is needful. "Giving style" to one's character—a great and rare art! It is exercised by those who see all the strengths and weaknesses of their own natures and then comprehend them in an artistic plan until everything appears as art and reason and even weakness delights the eye. Here a large mass of second nature has been added; there a piece of original nature has been removed; both by long practice and daily labor. Here the ugly which could not be removed is hidden; there it has been reinterpreted and made sublime. . . . It will be the strong and domineering natures who enjoy their finest gaiety in such compulsion, in such constraint and perfection under a law of their own; the passion of their tremendous will relents when confronted with stylized, conquered, and serving nature; even when they have to build palaces and lay out gardens, they demur at giving nature a free hand. Conversely, it is the weak characters without power over themselves who *hate* the constraint of style. . . . They become slaves as soon as they serve; they hate to serve. Such spirits—and they may be of the first rank—are always out to interpret themselves and their environment as free nature—wild, arbitrary, fantastic, disorderly, astonishing; and they do well because only in his way do they please themselves. For one thing is needful; that a human being attain his satisfaction with himself—whether it be by this or by that poetry and art; only then is a human being at all tolerable to behold. Whoever is dissatisfied with himself is always ready to revenge himself therefor; we others will be his victims, if only by always having to stand his ugly sight. For the sight of the ugly makes men bad and gloomy.

— *The Gay Science*

[29]

From a doctoral examination. "What is the task of all higher education?" To turn men into machines. "What are the means?" Man must learn to be bored.

• • •

The natural value of egoism. Self-interest is worth as much as the person who has it: it can be worth a great deal, and it can be unworthy and contemptible.

— *Twilight of the Idols*

Finally, there is the later philosophy of Ludwig Wittgenstein. Earlier in this chapter, we introduced you to the outline of his *Tractatus Logico-Philosophicus,* which he wrote during World War I. By 1940, he had changed his mind, and produced several books of aphorisms, all of which presumed intimate knowledge with the whole of contemporary philosophy and his own philosophy in particular. The following aphorism, from *Philosophical Investigations,* are carefully designed, for example, to challenge such standard philosophical beliefs as the idea that each of us has sensations that we can know better than anyone else:

"Imagine a person whose memory could not retain *what* the word 'pain' meant—so that he constantly called different things by that name—but nevertheless used the word in a way fitting in with the usual symptoms and presuppositions of pain"—in short he uses it as we all do. Here I should like to say, a wheel that can be turned though nothing else moves with it, is not part of the mechanism.

The essential thing about private experience is really not that each person possesses his own exemplar, but that nobody knows whether other people also have this or something else. The assumption would thus be possible—though unverifiable—that one section of mankind had one sensation of red and another section another.

Look at a stone and imagine it having sensations.—One says to oneself: How could one so much as get the idea of ascribing a *sensation* to a thing? One might as well ascribe it to a number!—And now look at a wriggling fly and at once these difficulties vanish and pain seems able to get a fooothold here, where before everything was, so to speak, too smooth for it.

Think of the recognition of *facial expressions.* Or of the description of facial expressions—which does not consist in giving the measurements of the face! Think, too, how one can imitate a man's face without seeing one's own in a mirror.

But isn't it absurd to say of a *body* that it has pain?—And why does one feel an absurdity in that? In what sense is it true that my hand does not feel pain, but I [feel pain] in my hand?

What sort of issue is: Is it the *body* that feels pain—How is it to be decided? What makes it plausible to say that it is not the body?—Well, something like this: if someone has a pain in his hand, then the hand does not say so (unless it writes it) and one does not comfort the hand, but the sufferer: one looks into his face.

The form of philosophy is as important to the ultimate presentation of the project as the particular opinions in it. But regardless of your choice of form, the most important thing is that your writing represent careful and clear-headed thinking, and that it serve to introduce the reader and entice him or her to your own view of the world. Most philosophers—even the great aphorists—begin with a straightforward presentation, at least in order to make their ideas clear. (Even Plato wrote straightforward essays, but we have lost them.) The most sensible way to start, therefore, is by straightforwardly setting down your main ideas, ordering them in a brief (one-page) argument, and then filling out the details, providing quotations and examples as you expand the presentation. Then, if you feel like experimenting, you might want to try your hand at a short dialogue, or at a short series of aphorisms to supplement what you have done. But the overall effect—always—must be an impression of clear thinking and passionate involvement in thinking. Philosophy, in any of its forms, is never anything else.

APPENDIX II

DEDUCTIVE LOGIC
VALID ARGUMENT FORMS

In "A Little Logic," we introduced the distinction between the truth (or falsity) of a statement and the validity (or invalidity) of a deductive argument. It is possible for an argument to be valid even if its premises and conclusion are false. For example:

> All dogs are green
> Socrates is a dog
> _____
> Therefore, Socrates is green.

This is a valid argument, even though both the premises and the conclusion are false. For a deductive argument to guarantee the truth of its conclusion, the premises must be true *and* the argument must be valid. Here we will say a little bit more about what it means for an argument to be valid.

A valid argument has the right *form:* invalid arguments do not. The right form of an argument is based on a list of basic rules of inference, such as the following:

The syllogistic form

> All P's are Q's.
> S is a P.
> _____
> Therefore, S is a Q.

is a valid form, as we saw above. But

> All P's are Q's.
> S is a Q.
> _____
> Therefore, S is a P.

is not. How do we know? Since the definition of a (valid) deductive argument is that the truth of the premises guarantees the truth of the conclusion, we try to find an argument that fits the form that does indeed have true premises and a false conclusion. If there is no such argument, the form is a valid argument form. If there is *any* such argument, then it is not a valid argument form. So,

There is one danger that we must guard against, Socrates said.

What sort of danger? I asked.

Of becoming misologic [hating logic], he said, in the sense that people become misanthropic. No greater misfortune could happen to anyone than that of developing a dislike for argument. Misology and misanthropy arise in just the same way. Misanthropy is induced by believing in somebody quite uncritically. You assume that a person is absolutely truthful and sincere and reliable, and a little later you find that he is shoddy and unreliable. Then the same thing happens again. After repeated disappointments at the hands of the very people who might be supposed to be your nearest and most intimate friends, constant irritation ends by making you dislike everybody and suppose that there is no sincerity to be found anywhere. . . .

The resemblance between arguments and human beings lies in this: that when one believes that an argument is true without reference to the art of logic, and then a little later decides rightly or wrongly that it is false, and the same thing happens again and again . . . they end by believing that they are wiser than anyone else, because they alone have discovered that there is nothing stable or dependable either in facts or in arguments, and that everything fluctuates just like the water in a tidal channel, and never stays at any point for any time. . . .

But suppose that there is an argument which is true and valid but someone spent his life loathing arguments and so missed the chance of knowing the truth about reality—would that not be a deplorable thing?

(336 words, Hugh Tredennick, The Last Days of Socrates *[Phaedo 89d-90e] (Harmondsworth, MD: Penguin, 1954).*

we know that the above form is invalid because we can make up an example such as:

> All lemons are yellow.
> Sam (the canary) is yellow.
>
> ---
>
> Therefore, Sam is a lemon.

When you suspect that an argument in philosophy is invalid, translate the argument into formal symbolism ("All P's are S's . . .") and then find another argument with true premises and a false conclusion that fits the form ("That's like arguing that . . ."). If even one such instance of an argument form is invalid, then the form itself is not a valid argument form.

The most familiar form of deductive argument, the form illustrated above, is the **categorical syllogism**. A syllogism consists of three lines—two premises and a conclusion—and contains three terms or categories. (The term that appears in both premises is called the middle term.) The form of the statements themselves is quantitative, preceded by "all," "some," "no . . ." and "not all . . ."

But not all deductive arguments are syllogisms; others involve a variety of inferences and complexities. Two of the most frequently used and best-known have the Latin names ***modus ponens*** and ***modus tollens.*** *Modus ponens* has the form:

> If P then Q.
> P.
>
> ──────────
>
> Therefore, Q.

For example,

> If Socrates keeps annoying people, he'll get in trouble.
> Socrates won't stop annoying people.
>
> ──────────────────────────────
>
> Therefore, he'll get in trouble.

Modus tollens has the form:

> If P then Q.
> Not Q.
>
> ──────────
>
> Therefore, not P.

For example,

> If you care enough, you'll send the very best.
> You are not sending the very best.
>
> ──────────────────────────
>
> Therefore, you do not care enough.

Although any argument that fits one of these forms is valid, whether or not it is also sound depends on the truth of its premises.

There are two arguments that superficially look like *modus ponens* and *modus tollens* but are in fact invalid. They are:

> If P then Q.   If P then Q.
> Q.   Not P.
>
> ──────────   ──────────
>
> Therefore, P.   Therefore, not Q.

For example,

> If you stay up too late, you'll miss breakfast.
> You missed breakfast.
>
> ──────────────────────────
>
> Therefore, you stayed up too late.

RULES OF INFERENCE

$\supset$ = if, then
$\frown$ = not
$\cdot$ = and
$\vee$ = or
$\therefore$ = therefore

1. *Modus Ponens* (M.P.)
   $p \supset q$
   p
   $\therefore q$

2. *Modus Tollens* (M.T.)
   $p \supset q$
   $\frown q$
   $\therefore p$

3. Hypothetical Syllogism (H.S.)
   $p \supset q$
   $q \supset r$
   $\therefore p \supset r$

4. *Disjunctive Syllogism* (D.S.)
   $p \vee q$
   $\frown p$
   $\therefore q$

5. *Constructive Dilemma* (C.D.)
   $(p \supset q) \cdot (r \supset s)$
   $p \vee r$
   $\therefore q \vee s$

6. *Absorption* (Abs.)
   $p \supset q$
   $\therefore p \supset (p \cdot q)$

7. *Simplification* (Simp.)
   $p \cdot q$
   $\therefore p$

8. *Conjunction* (Conj.)
   p
   q
   $\therefore p \cdot q$

10. *Addition* (Add.)
    p
    $\therefore p \vee q$

Irving Copi, Introduction to Logic, *7th edition (New York: Macmillan, 1986), 311-12.*

If you stay up too late, you'll miss breakfast.
You didn't stay up too late.

Therefore, you didn't miss breakfast.

These two fallacies are called *the fallacy of affirming the consequent* and *the fallacy of denying the antecedent.* They must always be avoided!

One type of argument, which is really a kind of *modus tollens,* is of special use in philosophy. It is called the *reductio ad absurdum* or "reduction to absurdity." One philosopher argues that P (e.g., "Justice is whatever the strongest person insists on."). Her opponent argues that If P then Q (e.g., "If justice is the will of the strongest, then it is just for the strongest to be unjust."). But Q in this case is obviously absurd and therefore false—so the original claim P must be false as well. (The example is a famous argument by Socrates.) One good way to attack a philosophical position is to show that regardless of the apparent logic, its consequences are absurd.

APPENDIX III
COMMON INFORMAL FALLACIES

"INFORMAL" FALLACIES

Many intended arguments are fallacious even though they are, formally, valid arguments. That is, they do not violate the rules of inference and the proper forms of deductive argument. They are, nevertheless, bad arguments. A tautology, for example, is a straightforwardly valid argument ("If p, then p"). But obviously such an argument, in the context of a discussion or a philosophy paper, does nothing to further the point to be made. The following is a list of often made but almost always bad "informal" fallacies:

MERE ASSERTION   The fact that you accept a position is not sufficient for anyone else to believe it. Stating your view is not an argument for it, and unless you are just answering a public opinion survey, every opinion always deserves a supporting argument. There are statements, of course, that everyone would accept at face value, and you need not argue those. But that does not mean that they cannot be argued, for even the most obvious facts of common sense must be argued when challenged—this is what much of philosophy is about.

BEGGING THE QUESTION   Another fallacy is something that looks like an argument but simply accepts as a premise what is supposed to be argued for as a conclusion. For example, suppose you are arguing that one ought to be a Christian and your reason is that the Bible tells you so. This may, in fact, be conclusive for you, but if you are trying to convince someone who doesn't believe in Christ, he or she will probably not believe what the Bible says either. As an argument for becoming a Christian, therefore, referring to the Bible begs the question. Question begging often consists of a reworded conclusion, as in "this book will improve your grades because it will help you to do better in your courses."

VICIOUS CIRCLE   Begging the question is similar to another error, which is often called arguing in a "vicious circle." Consider a more elaborate version of the above fallacy. A person claims to know God exists because she has had a religious vision. Asked how she knows that the vision was religious rather than just the effect of something she ate, she replies that such an elaborate and powerful experience could not have been caused by anyone or anything but God. Asked how she knows this, she replies that God Himself told her—in the vision. Or, "he must be guilty because of the look on his face." "How do you know that he looks guilty rather than frightened or sad?" "Because he's the one who did it, that's why!" If you argue A because of B, and B because of C, but then C because of A, you have argued in a vicious circle. It is vicious because, as in begging the question, you have assumed just what you want to prove. But the following is worth remembering: Ultimately, all positions may come full circle, depending upon certain beliefs that can be defended only if you accept the rest of a great many beliefs. Debates between religious people and atheists are often like this, or arguments between free-marketeers and Marxists, where many hours of argument show quite clearly that each person accepts a large system of beliefs, all of which depend on the others. Some logicians call this a "virtuous circle," but this does not mean that there are no vicious circles. A virtuous circle is the development of an entire worldview, and it requires a great deal of thinking and organizing. Vicious circles, like begging the question, are usually shortcuts to nowhere that result from careless thinking.

IRRELEVANCIES   You have seen people who argue a point by arguing everything else, throwing up charts of statistics and complaining about the state of the universe and telling jokes—everything but getting to the point. This may be a technique of wearing out your opponent; it is not a way of persuading him or her to agree with you. No matter how brilliant an argument may be, it is no good to you unless it is relevant to the point you want to defend.

AD HOMINEM ARGUMENTS   The most distasteful kind of irrelevancy is an attack on your opponent personally instead of arguing against his or her position. It may well be that the person you are arguing against is a liar, a sloppy dresser, bald and ugly, too young to vote or too old to work, but the only question is whether what he or she says is to be accepted. Harping on the appearance, reputation, manners, intelligence, friends, or possessions of your opponent may sometimes give your readers insight into why he or she holds a certain position, but it does not prove or disprove the position itself. As insight into an opponent's motives, personal considerations may, in small doses, be appropriate. But more than a very small dose is usually offensive, and it will usually weigh more against you than against your opponent. Whenever possible, avoid this kind of argument completely. It usually indicates that you don't have any good arguments yourself.

UNCLEAR OR SHIFTING CONCLUSIONS   One of the most frustrating arguments to read is an argument that has a vague conclusion or that shifts conclusions with every paragraph. If something is worth defending at all, it is worth stating clearly and sticking with it. If you argue that drug users should be punished, but aren't clear whether you mean people who traffic in heroin or people who take aspirin, you are not worth listening to. If you say that you mean illegal drug offenders, don't argue that drugs are bad for your body, since this is equally true for both legal and illegal drugs. If you say that you mean amphetamine users, then don't switch to talking about the illegality of drugs when someone explains to you the several medical uses of amphetamines. Know what you are arguing, or your arguments will have no point.

CHANGING MEANINGS   It is easy to miss a fallacy when the words seem to form a valid argument. For example, consider this:

> *People are free as long as they can think for themselves.*
> *Prisoners in jail are free to think for themselves.*
> *Therefore, prisoners in jail are free.*

This paradoxical conclusion is due to the ambiguity of "free," first used to refer to a kind of mental freedom, second to refer to physical freedom. An interesting example is the argument often attributed to the famous British philosopher John Stuart Mill: "Whatever people desire, that is what is desirable." But notice that this argument plays with an ambiguity in the English language. Not everything that is in fact desired *should* be desired (for example, alcohol by alcoholics), so the argument is deductively invalid. (Mill makes the case, however, that the only evidence that *x* is desirable is that people in fact desire it.) Be careful that the key terms in your argument keep the same meaning throughout.

DISTRACTION   Another familiar form of fallacy is the "red herring," the sometimes long-winded pursuit of an argument leading away from the point at issue. For example, in the middle of an argument about the relation between the mind and the brain, a neurologist may well enjoy telling you, in impressive detail, any number of odd facts about neurology, about brain operations he or she has performed, about silly theories that neurology-ignorant philosophers have defended in the past. But if these do not bear on the issue at hand, they are only pleasant ways of spending the afternoon, not steps to settling a difference of opinion. Distraction is a fallacy that is especially advantageous when the time for argument is limited. (For this reason, it is particularly prevalent in the classroom.)

PSEUDO-QUESTIONS   Sometimes fallacious reasoning begins with the very question being asked. For example, some philosophers have argued that asking such questions as "How is the mind related to the body?" or "Could God create a mountain so heavy that even He could not move it?" are pseudo-questions; that is, they look like real questions—even profound questions—but are ultimately unanswerable because they are based on some hidden piece of nonsense. (In these two cases, it has been suggested that there is no legitimate distinction between mind and body, and therefore any question about how they are "related" is pointless; the second question presumes that God is "omnipotent" in the sense that He can do the logically impossible, which is absurd.) Pseudo-questions, like distractions, lead us down a lengthy path going nowhere, except that, with pseudo-questions, we start from nowhere as well.

DUBIOUS AUTHORITY   We mentioned earlier that modern philosophy is based on the assumption that we have a right—and sometimes a duty—to question authority. Yet, most of our knowledge and opinions are based on appeals to authorities— whether scientists or "the people" are particularly wise or not. It would be extremely foolish, if not fatal, not to so appeal to authorities, especially in a world that has grown so technologically and socially complicated. We ask an economist what will happen if interest rates fall. We ask Miss Manners which fork to use for the salad. The fallacy of dubious authority arises when we ask the *wrong* person, when we appeal to an expert who is not in fact an expert in the area of concern. For example, when physicians are asked questions about nuclear policy or physicists are asked questions about high school education, their expertise in one field does not necessarily transfer to the other. Appealing to opinions in books and newspapers depends on the authority of the authors and publications in question. What is in print is not necessarily authoritative.

SLIPPERY SLOPE   Metaphors often pervade arguments. One of the more common metaphors is the "slippery slope," the greased incline that, once trod, inevitably carries us to the bottom. (In politics, it is sometimes called "the chilling effect" or "the domino theory.") For example, it is argued that any interference with free speech whatsoever, even forbidding someone to scream "fire" in a crowded auditorium,

INFORMAL FALLACY EXAMPLES:

Changing meaning:

> Power tends to corrupt (Lord Acton).
> Knowledge is power (Francis Bacon).
> Therefore knowledge tends to corrupt.

Begging the question:

> She says that she loves me,
> and she must be telling the truth,
> because she certainly wouldn't lie to someone she loves.

Pity and other emotional appeals:

> Mr. Scrooge, I certainly deserve a raise in pay.
> I can hardly manage to feed my children on what
> you are paying me. And my youngest child, Tim,
> needs an operation if he is ever to walk without crutches.

All from: Irving M. Copi, Informal Logic *(New York: Macmillan, 1986).*

will sooner or later lead to the eradication of free speech of every kind, including informed, responsible political discussion. But is it the case that, by attacking an extreme instance, we thereby endanger an entire institution? Sometimes, this may be so. But more often than not, the slippery slope metaphor leads us to think that there is such inevitability when in fact there is no such thing.

ATTACKING A STRAW MAN   Real opponents with real arguments and objections are sometimes difficult to refute, and so the easy way out is to attack an unreal opponent with easily refutable arguments and objections. This is called *attacking a straw man.* For example, French existentialist Jean-Paul Sartre argued that human beings have "absolute freedom," meaning that they could always find *some* alternative way of dealing with a difficult situation. But unsympathetic critics quickly interpreted his claim to mean that a person can do absolutely anything he wants to do, for example, fly to the moon by flapping his ears—believing they had refuted Sartre with such silly examples.

PITY (AND OTHER EMOTIONAL APPEALS)   Some forms of fallacy appeal to the better parts of us, even as they challenge our fragile logical abilities. The appeal to pity has always been such an argument. Photographs of suffering people may well be an incentive to social action, but the connection between our pity—which is an undeniable virtue—and the social action in question is not yet an argument. The appeal to pity—and all appeals to emotion—have a perfectly legitimate place in philosophical argument, but such appeals are not yet themselves arguments for any particular position. An orator may make us angry, but what we are to do about the problem must be the product of further argument.

APPEAL TO FORCE   Physical might never makes philosophical right. Sometimes a person can be intimidated, but he or she is not thus refuted. Sometimes one has to back up a philosophical conviction with force, but it is never the force that justifies the conviction.

INAPPROPRIATE ARGUMENTS   The last fallacy we will mention has to do with choice of methods. To insist on deductive arguments when there are powerful inductive arguments against you is a fallacy too—not a fallacious argument, perhaps, but a mistake in logic all the same. For example, if you are arguing deductively that there cannot be any torture going on in a certain country, since Mr. Q rules the country and Mr. Q is a good man (where the implicit premise is that "good men don't allow torture in their country"), you had better be willing to give up the argument when dozens of trustworthy eyewitnesses publicly describe the tortures they have seen or experienced. To continue with your deduction in the face of such information is foolish. This may not tell you where your argument has gone wrong: Perhaps Mr. Q is not such a good man. Or perhaps he has been overpowered. Or perhaps good men can't prevent torture if they aren't told about it. But in any case, the argument must now be given up.

The same may be true the other way around. Certain abstract questions seem to be answerable only by deduction. When arguing about religious questions, for example, looking for evidence upon which to build an inductive argument may be foolish. What is at stake are your basic concepts of religion and their implications. Evidence, in the sense of looking around for pertinent facts, may be irrelevant. Very abstract questions often require deductive arguments only.

To be caught in one of these fallacies is almost always embarrassing and damaging to your overall argument. If you have a case to make, then make it in the most powerfully persuasive way. An intelligent combination of deductive and inductive arguments, coupled with analogies and proper criticisms of alternative positions, is the most effective persuasion available. If you think your opinions are important, then they deserve nothing less than the best supporting arguments you can put together.

BRIEF BIOGRAPHIES

Anselm, Saint (1033–1109) Archbishop of Canterbury and author of the ontological argument for God's existence. He is best known for his *Monologion* and *Proslogion*.

Aquinas, Saint Thomas (1225–1274) Author of the *Summa Theologica*, the most comprehensive "official" theological statement of the Roman Catholic Church.

Aristotle (384–322 B.C.) Plato's student for eighteen years, he learned and then parted from Plato's views. In addition to his biological studies, Aristotle virtually created the sciences of logic and linguistics, developed extravagant theories in physics and astronomy, and contributed to ethics, epistemology, metaphysics, politics, and aesthetics.

Augustine, Saint (354–430) The preeminent figure in the development of medieval Christian thought from its roots in classical Greece and Rome. He is best-known for his theological treatise *The City of God* and for his extremely personal *Confessions*.

Bentham, Jeremy (1748–1832) A leader in the legal reform movement in England and the founding father of that ethical position called utilitarianism. His best-known work is his *Introduction to the Principles of Morals and Legislations*.

Berkeley, Bishop George (1685–1753) He wrote most of the works that brought him fame before he turned twenty-eight. Concentrating on perception, his entire philosophy is aptly summarized in his famous phrase: "To be is to be perceived." Berkeley's arguments for this proposition are most thoroughly outlined in his *Treatise Concerning the Principles of Human Knowledge*.

Butler, Bishop Joseph (1692–1752) English theologian who formulated the standard arguments against psychological egoism in his *Fifteen Sermons*.

Confucius (551–479 B.C.) Classic Chinese philosopher who defended the centrality of personal virtue and family piety, author of the *Analects*.

Descartes, René (1596–1650) French mathematician and philosopher considered the "father of modern philosophy." He developed a philosophical method that could be adapted to individual reason. Descartes sought a basic premise from which, as in a geometrical proof, he could deduce all the principles that could be known with certainty.

Dewey, John (1859–1952) One of the leading American pragmatists, and an often outspoken social critic. His views on education have been especially influential. His many books include *Reconstruction in Philosophy* and *Human Nature and Conduct*.

Diogenes (d. ca. 320 B.C.) Cynic philosopher who lived an extremely simple life. Offered anything he wanted by Alexander the Great, Diogenes replied, "Get out of my light."

Epicurus (341–270 B.C.) Greek philosopher who argued that the good life was pleasure.

Hegel, Georg Wilhelm Friedrich (1770–1831) German philosopher who, during the age of Napoleon, wrote his *Phenomenology of Spirit* (1807)—the single most powerful influence in European history (after Kant's works) for the next one hundred years.

Heidegger, Martin (1889–1976) German phenomenologist and student of Edmund Husserl, whose rebellion against his teacher became the "existential" movement in phenomenology. Heidegger's best-known work is *Being and Time* (1927).

Heraclitus (*ca.* 540–*ca.* 480 B.C.) Pre-Socratic philosopher who taught that the basic element of reality is constantly changing, like fire, with an underlying *logos*.

Hobbes, Thomas (1588–1679) One of England's first great modern philosophers. Hobbes argued that people were motivated to become part of society for their mutual protection. His best-known work is *Leviathan* (1651).

d'Holbach, Baron Paul Henri (1723–1789) French philosopher and one of the leaders of the Enlightenment.

Hume, David (1711–1776) Often noted as the outstanding genius of British philosophy. In his major works, *Treatise of Human Nature* (1739) and *Inquiry Concerning Human Understanding* (1748), Hume argued that there is no knowledge of right and wrong and no rational defense of moral principles. His epistemological enquiries led him to embrace a form of skepticism.

Husserl, Edmund (1859–1938) German-Czech philosopher and mathematician who founded phenomenology. His best-known works are *Ideas,* I (1913) and *Cartesian Meditations* (1931).

James, William (1842–1910) James developed the American philosophy of pragmatism. His best-known works are *Pragmatism: A New Name for Some Old Ways of Thinking* (1907) and *The Varieties of Religious Experience* (1902).

Jefferson, Thomas (1743–1826) Primary author of the Declaration of Independence and third president of the United States.

Kant, Immanuel (1724–1804) German philosopher; probably the greatest philosopher since Plato and Aristotle. His philosophical system—embodied in three huge volumes called *Critique of Pure Reason* (1781), *Critique of Practical Reason* (1788), and *Critique of Judgement* (1790)—changed philosophy as much as the revolution changed France.

Kierkegaard, Søren (1813–1855) Danish philosopher and theologian who is recognized as the father of existentialism. His basic tenet is the need for each individual to choose his or her own way of life. *Either/or,* and *The Concept of Dread* are among his best-known works.

Lao-Tze (6th century B.C.) Early Chinese Taoist and author of the *Tao Te Ching*.

Leibniz, Gottfried Wilhelm (1646–1716) He has been called "the last of the universal geniuses." Leibniz was one of the inventors of calculus, the father of modern formal linguistics, the inventor of a primitive computer, a physicist, and most of all a great philosopher. His concise *Monadology* (1714) summarizes his mature metaphysical theories.

Locke, John (1632–1704) English philosopher and politician credited not only with founding British empiricism but with fathering modern political liberalism as well. His best-known works are *Treatises of Government* (1689) and *Essay Concerning Human Understanding* (1690).

Marx, Karl (1818–1883) German philosopher and social theorist who formulated the philosophical basis for one of the most powerful political ideologies of this century. His most famous works are *Capital* and *The Communist Manifesto*.

Mill, John Stuart (1806–1873) English philosopher and economist best known for his moral and political writings, particularly *On Liberty* (1859) and *Utilitarianism* (1861).

Nietzsche, Friedrich Wilhelm (1844–1900) German philosopher who declared himself the archenemy of traditional morality and Christianity. His most sustained and vicious attack is one of his last books, *Antichrist* (1888).

Parmenides (*b. ca.* 515 B.C.) Pre-Socratic philosopher who taught that reality was eternal and unchanging, and that therefore we could not know it as such.

Pascal, Blaise (1623–1662) French mathematician and philosopher with mildly mystic tendencies. Pascal stressed confidence in "the Heart" rather than reason. However, he was also one of the inventors of the computer.

Plato (*ca.* 428–347 B.C.) Greek philosopher who fell under the influence of Socrates. Plato devoted his life to continuing the work of Socrates (following Socrates' death). He set up the Academy (the first university in the West) for this purpose, spending the rest of his life teaching there. Plato first set down his reminiscences of Socrates' life and death and, using the dialogue form, with Socrates as his spokesman, extended Socrates' thought into new areas. Because we have nothing from Socrates himself, it is difficult to know how much is original Plato and how much is transcribed Socrates.

Pythagoras (*ca.* 580–*ca.* 500 B.C.) The Greek religious mystic who believed that numbers were the essence of all things.

Rousseau, Jean-Jacques (1712–1778) French Enlightenment philosopher who is most famous for his conceptions of "the noble savage" and "the social contract." Rousseau's writings were condemned, and he spent most of his life running from the police. After his death, his political ideas became the ideology of the French Revolution.

Russell, Bertrand (1872–1970) One of the greatest philosophers of our century. He wrote an enormous number of philosophical books on virtually every topic, from mathematical logic to marriage and the family.

Sartre, Jean-Paul (1905–1980) Contemporary French philosopher. Sartre is generally regarded as the main proponent of the philosophy of "existentialism." In his greatest work, *Being and Nothingness* (1943), Sartre argues the centrality of freedom in human existence.

Schopenhauer, Arthur (1788–1860) German philosopher who developed Kant's idealism into his own unique system. Famous for his pessimism, Schopenhauer declared the ultimate reality to be an irrational and insatiable Will. His main work is *The World as Will and Idea*.

Socrates (*ca.* 470–399 B.C.) Athenian philosopher with a gift for rhetoric and debate. Socrates urged a return to the ideals of wisdom, virtue, justice, and the good life.

Spinoza, Benedictus de (1632–1677) Dutch-Jewish philosopher. His best-known book is *Ethics* (1677), a radical reinterpretation of God as identical to the universe (pantheism).

Thales of Miletus (625?–547? B.C.) The earliest-known Greek philosopher. Thales taught that all things were composed of water.

Tillich, Paul (1886–1965) Among the best-known modern theologians. Tillich emphasized emotion and "concern" rather than reason in religion. In Tillich's philosophy, God is simply the symbol of our "ultimate concern" and not the transcendent judge of the scriptures.

Voltaire (1694–1778) Voltaire, whose real name was François-Marie Arouet, was a celebrated man of letters and a trenchant critic of religious dogmatism and political authoritarianism. His philosophical views, while not especially original, reflect perfectly the spirit of the Enlightenment. His most widely read work is the satirical novel *Candide.*

Whitehead, Alfred North (1861–1947) Famous English logician who, with Bertrand Russell, established the basis of modern logic. Late in life Whitehead turned to metaphysics and "process philosophy."

Wittgenstein, Ludwig (1889–1951) Austrian-born philosopher who became the most powerful influence on twentieth-century "analytic" philosophy.

GLOSSARY

This glossary of key terms serves also as a subject index to the important philosophical concepts discussed in the book. The page numbers in brackets at the end of the entries refer to the major text discussion of the concept. A name index of the philosophers and their works appears at the end of the book.

absolute freedom: freedom from *all* constraints (which is impossible). Jean-Paul Sartre uses the term to insist that a person is *always* free to choose, no matter how confined or restricted by circumstances, but he does not thereby mean that a person is ever free from constraints. [p. 222]

absolutism (in ethics): the thesis that there is a single set of correct moral standards, applicable to all societies. [p. 266]

absurd, the "absurd": unreasonable, irrational, without meaning. Albert Camus uses the term to refer to "the confrontation of reasonable man and an indifferent universe," a world that seems unresponsive to our demands for justice and meaningfulness. [p. 49]

ad hominem: an argument aimed at the individual but ignoring the issue completely (also called *ad feminam*). [p. 21]

aesthetics: the branch of philosophy concerned with beauty, especially as it appears in works of art, and with the judgments we make about the artistic value of such works. [p. 8]

agnosticism: the refusal to believe either that God exists or that He does not exist, usually on the grounds that there can be no sufficient evidence for either belief, **agonistic**: a person who accepts agnosticism. [p. 68]

altruism: the thesis that one ought to act for the sake of the interests of others, rather than one's own interests alone. *See also* **ethical altruism**; **psychological altruism**. [pp. 60, 251]

analogy: similarity, comparison. An argument by analogy is a demonstration that two things are similar in certain crucial respects and therefore are probably similar in other respects. [pp. 16, 202]

animism: the view that everything—perhaps even the universe as a whole—is alive. [p. 320]

anthropomorphic: humanlike. An anthropomorphic conception of God ascribes human attributes to Him, usually personality traits, such as a sense of justice or jealousy, sometimes (as in Greek mythology or children's stories) physical attributes as well. [p. 73]

appearance and reality: in metaphysics, a traditional contrast between things as they *seem* to be and things as they actually are. The question the logically follows is:

371

How can we be sure that the appearances we know are an accurate representation of reality? [p. 110]

a priori **(knowledge)**: "before experience," or, more accurately, independent of all experience. *A priori* knowledge is always necessary, for there can be no imaginable instances that would refute it and no intelligible doubting of it. One might come to know something *a priori* through experience (for example, you might find out that no parallel lines ever touch each other by drawing tens of thousands of parallel lines), but what is essential to *a priori* knowledge is that no such experience is needed. [pp. 7, 131]

argument: process of reasoning from one claim to another. An argument may, but need not be, directed against an explicit alternative. A philosophical argument does not require an opponent or a disagreement. [pp. 5, 16]

argument from design (for God's existence): an argument that attempts to "prove" that God exists because of the intricacy and "design" of nature. The basis of the argument is that, since the universe is so well designed, it must have a designer. The analogy most often used is our inference from finding a complex mechanism on the beach (for example, a watch) that there must have been some intelligent being who created it. [p. 91]

asceticism: a philosophy of rigorous self-discipline and abstinence, rejecting as much as possible the comforts, luxuries, and pleasures of the world. [pp. 246–247]

assumption: a principle taken for granted, without argument or proof. [pp. 138, 155]

atheism: the belief that there is no God, **atheist**: a person who doesn't believe in God. [p. 68]

atom: one of the smallest possible material bodies. Atoms are the building blocks of reality. Democritus is credited with the first atomic theory. John Dalton is the father of the modern theory, which is the basis of modern chemistry. [p. 114]

authentic self: in existentialism, the genuine, individual self-identity, to be distinguished from the inauthentic, merely role-playing and public identity. The term has become prominent through the philosophy of Martin Heidegger in this century. *See also* **essential self**. [p. 192]

authority: legitimate power. [pp. 19–20, 281]

autonomy: independence. *Intellectual* autonomy is the ability of a rational person to reach his or her own conclusions about what to believe and what not to believe. *Moral* autonomy is the ability of a rational person to reach his or her own moral conclusions about what is right and what is wrong. (This does not mean that they will therefore come to different conclusions.) [p. 259]

axiom: a statement that is true by definition or is so obviously true that it need not be proved, and so may be used without further debate as a starting point of argument. [p. 17]

bad faith: Sartre's characterization of a person's refusal to accept himself or herself: this sometimes means not accepting the facts that are true about you. More often, it means accepting the facts about you as conclusive about your identity, as in the statement, "Oh, I couldn't do that, I'm too shy." [p. 192]

begging the question: assuming the truth of the point at issue in a question. E.g., How do I know God would not deceive me? Because the natural light of reason with which He endowed me tells me so. (In popular writing nowadays the phrase "begging the question" is often used very loosely to mean something like "inviting the question.") [p. 21]

behaviorism: the thesis that there are no mental events (or that they are of no scientific importance). What we call by mentalistic names (pains, emotions, motives) are actually patterns of behavior, misnamed and mistakenly supposed to be inner, "ghostly" occurrences. [pp. 196–197]

Bodhisattva: in Buddhism, an enlightened person devoted to the enlightenment of others. [p. 309]

Buddhism: a religion founded in India by Gautama Buddha (*ca.* 566–480 B.C.), derived from **Hinduism** and teaching that suffering is the universal condition of human existence. [pp. 308–316] **Zen Buddhism**: a more recent development of Buddhism that stresses the importance of meditation and teaching. [p. 78]

capitalism: an economic system based on private ownership and the freedom of producers and consumers to sell and buy as they choose. [p. 204]

categorical imperative: in Kant's philosophy, a moral law, a command that is unqualified and not dependent on any conditions or qualifications. In particular, it is that rule that tells us to act in such a way that we would want everyone else to act the same way. [pp. 259–260]

certain: beyond doubt. But it is important to insist that certainty in the philosophical sense is more than the common psychological use of "certain" ("feeling certain"). One can feel certain and yet be wrong or foolish. One can be certain, in this philosophical sense, only if one can prove that the matter is beyond doubt, that no reasons for doubt could be raised. [p. 158]

climate of opinion: a shared set of ideas and beliefs, and the intellectual atmosphere in which these are generally acceptable. [p. 10]

coherence theory of truth: the theory that a statement or belief is true if and only if it "coheres" with a system of statements or beliefs. Since we can never get "outside" our experience, the only sense in saying that a belief is true (according to this theory) is that it "coheres" with the rest of our experience. [pp. 170, 173]

commitment: a binding obligation formed voluntarily. [p. 82]

compassion: fellow feeling, sympathy, the sharing of another's suffering. [pp. 232, 252]

compatibilism: the thesis that both determinism (in some interpretations) and free action can be true. Determinism does not rule out free action, and the possibility of free action does not require that determinism be false. They are *compatible* positions. [p. 232]

concept: an idea, usually of a *kind* of object or state of affairs, usually expressed by a word or phrase. (Concepts are sometimes said to be the *meanings* of words.) [p. 6]

conceptual framework: a system of concepts within which objects are classified and recognized in a certain way and in which certain interpretations and ideas are given priority. In a scientific conceptual framework, for example, we tend to talk in terms of *physical* forces; in a religious conceptual framework, we tend to talk in terms of *spiritual* forces; in an economic conceptual framework, we tend to talk in terms of price, cost, supply, and so on. (Compare, for example, the very different ways we would discuss the building of a new steeple on a church in scientific, religious, and economic terms.) [pp. 6, 9]

consciousness: mental awareness (not to be confused with conscience). [pp. 184–189]

conclusion: the end of an argument; the final claim. [pp. 17, 23]

consequentialism (in ethics): the view that the goodness or badness of an action depends on its actual consequences (e.g., who is helped, who is harmed). [pp. 262–264]

contemplation (the life of): according to Aristotle (and other philosophers), the happiest life, the life of thought and philosophy. [pp. 60, 62]

contingent: not necessary, could have been otherwise. What we believe (or a state of affairs) is contingent if we can imagine its being other than it is. [p. 147]

contingent falsehood: a statement that is false but might not have been so. "The earth has two moons" is a contingent falsehood, for we can imagine what it would be for the earth to have two moons. [p. 147]

contingent truth: a true statement that could have been otherwise. It is contingent that heavy objects fall toward the earth, since we can easily imagine what it would be like if they did not. This is so even though it is physically necessary that heavy objects fall. [p. 147]

contract: *see* **social contract**.

contradiction: two statements, both of which cannot be true; neither can they both be false. For example, "It is raining" and "It is not raining," said of the same phase place at the same time. [p. 21]

correspondence theory of truth: the theory that a statement or belief is true if and only if it "corresponds" with "the facts." Even when restricting our attention to statements of fact, however, this commonsensical "theory" gets into trouble as soon as it tries to pick out what corresponds to what. How can we identify a "fact," for example, apart from the language we use to identify it? And what does it mean to say that a statement "corresponds" to a fact? [pp. 168, 173]

cosmological argument: an argument (or set of arguments) that undertakes to "prove" that God exists on the basis of the idea that there must have been a first cause or an ultimate reason for the existence of the universe (the cosmos). [p. 90]

cosmology: the study of such questions as how the universe came into being, the nature of space and time, the dimensions of the universe. [p. 112]

critical thinking, criticism: thinking carefully. It does not necessarily mean attacking anyone else's ideas. [p. 20]

deduce: to reason from one principle to another in accord with accepted rules of inference. What is crucial to deduction or deductive argument is that the conclusion is guaranteed as much certainty as the premises. [pp. 17–23]

deduction: sometimes defined more narrowly as the inference from a general premise to a particular conclusion by means of a syllogism: for example, from "All men are mammals," and "Socrates is a man" to "Socrates is a mammal." This is not what is meant by deduction in general, however, and it is not what Descartes intends by that term. [p. 17]

deism: a variation of the Judeo-Christian tradition that was extremely popular in the science-minded eighteenth century. Deism holds that God must have existed to create the universe with all its laws (and thereby usually accepts some form of the cosmological argument), but it also holds that there is no justification for our belief that God has any special concern for man, any concern for justice, or any of those anthropomorphic attributes for which we worship Him, pray to Him, and believe in biblical stories about Him. [p. 70]

determinism: the view that every event in the universe is dependent upon other events that are its causes. In this view, all human actions and decisions, even those we would normally describe as "free" and "undetermined," are totally dependent on prior events that cause them. *See also* **"hard" determinism**; **"soft" determinism**. [pp. 40, 216]

dialectic: a philosophical method, used extensively by G. W. F. Hegel and Karl Marx, in which contradictions are played against one another to arrive at the truth. The origins of dialectic are to be found in ancient Greek philosophy. [p. 139]

duty-defined morality: the view that moral right and wrong are determined first of all by the concept of a person's duties and obligations. [p. 242]

egocentric predicament: the problem that seems to follow from the view that we know only our *own minds* directly—that is, that we might never know anything or anyone else. [p. 201]

egoism: the thesis that people act for their own interests. *See also* **ethical egoism**; **psychological egoism**. [pp. 250–255]

empirical (knowledge): derived from and to be defended by appeal to experience. Empirical knowledge can only be so derived and so defended (as opposed to *a priori* knowledge, which need not be). [p. 7]

empirical truth: a statement that is true because of the facts and knowable through experience. [pp. 147–148]

empiricism: the philosophy that demands that all knowledge, except for certain logical truths and principles of mathematics, comes from experience. British empiricism is often used to refer specifically to the three philosophers Locke, Berkeley, and Hume. It is still a very much alive movement, however, and includes Bertrand Russell and other contemporary philosophers. [pp. 129, 150–151]

Enlightenment: The dominant cultural movement of the eighteenth century characterized by the rejection of the church's authority in intellectual matters, enthusiasm for modern science, and faith in the power of human reason to attain knowledge and promote social progress. [p. 70]

entitlement: having a right to something. A central concern of justice is entitlement—the right to keep what one already possesses, the right to keep what one earns or is given. [p. 287]

epistemology: the study of human knowledge, its nature, sources, and justification. [pp. 8, 145]

equality: in concerns of justice, having the same rights and status before the law as others, being given the same opportunities for advancement. [pp. 288–291]

essential self: the characteristics that make a person *that particular person. See also* **authentic self**. [p. 182]

ethical altruism: the thesis that people *ought* to act in the interests of others. [pp. 251–252]

ethical egoism: the thesis that people *ought* to act in their own self-interest. [pp. 251–252]

ethics: the study of a way of life and its values, including a system of general moral principles and a conception of morality and its foundations. Sometimes, the study of moral principles. [pp. 8, 243]

eudaimonia: Aristotle's word for "happiness," or, more literally, "living well." [p. 250]

evidence: reasons to believe, based on experience. [p. 19]

existentialism: a twentieth-century philosophical movement that developed in France and Germany through the work of Martin Heidegger, Jean-Paul Sartre, and others. Its basic theme is human freedom and responsibility, the lack of any given rules, and the need for us to be responsible for our actions. [pp. 40, 70]

facticity: Sartre's term for the totality of facts that are true of a person at any given time. [p. 190]

factual truth: *see* **empirical truth**.

faith: in the popular sense, a belief in something for which you have inadequate evidence or little good reason. In theology, faith usually refers to the trust a believer should have in God's ultimate grace and fairness. Sometimes, faith is defended as a rational belief in God (for example, in Kant). [p. 242] More often, faith is defended *against* rationality (as in Kierkegaard). [p. 95]

fallacy: an invalid argument. [pp. 21, 23]

fascism: the view that the state has the right to control virtually every aspect of individual life, since the state is of primary importance, the individual only secondary. (Also sometimes called *totalitarianism*.) [p. 217]

Form: the structure of a thing, that which identifies it as a particular thing or kind of thing. In Plato, a Form is an independently existing entity in the World of Being, which determines the nature of the particular things of this world. In Aristotle, forms are merely the essential characteristics that identify a thing as what it is, without independent existence. [p. 119]

freedom: the idea that a human decision or action is a person's own responsibility and that praise and blame may be appropriately ascribed. The most extreme interpretation of "freedom" is the absence of any causes or determinations. Thus an indeterminist would say that an event was free if it had no causes; some philosophers would say that a human act was free if it was only self-caused but not determined by anything else (including a person's character). Certain determinists, however (**"soft" determinists**), would say that an act is free only if it is "in character" and based on a person's desires and personality. Most generally, we say that a person's act was free, whether or not it was the result of a conscious decision and whether or not certain causes may have been involved, if we would say he or she could have done otherwise. [pp. 214–237]

free market: a system of voluntary exchange in which every agent is free to produce, buy and sell as "the market will bear," without interference or standards set by any outside authority. [pp. 283–284]

free will: among philosophers, a somewhat antiquated expression (as in "he did it of his own free will") meaning that a person is capable of making decisions that are not determined by antecedent conditions. Of course, there may be antecedent considerations, such as what a person wants or what a person believes, but free will means that such considerations never determine a person's decision. At most they "enter into the decision." [pp. 40, 87]

functionalism: the theory that mental events are identical to certain processes in the brain, but that similar processes in another medium (like a computer) would have similar mental manifestations. [pp. 197, 200]

General Will (in Rousseau): the collective desires and determinations of a people. [p. 292]

generalization from experience, inductive generalization: inference from observation, experience, and experiment to a generalization about all members of a certain class. For example, a researcher in a laboratory finds that certain experiments on tobacco plants always have the same result. He or she generalizes, through induction, from experimental observations to a claim (or *hypothesis*) about all tobacco plants. But notice that this generalization is never certain (like the generalization in geometry from a proof of a theorem about this triangle to a theorem about all triangles). It might always turn out that there was a fluke in the experiment or that the researchers chose a peculiar sample of plants. [p. 18]

good life: a life well lived; the most desirable way to live. [p. 242]

happiness calculus: a technique developed by Jeremy Bentham to calculate right action in terms of the quantity of pleasure and pain it produces. Pleasures are weighed against one another and balanced against the pain produced by an action, and the action that produces the most pleasure for the most people and the smallest amount of pain is the action that should be done. [p. 264]

"hard" determinism: determinism uncompromised and unqualified. [p. 232]

hedonism: the conception of the good life that takes pleasure to be the ultimate good. [pp. 10, 243–244]

Heisenberg Uncertainty Principle (in physics): the hypothesis that one cannot know both the motion and the position of a subatomic particle. [p. 230]

Hinduism: ancient religion of India, in which the conception of ultimate reality does not include a conception of what we call "God." Hinduism stresses the unity of life and the ideal of being "at one" with the cosmos. [p. 78]

Hume's Fork: David Hume's argument that every justifiably true statement is either a "truth of reason" or a "matter of fact." [p. 159]

hypothesis: a statement to be confirmed—or disproved—by appeal to experience and the facts of the case, to be ascertained through experiment and observation. [p. 19]

idealism: the metaphysical view that only minds and their ideas exist. [p. 129]

identity theory (of mind and body): the thesis that mental events and physical events are the same, just different aspects of neurological processes in the brain. [p. 197]

ideology: a system of values and ideas through which actions and events are interpreted and evaluated. [p. 9]

immanent (God): God defined as *within* the world and the human spirit, rather than distinct from humanity and the universe He created. [p. 75]

immaterialism: the metaphysical view that accepts the existence of nonmaterial entities. The weak version asserts merely that there are such entities. The strong version, idealism, asserts that there are only such entities (that is, there are no material objects). [p. 118]

incoherent: lacking coherence; not fitting together in an orderly or logically agreeable fashion. Using fancy jargon that has no precise meaning may be a source of incoherence. So is a mere list of random beliefs, without any order or logic to hold them together. (They may even contradict each other as well.) An incoherent philosophy may be insightful and true in parts, but, because it never coheres into a single system, it may well appear to be nonsense or simply a jumble of words and phrases. In other cases, an incoherent philosophy may be one that makes no sense, whose terms are utter gibberish or whose principles are mere ramblings without intelligible connection or interpretation. [p. 21]

indeterminism: the thesis that at least some events in the universe are not determined, are not caused by antecedent conditions, and may not be predictable. [pp. 228, 232]

indubitable: not susceptible to being doubted. [p. 158]

induction, **inductive reasoning**, **inductive generalization**: the process of inferring general conclusions (for example, "all swans are white") from a sufficiently large sample of particular observations ("this swan is white, that swan is white, and that one, and that one, and that one . . ."). It is usually contrasted with **deduction** in that, while deductive reasoning guarantees that the conclusion shall be as certain as the premises, induction never gives us a conclusion as certain as the premises. Its conclusions are at most, merely probable. (There might always be some black swan somewhere—and there are, in western Australia.) [p. 17] **Inductive logic** is the study of induction and inductive reasoning. [p. 19]

ineffable: impossible to describe. [p. 97]

inference: the process of reasoning from one set of principles to another, as in an argument. *Deductive inference* is but a single kind of inference. [p. 17]

innate ideas: ideas that we are born with, which may include tendencies to think in certain ways that are "hardwired" into our minds. [p. 154]

interpretation: a way of understanding, a view of a set of facts, from a certain perspective. [p. 150]

intuition: direct, unmediated awareness. As the word is commonly used—for example, when people talk of feminine intuition—some sort of mysterious mode of knowing is implied. As a technical philosophical term, however, "intuition" need not have this connotation. Thus Kant describes sense perception as a form of intuition.

invalid: not valid; not correctly following agreed-upon rules of inference in an argument. Properly applies to arguments, not to statements. [pp. 17, 23]

irrational: going against the rules of reason. (Not the same as *non*rational, such as when we say that worms and fish are "not rational animals.") Only rational (that is, thinking, planning, calculating) creatures can be *ir*rational. [pp. 97, 176]

Jainism: the third of the great Indian religions, committed to a life of non-harm. [p. 309]

justice: the administration of fair rewards, punishments, benefits, and responsibilities in society. **Distributive justice**: the fair apportionment of goods and services. **Retributive justice**: the fair use of punishment. [pp. 284–288]

leap of faith: in Kierkegaard, believing on faith what one cannot prove. [p. 82]

legitimacy: conforming to standards of law or propriety. [p. 281]

life-style: a way of living, with certain values and concepts. [p. 9]

logic: that part of philosophy that studies the structure of *rational arguments,* in particular the rules of valid inference and the rules of inductive generalization. In general, logic simply means "order." [pp. 8, 16]

Logos: (Greek) word, reason, logic, especially the "logic" underlying reality, giving the world order. [p. 117]

materialism: the metaphysical view that only physical matter and its properties exist. Seemingly nonmaterial entities are really physical bodies: to talk about energy, for example, is, in a way, to talk about physical potential; to talk about minds is, as a kind of shorthand, to talk about behavior; to talk about ideas is, in a misleading way, to talk about the various structures and interrelationships between objects. Numbers have no existence of their own but only represent sets of sets of objects (the set of all sets of eight things is the number eight, for example). Materialism has always been a powerful worldview in modern scientific culture. It was also the most common view among the pre-Socratic philosophers. [pp. 118, 293]

"matter of fact": in Hume, an empirical claim, to be confirmed or falsified through experience. [pp. 159–160]

metaphysics: most simply, the study of the most basic (or "first") principles. Traditionally, the study of ultimate reality, or "Being as such." Popularly, any kind of very abstract or obscure thinking. Most philosophers today would define metaphysics as the study of the most general concepts of science and human life, for example, reality, existence, freedom, God, soul, action, mind. [pp. 8, 112]

method of doubt, methodological doubt: Descartes' technique for discovering those principles of which we can be "perfectly certain"; namely, doubt everything, until you discover those principles that cannot be doubted. [pp. 157–158]

mind-body problem: how mental events (pains, thoughts, feelings) are related to the body—in particular, the brain. [pp. 195–211]

monad: in Leibniz, the simple immaterial substances that are the ultimate constituents of all realty. God, the one uncreated monad, created all of the others as self-enclosed ("windowless") predetermined entities. [p. 127]

monism: the metaphysical view that there is ultimately only one substance, that all reality is one. Less strictly, it may be applied to philosophers who believe in only one kind of substance. [p. 127]

monotheism: the belief in one God. [p. 72]

morality: in general, the rules for right action and prohibitions against wrong acts. Sometimes morality is that single set of absolute rules and prohibitions that are valid for all men at all times and in all societies. More loosely, a morality can be any set of ultimate principles and practices basic to a society. [pp. 8, 242–271]

moral philosophy: the study of right and wrong actions, moral values, and principles. [pp. 8, 241]

mukti: Hindu bliss in liberation. [p. 309]

mysticism: the belief that one can come to grasp certain fundamental religious truths (the existence of God, the oneness of the universe) through direct experience of a very special kind, different from ordinary understanding and often at odds with reason. [pp. 97, 309]

necessary truth: something that cannot be otherwise and cannot be imagined to be otherwise. In philosophy, it is not enough that something be "necessary" according to physical laws (for example, the law of gravity) or "necessary" according to custom or habit (for example, the "necessity" of laws against tax evasion or the felt necessity of having a cigarette after dinner). Necessity does not allow for even imaginary counterexamples; thus it is a necessary truth that two plus two equals four; not only do we believe this with certainty and find ourselves incapable of intelligibly doubting it, but we cannot even suggest what it might be for it to be false, no matter how wild our imaginations. [pp. 147–148]

nihilism: the view that nothing has any value. [p. 50]

nirvana: in Buddhism, the ideal state of peacefulness. [p. 309]

objective truth: truth independent of our personal opinions and demonstrably true to anyone (who is in the proper position to observe, who has the right testing equipment, and so on). [p. 175]

obvious: taken to be true without argument or proof; apparently indubitable. [p. 145]

omnipotent: all-powerful, usually said of God. [p. 69]

omniscient: all-knowing, usually said of God. [p. 69]

ontological argument: an argument (or set of arguments) that tries to "prove" the existence of God from the very concept of "God." For example, "God," by definition, is that Being with all possible perfection; existence is a perfection; therefore God exists. [p. 93]

ontology: the study of being: "What is most real?"; "What is it for a thing to exist?" **ontological**: having to do with the idea of existence. [pp. 8, 109]

pantheism: the belief that everything is God. Spinoza, for example, was a *pantheist*. Hinduism is, in part, a form of pantheism. [p. 76]

paradox: a self-contradictory or seemingly absurd conclusion based on apparently good arguments. [p. 22]

Pascal's wager: the argument that it is prudent to believe in God because if He exists and you believe, you will be eternally rewarded; but if He exists and you don't believe, you will be eternally punished. Suggested by the French philosopher Blaise Pascal in the seventeenth century. [p. 95]

pessimism: the view that life is no good and ultimately serves no purpose. Loosely speaking, a *pessimist* is a person who expects things to turn out for the worst. Arthur Schopenhauer, a nineteenth-century German philosopher and follower of Kant (who was not at all a pessimist), was one of the leading pessimists of all time. [p. 133]

pluralism: the metaphysical view that there are many distinct substances in the universe and, perhaps, many different kinds of substances as well. [p. 268]

pluralism (in ethics): acceptance of the coexistence in a society of several different ethical value systems—whether or not they actually contradict one another. [p. 123]

polytheism: belief in many gods and goddesses. [p. 72]

positive and negative freedom: *positive* freedom is the freedom *to* realize one's potential (by following rules, getting a good education, learning through experience); *negative* freedom is freedom *from* constraints (such as not being in prison or threatened with imprisonment or, worse, not being prevented from doing what one chooses). These are opposite aspects of the same considerations; every instance of being free *from* constraints is at the same time the freedom *to* do something, and vice versa. [p. 221]

positivism: this term used to be used as a synonym for **empiricism**. In recent times it has come to mean the outlook advanced by logical positivists who hold that only sentences capable of empirical verification are really meaningful. [pp. 129, 150–151]

power: the ability to get something done. It is sometimes defined as power *over other people,* but this applies only sometimes, when to get something done requires moving or getting around others to do it. [p. 282]

practical reason: the application of our rationality to practical problems—particularly moral problems—the solution to which consists in an action (as opposed to a statement or a theory). [p. 234]

pragmatic theory of truth: the theory that a statement or belief is true if and only if it "works," that is, if it allows us to predict certain results or function effectively in everyday life, or if it encourages further inquiry and helps us lead better lives. [pp. 170, 173]

premise: a statement that is accepted from the start of an argument and is not itself argued. "I think" is the premise of the argument "I think, therefore I am." [pp. 17, 23]

presupposition: a principle that is assumed as a precondition for whatever else one believes but that itself may remain unexamined and uncriticized throughout the argument. For example, a lawyer presupposes that the court aims at justice and has some idea what is just. It is the philosopher, not the lawyer, who challenges those claims. [p. 153]

principle of universal causality: the belief that every event has its cause (or causes). In scientific circles, "its sufficient natural cause" is usually added in order to eliminate the possibility of miracles and divine intervention (which are allowed in Leibniz's similar but broader Principle of Sufficient Reason). [pp. 153, 216]

problem of evil: the dilemma that emerges from trying to reconcile the belief that God is omnipotent, omniscient, and just with the suffering and evil in the world. [p. 83]

psychological altruism: the thesis that people "naturally" act for the well-being of others. [pp. 251–252]

psychological egoism: the thesis that people always act for their own self-interest, even when it seems as if they are acting for other people's benefit (for example, in giving to charity, the egoist would say, the person is simply making himself or herself feel self-righteous). [pp. 251–252]

rational: in accordance with the rules of effective thought concerning coherence, consistency, practicability, simplicity, comprehensiveness, looking at the evidence and weighing it carefully, not jumping to conclusions, and so on. Rationality may not guarantee truth; all the evidence and everything we believe may point to one conclusion, and yet later generations, who know things that we do not, may see that our conclusion was incorrect. It was rational thousands of years ago to believe that the earth was flat, even though it was not true. It is not rational for us to believe the same thing, for our evidence and all sorts of other beliefs indicate, rather, that it is rational to believe that the earth is (more or less) spherical. [pp. 89, 95]

rationalism: that philosophy that is characterized by its confidence in reason, and intuition in particular, to know reality independently of experience. *Continental rationalism* is usually reserved for three great European philosophers, Descartes, Spinoza, and Leibniz. [pp. 150–151]

rationality: primarily, the ability to think and to act according to goals, plans, and strategies. Rationality is also thinking well and effectively and having good, well conceived goals, plans, and strategies. In the first instance, rationality is to be contrasted with *non*rationality; in the second instance, it is contrasted with *ir*rationality. Worms are nonrational; fools and fanatics are irrational. [p. 172]

reality: everything that actually is, as opposed to what merely appears to be, might have been, or is not. A term of metaphysical praise, as in "what is most real is . . ." [pp. 107, 111]

reason: the ability to think abstractly, form arguments, and make inferences. Sometimes referred to as a "faculty" of the human mind (a leftover from eighteenth-century psychology). In metaphysics, however, it often has a more controversial meaning; namely, that human ability to go beyond experience to determine, through thought alone, what reality is really like. [pp. 32, 89]

reasons: evidence or arguments in support of a belief or statement. A belief or statement is *reasonable* if it is or can be supported by sufficient evidence or arguments. [pp. 16, 23]

reductio ad absurdum: a form of argument in which one refutes a statement by showing that it leads to absurdity. [p. 21]

Reformation: sixteenth-century religious movement, initiated by Martin Luther in Germany, which resulted in the splitting of the Christian church and the establishment of *Protestantism*. [p. 75]

refute: to reject for good, convincing reasons. One refutes a statement by showing that it is false; one refutes an argument by showing either that it is invalid or that its conclusion is false, or both. [pp. 17–23]

relativism (in ethics): the view that societies differ in their basic ethical values. *Cultural relativism* is the thesis that societies in fact so differ. *Ethical relativism* is the more radical thesis that what is considered right (or wrong) in a given society *is* therefore right (or wrong) in and for that society. [pp. 266–268]

right: a claim or title justified by law, custom, or morality. [p. 294]

rule of inference: a generally accepted principle according to which one may infer one statement from another. [p. 17]

self-contradictory: indicating a contradiction within one and the same statement or set of statements. What I say may contradict what you say; but what I say might also contradict something else that I said, in which case I am being self-contradictory. Moreover, in a few strange cases, my own statement may be self-contradictory; for example, "I do not exist." [p. 22]

self-evident: obvious and acceptable without argument. The Declaration of Independence begins by making certain arguments impossible, for example, by declaring certain truths to be "self-evident." [p. 145]

self-identity: the way you characterize yourself, either in general (as a human being, as a man or woman, as a creature before God, or as one among many animals)—or in particular (as the person who can run the fastest mile, as in all-C student, or as the worst-dressed slob in your class). Self-identity of a person, in other words, is not merely the same as the identity of a "thing," for example, the identity of a human body. It is a question of "who," not only "what," I am. [p. 184]

Sisyphus (myth of): in Greek mythology, the story of Sisyphus, whom the gods punished by making him spend all eternity pushing a rock up a mountain only to have it fall back down again. Albert Camus uses Sisyphus as a model for the "absurdity" of human life in general. [p. 49]

skepticism: the philosophical belief that knowledge is not possible, that doubt will not be *overcome* by any valid arguments. A philosopher who holds this belief is called a *skeptic*. Skepticism is not merely personal doubt; it requires systematic doubt, with reasons for that doubt. [p. 157]

social contract: an agreement, tacit or explicit, between all members of society, in which each citizen gives up certain rights and privileges in return for the protection and mutual advantage of society. [pp. 291–294]

"soft" determinism: a thesis that accepts **determinism** but claims that certain kinds of causes—namely, a person's character, will allow us to call his or her actions "free." The soft determinist is therefore a **compatibilist**, who believes in both freedom and determinism. [p. 232]

solipsism: the view that we can know only of the existence of our own minds: sometimes called the **egocentric predicament**. [p. 185]

soul: what is most essential to individual human existence; in Christianity, that aspect of the person that survives death. More generally, we use the word "soul" to refer to whatever is basic and "deep down" in a person. [p. 182]

sound (argument): a good argument; a deductive argument which is valid and has true premises. [p. 18]

Spirit: in Hegel's philosophy, the all-embracing idea that includes the entire universe and all of humanity. More generally, Spirit means enthusiasm (as in "team spirit" or "when the spirit moves me"); in religion, Spirit usually refers to an intangible being, such as God or, sometimes, the human soul. [pp. 80, 134]

Stoicism: an ancient movement in philosophy that taught self-control and minimized passion, with a willingness to endure whatever fate has in store. [pp. 61–62]

strong (argument): an inductive argument whose evidence makes the truth of the conclusion highly probable. [p. 18]

subjective truth: an idea that might be said to be true for the person who believes it but possibly for no one else. In Kierkegaard, a subjective truth is an idea (for example, belief in God) that is believed passionately but is not objectively true or false. [p. 175]

substance: the essential reality of a thing or things that underlies the various properties and changes of properties. Its most common definitions: "that which is independent and can exist by itself"; "the essence of a thing which does not and cannot change." In traditional metaphysics, substance is the same as "ultimate reality," and the study of substance is that branch of metaphysics which studies reality, namely, **ontology**. [pp. 121, 135]

syllogism: a kind of deductive reasoning. The best-known examples are those arguments of the form.

> All Ps are Qs. (Major premise)
>
> S is a P. (Minor premise)
>
> _____
>
> *Therefore,* S is a Q. (Conclusion)

The major premise is a general claim, the minor premise is usually (but not always) a particular claim. [p. 17]

tabula rasa: in Locke's philosophy, the "blank tablet" metaphor of the mind, in opposition to the doctrine that there are innate ideas. In other words, the mind is a "blank" at birth, and everything we know must be "stamped in" through experience. [p. 151]

teleology: the belief that all phenomena have a purpose, end, or goal (from the Greek *telos,* meaning "purpose"). Aristotle's metaphysics is a teleology, which means that he believes that the universe itself—and consequently everything in it—operates for purposes and can be explained according to goals. A *teleological view* of the universe (or of any specific phenomenon) is a view that tries to explain in terms of purposes, rather than in terms of cause and effect or origins. [p. 134]

theism: belief in God. [p. 68]

theology: the theoretical study and interpretation of religious doctrines, practices, and experiences. [pp. 68–100]

thinking self: in Descartes, the real self, the self that discovers its own existence (beyond any doubt) by catching itself in the act of thinking (about itself). [p. 185]

transcendent: independent of. In the philosophy of religion, a *transcendent God* is one who is distinct and separate from the universe He created. This is contrasted with the concept of an **immanent** God, for example, in pantheism, where God is identical with His creation, or, to take a different example, in certain forms of humanism, in which God is identical with humankind. (Hegel argued such a thesis.) [pp. 75, 190]

"truth of reason": in traditional rationalism, a belief that can be justified solely by appeal to reason, through intuition or by deduction from premises based upon intuition. Arithmetic and geometry were, for the rationalists as for the empiricists, a paradigm case of such truths. They disagreed mainly on the scope of such truths and on the restrictions to be placed on the problematic appeal to intuition. [pp. 156–159]

***Übermensch* (German)**: Nietzsche's conception of a superior person, who might replace us in the future. [p. 269]

universalizability: the ability to be applied to everyone without exception. This is an essential feature of moral principles, according to Kant and others. [p. 261]

unsound (argument): a bad argument; a deductive argument that is either invalid or has false premises (or both). [p. 18]

utilitarianism: the moral philosophy that says that we should act in such ways as to make the greatest number of people as happy as possible. [p. 262]

utopia: a vision of the ideal society, usually without much indication about how one could possibly get there. [p. 278]

valid: said of an argument that correctly follows agreed-upon rules of inference. Always applies to arguments, not statements. [pp. 17, 23]

virtue: an admirable personal quality; an aspect of good character. [p. 265]

virtue ethics: the view that the central feature in the evaluation of people and their actions should be the character of the agent. [pp. 264–266, 326]

weak (argument): an inductive argument whose evidence does not make the truth of the conclusion very probable. [p. 18]

***Weltanschauung* (German)**: "worldview"; a way of looking at and understanding the world. [pp. 10, 131]

will: the power of mind that allows us to choose our own actions, or at least choose what we will try to do. In Kant, a good will is the only thing that is good "without qualification": in other words, acting for the right reasons and with good intentions. [p. 133]

wisdom: the ideal of human thinking—although it is by no means agreed what sorts of principles or personalities are most wise. Wisdom is essentially practical as well as abstract or theoretical knowledge, including "how to live (and live well)." [p. 62]

World of Becoming: in Plato's metaphysics, the world we live in, the world of change and objects perceived by the senses. [p. 119]

World of Being: in Plato's metaphysics, the world of ideal Forms, a world that is unchanging, a world we can know only through reason and thinking. [p. 119]

worldview: a way of seeing the world, a way of understanding the "larger perspective." [p. 10]

Zen Buddhism: *see* **Buddhism**. [p. 78]

INDEX